1919
AMERICA'S LOSS
OF INNOCENCE

1919
AMERICA'S LOSS

OF INNOCENCE

Eliot Asinof

DIF

DONALD I. FINE, INC.
New York

Library of Congress Cataloging-in-Publication Data

Asinof, Eliot, 1919-
   1919 : America's loss of innocence / by Eliot Asinof.
     p. cm.
   ISBN 1-55611-150-9 (alk. paper) :
     1. United States—History—1913-1921. I. Title.
   E766.A85 1990
   973.91—dc20   89-45335
                                                 CIP

Manufactured in the United States of America
10 9 8 7 6 5 4 3 2 1

DESIGNED BY IRVING PERKINS ASSOCIATES

to I.F. Stone

Things fall apart; the center cannot hold;
Mere anarchy is loosed upon the world,
The blood-dimmed tide is loosed, and everywhere
The ceremony of innocence is drowned;
The best lack all conviction, while the worst
Are full of passionate intensity.
Surely some revelation is at hand;
Surely the Second Coming is at hand;
The Second Coming!

—WILLIAM BUTLER YEATS
The Second Coming

Foreword

History is the record of man's struggle to survive his own venality.

—Frederick L. Schuman
Professor of history
Williams College

1919 began on a magnificent high. The war had just ended and Americans believed they had won it. As Frederick Lewis Allen described the scene: "The great majority...had real faith that this war could be the last one ever, that victory would bring a new day of universal freedom." Newspapers rejoiced in the new American power and prestige, boasting of a nation wealthier than all others. The New Year marked "the dawn of a new era on earth." 1919 would be "a year of jubilee."

As it turned out, it was a year of compounding disasters, a year of sea-changing values wherein freedom, democracy, and the rule of law became shadowy myths. Suddenly, the great democratic process was rendered irrelevant as Americans ran rampant in its debasement like looters after an earthquake. Americans not only went mad, they reasoned that it was virtue.

1919 was cursed with hypocrisy. To record its events is to suffer the biliousness of its leading spokesmen whose rhetoric spilled over with noble pieties while they violated the public welfare.

All this was part of the great love affair Americans have always had with their country. Long before Irving Berlin, our abiding passion was "God bless America, land that I love." Nor was it difficult to understand the romance, for everyone in the world

11

envied us. And, like all lovers, we were blind, concealing and denying all blemishes. It was sometimes astonishing how readily this could be accomplished. We became masters of obfuscating reality, geniuses in the art of the cover-up, anything to save face with our romance. In the end, we deluded only ourselves.

1919 was the year when the romance turned sour. We awoke to discover the mark of the cuckold. It was a year of shock, of shame and finally of not giving a damn. The passions of 1919 were contrary, creating a year of disenchantment made giddy by money to spend, especially after having saved it to preserve the great war romance. It was, then, a year of abandonment to forget the war. And how the changing styles and tastes reflected it! Silk stockings beneath higher and higher hemlines suddenly all of six inches above the floor. New clothes featured a diaphanous look. Girls began to use rouge and makeup and wear their hair shorter. Automobiles were everywhere, mostly open Model T Fords, hand crank to start, thirty miles per hour limit on rough roads. In the cities, there was dancing to jazz. Everyone went to see the movies of Charlie Chaplin, Mary Pickford, Douglas Fairbanks and Theda Bara. Adults played the stock market and auction bridge.

In contrast to battle lines and casualty lists, the newspapers offered a frivolous excitement to celebrate the liberation. Jack Dempsey, the great white heavyweight, knocked out Jess Willard. Babe Ruth hit phenomenal home runs. Alcock and Brown flew the Atlantic nonstop. It was all to smother a continuing pain. Even the soaring cost of living did not stop people from spending. Milk jumped from nine cents a quart to fifteen cents, steak from twenty-seven cents a pound to forty-two cents. Rents skyrocketed, and landlords were the eternal villains. Profiteers were despised but nothing was done to stop the profiteering. Demobilization was devoid of plan or structure as millions of servicemen were discharged into a diminished job market while the advent of Prohibition denied them the pleasures of an honest glass of beer. Sinclair Lewis wrote *Main Street* in 1919, depicting the stultifying culture of small-town America as if its independent spirit had been immersed in a barrel of Jergens lotion and was softening to death. The social rebellion in cities would liberate young people from old moral strictures but hold their minds in sugary ignorance, proving only that licentiousness was a lot more fun than the old inhibitions.

Above all, the government lost touch with the people and the people lost regard for the government.

1919 was the year of postwar chaos, American style. The war was over Over There, but no one except those who had survived the worst of it knew the enormity of its horrors. The rest of America was forever safe on the safe side of the Atlantic. How quickly the war itself would lose the passion that justified it! The more high-sounding its alleged purpose, the more complete was the subsequent revulsion. Nothing appeared to gratify us more than to renounce the Wilsonian idealism, then have a good time as a reward for having secretly rejected it in the first place.

1919 was the year of the jellyfish, the rat, the mad dog—a year of cowardice, of gross political opportunism, of furies unleashed. In 1919, America gave way to false values and impossible hopes. The essence of our failures can be illustrated best in four major events that were spawned in that year, as vital for their symbolic impact as for their reality: (1) Woodrow Wilson's defeats at the Paris Peace Conference and the subsequent rejection of the League of Nations by the United States Senate; (2) the Red Scare and the start of what would eventually become known as the Cold War with the Soviet Union; (3) the enactment of the Eighteenth Amendment and the advent of Prohibition; (4) the fixing of the World Series, which became known as the Black Sox Scandal. Each contributed to the breakdown of our ethic, the diminishing of our pride, the shattering of our hopes. They were, in fact, all of a piece, their origins intertwined as though cut from the same shabby cloth. To understand the failure of the peace conference is to know the roots of the Cold War and the oncoming Red Scare. The social forces that fanned these flames were the religious and political soul of Prohibition. The Black Sox Scandal emerged from the cynicism of a failed idealism and, like the other three legs of the shaky table, served to exacerbate that cynicism in vicious cycles.

For it all, the war was the fountainhead spraying its foul waters over everything in our lives. No matter that it had ended or that we had won, there were no rewards for the victory. War, by its nature, distorted the body politic. It created its own lies, then fed on them. War was the ultimate degradation extolled as the opposite. America tried desperately to forget it but ended up paying its dues. In 1919, everything came to crisis, wrenching the national psyche as if we were wrestling with a guilty collective conscience. And what a mess we made of the battle!

It is the premise of this book that the vitality of our history lies in confronting the essence of what we are as a people, otherwise we cannot deal with what we ought to be. How does it profit our collective wisdom to be seduced into lassitude while the rats are gnawing in the woodwork? Who gains by the vain and pompous references to glorious cities on the hill but the rats themselves? This account is not a pretty one with inspiring American heroes and sacrificial profiles in courage. More likely, it assembles a collection of opportunists and self-deceivers whose manipulations deceived us all, always in the name of the public welfare.

On the eve of my induction into the Army in the fall of 1941, I visited the journalist I.F. Stone at the newspaper *PM*, where he was kind enough to listen to my confusions. As a history student, I had learned enough to understand the futility of wars. I was frustrated and frightened at the prospect of soldiering in still another war for the preservation of democracy. As I saw it, the same forces that created Hitler and permitted him to run rampant over the European continent would then preside over the peacemaking for another turn in the eternal cycle. What, in effect, was I to believe in?

He took no delight in my question, especially for the gravity of what was at stake. His response was wonderfully sympathetic and perceptive. History, he explained, has always imposed such unjust burdens, and that they should fall on me was merely the unfortunate result of being of age at such a time. His point was, Fascism had to be destroyed. Even if there were no guarantees at what followed, Fascism had to be destroyed. He likened it to a plague. No matter that new diseases or variables of the old persisted, the plague must be wiped out or civilization would itself be destroyed. It was up to me to make peace with that, but always with the understanding that the historical rewards for my sacrifices will inevitably be less than what I would like them to be.

Nonetheless, he felt that history had a remarkable way of working out, if not for the best then for the better. The war would be fought for the better reasons—and when it was won, we would have to work for a better peace.

When I blanched at such a feeble prospect, he suddenly assumed an astonishing pugnacity, fist rapping on the desk top as he spoke: "We simply mustn't let them get away with anything less!"

To re-create that scene so many years later can only trivialize its impact. I felt, if not the best, then definitely the better for it, and I went off to become part of history that much better to understand it. As it turned out, "they" have gotten away with far too much. Reading I.F. Stone's work over the ensuing years makes that all too clear. But always, there was his pugnacious pose to keep me involved. In this book, I offer some of my own. I would show how it was seventy years ago in our eternal struggle with venality. On the record, at least, I would not let them get away with it.

For its telling, I am indebted to the many excellent sources listed in the subsequent pages and bibliography. I am especially grateful for access to the Edsel Ford Memorial Library at the Hotchkiss School in Lakeville, Connecticut, and the Williams College Library in Williamstown, Massachusetts.

—E.A.

1. WOODROW WILSON'S WAR FOR DEMOCRACY

I wish there were some great orator who could make men drunk with the spirit of self-sacrifice.

—WOODROW WILSON

Paris, January 18, 1919

At the Quai d'Orsay, the Salon de la Paix offered a garish setting with thick red carpets, heavy cream-colored drapes along towering walls, crystal chandeliers suspended from gold frescoes on a white ceiling, frolicking cupids along spacious borders like a Hollywood movie set for the crowning of an emperor. Plenipotentiaries from all over the world assembled here in their elegant cutaways, their staffs of experts and special commissions in attendance like royal retainers. In this palatial ambience, a conference was held to resolve the conflicts of the world after the most devastating war in history. Its aim was to make the peace.

In contrast, hardly an hour's drive would take one to the sites of carnage, a wasteland of shattered homes and decimated forests, of rotting fetid trenches where millions died in over four years of unrelenting slaughter. Who would note the contradictions of peacemaking in such opulence by old men who had never suffered the subhuman horror of those trenches, never been assaulted by the barbarity of poison gases, never cringed under thunderous artillery barrages or lived with the rotting stench of the death of friends?

Incredibly, however, the people of the world were alive with hope. No matter that this had been just another war in the endless cycle of wars. No matter that eight million soldiers had been killed and twenty million more maimed, that twenty-two million civilians were casualties. The accompanying flu epidemic had killed six million more. Thirteen million tons of shipping had been sunk, twelve thousand square miles of France had been ravaged, hundreds of thousands of buildings, including twelve thousand churches, destroyed. In spite of famine accompanied by epidemics of cholera and typhus, in spite of the chaos and challenge of revolution, indeed, in spite of everything, among the great mass of the world's victims there was hope. There was a world leader who gave them reason to, one man in that mass of well-stuffed diplomatic suits with the power to change the world. He was Woodrow Wilson, president of the great American democracy. Woodrow Wilson, who had brought the war to an end, would lead the world to peace. Had he not declared the intention of his country "to make the world safe for democracy in a war to end all wars"? Had he not dared to demand "a peace without victory"? Had he not stated a program of Fourteen Points to free the world of tyranny and exploitation with a League of Nations to secure the brotherhood of man?

How like a god he was! The first American president to cross the seas while in office, that he might personally implement his ends. And how magnificent had been his greeting! He had come to Paris to experience a reception that no man had ever known, a sea of humanity surging through the streets, a solid moving mass, weeping, cheering, waving, emitting a deafening roar as he drove by. "Honor to Wilson the Just!" they cried out. Never had anyone seen so many whose hearts reached out to him nor heard such sounds of love and gratitude. To Wilson, this had been as a message from God himself. And so it had been in London. Millions more came to see him—children with flowers they tossed before his carriage and, above all, working people who called him "the Savior" as he rode by with the king and queen, cannons roaring in the distance. Then, again in Italy, he was greeted with a boundless joy that seemed almost hysterical. In the industrial north, hordes of peasants poured into cities for a glimpse of him, people of all classes mingling for the first time, overwhelmed by a mutual cmotion, many kneeling in filthy streets to pray. He was hailed everywhere as the Prince of Peace, worshipped as if sent from heaven to help the poor, the helpless, the sufferers of war's brutalities. Many had knelt beside the tracks as his train went by, children had thrown flowers, every hut in Italy had a candle burning beneath his picture torn from newspapers, a saint to be worshipped. They would call this the Second Coming of the Messiah.

All over the world there was a tidal wave of hope, so effusive, so all-powerful, it appeared that civilization had finally reached a turning point. Peace would overwhelm the decadence of the warmakers. The people were as one in their demand for change. And here, at last, was the man who would bring it about. From that sanctuary of hope across the Atlantic, here was Woodrow Wilson, who had pledged to implement that change.

"... We seek no indemnities ... no material compensation; we desire no conquest, no dominion," Wilson said to the Joint Session of Congress, April 3, 1917. "We have no selfish ends to serve.... We would fight for the principles that gave this country birth ... for the things which we have always carried nearest our hearts ... for a universal dominion of right by such a concert of free peoples as shall bring peace and safety to all nations and make the world itself free...."

In these words, he had asked the United States Congress to declare war as a crusade for humanity. There was no bitterness in his speech, no cry for vengeance, no hatred toward human enemies. He had committed his country to serving the highest purpose of all: the liberation of mankind from oppression and the preservation of democracy throughout the world. This, then, was the cause that had brought him to Paris and inspired the crucial conflicts of 1919. Before the year was out, the hopes of millions would be shattered.

Woodrow Wilson's war was a myth, a mystique, a masquerade. He did not understand it, but thrived on his pretensions like a man wedded to a shrew, forever convinced that she was an angel. From the moment the war erupted in Europe, he was caught in its spiraling confusions. He kept trying to put square pegs in round holes and never abandoned the effort. Because of the war, he was forced to run away from the world he knew; inevitably, the world would catch up with him.

For Wilson and his presidency, the problem had no right to exist. He had had no knowledge of foreign policy. He was a pacifist by personality as well as political persuasion. When he was made to face the war, he did everything he could to keep America out— except to bring us in. And when he did with that transcendental speech, Woodrow Wilson at the Paris Peace Conference in 1919 was doomed.

There have always been presidents who were prepared to make war as if it were a feast for a hungry man (Theodore Roosevelt was a prime example), but Wilson found surcease only in the role of peacemaker. In 1914, the eruptions of Europe seemed like utter madness to him, their roots imbedded in old-world rivalries of which he had no understanding. The assassination at Sarajevo, Bosnia, was itself a distant and preposterous event; the Austro-Hungarian Archduke Ferdinand von Este, shot by a Serbian, died largely because he preferred a uniform so tight-fitting that he had to be sewn into it, whereupon the doctor who tried to save him lost too much time cutting him out of it. On such preposterous characterizations did the history of the world turn, and twenty million more would die as a result of it.

With astonishing suddenness the nations of Europe began declaring war on each other, the outgrowth of ententes and secret treaties allegedly designed to prevent it. The response of the belligerent capitals was a pageantry of ecstatic cheers, patriotic singing, parades, celebrations of national pride and heartfelt prayers for eventual victory. War, in the traditions of Europe, was a liberation.

In Washington, D.C., Woodrow Wilson sat by his beloved wife's bedside and watched her die, sinking into such despair he seemed on the brink of collapse. Europe appeared to mean nothing to him. On a visit to his dear friend and adviser, Colonel Edward House, in New York, he insisted on taking a walk through the crowded downtown streets at night, just the two of them. To House, fearing for his safety, the experience was a nightmare: "I thought at that time, and on several occasions afterward, that the president wanted to die."

In time, Wilson responded to the world crisis, establishing a national policy of neutrality "in thought as well as deed." The country agreed. "The war is none of our business," it was said, a locution that denied what became the true American purpose. The transition that followed seemed inexorable. Within months, our neutral attitudes began to change. Since the British Navy controlled the seas, England immediately cut Germany's Atlantic cable. All telegraphic communication would, from then on, come out of London; England would censor everything that was cabled to America. United States correspondents immediately went to cover the war exclusively with Allied armies. When Germany violated Belgium's territory, its invasion was made to appear a crusade in sadism—raping nuns, severing hands of Belgian babies, bayoneting old women, shipping corpses back to German soap factories, dressing German soldiers in nuns' habits for spying purposes. To the disseminators of war news, no horror was too extreme. No matter that no atrocity was substantiated, this was the stuff of acceptable journalism.

Whatever our so-called neutrality, it was far more satisfying to take sides. Because of a common language and heritage, it was easier to side with Britain. There was something touching about "It's a Long Long Way to Tipperary" as compared to the imperious image of the militarist Prussian Junkers. The Kaiser himself, with his arrogant twirling moustache, was an easy target for democratic barbs.

The neutrality of deed was even more difficult to maintain with so much money to be made for violating it. There was simply no getting around the British Navy's control of trade. The law of the seas was not law but whatever the controlling sea power dictated. England permitted shipping only in Allied ports. They would haul our bottoms into British ports, search them at leisure, rifle the mails, steal trade secrets. American exporters to other countries, neutral or otherwise, had to get British permission. England actually blacklisted American companies who chose to trade with Germany. United States protests to these gross violations of neutral rights got nowhere. Our ambassador to England, Walter Hines Page, almost as pro-British as pro-American, was always there to soften them.

Meanwhile, the war became a blessing to American business, lifting the economy from a lingering depression. And with it came the inevitable dissolution of neutral opinion. That this conformed with Wilson's (and Colonel House's) love of the English was a convenient factor in its blessings, whatever the violations of neutral rights. J. P. Morgan's National City Bank had made huge loans, $10 million to France, $500 million more to Britain through a consortium of banks. By April 1917, when we went to war our-selves, over $2 billion had been raised in Allied war bonds (and barely $20 million for Germany). With these loans, production and profit turned depression into instant prosperity. Prices began to climb. Wheat rose to its highest level in years. Cotton prices tripled, hogs as well. The price of steel leaped with every new order. As William A. White wrote: "War was producing . . . its own intoxication, a kind of economic inflation that had spiritual re-flexes. People felt happy because they were busy making money—naturally, as the Allies were our customers, they became our true friends."

Wilson was more poetic, and much less candid. "To develop our life and our resources, to supply our own people and the people of the world as their needs arose from the abundant plenty of our fields and our marts of trade; to enrich the commerce of our own states and of the world with the products of our farms, and our factories with the creations of our thought and the fruits of our character." Or, as the dissident Wisconsin senator Robert La Follette put it: "Neutrality for profit and glory."

When the established credit line became overextended, there was a question as to whether more loans were advisable. Secretary of State William Jennings Bryan was vigorously opposed—at first. Secretary of the Treasury William G. McAdoo was a Morgan sym-pathizer. "Great prosperity is coming," he advised Wilson. "It will be tremendously increased if we can extend financing. Otherwise, it may stop and that would be disastrous." Robert Lansing of the State Department was even more graphic: ". . . the result [of its denial] would be restriction of output, industrial depression, idle capital and idle labor, numerous failures, financial demoralization and general unrest and suffering among the laboring classes . . . ," adding in a remarkable confession of our inherent duplicity: "Can we afford to let a declaration as to our conception of 'the true spirit of neutrality' stand in the way of our national interests which seem to be seriously threatened?"

Meanwhile, as early as October 1914, barely two months after the outbreak of war, E. I. Du Pont had received its first war contract: Russia ordered 960,000 pounds of TNT. Four days later, France ordered eight million pounds of cannon powder and 1,250,000 pounds of gun cotton for making explosives. By December, the Allies had bought 15,600,000 pounds of Du Pont powder. By March 1915, orders increased 350 percent. Charles Schwab, head of Bethlehem Steel, went immediately to London to do business and came home with a $50 million order. Heavy industry was reviving, and J. P. Morgan was there to finance it with extensive credits. All for the Allies, since the British Navy had blockaded German ports.

Not without threatening implications, as everyone realized. There were cautionary senatorial proposals for an embargo on arms sales to belligerent nations. It was one thing to make money on the wars of others; it was quite another to supply, and invest in, only one side. For weeks, Wilson "pondered the perplexing issue," then publicly declared that "the duty of a neutral to restrict trade in munitions of war has never been imposed by international law." And in that one feeble legalistic phrase, whatever his desire to keep America out of the war, he had committed us.

In May 1915, England placed a new order for $100 million worth of shells and shrapnel with Bethlehem Steel. Du Pont's profits were running 100 percent ahead of 1914. Businessmen poured into New York City vying for subcontracting orders. Daniel Guggenheim, a copper magnate, commented with ponderous righteousness that "These men have become wealthy because they have been thrifty." Franklin D. Roosevelt, under secretary of the Navy, protested the rising prices of copper, suggesting that Guggenheim also make *his* wealth, not by greed but by thrift. Frederick Howe, commissioner of Immigration, proposed that all munitions manufacturers be stripped of profits. William A. White was in favor of government ownership of all plants making munitions of every kind. *La Follette's Weekly* was brutally critical: "When you can boom stocks 600 percent in manufacturing munitions—to the Bottomless Pit with Neutrality! What do Morgan and Schwab care for world peace when there are big profits in World War?" White added: "...we are rich with blood money. We have built up our own wealth on the lives of others. Our Prosperity is cursed and tainted." Henry Ford, greatest of all automobile manufacturers, was a determined pacifist who refused to accept any war orders, fulminating against American profiteers. "Take away the capitalists and you will sweep war from the earth."

Meanwhile, Colonel House, Wilson's emissary to the diplomatic centers of the war, was being advised by the German government that if the United States wished to remain at peace, it had better embargo the shipments of munitions. The German invasion of France had been stopped short of Paris, frustrating the quick victory anticipated by the High Command. Time suddenly appeared to side with the British blockade, destined to starve out the Central Powers. Significantly, American trade with Germany diminished from $345 million in 1914 to a minuscule $2 million in 1916 even as it boomed to $2.7 billion with the Allies. Against this crushing disparity, Germany had one recourse: submarines. Hundreds of U-boats were roaming the seas surrounding the British Isles and continental ports, torpedoing cargo ships in ever-increasing tonnage. The British took their losses, and produced more and more ships. Inevitably, American lives were lost, whereupon Wilson protested this violation of neutral rights with strident notes to the German government. Germany expressed regrets, but how else could she sustain her war effort? Did not England also violate American neutrality with its seizures of ships? U-boat sinkings were different, it was argued, for killing was not akin to property damage. The Germans argued it could not be otherwise. They could not issue warnings before torpedoing, for an exposed submarine was too easy a target. Were not British ships advised to ram U-boats if they surfaced? Were not merchant ships armed? It was like asking a man fighting for his life not to shoot his assailant for fear of hitting a passerby.

Then, in May 1915, came the turning point. The British Cunard Line queen ship, the *Lusitania,* set sail from New York to Liverpool, a magnificent four-stacker, 755 feet long, eighty-eight feet wide, four propellers—the largest and most luxurious ship afloat for three thousand passengers, capable of speeding to twenty-five knots in a record crossing of four days, eleven hours, four minutes. On the day before its sailing, the German government issued a warning with an ad in New York newspapers: "NOTICE ... Travellers ... are reminded that a state of war exists ... vessels flying the flag of Great Britain ... are liable to destruction."

One thousand two hundred and fifty-seven passengers, 188 of whom were Americans, and a crew of 667 paid no heed to it. On May 7, land was sighted off the coast of Ireland, green hills and white cottages in the midday sun, a fittingly lovely sight to end a luxurious week. If there was no convoy of destroyers to escort them to port, that too seemed reassuring.

In the midst of this serenity, suddenly there was a pounding thud, and almost immediately, a tremendous blast. As reported in the ship's log: "An unusually heavy detonation followed with a very strong explosive cloud...."

The great ship heeled to starboard and sank in eighteen minutes. As the U-boat captain reported, other ships similarly struck did not sink at all, or sank slowly. Most required a second torpedo. Since the *Lusitania* was equipped with a technology designed for unsinkability, the only explanation was the extraordinary second blast caused by explosive munitions in the hold. At a subsequent committee of inquiry, the *Lusitania* captain admitted he had been instructed by the Admiralty to steer a midchannel course and to avoid areas known to be dangerous, to proceed at high speed in a zigzag pattern. All this he had disregarded. When torpedoed, he was going only eighteen to twenty-one knots in order not to arrive in Liverpool at a time of unfavorable tides—which he could have safely accomplished by a high-speed roundabout course as instructed. This too he admitted.

The *Lusitania* had apparently been turned into a sitting duck.

Nothing in the war, before or after, so wrenched the American people, especially under the force of British propaganda. "Sunk without warning!" went the battle cry of horror. No matter that there *had* been reasonable warning. Months before the tragedy, Germany had repeatedly warned of such sinkings. There were twenty-two more sinkings even while the *Lusitania* was in passage. No matter that Americans could have sailed a few hours later on *The New York*, a neutral liner and thus without risk. It was the loss of 114 American lives that was so inexcusable. During the same week of the *Lusitania* disaster, the British Navy was preventing American merchant ships from entering neutral ports in Scandinavia and almost a billion dollars' worth of meat products was detained. Meat packers, cotton dealers and western miners were all protesting the arbitrary British seizures. Lansing at the

State Department agreed that "the conduct of Great Britain was unbearable." Said William Jennings Bryan: "Why are we more stern with Germany than England? They kill thousands (with U-boats) while the British blockade starves millions. What do you expect Germany to do?"

Along the Eastern seaboard, there was considerable talk of war. Those who had sought it from the onset now felt free to speak openly. The propaganda value of the *Lusitania* seemed akin to the sinking of the *Maine* in 1898, also under a highly suspicious set of circumstances. (Indeed, the true story of the famous Boston Massacre in 1775 suggested more than raw British butchery.) Teddy Roosevelt was his usual bombastic self: "Wilson and Bryan . . . are both such abject creatures, they won't go to war unless they are kicked into it." Bryan more than Wilson, as it turned out, as they clashed over the sternness of Wilson's communications to Berlin.

Colonel House was in London when the *Lusitania* went down, full of British excitation at the prospects of a pro-war American response. "I believe an immediate demand should be made upon Germany for assurance that this shall not happen again," he cabled Wilson. To Ambassador Page, he commented with reassurance: "We shall be at war within a month."

In the States there was confusion. Polls taken of congressmen showed agreement at the horror of the sinking, but only three opted for war. The same feelings prevailed in a sampling of newspaper publishers throughout the country.

Five days after the sinking, Wilson's speech to Congress was classic: "The example of America must be a special example . . . not merely of peace because it will not fight, but of peace because peace is the healing and elevating influence of the world and strife is not. There is such a thing as a nation being so right that it does not need to convince others by force that it is right. . . . There is such a thing as a man being too proud to fight."

Again, the country responded well to this position. There would be business as usual while the polarizing continued. As German Ambassador von Bernstadt put it: "Our propaganda has collapsed completely." The country was awash with anti-Hun jingoism. Hyphenated Americans with foreign accents were made to seem threatening. T.R. bellowed for 100 percent Americanism.

Pacifists were called pro-German and traitors. The simplistic battle raged: "Would you fight if a German soldier struck your mother?" versus "I didn't raise my boy to be a soldier." Overall, it was easier to hate than abstain.

The battle over policy continued, especially vis-à-vis Americans who sailed on Allied ships. Bryan advocated that this be restricted, pointing out that hardly a year before, when hundreds of Americans were killed during revolutionary outbreaks in Mexico, Wilson had warned them to leave Mexico or remain at their own risk. In the present crisis, however, Wilson reversed gears: "I cannot consent to any abridgment of the rights of American citizens. Once accept a single abatement of right, and many other humiliations would follow." To La Follette, for one, this was specious and insulting. How many abatements had already been suffered at the hands of the British? "To be neutral was to refrain from provocations. Wilson was simply endorsing a program for war without actually declaring it!"

Meanwhile, as German propaganda had collapsed, British propaganda may well have reached its zenith, releasing a report "on alleged German atrocities" by a committee of distinguished British intellectuals headed by Viscount James Bryce, noted historian and diplomat, and long one of Wilson's heroes. In it, the Germans were charged with having committed every sadistic act imaginable, deeds so degenerate as to suffer total revulsion at its reading. The publishing of this document in American newspapers, hardly a week after the *Lusitania*, was a knockout blow in the propaganda war. No matter that a number of celebrated American correspondents who had experienced the war expressed astonishment at its contents. Their jointly signed cable to the Associated Press in New York stated categorically as to its falseness: "IN SPIRIT OF FAIRNESS WE UNITE IN DECLARING GERMAN ATROCITIES GROUNDLESS." But any denial was a mere prick at the giant hide of hate. America was losing what was left of its lingering neutrality.

There was enormous power and big money behind the prowar movement. Important industrialists of the East formed the National Security League with over one hundred thousand members in hundreds of branches throughout the country, dedicated to support the Allies on the patriotic premise that our country's survival depended on their victory. In New York, a committee of authors, artists, editors and educators dedicated their talents to fight for America's honor in denouncing pacifism, promoting what came to be called preparedness. They never stopped attacking public officials who opposed them, especially Robert La Follette. They called themselves the Vigilantes. Then there was Thomas Dixon, author of *The Clansman,* from which *Birth of a Nation* was adopted, whose new best-selling novel, *The Fall of a Nation,* attacked advocates of peace who left America helpless before the Hunlike invader until, not the Ku Klux Klan but a modern Joan of Arc organized a secret clan of women who led the men to overthrow the conqueror and restore democracy. *Lysistrata* was stood on its head. As for Teddy Roosevelt, ever the raging Bull Moose, Wilson's duplicity was intolerable. "President Wilson took forty-one different positions about preparedness... the weasel words of one position took all the meaning out of the words used in another."

Wilson was a president without a position or an identifiable point of view. His pledge for neutrality had become victim of his own inability to be neutral. Once he allowed Americans to sail on British ships, or to send munitions and supplies exclusively to Allied ports, any indignation at German retaliation, at whatever cost to American lives, was pure sophistry. When he permitted the extension of credit for Allied purchases, he immediately committed United States financial power groups to an Allied victory to secure those loans. Behind them, then, the manufacturers, the stockholders, the workers and owners all became beholden to this credit line. And the newspapers, largely owned and dominated by the beneficiaries of this policy, spelled out the news as they saw fit. If war was to be avoided, then neutrality could not be compromised. There were no international rights or liberties, no national honor that justified any violation of that neutrality. Only money was involved. Put it simply: No credit to belligerent nations. No shipments of arms or munitions to anyone, even for cash and carry. No Americans permitted to sail on belligerent ships. Of course, Wilson understood this. He also understood that prosperity was at issue, that 1916 was an election year, and that the blustering ever-popular Teddy Roosevelt was baying at his heels.

Then, much to his (and everyone else's) astonishment, the

president fell in love. A desperately grieving widower over sixty years old, he rediscovered love and the joys of a rejuvenated sex life. His Secret Service guardian, Edmund Starling, wrote that this normally dour man, on the morning of his honeymoon, was seen in his private railway car kicking up his heels, singing "Oh You Beautiful Doll." She was Edith Bolling Gault, an attractive and spirited Washington widow who became a perfect wife for him, so much so, in fact, that he seriously considered retiring from the presidency. All this ecstasy stunned House, the more so for its intrusion on their relationship. House, however, was smart enough to play his cards well, eventually using the romance to increase his own power.

With House at work, there would be no retreat by the president, no abandonment of his God-given responsibility to his people for the pleasures of love. The 1916 election was around the corner and he would be wise to prepare for it. And the changing mood of the electorate, or so House saw it, was wrapped up in a single word: preparedness.

The president responded. He toured the country, an opening gun in his campaign, as it were, and another occasion to gratify his penchant for oratory. With old Wilsonian rhetoric, he played the war/peace game to a stirring draw: "This country should prepare herself, not for war . . . but for adequate national defense . . . the prosecution of peace. . . . There is danger to our national life. . . . I pledge you my word that, God helping me, I will keep this nation out of war if it is possible."

Meanwhile, the regular army was to be increased to 186,000, a federalized National Guard to 425,000 and the Reserved Officers Training Corps was to be established at universities. However slightly, the military boot was now in the door—enough to infuriate both sides of the issue. T.R., for example, was fuming. If he were president, America would be in the war and T.R. would be in France leading the attack. "I am sick at heart over the reactions of Wilson," Roosevelt told the British ambassador. "Your country is passing through the flame and will come out cleansed and refined to lofty nobleness. Mine is passing through the thick yellow mud-streak of 'safety first.' "

As it turned out, Wilson was much closer to the American mainstream. In addition, sensitive to the dynamics of this coming

presidential election, the German government stopped all provocative U-boat attacks on neutral shipping. The screaming headlines of death on the high seas, and more dead Americans, became
a thing of the past. Wilson, it seemed, had brought America
through the worst of it. Roosevelt failed to win the Republican
nomination, having incurred the resentment of the old guard at
his defection to the Progressives in 1912. Wilson, who had
squeaked into office because of the Republican split, now faced a
united party under the candidacy of Charles Evans Hughes. In
spite of Wilson's incumbency and the political achievements of his
administration, his reelection was in doubt. The Republican Party
had been the dominant one since 1886. For Wilson to win, the
Democrats needed a battle cry around which to rally the American
people, a popular slogan to pin on the president's rhetorical style.
Wilson himself had recommended a plea for patriotism, to steal
T.R.'s thunder. Quite by accident, the solution popped out of a
dreary keynote speech by New Jersey Governor Martin Glynn
who ran on about the way Wilson had "sent notes instead of guns"
to Germany, listing outrage after outrage that did not end up in
war. "What *did* he do?" someone cried out, to which the delegates
cried out in a rousing response: "He kept us out of war!" And
suddenly, the crowd was bellowing this phrase over and over,
snake-dancing down the aisles, flags waving in a near-hysterical
demonstration as they chanted, "He kept us out of war!"

Wilson was nominated on the first ballot, but he did not recognize the source of his political power. Too honest to exploit this
new slogan, his acceptance speech reflected his fears: "No nation
can any longer remain neutral as against any willful disturbance
of the peace of the world." But his campaign manager, the advertising professional George Creel, did not hesitate to reap the
harvest of the campaign phrase.

Even then, the results were so close it wasn't until Friday,
three days after election day, that the California vote was finally
counted. Wilson had won by a bare 3,773 votes, giving him 277
electoral college votes to Hughes's 254—a curious election that
the Republicans celebrated but the Democrats won. Said the dis-
traught British ambassador, "The elections have clearly shown
that the great mass of Americans desire nothing so much as to
keep out of the war."

If the president opposed it in support of the public will, what, then, could bring us in? The answer became evident at the proposed resolution in Congress that all Americans be warned not to travel in war zones, for there was no greater *causus belli* than American deaths at the hands of a hostile foreign power. Had not the president issued precisely the same warning to Americans vis-à-vis Mexico several years before for precisely the same reason? But here, when the dangers were far greater, he chose to block the resolution from even coming to a vote. As he saw it, how could we stay out of war zones and continue to ship war goods? The issue was America's rights as a neutral—a euphemism for money-making. Besides, would Germany dare to sink more American ships at the risk of provoking us? Did their survival lay more in blocking Allied supply lines than in avoiding our entrance? Wilson declared that such a resolution was an attack on his presidential leadership. To keep his options open, he insisted on determining all matters concerning war and peace.

Thus he would lead America into the coming months like a man on a tightrope.

Meanwhile, in France, the war was a continuing slaughterhouse. The poet Edwin Dwight said it best in his portrait of "Victory":

> Five hundred miles of Germans
> Five hundred miles of French
> And English, Scotch, and Irishmen
> All fighting for a trench;
> And when the trench is taken
> And many thousands slain,
> The losers, with more slaughter,
> Retake the trench again.

Wilson, endowed with a mandate of popular will, became consumed by a new messianic notion that he could end the war without fighting in it. The battlefield stalemate and the millions already dead would be his ticket to the negotiating table. The Kaiser was said to be agreeable. Wilson rushed into the breach, offering to use the power and prestige of America as mediator for a mutually satisfying agreement that would end the war and establish an international association that would keep the peace. To Wilson's dismay, the Allies declined, determined to capture the spoils for which they had entered the war in the first place. Wilson remained undeterred, even though House opposed this view, for the colonel was convinced that the best course was to enter the war as quickly as possible. Wilson argued, "This country does not intend to become involved.... We are the only one of the great white nations that is free from war today, and it would be a crime against civilization for us to go in." In late January 1917, he made a distinguished speech before the Senate that might have altered history had the combatants seen fit to comply. "Peace without victory!" he proposed. "Victory would mean peace forced upon the loser, a victor's terms imposed upon the vanquished.... Only a peace between equals can last. Only a peace ... of equality and a common participation in a common benefit."

The words were gloriously civilized but they did not satisfy the needs of the warriors. National leaders who had brought their people into war for specific conquests were not about to make peace without having achieved those conquests. After all the carnage, how could they justify it? How long would they remain in power? Whatever the current stalemate on the battlefront, no war office was going to concede anything less than a coming victory. The Allies rejected the Wilson proposal as unrealistic. Germany, meanwhile, was preparing a massive assault in the spring backed by another massive submarine attack on Allied shipping that was guaranteed to starve out Britain—or so the High Command advised the Kaiser.

But even as these preparations were evolving, the German Foreign Office paid homage to Wilson's peace offer. The German ambassador advised Wilson of his government's desire to negotiate. And Wilson, ever responsive to the potential of his role as peacemaker, was elated. Hardly a week after his speech, however, he was shocked by the German government's declaration to resume unrestricted submarine warfare. In New York, House read of it in screaming headlines, then took the midnight train to Washington. He found the president deeply depressed. "He said he felt as if the world had suddenly reversed itself ... he could not get his balance." The crown of the peacemaker was being knocked off his head.

Immediately, Wilson met with his cabinet to hear them out. Then he went before Congress to advise that he was severing diplomatic relations with Germany. This, he made clear, did not mean war or even that he had any intention of leading the country into war largely because of what he understood to be the selfishness of its underlying causes. "The singularity of the present war is that its origins and objects have never been fully disclosed," he said.

The president was making his last stand with this declaration, quite remarkable as a statement before Congress, for it suggested the dubious validity of the war itself. House, who had objected to these words, was careful to avoid making an issue of them. Any suspicion of a radical idea in the president's head was anathema to him but he knew how to ride out these little storms—especially now when the drift toward war was so evident.

To the war crowd, this was one more illustration of Wilson's "lily-livered failure to defend America's honor." Once again, in full voice, Teddy Roosevelt led the pack in his contempt for Wilson's pacifism. The British government, which had infuriated Wilson for its refusal to accept his peace offering, was now equally furious at his refusal to join the war. It had, however, one amazing card up its sleeve, one it was extremely reluctant to use. Having broken the German secret code weeks before, British intelligence had intercepted a telegram from Germany's new foreign secretary, Arthur Zimmermann, to its ambassador in Washington, that read: "On the first of February, we intend to begin submarine warfare unrestricted. In spite of this, we intend to keep neutral the U.S. of A. If this attempt is not successful, we propose an alliance of Mexico on the following terms: that we shall make war together, make peace together, provide generous financial support and an understanding . . . that Mexico is to reconquer its lost territory in New Mexico, Texas, and Arizona. . . . Please call the president's attention to the fact that unrestricted employment of our submarines now offers the prospect of compelling England to make peace within a few months. . . ." England had withheld this telegram from release lest the Germans realize that the code had been broken. But with Wilson's refusal to declare war, they had no choice but to risk the consequences.

So the Zimmermann telegram was secretly dispatched to Secretary of State Robert Lansing, long a British sympathizer, and just as secretly released through the Associated Press without identifying the source. On February 28, every newspaper in America was asked to headline its contents. The news shocked the country. Many immediately doubted its authenticity. Hundreds of reporters stormed the State Department to challenge it, firing questions at Lansing. Yes, he admitted, the AP story was indeed authentic. Since British propaganda had so tainted the truth for so long, however, stories persisted that this was just another illustration of British guile. Then, to everyone's astonishment, Arthur Zimmermann himself admitted in Berlin that he had sent it!

In America, the Western states, rock-hard resisters against entry into the war, now became terrorized by reports of a hundred thousand Germans in Mexico, ready to invade. T.R. became apoplectic, unleashing a stream of invective against Wilson that bordered on the unprintable. "This man is enough to make the saints and the angels—yes, and the Apostles—swear, and I would not blame them. *My God, why doesn't he do something!*"

Through it all, Wilson's resistance had been remarkable. In spite of his anger against the deceits of the German government which had played him for a fool; in spite of the rising tide of pro-war American sentiment, which, for the first time, appeared to dominate the American consensus; in spite of the pressures of Colonel House and his cabinet, he still resisted. In his torment, he sustained sleepless nights, suffered attacks of his old dyspepsia and was constantly unnerved and irritable. He prayed for guidance as he struggled for a way to proceed. To his everlasting credit, he saw that, German perfidy notwithstanding, the cause was not worth the potential sacrifice. Even with eventual victory, he could foresee the consequences, the self-seeking motives of his Allies that would dominate the terms of the peace. He could not see himself leading his people into the bloodbath for such dubious prospects. There was no question but that the alternatives before him were a continuing source of torment. Could he simply take the position that the German government had forced him into war? Or the reverse position, that, in spite of these provocations, he must continue to refuse, no matter that this might make him and the United States appear as a spineless international joke?

In the midst of these conjectures came a completely startling event that would alter the course of history: the Russian people overthrew the tyrannical government of the Romanov tsars and set up a provisional government under Aleksandr Kerensky. To Wilson, there was nothing more gratifying than that this new ideology would suddenly purify the Allied cause. (Indeed, one might wonder at the ideological confusion had the German people overthrown the Kaiser and the Hohenzollerns.) His friend, Colonel House, immediately took pains to flatter the president that this great event was no doubt the result of his influence. Said Wilson with incredible innocence, "Russia was known by those who knew it best to have been always, in fact, democratic at heart."

For all its grandeur, for the Allies the revolution created a new wariness. For one thing, how many divisions would this new government be able to mount against the Germans on the eastern front? How effective would they be as a fighting force? King George V of England cabled condolences to his cousin, Tsar Nicholas, reassuring kinship in the "great war for democracy." Another cable went to the British ambassador to warn the provisional government that any violence done to the tsar or his family would have a deplorable effect on British public opinion. Wilson, meanwhile, immediately sent a delegation to Petrograd to support Kerensky and the Russian war effort, astonishing everyone, including the Russians, by appointing Elihu Root, a snobbish ultraconservative Republican, to head it. Root, along with American Ambassador David Francis, could hardly resist alienating the new regime even as they offered military support worth $325 million and a vital Red Cross presence. It appeared not to concern any of them that the Russian aristocracy had brought the revolution on itself. The American journalist John Reed wrote of it: "Graft in (Tsarist) Russia is on such a naively vast scale that it became almost grotesque.... Exposure after exposure revealed that the entire intendency was nothing but a mass of corruption; but the trail always led so far and so high that it had to be choked off.... In the caste-controlled Russian Army, millions of soldiers had to fight almost bare-handed, suffering hunger, cold, disease, all because of the incredible cupidity and incompetence of their superior officers."

Because of this, there were more Russian casualties than in all other armies combined. To the peasants, withdrawal from the slaughter was at the essence of the revolution. As it turned out, the continuing Russian involvement in the war, implemented by Kerensky to insure Allied support for his government, became the principal cause of his downfall.

Wilson, meanwhile, was under enormous pressure by an ever-increasing American war spirit. In the end, his decision was arrived at with typical Wilsonian righteousness. To justify so devastating an action as asking America to go to war, he would convince himself that it would be a noble crusade. Whatever the facts that brought him so much torment, whatever the dismal prospects for peace as he anticipated them, once he committed himself to war he had to disregard them. His identification with Christ and the word of God would not permit him to proceed otherwise. He could not go before Congress and the American people unless he believed in the effect of his own words.

The night of March 31, he left his bed for his desk in slippers and robe, sat at his old portable typewriter and punched out a final draft of that decision. This would be his speech before the Joint Session of Congress he had summoned for April 2 "to receive a communication concerning grave matters."

Its thrust was a message less of vengeance against ruthlessness or even the defense of America's honor than of the nobility of our cause. "Germany's war was against all nations . . . a challenge to all mankind . . . against the rights and liberties of small nations. This would not be a war driven by hatred. We have no quarrel with the German people. We have no feeling toward them but one of sympathy and friendship. It was not upon their impulse that their government acted in entering the war . . . provoked and waged in the interests of dynasties accustomed to use their fellow men as pawns and tools." But the key phrase, more loaded with consequence than the rest, was the ultimate in mischievous fantasy: "The world must be made safe for democracy." Above all else, it would justify the godliness of his purpose. Nonetheless, he had yet to fully convince himself that this was necessary. He summoned his friend Frank Cobb, editor of the *New York World*. Cobb arrived late that night. (House would not appear until the next morning.)

Cobb found Wilson in poor shape, desperate to talk, seeking an alternative to his decision, any possible way of avoiding it. Cobb replied that America's hand had indeed been forced. Wilson continued to protest, overwhelmed by what he took to be the prospects. War would overturn the world as we knew it. "It would mean that we should lose our heads along with the rest and stop weighing right from wrong. It would mean that a majority of people would go war mad." It would mean that Germany would be beaten so badly, in fact, that there would be a dictated peace and "...at the end of the war there will be no bystanders with sufficient power to influence the terms. There won't be any peace standards left to work with. There will be only war standards." He despised the thought that the Allies would expect to have their way with the very things he was so opposed to. Nor did he have any illusions about the impact of war on the American people, for when a war got going, a nation gave up its freedom—everything became dictated to support the war effort. We could not maintain democratic traditions in war. We would, in effect, become like the Germans themselves.

"Once lead the people into war," Wilson told Cobb in considerable anguish, "and they'll forget there ever was such a thing as tolerance.... Conformity would be the only virtue, and every man who refused to conform would have to pay the penalty." He begged Cobb: "If there is any alternative, for God's sake, let's take it!"

Cobb could offer none.

As extracted from Edward Robert Ellis's excellent history, the following day was overloaded with drama. Washington was bristling with predictable tension. Colonel House arrived at the White House in time for breakfast in hopes of talking things over with the president, but Wilson chose to play golf with his new wife in the light spring rain. It wasn't until afternoon that Wilson read him the speech, no doubt in the way of rehearsal. House immediately commented on its brilliance—but for one phrase, "until the German people have a government we can trust," which he felt "looked too much like inciting revolution" (which was, apparently, more threatening than war itself). Wilson agreed and deleted it.

Thousands of pacifists, aware of the pending speech, were rolling into Washington in trains from all over the country. It was well known that midwesterners, many of whom were of German descent, did not want war. Their arm bands were white, and their badges read "KEEP OUT OF WAR," and others carried white tulips in keeping with Easter. They tried to see the president but were denied. They tried to storm the State-Navy-War Department Building but again were repulsed. They sat on steps, drifted up and down Pennsylvania Avenue. Others went into the Senate Office Building, most prominently, the Massachusetts delegation, who demanded to see Henry Cabot Lodge. When the senator finally came out, their spokesman, an ex-semipro baseball player named Alexander Bunnwart, asked what Lodge intended to do. Lodge replied that he would support the war; at once, they began to argue against this, and Lodge became irritated at their objections. "National degeneracy and cowardice are worse than war!" he declared. "Anyone who wants to go to war is a coward!" Bunnwart replied. "You're a damned liar!" Lodge shouted at him, then hit him. Bunnwart hit back, and in the resulting melee, was beaten and jailed for assault. When the news ran through the Senate Office Building, it was said that Lodge had struck the first blow for freedom.

Meanwhile, newspapers reported a quote from Dr. John Haynes Homes, pastor of New York's Community Church: "If war is right, then Christianity is false, a lie. If Christianity is right, then war is wrong, false, a lie." In the new Congress, its first woman, Jeannette Rankin, pacifist from Montana, took her seat carrying a bouquet of flowers. In the spectator's gallery, a general's wife told a Congressman's wife: "We are utterly unprepared [for war], and we will just be annihilated—the Germans would just come over in their ships and submarines and *do* it."

The president waited nervously in the White House, then at last got word that Congress would receive him at 8:30 P.M. His party left at 8:20 into streets guarded by Marines, foot soldiers, two troops of cavalry. There were armed men everywhere, police, secret service agents—all to guard against the pacifists.

Inside, the House chamber was jammed and brilliantly lit. In front, Supreme Court justices were dressed in suits, not robes, most prominent of whom was Chief Justice Edward White. Behind them sat the cabinet. Above were the wives in glittering evening gowns, foreign diplomats in full regalia. This was an affair of state. The House was called to order, and in came Vice President Thomas Marshall followed by senators carrying or wearing flags. Lodge appeared, his face puffy and bruised. At 8:32, Wilson was greeted with an ovation. He was conspicuously pale, his facial skin taut, muscles knotted like marble.

Then he began, and the hall became deathly silent. In time he spoke the dramatic words: "There is one choice we cannot make, we are incapable of making: we will not choose the path of submission...." At this first suggestion of commitment, the chief justice leaped to his feet, hands clasped over his head ("looking ten feet tall," wrote secret service agent Edmund Starling), and from his throat ripped the rebel yell, the Confederate war cry. This provoked an avalanche of applause, White himself trembling with emotion, tears streaming down his craggy old face.

Wilson continued with thirty-six minutes of beautiful rhetoric and balanced phrases, golden images, building at last to his request that Congress declare "the recent course of the imperial German government to be in fact nothing less than war against the government and people of the United States.... To such a task we can dedicate our lives and fortunes, everything that we are and everything that we have, with the pride of those who know that the day will come when America is privileged to spend her blood and her might for the principles that gave her birth and happiness, and the peace which she has treasured. God helping her, she can do no other."

When he lowered his head, there followed a long moment of silence as if in reverence, then the huge crowd leaped to its feet, screaming, cheering, waving little flags—except for Senator Robert La Follette, who sat with tight lips sealed, arms folded across his chest in defiance. There were a few others, but that was all.

Wilson was completely exhausted. In deference to his mood, there was no celebration at the White House with his family and Colonel House. Late that night, he sat with Joseph Tumulty in the Cabinet Room, once again overwhelmed by a need to find an outlet for his confusions. The massive response to his war speech was a brutal reminder of the reality he could not repress. As he had with Frank Cobb barely twenty-four hours earlier, he exposed crushing doubts that his crusade for freedom and democracy were not what others had in mind.

As Tumulty wrote of this moment: "For a while, he sat silent and pale . . . at last he said, 'Tumulty, think what it meant—the applause of the people at the Capitol and the people lining the avenues as we returned. My message was a message of death to our young men. How strange to applaud that!' As he said this, the president drew his handkerchief from his pocket, wiped away great tears . . . and then laying his head on the cabinet table sobbed as if he had been a child."

It was, perhaps, Wilson's finest hour, a confession of horror at what he had unleashed. It was also prophetic, for the forces that had driven him to it were now more dominant than ever. He would weep at this rejoicing of his people about to go to war. He would weep again when there would be no rejoicing at the peace.

Teddy Roosevelt returned from a fishing expedition in the Gulf of Mexico, where he had rammed a harpoon into a giant devilfish that towed his party's launch over half a mile before they could haul it aboard. "Good sport—but not the sort of thing to recommend to a weakling," he bragged to the press. In Washington, he went to the White House to congratulate the president— who was too occupied with his cabinet to see Roosevelt. So he visited with his friend Henry Cabot Lodge, whom he congratulated instead for punching the pacifist.

On the following day, it was reported that Wilson's speech was praised everywhere. Commented Franklin D. Roosevelt, "It will be an inspiration to every true citizen no matter what his political faith, no matter what his creed, no matter what the country of his origin." Ignacy Paderewski, prime minister of Poland and celebrated pianist, declared that the world had never seen Wilson's equal. Wilson's name was, at last, cheered in the British House of Commons. In France, the war message was read to schoolchildren. British aviators dropped translations in leaflets behind German lines. Italians did the same over Austria.

In New York, the stock market recorded huge gains.

In the Senate, however, Robert La Follette protested when faced with a proposal for unanimous consent to the declaration of war, insisting on the Senate rule to compel a one-day delay of any legislation to give time for study. As a result, the stock market slumped, reportedly in response to La Follette's tactics. Said "Fighting Bob": "Wall Street's anger is a matter of utter indifference to me. . . . I have never experimented with the dubious business of trying to serve two masters: the people of this country and the interests of Wall Street." For this, other senators—no doubt with sizable investments—suggested he was treasonable, a word that would soon run wild over the national psyche. A Columbia University professor likened La Follette to Benedict Arnold and Judas Iscariot. Students from M.I.T. burned him in effigy.

After the Senate voted eighty-two to six for war, La Follette was shunned by his colleagues. On his departure from the Senate floor, a man stepped forward and handed him a rope. In the House of Representatives, Jeannette Rankin responded haltingly to the roll call, "I want . . . I want . . . to stand by my country but I cannot vote for war. I vote 'No,'" and broke down in tears. The House voted 373 to fifty, approving the declaration.

On April 6, 1917 (Good Friday), Wilson's lunch with his wife was interrupted by the arrival of the joint declaration, already signed by the vice president and the speaker of the House. At 1:20 P.M., with a pen handed to him by his second wife, Edith, the president signed. The news was signaled to the nearby State-Navy-War Department Building and immediately wired to bases all over the world.

America would never be the same.

"War is the health of the State," the young American radical Randolph Bourne wrote. This was what the state established itself to do, the historical genesis for the protection and security of its people against all enemies. Especially in time of war, the military becomes the strength of the state; there can be no interference with the recruiting of an army, for example, wherein the critics of conscription suffer the full condemnatory power of the law. No sabotaging of war production for profiteering purposes, however greatly it may have harmed the war effort, was ever prosecuted with the fury of punishing a draft dodger. Nor did it matter that the entrance into the war might be unpopular with a majority of the people; no legislative body ever denied a president the right to bring us in—even though he had brought the nation to it without its intimate knowledge of the cause. It was one of Wilson's most specious distortions when he claimed "friendship with the German people," who had no say in their government's war policy—for the presumption was that the American people did. Yet there was no American referendum on that matter, not even a legitimate polling of the public mind. If Congress had voted to declare war with barely a ripple of dissent, it was because all the well-oiled wheels of news and sermons were trained to spin the universal message of patriotism. The public accepted these dictates as though it had decided on them itself. Once the machine began to roll, there would be no stopping its engines, no questioning its direction. The rules of peacetime would be abandoned. Power would become rigidly exercised with a thoroughness that existed at no other time.

As H. L. Mencken put it, Americans had viewed the European war "idly and unintelligently—as a yokel might stare at a sword swallower. Then, suddenly seeing a chance to profit, found good reason to jump in." Or La Follette: "Woodrow Wilson's declaration of war was not written on his White House typewriter on April 2, 1917, it was written when the House of Morgan floated the first Anglo-French Bond Issue with the consent of the United States Government." Or *McClure's Magazine:* "The coming ism is no longer Socialism—it is patriotism."

Immediately after legislating conscription, Congress passed an espionage act that made it a crime to suggest or do anything that might be considered pro-German. The act was upheld by the Supreme Court, the great libertarian justice Oliver Wendell Holmes assenting: "Free speech can legitimately be restricted on the grounds of clear and present danger."

The state became extremely unhealthy. Said the radical Max Eastman: "They give you ninety days for quoting the Declaration of Independence, six months for quoting the Bible, and pretty soon somebody is going to get life for quoting Woodrow Wilson in the wrong connection."

To Mencken, the American people had already been led to believe that (a) the Germans were about to invade our shores, rape our women, pillage our homes and (b) our entrance into the war would end it quickly, our forces being so overwhelming that we would be invulnerable. Both arguments were grounded on the theory that to make the mob fight, first scare it to death, then convince it that the fight would be without risk—and profitable. All of Wilson's idealistic nonsense was simply icing on the cake, most of which would be abandoned anyway "as soon as the bullets began to fly."

What America needed was a shot in the arm. Immediately after the stirring impact of Wilson's speech subsided, there was a giant wave of apathy. To most, the war was still three thousand miles across the Atlantic (and a lot further to Westerners). Even in Congress, the sound and fury had faded. La Follette was amused at the "disappearance of all the bravado...a gradual lengthening of faces, hats not so much on one side.... The awful seriousness of the thing was beginning to sink in, expecting, perhaps, the president had some big concealed plan by which peace with a glory that would exalt him before all presidents was to be achieved in a few weeks."

Came, then, George Creel, ex-adman, recently Wilson's campaign manager, now the presidential appointee for the Herculean task of rallying the American people to the war effort. Never would anyone do so much for a war. His agency was called the Committee for Public Information.

Creel was not the first to recognize the importance of propaganda in war, but the audacity and thoroughness with which he ran this show was extraordinary. This would not be propaganda but information, he pledged—except when classified for security purposes. The premise on which he operated, however, was that the effective execution of the war could come only out of hate. Hating the enemy was as vital as ammunition, and like ammo, it had to be manufactured. Creel gathered in Washington a vast group of novelists, essayists, publicists to join this team. The CPI printed a newspaper, one hundred thousand copies a day. Famous artists drew thousands of pictures over the next eighteen months. He had photographers from all over the country as well as from Europe, flooding the country with selected shots. In Hollywood, movie studios would turn out pictures under his supervision: *Pershing's Crusaders, America's Answer, Under Two Flags.* In these days before radio, he conceived and organized an extraordinary technique in reaching the people, the Four-Minute Men, they were called. One hundred and fifty thousand public speakers, they moved through five thousand communities, trained to deliver the CPI message in the most effective manner. They spoke everywhere: public parks on weekend afternoons, school auditoriums, theaters before moving pictures, club lunches and civic banquets, ferries and riverboats, even private parties.

The contents changed weekly as the CPI released new subjects backed by research material, news reports, special items of information. All aspects of the war and the war effort were dealt with, but never for more than four minutes, a well-considered estimation of attention span. "The Importance of Speed," "Maintaining Morals and Morale," "The Meaning of America," "Where Did You Get Your Facts?" Everything from war news to exhortations to buy Liberty Bonds to reporting slackers or draft dodgers to authorities.

Creel reported that over 7,500,000 speeches were made to over three hundred million people (three times the total population). He rallied singers to spread the word with patriotic songs using movie theaters for sing-alongs. He mobilized celebrated college professors to write and address great gatherings. He invited Allied speakers to tour the country with firsthand accounts of the war. His pamphlets were translated for foreign distribution as well as for millions of American immigrants. He issued over seven million copies of a popular pamphlet titled "How War Came to America," plus untold millions of other tracts for use in schools and as supplements for speakers, newspaper editors, even government officials. He flooded the country with posters (the most famous of which was the finger-pointing Uncle Sam I WANT YOU, drawn by James Montgomery Flagg), in subway stations, on barn walls, in schools, billboards on highways and signs in streetcars. "The Battle of the Fences," he called it. Through it all, he created and delivered The Word, the acceptable official patriotic word. And though his terminology was "strictly by voluntary agreement" of all involved in its dissemination, any dissidence was rigorously suppressed.

Behind it all was Creel's selling premise: the fundamental greatness of America. To sell the war, he had first to sell America. He created a shining picture of democracy, the glorious city on the hill. To the adman, the obligatory accent-on-the-positive would saturate the public mentality. There would be no mention of the corruption of cities still rampant throughout the country, or the arrogance and greed of American robber barons or the viciousness of racist domination of colored people. Creel's brush was made to whitewash the entire history of America, and he had the war to justify it. Democracy was, after all, the last and best hope of the entire world. There could be no compromise with a war for its survival. Every word of its virtues would be repeated a thousand times. America the pure, the beautiful, the blessed by God; America the redeemer, the hope of the oppressed. The whole world was subjected to this, another of his achievements, for everyone was desperate for something to believe in. As Creel boasted of his work: "Before the flood of our publicity... from being the most misunderstood nation, the United States became the most popular." It was, as he would later put it, "The world's greatest adventure in advertising."

To American intellectuals, the war process became the meat of their existence—whatever they might have thought of Creel's creations. The same writers, artists and teachers who had so vociferously condemned their German counterparts in 1914 for singing the praises of German militarism now rallied behind the CPI. Randolph Bourne had a field day with this turnabout. "Intellectuals are now complacently asserting that it was they who effectively willed it (our entrance into the war) against the hesitation and dim perceptions of the American democratic masses." He warned them of their alliance with the most reactionary groups in the country, the very forces they had spent their lives opposing. "What we have is an intellectual class entering the war at the head of illiberal cohorts in the avowed cause of world liberalism."

At the top of this list was twenty-seven-year-old Walter Lippmann, who foresaw a world democratically united by the eventual Allied victory, then led by a progressive America. This conception of the liberal using war to achieve power left Bourne bemused. Can a child on the back of a mad elephant be any more effective in controlling the beast than a child on the ground? According to Bourne, "We manufacture consolations here in America, while there are probably not a dozen men fighting in the trenches of France who did not long ago give up every reason for being there except that nobody knew how to get them away." In his trilogy *U.S.A.*, John Dos Passos eulogized Bourne:

> This little sparrowlike man,
> tiny twisted bit of flesh in a black cape,
> always in pain and ailing,
> put a pebble in his sling
> and hit Goliath square in the forehead with it.

War, he wrote, is the health of the State.

Half musician, half education theorist (weak health and being poor and hunchback, twisted in body and on bad terms with his people hadn't spoiled the world for Randolph Bourne; he was a happy man, loved *die meistersinger* and playing Bach with his long hands that stretched so easily over the keys and pretty girls and good food and evenings of talk.)...Bourne seized with feverish intensity on the ideas then going around Columbia, he picked rosy glasses out of the turgid mumble of John Dewey's teaching through which he saw clear and sharp.
> the shining capitol of reformed democracy,
> Wilson's New Freedom;
> but he was too good a mathematician; he had to work the equations out;

> with the result
> that in the crazy spring of 1917 he began to get unpopular where his bread was buttered at The New Republic;
> for the New Freedom read "Conscription," for Democracy read "Win the War," for Reform "Safeguard the Morgan Loans."
> for Progress Civilization Education Service
> Buy a Liberty Loan,
> Staff the Hun
> Jail the Objectors.

He was cartooned, shadowed by the espionage service and the counter espionage service; taking a walk with two girlfriends at Wood's Hole he was arrested, a trunk full of manuscripts and letters stolen from him in Connecticut. (Force to the utmost, thundered Schoolmaster Wilson.)

He didn't live to see the big circus of the Peace at Versailles...

Six weeks after the armistice, he died planning a message on the foundations of future radicalism in America.

If any man has a ghost,
Bourne has a ghost,
a tiny twisted unscared ghost in a black cloak
hopping along the grimy old brick and brownstone streets
still left in downtown New York,
crying out in a shrilled soundless giggle;
War is the health of the state.

Wilson thrived on the new patriotism that now replaced the new freedom. He had never been tolerant of opposition, and now he heard little of it. "Force!" he cried out on Flag Day. "Force to the utmost, force without stint or limit, the righteous and triumphant force which shall make right the law of the world, and cast every self-dominion down in the dust."

All power to the war effort; no matter what the means, the end would justify it. Democracy must be saved—even if it first was necessary to destroy it. And Wilson would preside over its destruction.

His postmaster general, Albert Burleson (a Texas friend of Colonel House), supervised the mails as though the enemy was about to subvert the national will behind a postage stamp. He assumed dictatorial powers of what was permissible and patriotic use of the mail and what was not. Seditious literature was anything that violated his personal view of Americanism. The extent of his censorship became so preposterous that Wilson's oldest and most ardent supporters were being barred from using the postal services. No matter that they protested to Wilson himself. The president did not intercede.

His departments of war, navy and state created their own intelligence agencies to collect information on anyone suspected of subversive thought—from anarchists and Industrial Workers of the World (IWW) union members to philosophers at obscure colleges. The Department of Justice was transformed into a nationwide system of counterspying. Attorney General Thomas Gregory, another son of the Confederacy brought to the cabinet by Colonel House, organized the American Protective League, an idea conceived by a Chicago adman named A. M. Briggs. Its membership included anyone who wished to join. Two hundred and fifty thousand citizens in every major city became spies and informers allegedly to protect the security of the country, and bought out the entire supply of badges at seventy-five cents each. Inscribed AMERICAN PROTECTIVE LEAGUE, SECRET SERVICE DIVISION, they were to be well concealed, but displayed on demand. Said Gregory: "They kept an eye on disloyal individuals . . . made reports of disloyal utterances, seeing that the people of the country were not deceived." They assumed the powers of policemen, judges, juries. They invited and provoked, then arrested fellow citizens. Their simplistic conceptions of patriotism quickly became the norm, soon leading to the proliferation of the Ku Klux Klan, Knights of Liberty, Anti-Anarchy Association and a slew of bigoted groups intent on purging whomever they chose to purge.

J. Edgar Hoover became a leading organizer of the American Protective League in June 1917, his first assignment in the Department of Justice. His principal contribution was the creation of lists and files of subversive peoples and groups.

The results were frightening.

A man was sentenced to five years at hard labor for speaking critically of the president—on the testimony of his own daughter. In Illinois, a German-born American named Robert Paul Prager was rumored to be hoarding dynamite in his cellar, no doubt because he had spoken well of socialism to his fellow coal miners. As rumors spread, a mob went after him and lynched him. For this, eleven men were indicted—but acquitted by a jury in less than half an hour on the grounds that this was "patriotic murder."

Elihu Root, ex-secretary of state and a highly respected dignitary of the Republican Party, recommended that there were men walking the streets of New York who should be shot for treason. Pacifists were warned that "there is no shortage of hemp or lampposts." Teddy Roosevelt roared: "He who is not with us, absolutely and without reserve of any kind, is against us and should be treated as an enemy alien." A Texas federal judge said that La Follette should be executed by a firing squad. Nicholas

Murray Butler, Columbia University president, said of La Follette: "You might just as well put poison in the food of every American boy that goes to his transport as permit this man to talk as he does."

To justify it all, Woodrow Wilson proposed to Congress in 1918 that the Espionage Act of 1917 be taken one step further. The new Sedition Act specified a fine of $10,000 and/or sentence of up to twenty years for obstructing the sale of Liberty Bonds; inciting to insubordination; discouraging of recruiting; uttering, writing, publishing "any disloyal, profane, scurrilous or abusive language about the flag, the armed forces, their uniforms, the Constitution or the American form of government." The specific meaning of such vague terminology was left to any court to interpret as it wished.

Over fifteen hundred people were arrested for mere utterances, and many served long sentences. The president was putting his enemies in power and his friends in jail. Thousands more were charged. Rose Pastor Stokes was sentenced to ten years in prison for writing a letter to a Kansas City newspaper denouncing war profiteers. Judge Kenesaw Mountain Landis sentenced the Socialist congressman Victor Berger for less, even as he was reelected. Eugene V. Debs was jailed for objecting to the draft. William Powell of Detroit got the maximum for daring to disbelieve German atrocity stories.

The entire country became washed under a tidal wave of anti-German propaganda. The Kaiser was referred to as "The Werewolf of Potsdam" or "The Beast of Berlin." Delivering the invocation at one session of Congress, the evangelist Billy Sunday said this about Germany: "Thou knowest, O Lord, that no nation so infamous, vile, greedy, sensuous, bloodthirsty ever disgraced the pages of history." Sauerkraut became known as Victory Cabbage. You could not say "auf Wiedersehen" without creating suspicion. Dachshunds were to be called Liberty Pups. A trifling, not abnormal epidemic of diarrhea was proof that German spies had poisoned the water system. Any failure in production at a war plant was caused by German saboteurs. In Cincinnati, pretzels were taken off tavern counters. Fritz Kreisler, world-famous violinist, was denied the right to perform by the mayor of East Orange, New Jersey.

For it all, not one single German spy was caught.

The country had gone mad, but the madness became normal. The submission of individual liberties to the dictates of the state was the greatest in our history. The government had succeeded in taking away—and the individual in giving up—the rights it had taken centuries to win. That this could happen so readily became a message for demagogues to come. With war, or threat of war, people could be led to mass solidarity with cheap slogans from gushing admen and acquiescence from the president. The typical American was no longer a lover of liberty. He could be lied to and kicked around and betrayed without his feeling any real resentment. If he rebelled, that rebellion would be used to justify further suppression. The mystery was the ease with which this was accomplished while the average American continued to believe he was free.

It followed that the conscription of the American mind was more effective than the conscription of American business. Somewhere it was written that wars were good for business, and any challenge to this truism would be treasonable. Any wartime administration quickly learns the limits of its power to ensure the manufacture of cannons, for example, or even battleships, without guarantees that profits will not be sacrificed. It was far simpler to put several million men into service than to supply them with armaments. Nowhere was this more apparant than in dealing with the United States Steel Company, which demanded 4.5 cents per pound for plates needed to build battleships. Bernard Baruch, head of the War Industries Board, knew this was an inflated price; but Judge Elbert Gary, head of the company, refused to discuss the matter, even with the president of the United States. It took months of negotiations to arrive at a compromise price, and then only when the government threatened to commandeer the entire U.S. Steel Company did Gary comply. Nor was it different with the heavy metal industry, which refused to convert to the manufacturing of cannons, preferring production of civilian hardware at unlimited profits than dealing with the government at cost-plus 5 percent. Thousands of men were prosecuted and jailed for draft evasion and conscientious objection, but not one manufacturer was prosecuted for profiteering. War, as the saying went, was a rich man's quarrel and a poor man's fight.

The congressional battle over the new excess profits tax was equally illustrative. Largely because of Senator Robert La Follette, the Senate made responsive noises at the inequity of sending young men off to fight while others at home got wealthy from it. Even in the ostensibly plutocratic nations of Europe, tax rates rose to 50 percent and more. England jumped to 80 percent of all personal income. Others went as high as 90 percent. In the United States, however, the excess profits tax rate was held at 30 percent, forcing the principal revenue to come from the public sale of bonds, thereby placing the financial responsibility for the war on the working and middle classes. Again, La Follette was furious: "It was part of [the] history of all great wars that the wealthy demanded the minimum of taxation and the maximum of loans." He cited leading economists (Adam Smith, David Ricardo, John Stuart Mill) on the efficacy of high taxation during wartime. His plea for an 80 percent tax levy was rejected almost exclusively by those who had been most ardently for the war. He also attempted to get legislation passed to raise overseas pay to $50 a month— as in Canada—the revenue for which would come from taxing incomes over $25,000. That too was voted down. In *Colliers Magazine*, it was written of "Fighting Bob" that "No man in Congress would have made so useful a contribution to the conduct of the war as the one who most stubbornly resisted our entering it."

So it was that American industry made net profits of $8,766,000,000 in 1916, and over $10 billion in 1917. It was also of note that U.S. Steel, America's largest industry, showed an increase of dividends from 1913 to 1917 that was three times higher than the increase in wages—this at a time when the cost of living was soaring.

Years later, in congressional hearings, the history of the war was called "the greatest business proposition since time began."

In his speech for the declaration of war, Wilson had said: "To such a task we dedicated our lives and our fortunes..." Forty-three thousand Americans lost their lives in that dedication—but not one fortune.

*   *   *

Meanwhile, in Russia, Kerensky's provisional government tried desperately to serve the Allies by maintaining the Eastern Front against the German army. As John Reed had predicted, it would cause his collapse. The peasants had had more than enough of slaughter. The Bolsheviks alone realized this, and on their pledge to the Russian people that they would pursue peace, they swept into power in November 1917. For the exhausted country, the war against Germany was over. The tsar was executed. The royal family fled. Suddenly there was Vladimir Ilyich Lenin (or "Lenine," as his name appeared in the Western press), and beside him was Leon Trotsky, late of the Lower East Side of New York.

And now, the new pure Allied war was exposed to the world not as a war for democracy but as an old-fashioned cutthroat, imperialist power fight for the exploitation of spoils: hardly had the new Bolshevik regime taken power before its officials had drawn from the tsar's files the secret treaties between the Allies, the real reasons why they went to war.

The Sazonov-Paléologue Agreement of 1915. The Sykes-Picot Treaty of 1916. The Treaty of Saint-Jean de Maurienne, 1917. The Treaty of London, 1917. In these documents, Britain and France conceded to Russia the annexation of Constantinople, the west coast of the Bosporus, Sea of Marmara and the Dardanelles and more. In return, Russia agreed to the incorporation of the neutral zone in Persia into the oil-hungry British sphere of interest. Persia and the Ottoman Empire would be dismembered and partitioned, their pieces scattered in support of Allied vested interests. Italy, then on the side of the Central Powers, was seduced to join the Allied side with an out-and-out bribe, was promised Trieste, Trentino, South Tirol at the Brenner frontier, a chain of African territories that would lead to control of Abyssinia. France and Russia had conducted secret negotiations by which Poland (that crown jewel in the crown of the tsar) was recognized as a Russian sphere of interest in return for France's right to Alsace-Lorraine *plus* the Saar Basin and the cutting off of a huge swath of the Rhineland for French military occupancy.

Assemble the pieces of the insidious jigsaw portrait: Italy was but a jackal determined to feed off whatever loot it might accumulate; Britain, the eternal imperialist, was intent on gobbling up colonies to exploit by dint of its dominant naval force and mercantile trading power; France, dominated by a wretched, illiberal bourgeoisie, based its survival on the destruction and exploitation of German industry; imperial Russia was a tyranny so backward as to be suggestive of the worst of the Middle Ages; Poland was under the control of a royalist landowning anti-Semitic oligarchy with grandiose military aspirations. This, Lenin argued, was what the working people of the Allied armies were being asked to die for.

What followed was the more repellent for its predictability—the secret treaties would be kept secret from the American people. In Washington, Woodrow Wilson spoke not one public word of dismay. The great war leaders, having committed the American people to their sacrificial Christian duty, were not about to qualify that commitment simply because it had turned out to be the devil's work. The great independent newspapers of America, the main source of people's information, saw no reason to publish their existence, much less their contents. (Only two so much as mentioned them.) This vast conspiracy of silence was, in an odd way, the biggest story of the American war effort. The enormity of its implications could be calculated only through its disastrous consequences. There would be no understanding of the war because there would be no information about it except what was deemed suitable—especially as it applied to the Russian Revolution, about which the only news reported was directed toward its overthrow. For delivering the bad news of the great Allied perfidy, the messenger would have to be killed. In the end, this policy would contribute to the killing of the peace treaty in Paris.

Meanwhile, the overthrow of Russian capitalism sent shock waves through Allied capitals. The release of the secret treaties became known as a Bolshevik assault on the premise by which all so-called civilized governments carried on diplomacy. How else could nations survive each other's encroachments? How else could wars be fought, this one above all? The Allies sensed their vulnerability, especially in the trenches, frightened of soldiers rebelling at the realization of this defamation of the war itself.

In Washington, Wilson was quick to see the competitive threat to his altruistic purposes. As in all such crises, he dove into the breach, resorting to his passion for oratory. With a sudden call for a joint session of Congress on January 8, 1918, he made still another of his great speeches to declare himself, and America, world leader in the cause of peace with justice and freedom: "Whether their present leaders believe it or not, it is our heartfelt desire and hope that some way may be opened whereby we may be privileged to assist the people of Russia to attain their utmost hope of liberty and ordered peace."

To implement the unselfish American war aims, he introduced a new program, "the only possible program . . . ," which he called the Fourteen Points:

I. Open covenants of peace, openly arrived at, after which there shall be no private international understandings of any kind, but diplomacy shall proceed always frankly and in public view.

II. Absolute freedom of navigation upon the seas, outside territorial waters, alike in peace and in war, except as the seas may be closed in whole or in part by international action for the enforcement of international covenants.

III. The removal, as far as possible, of all economic barriers and the establishment of an equality of trade conditions among all the nations consenting to the peace and associating themselves for its maintenance.

IV. Adequate guarantees given and taken that national armaments will be reduced to the lowest point consistent with domestic safety.

V. Free, open-minded and absolutely impartial adjustment of all colonial claims, based upon a strict observance of the principle that in determining all such questions of sovereignty the interests of the populations concerned must have equal weight with the equitable claims of the government whose title is to be determined.

VI. The evacuation of all Russian territory and such settlement of all questions affecting Russia as will secure the best and freest cooperation of all other nations of the world in obtaining for her an unhampered and unembarrassed opportunity for the independent determination of her own political development and national policy and assure her of sincere welcome into the society of free nations under institutions of her own choosing; and, more than welcome, assistance also of every kind that she may need and may herself desire. The treatment accorded Russia by her sister nations in the months to come will be the acid test of their goodwill, of their comprehension of her needs as distinguished from their own interests and of their intelligent and unselfish sympathy.

VII. Belgium, the whole world will agree, must be evacuated and restored, without any attempt to limit the sovereignty which she enjoys in common with all other free nations. No other single act will serve as this will serve to restore confidence among nations in the laws which they themselves have set and determined for the government of their relations with one another. Without this healing act the whole structure and validity of international law is forever impaired.

VIII. All French territory should be freed and the invaded portions restored, and the wrong done to France by Prussia in 1871 in the matter of Alsace-Lorraine, which has unsettled the peace of the world for nearly fifty years, should be righted, in order that peace may once more be made secure in the interest of all.

IX. A readjustment of the frontiers of Italy should be effected along clearly recognizable lines of nationality.

X. The peoples of Austria-Hungary, whose place among nations we wish to see safeguarded and assured, should be accorded the freest opportunity of autonomous development.

XI. Rumania, Serbia and Montenegro should be evacuated; occupied territories restored; Serbia accorded free and secure access to the sea; and the relations of the several Balkan states to one another determined by friendly counsel along historically established lines of nationality; and international guarantees of the political and economic independence and territorial integrity of the several Balkan states should be entered into.

XII. The Turkish portions of the present Ottoman Empire should be assured a secure sovereignty, but the other nationalities which are now under Turkish rule should be assured an undoubted security of life and absolutely unmolested opportunity of autonomous development, and the Dardanelles should be permanently opened as a free passage to the ships and commerce of all nations under international guarantees.

XIII. An independent Polish State should be erected which should include the territories inhabited by indisputably Polish populations, which should be assured a free and secure access to the sea, and whose political and economic independence and territorial integrity should be guaranteed by international covenant.

XIV. A general association of nations must be formed under specific covenants for the purpose of affording mutual guarantees of political independence and territorial integrity to great and small states alike.

At the conclusion of this staggering set of proposals, Congress was jubilant. As John Dos Passos reported: "Senators and representatives jumped on chairs and waved their arms as if they were at a football game." The entire nation appeared to respond in kind. It was a magnificently unifying speech. Such normally diverse Republicans as Theodore Roosevelt and Senator William Borah voiced approval, and so too did the radicals.

Hostile Republican newspapers such as the *New York Tribune* added words of support: "As Lincoln freed the slaves of the South half a century ago, Mr. Wilson now pledges his country to fight for the liberation of the Belgian and the Pole, the Serb and the Rumanian.... Today, as never before, the whole nation marches with the president, certain alike of the leader and the cause."

It remained for the Allies to take exception, and immediately there was a demonstrable erosion of Wilson's goals. To the British, for example, "freedom of the seas" was a direct assault on their age-old hegemony. To the French, though pleased at the return of Alsace-Lorraine, there was in Wilson's words no guarantee of their security. To the Italians, the "readjustment of frontiers along

clearly recognizable lines of nationality" was infinitely less satisfying than the reasons for their entrance into combat.

Even Germany objected, not only to the return of Alsace-
Lorraine to France, but to what the government considered to be
naively idealistic conceptions of such a thing as a community of
"peace-loving nations."

As for Russia, Lenin stated his approval: "It is a great step
toward the peace of the world." He also stated his skepticism:
"This is all very well as far as it goes, but why not formal recognition and when?"

In the end, the determination of the Bolsheviks to withdraw
from the war became a turning point. To make peace with Germany was deemed to be a betrayal, for it would release over a
million German troops to the Western front. Immediately, the
presumption was offered that the revolution itself had been inspired by the German government, that Lenin and Trotsky were
financed by them, that they were, actually, German agents.

Allied capitalism, then, saw no other recourse but to destroy
the revolution—even if it meant jeopardizing the war against Germany. In the British War Cabinet, Winston Churchill emerged as
the first great Allied anti-Bolshevik ideologue, desperately seeking
a likely White Russian leader around whom the counterrevolution
could rally. His choices were typical of that desperation: Kornilov,
Kaledin, Deniken, Semenov, a collection of brutally corrupt ex-
tsarists, tyrants, anti-Semites, butchers; but all were heralded by
the Allied press as heroic representatives of the democratic Russian people. They were given Allied money and munitions and,
soon enough, troops. While the trench war continued in France,
these White Russian armies ran rampant across the devastated
Russian countryside, slaughtering people they were sent there to
lead, looting the villages, stealing crops and cattle. Any military
advance was proclaimed as the forerunner of victory. All Bolshevik resistance was crumbling. To Churchill it was only a matter
of time before the revolutionary government would be ousted.
No American official doubted it. In a study made a few years later
by Walter Lippmann, the prestigious *New York Times* was shown
to have published a succession of distortions and outright lies, its
correspondent so obviously biased against the revolution he was

unable to perceive the reality. Insofar as Russia was concerned, we were perhaps the most ill-informed nation on earth.

Nor was it accidental that Wilson would eventually get sucked into the churning whirlpool. He would tell Congress that the Russian Revolution had been betrayed. He had come to the conclusion that it was all part of a new conspiracy hatched in Berlin. There would be no support granted to the Bolshevik government, no recognition of its legitimacy to represent the great Russian people (lest it encourage Bolshevik sympathizers in other areas). Edgar Sisson, Wilson's emissary from the Committee for Public Information, discovered new "secret papers" to prove the German connection, documents tying Lenin and Trotsky to the highest levels of the German government. Wilson endorsed the release of these papers to American newspapers; no matter that they turned out to be forgeries, the risk was worth the message. Their release, then, would justify the most extraordinary shift of policy in the complex diplomatic history of the war: Wilson would send American troops into Russia as part of the Allied intervention to overthrow the Bolshevik government.

It was an invasion so blatantly ideological, no rationalization could dissuade the Russians from understanding its true intent. American troops landed at Archangel on the Baltic Sea allegedly to prevent Germany from capturing a vast supply of war goods shipped to the Russian armies of the provisional government, but it was the Russian Red Army the Americans battled. Another force was dispatched to Vladivostok in Siberia, allegedly to contain what became a huge Japanese presence, or to help Czech soldiers return to the front, or to prevent another shipment of arms from falling into German hands, but it was the counterrevolutionary White Russians our troops were made to support, and again, it was the Russian Red Army they battled. This illegal intervention would make little military progress, and American soldiers were bewildered at what they were doing in such godforsaken circumstances. But the impact on the Bolshevik government was an unmistakably compelling one. No matter that our forces were limited to ten thousand here, 7,500 there; we were irritating thorns pricking the Russian bear as it was being surrounded by a hoard of savage wolves. To the Bolsheviks, this was proof of American enmity, not for reasons of conquest or territorial disputation or defense of American rights; the intervention was understood to be intended purely for the purpose of assisting in the overthrow of the revolution. It was this declaration of American policy that would segue from these absurd military incursions to the endless decades of what came to be called the Cold War.

All this was happening in the midst of the war with Germany. The Allies did not recognize that Bolshevism was, in fact, an ally against the imperial German government, ignoring the possibility that the Kaiser et al. might well go under because of the thrust of revolution. Bruce Lockhart, a highly perceptive British agent in Russia, was persistently indignant at his government's failure to understand this. He would even suggest that there were forces in the war cabinet "who would rather have lost the war than run the risk of social unrest at home." Indeed, under Churchill's domination, the War Office thought only in terms of destroying the revolution at whatever cost in protracting the war with Germany. Georges Clemenceau, premier of France, actually ordered a French general in charge of the Balkan command to halt his pursuit of German forces retreating across the Danube and divert his army to the east in order to assist the White Russians in another desperate battle against the new Red Army. In America, Secretary of State Lansing warned that the Bolshevik regime with its overt denial of the rights of property was at least as great a threat to America as German militarism. The war, then, was no longer a fight against Prussian military domination, or "to make the world safe for democracy," but coldly and defiantly, for the ultimate protection of property rights.

"The war against the Boche was turning into a war against the Bolshie," it was said. Not the least of the spreading implications were reactions to the growing domestic unrest in Allied countries. Radical protest, it seemed, was due to the influx of Russian gold just as the revolution itself was due to German gold. The result of such tortured reasoning reached its apogee for Lockhart at a dinner with the son of the millionaire businessman Alfred Nobel (creator of the Nobel Peace Prize) with large commercial interests throughout Russia, wherein Nobel suggested that Britain and the Allies *join with Germany* for intervention to overthrow the Bolsheviks.

The consequences of this extraordinary orientation were, to

put it mildly, unhealthy. For one thing, they raised hopes of successful counterrevolution rooted in a flood of false information. For another, they intensified a civil war that sent many thousands more Russians to their deaths, mostly by the brutal men Churchill et al. had chosen to be their leaders. In the end, the effect was a terrible tarnishing of Allied diplomacy at a time when sensible leadership was a prerequisite to the successful conclusion to the war. The Russians were thus forced to sign a punishing peace with Germany at Brest Litovsk (brought about largely by Allied blundering), then condemned by the Allies for cowardly deserting the war, who justified the entire canard by insisting that the Bolsheviks were German agents in the first place.

Meanwhile, Wilson's Fourteen Points speech was being circulated among the people of the world as if it were the Sermon on the Mount. George Creel saw to that. Hundreds of thousands of copies were printed in a variety of languages and distributed throughout Europe, especially behind German lines. By late summer 1918, the greater the power of the fresh American expeditionary force on the battlefields, the more effective became the propaganda. With every military victory, Wilson's continuing pledge of friendship for the German people helped bring the collapsing imperial German government to its knees.

Field Marshal Paul von Hindenburg would confess just after armistice, "In the end, the extraordinary fighting ability of American soldiers defeated us," but to the new German government, it was the Russian, then the Austrian, then the German revolutionary movements that forced its capitulation. Germany preferred to deal with Wilson and the Allies than its own working people. As John Toland recounted in his highly documented history *No Man's Land,* the new Centrist leader of the Reichstag, Matthias Erzberger, pleaded with Marshal Ferdinand Foch on November 8 for no delay of the armistice: "For God's sake, monsieur le maréchal . . . stop the hostilities this very day. Our armies are a prey to anarchy. Bolshevism threatens them: and Bolshevism may gain ground over the whole of Germany and threaten France herself!"

So, at last, the great war ended at 11 A.M., November 11, 1918. When Woodrow Wilson learned of it, he released all government workers and penciled his statement to the American people:

> The armistice was signed this morning. Everything for which America fought has been accomplished. It will now be our fortunate duty to assist by example, by sober, friendly counsel and by material aid in the establishment of just democracy throughout the world.

There seems to be no question but that he genuinely believed every pious word of it. That, of course, was Wilson's way.

2. WOODROW WILSON'S STRUGGLE FOR POWER

I believe in Divine Providence. If I did not, I would go crazy.

—WOODROW WILSON

Thomas Woodrow Wilson was born in the manse of a Presbyterian church in Staunton, Virginia, where his father was minister, his mother the daughter of a Presbyterian minister of Scots-Irish Presbyterian heritage. His father, John Ruggles Wilson, was a handsome, vigorous man, proud of his appearance and prouder yet of his command of language. Tommy, as he was called then, was a healthy baby but became sickly as a child, afflicted by dyspepsia and frequent headaches. Above all, he loved his father. In his sheltered boyhood, he saw the reverend as the interpreter of God's word on earth. For the rest of his life he prayed on his knees every day, said grace before every meal. He believed absolutely in the immortality of the soul. He never doubted. To have doubted would have been tantamount to doubting his own father.

As John Dos Passos wrote in *U.S.A.:* "The Wilsons lived in a universe of words linked to an incontrovertible firmament by two centuries of Calvinist doctrines. God was the Word and the Word was God. Dr. Wilson was a man of standing who . . . talked to God every day at the family prayers; he brought his sons up between the Bible and the dictionary."

"My incomparable father," Wilson would call him. "My beloved father." Until after age forty, Wilson constantly sought his father's advice. The formidable minister was everything the son wished to be and was not. Because of his fragility, he clung to his mother's apron strings, having inherited her feeble body, poor eyesight, her innate shyness with people. But his father remained his dominant inspiration.

His single passion was always with speech. The perfectionist father demanded precise usage at all times. As Wilson grew up, he began to see himself as an orator. He studied the great British speeches of Gladstone and Burke and exalted in the becoming of a leader through oratory. He would stand in front of a mirror practicing gesticulations and facial expressions as he spoke. He would go to his father's church, position himself at the podium and deliver great speeches before fantasy audiences. It was his father's wish that his son become a minister of God, but young Wilson saw himself only as a great statesman, chosen by God to do great things for humanity. Had he not received that call from God himself? God needed him. God would use him and preserve him until God's work was done. And because of it, whatever he did would be right. He need never doubt the wisdom and righteousness of his acts.

When he married, his wife Ellen Axson, like his mother, was a daughter of a Presbyterian minister—and mistress of the manse as well. The faith was always with him.

As Dos Passos extended his profile:

> "...he studied law at the University of Virginia; young Wilson wanted to be a Great Man, like Gladstone and the eighteenth century English parliamentarians; he wanted to hold the packed benches spellbound in the cause of Truth; but law practice irked him; he was more at home in the booky air of libraries, lecture rooms, college chapel, it was a relief to leave his law practice in Atlanta.... When he got his Ph.D. from Johns Hopkins he moved to a professorship at Wesleyan ... spoke out for Truth Reform Responsible Government Democracy from the lecture platform, climbed all the steps of a brilliant university career; in 1901 the trustees of Princeton offered him the presidency;
>
> he plunged into reforming the university, made violent friends and enemies, set the campus by the ears,
>
> and the American people began to find on the front pages the name of Woodrow Wilson.

and in 1910
the democratic bosses of New Jersey, hardpressed by muckrakers and reformers, got the bright idea of offering the nomination for governor to the stainless college president who attracted such large audiences.
by publicly championing Right.

When Mr. Wilson addressed the Trenton convention that nominated him for governor he confessed his belief in the common man (the smalltown bosses and the wardheelers looked at each other and scratched their heads); he went on, his voice growing firmer:
THAT IS THE MAN BY WHOSE JUDGMENT I FOR ONE WISH TO BE GUIDED, SO THAT AS THE TASKS MULTIPLY, AND AS THE DAYS COME WHEN ALL WILL FEEL CONFUSION AND DISMAY, WE MAY LIFT UP OUR EYES TO THE HILLS OUT OF THESE DARK VALLEYS WHERE THE CRAGS OF SPECIAL PRIVILEGE OVERSHADOW AND DARKEN OUR PATH, TO WHERE THE SUN GLEAMS.... THE SUN OF GOD,
THE SUN MEANT TO REGENERATE MEN....
The smalltown bosses and the wardheelers looked at each other and scratched their heads; then they cheered; Wilson fooled the wiseacres and doublecrossed the bosses, was elected by a huge plurality.

(Two years later) The bolt of the Progressives in Chicago from Taft to T.R. made the election sure...
and went to the White House
our twenty-eighth president.

When Wilson took office in 1913, America had no thought of war. In his inaugural address, he spoke of "a growing sense of community of interest among nations, foreshadowing an age of settled peace and goodwill...." Since the turn of the century, peace had become extremely fashionable. Over sixty peace societies were thriving. Never in our history had the word itself achieved such dignity. Said Dr. David Starr Jordan, director of the World Peace Federation: "What shall we say of the 'Great War in Europe,' ever threatening, ever impending, and which never comes? We shall say that it will never come. Humanly speaking,

it is impossible." The prestigious *Review of Reviews* would comment, "The world is moving away from military ideals; and a
period of peace, industry and worldwide friendship is dawning."
In the *New York Times,* an interview with David Lloyd George, then
chancellor of the exchequer, reported his comment that people
were sick of armaments; the time had come even for reducing
the giant British Navy. Americans heard that Kaiser Wilhelm,
emperor of imperial Germany, was an outspoken proponent of
world peace and was recipient of the world peace prize to prove
it. Ex-president Theodore Roosevelt, a visitor to the royal palace,
found him endearing. And weren't the Germans preparing to
construct a huge stadium in Berlin to host the 1916 Olympic
Games?

Nonetheless, there were wars. Every generation in every nation had suffered its soldiers in combat. In this century, barely a
dozen years old, the British had warred with the Boers in South
Africa. There was the Boxer Rebellion in China. In 1904, the
Russo-Japanese War. And always the colonial suppressions, savage beyond all humanness, in the name of the white man's burden. Belgians, Portuguese and Germans in Africa; America in
the Caribbean, the Philippines and Mexico. The British in Ireland and forever in India. France in Indo-China. Even as Wilson spoke of such benevolence, there was war in the Balkans.
The Turkish-Italian War had just ended—for a time. Foreign
officers of great nations kept playing the timeless diplomatic war
games in quest of dominance, all within what diplomatically was
called the balance of power. There were treaties and secret treaties and even more secret dealings in armaments. Above all,
there were alliances. The Triple Entente of Britain, France and
Russia versus the Triple Alliance of Germany, Austria-Hungary
and Italy. Smaller nations were seduced and bribed to join one
side or the other. For all the talk of peace, the world was a tin-
derbox waiting for a match.

Indeed, war was the obligatory international pastime, an extension of politics by other means, as commonplace as dueling,
ennobling to the national pride, an outlet for heroics, a challenge
to such virile virtues as courage and sacrifice. War was the ecstasy
of conquest written into history to symbolize the greatness of na-

tions, the embodiment of the patriotic spirit with parades and flags and marching bands to glorify the alleged triumph of good over evil.

War was as American as the star-spangled banner, a century and a half of continuous battles, 8,600 military engagements in 110 wars since the formation of the thirteen colonies. There were, in fact, only twenty individual years in which our military had not been in combat. Of twenty-eight presidents until Wilson, eleven had been generals. And through it all, over half the nation's expenditures had been allocated to its "defense."

But at last, in 1912, there was to be no more of it. Woodrow Wilson himself was an avowed pacifist. Unlike his political opponent, Theodore Roosevelt, there wasn't a shred of militarism in his nature. He often admitted that he'd never even had a fist-fight in his youth. Just to look at him, this was clear—a stiffly professorial type, he was rigorously moral without demonstrable passion. One could not picture such a man in military uniform. Indeed, he had never worn one. Bible in hand, he fought only with his mouth. He was a political force whose time had come.

In 1902, when he became president of Princeton, he was a staid conservative who believed that the automobile was the abhorrent forerunner of socialism, that labor unions were detrimental to the cause of industrial development and the best interests of the working man, that women had no need for the right to vote or for achieving equality. In his writings on American history and politics, he despaired of popular democracy with an active contempt for Jeffersonian democracy and its admiration for the French Revolution. Such crises of power in United States history as Shay's Rebellion and the Great Pullman Strike, Wilson saw through the eyes of a ruling-class mentality—even though they represented the people's needs under conditions of their greatest duress. He never had any direct contact with working people. He did not know the feel of calloused hands or the filth of a mine. He never absorbed the stench of poverty, the growing squalor of cities, the endless brutality of wage-slavery. He was forever distant from the people he preached to. To Wilson, the middle class represented the general welfare. With his limited vision, he would lecture that the abolitionist movement was pure fanaticism that helped bring on the Civil War. His God, after all, came out of the tradition of Southern slavery.

During his presidency, Wilson's postmaster general, A. S. Burleson, had segregated his department, which prompted a petition signed by twenty thousand "colored people." When their spokesman, W. W. Trotter, appeared before Wilson in protest, Wilson explained that the petitioners would surely be better off remaining among their own people; Trotter's objections so annoyed him that he threw the man out of his office. Nor was it surprising that, not two weeks later, he welcomed D. W. Griffith, motion picture producer of *Birth of a Nation*, and held the first preview at a presidential screening. Adapted from a novel by Thomas Dixon, *The Clansman*, the movie was a glorification of the Ku Klux Klan and its dedicated knights who combatted the intolerable menace of sexually voracious Negroes. Together with a fellow Southerner, Edward White, then chief justice of the United States Supreme Court, Wilson praised the movie, which, in no small part, was responsible for its incredible success. The movie grossed a phenomenal $50 million. To whites, it was a brilliant melodrama of white vengeance against Negro rape. To blacks it was brutally insulting. Its effect on American mores was unquestionably divisive. From Wilson, however, his constituency did not demand any compromise with his Southern heritage. Colored people did not vote in sufficient numbers since white power denied them. Wilson would preside over the violent fruits of a bigoted nation with its coming race wars and rampant lynchings, about which he had precious little to say. From his isolated aerie in the White House, Wilson simply played house with his beloved family, golf with his doctor and political games with his dear Texas friend, "Colonel" House. Except to a few intimates who thrived on telling him what they knew he wished to hear, Wilson's ear was not a sensitive one. He was enjoying himself more than he'd ever imagined possible.

Wilson had always been quick to adjust. His old aversion to Jefferson, for example, had disappeared quickly as he gauged the proper oratory for Democratic Party voters. The old Woodrow Wilson gave way to the new ambitions. He became a political man.

As governor, he had brazenly renounced the same bosses who

had paved the way for his election, and it brought him a new sense of political power-playing. With a resolute (and sometimes ruthless) hand, he had instituted admirable legislation: a progressive primary election law, a strong public utilities act, a corrupt practices act, an employees liability act, and he had become celebrated for turning New Jersey into a shining example of workable reform exactly when the country needed just that. All the while, he had his eye on bigger game. Trenton would be a stepping-stone to Washington. Even before he became known as a possible contender, he began ingratiating himself with the man who would be his principal adversary, William Jennings Bryan, the flamboyant Populist whom Wilson had always despised. (He had once written to a friend of his desire that Bryan be knocked "once and for all into a cocked hat!" a letter that would later surface, much to Wilson's embarrassment.) But since he needed Bryan, he invited him to a rapprochement dinner at Princeton. Said Wilson's wife Ellen Axson: "That dinner put Mr. Wilson in the White House."

Then, to smooth the way, there was Edward M. House, the quiet kingmaker, a man of almost Oriental modesty and self-effacement, his deferential acknowledgement of another's remarks a convincing "Why, that's true, yes, that's true." The nature of his meeting with Wilson was in itself symbolic. Wilson was governor of New Jersey at the time with a perky eye on the White House. He had the usual supporters in the smoke-filled rooms of the Democratic Party hierarchy, but he had good reason not to trust them. He had heard about House, an artificially designated nonmilitary Texas colonel, then living in New York City, who had made a large amount of money through various investments and had chosen to apply himself to his chosen hobby, political promotion, the better to use his skills as a power broker. House was said to be unique in his capacity for gaining influence, that he could charm the venom out of a cobra. As for his political preferences, they were perhaps best illustrated in a novel he had written, *Philip Dru, Administrator,* whose hero was a benevolent aristocrat who believed in government for the people but not by them. There is no record that Wilson ever read this book either before or after they met, or even if he had, how he might have responded. But meet House he did, in House's apartment on East Fifty-third Street, the governor visiting the colonel.

There was no agenda, certainly, and no stated purpose, but they both knew what was at stake, a silent understanding that they shared a mutual need. Wilson wanted help and guidance with someone he could trust, and House wanted a promising candidate on whose coattails he could ride to power—or, as it was said, a Machiavelli in search of a prince.

It was a fumbling affair at first, neither knowing quite what to say or what to make of the other. House, however, was a master at this sort of sociability. He could use his diminutive body, his soft blue eyes, his gentle voice, with consummate endearment. There was no doubt but that he had prepared himself like a graduate student at an oral examination for his doctorate. Even the initial fumbling would work to his advantage. Wilson quickly relaxed. He liked the look of the man, the narrow sloping shoulders, and the strong chin—quite the opposite of Wilson himself. He was taken by the soft Texas speech, barely above a whisper, and the accompanying shyness. Above all, he was gratified by House's wonderful capacity to listen, a quality Wilson always appreciated in a listener. House would listen and nod, soaking up Wilson's words spongelike, then return them in a corroborating style that lent dignity to the thought. One could imagine Wilson, the eternally antisocial creature, creaming at this entirely pliable personality. As Sigmund Freud defined it: "It was love at first sight."

And then, perhaps, blindness. Wilson had no hesitation about permitting House to take over, an advisor without portfolio who was always there for him, always careful never to step across that undefinable line. House read his speeches, discussed policy, recommended appointments. Even Cabinet posts were largely the choices of the colonel. Wilson rarely determined government policy without consulting him. His omnipresence in the White House was Washington's great nonsecret. The way to the president's ear was through the colonel. And the colonel always knew what the president wanted, sometimes even if the president did not know himself. Indeed, this arrangement continued without criticism, though some suspected it was much too artfully crafted by the little Texan. Less Machiavelli, perhaps, than a gentle Rasputin. The selection of Wilson's Cabinet, for example, was overloaded with a group of Southern Bourbons to whom House owed favors. Wilson did not care as long as they were obeisant. Only William Jennings Bryan as secretary of state had a willful mind of his own, and his had been an appointment that was politically an obligatory one. Wilson had even offered House a post of his choosing, but the colonel declined, preferring to keep a low public profile, no doubt the best means to maintain the serenity of their relationship. He was absolutely right about that. He was, in fact, almost always right; his genius was being an alter ego. House knew exactly what the president wanted, and when he didn't know, it was because the president himself did not know. And this was when House became dangerous. Someone described him as a man who walked into a room like an Indian on dry leaves.

In 1912, America was at its Progressive peak. The Democratic Party Populism of Bryan, the extraordinary popularity of Roosevelt's Progressive presidency were inescapable signs of the times. It was a movement of an American Protestant passion to redeem the world in its perpetual battle between the evils of greed and privilege and the rights of ordinary people. This had been dynamically articulated over the years by *McClure's Magazine*, an extraordinarily influential monthly that dignified the muckraking process. It featured such writers as Lincoln Steffens, who exposed what he called "The Shame of the Cities" and their corrupt political bosses; Ida Tarbell on the tyranny of the great Standard Oil Company; and Ray Stannard Baker on the growing corruptions within organized labor. The premise of these exposés was a faith in the American system as it was supposed to function, all partisans of the established order, reforms to be achieved under a more democratic capitalism. What they wrote, however, was so trenchant, it made them seem to be attacking what they were only trying to defend. Their fear was that powerful and sinister forces bent on crippling the democratic process might eventually destroy it. And since discontent was much on the rise, who knew where it would end? Indeed, these evils and injustices and corruptions had become so imbedded in the American ethic that responsibility for their reform had come to rest on the nation as a whole. Everyone had become a part of it. The average (middle-class) citizen would, in the end, get precisely what he asked for, but how could a Christian democracy explain the horror of the problem? Where, indeed, had it all begun?

Steffens tried to explain the conundrum: "Most people say it began with Adam. But Adam, you remember, said it was Eve, the woman, she did it. And Eve said no, no, it wasn't she, it was the serpent. And that's where the clergy have been stuck ever since. You blame that serpent. Satan. Now I come and I am trying to show you that it was, it is, the *Apple!*"

The quest for the apple became the great American seduction. Few wanted it any other way, even the hardworking man who saw himself as a soon-to-be capitalist fighting for a piece of the (apple) pie. Businessmen resisted good honest government the way they resisted a truly representative democracy. They had a common need for privilege. Franchises need special legislation, favors, protective tariffs, leniency, tax abatements, pull with officials, judges, prosecutors, even with the police. "The devil," said Steffens, "was privilege. Wipe out privilege and hope for privileges—and you destroy the apple."

Privilege, to be sure, had a way of maintaining itself. As Henry James wrote, "It is common prudence for those of us who have made it to the top floor to refrain from boring holes in it."

What was needed, then, was a fundamental change in American values. The philosopher John Dewey, in his prime, wrote: "Americans [have been] weened on the notion, sedulously created by the class in power, that the creative capacities of individuals can be evoked and developed only in a struggle for possessions and material gain. That class power was reactionary, resisting all social change . . . not in accord with its selfish needs . . . holding the people to identify their goals with the making of money—which only a small percentage could possibly do. It was all a fraud. . . . The persistance of an old horse-and-buggy individualism . . . worked to the utter undoing of the individual."

If Woodrow Wilson came late to progressive views, he was quick to capitalize on them. He had no difficulty in rationalizing these adjustments. Big money, the overpowering trusts, accumulated capital were, after all, immoral violations of middle-class and Christian capitalism. If he was also opposed to the power of organized labor—"as formidable an enemy to equality and freedom of opportunity as the so-called capitalist class"—he insisted that he was friendly with all working people. Socialism, a challenging minority force in the Western world, represented "a danger of the very sort we wish to escape, a danger of centralized and corruptible control."

"Mr. Wilson," said Eugene V. Debs, Socialist candidate for the presidency, "believes the poor working man should have the same freedom to sleep under a bridge as a stockbroker."

Wilson's solution to all problems was rooted in a moral regeneration. Evil lay in individuals, not in institutions. Individuals, then, must be punished, not corporations. "You do not arrest the speeding automobile; you arrest the driver. . . . One really responsible man in jail, one real originator of the schemes and transactions which are contrary to the public interest legally lodged in the penitentiary, would be worth more than a thousand corporations mulcted in fines. . . ." Thus, thousands of small stockholders would not suffer and all would prosper. No matter that corporations would continue to exploit the market by any means available; that because of their capacities for criminal excess, they controlled the courts that permitted those excesses; that the very system so brutally manipulated by those corporations would supply its own protection for both the speeding automobile *and* its driver. As a result, such pronouncements made Wilson a perfect candidate for conservative capitalists as well as the middle class. Significantly, his mentor for the presidency was Colonel George Harvey, publisher of *Harper's Magazine* and an associate of J. P. Morgan himself.

In the 1912 election year, Wilson became the ultimate spokesman, balancing traditional Wilsonian conservatism with the new progressivism. He settled comfortably between the reactionary Republicanism of President William Howard Taft and the Bull Moose liberalism of Teddy Roosevelt—but his principal strength came from those who leaned away from Taft. "The middle class is being squeezed out by the processes of big business prosperity," said Wilson. Big money interests squeezed out the smaller entrepreneur, crippled his credit, undersold him until his business withered, discriminated against competitive retailers, withheld raw materials from the small manufacturer. That was unfair competition. "What this country needs . . . is a body of laws which will look after the men who are on the make rather than the men who are already made."

He won with barely 40 percent of the vote. The jailed Debs pulled an amazing nine hundred thousand votes. Fifty-eight percent of the eligible voters turned out, reflecting the continuing downward trend since 1896. Barely 6 percent of the American population voted for Wilson, a statistic that appeared to bother no one in a position of power.

The election of Woodrow Wilson in 1912 epitomized the inadequacy of electoral democracy, for it failed to reflect or represent the conditions under which one hundred million people in America lived. A scant 2 percent of the population owned an incredible 60 percent of the country's wealth. Over 30 percent were aliens, most of whom lived in ghettoed poverty. Ten million more were "colored," a generation earlier freed from slavery but whose taste of freedom was anything but sweet. Nonetheless, at this time of the great Progressive crusade, the Wilson inaugural offered a promise of change.

"We have squandered a great part of what we might have used," he said, "[We have been] shamefully prodigal as well as admirably efficient. We have been proud of our industrial achievements, but disregarded the human cost . . . the fearful physical and spiritual cost to the men and women and children. . . . The groans and agony of it all had not yet reached our ears, the solemn moving undertone of our life, coming up out of the mines and factories. . . . The great government we loved has too often been made use of for private and selfish purposes, and those who used it had forgotten the people. . . ."

Thus the conservative-turned-liberal Wilson introduced what he called the New Freedom. With an eager and compliant Congress, his administration began to sweep away a mass of abuses with a new broom. First, the Underwood Tariff Act, the first substantial reduction in rates since before the Civil War. Wool was put on the free list. Tariffs on cotton were reduced almost to half. Barely five months in office, Wilson attacked the banking interests for failing to extend credit to small businessmen and especially farmers. He pushed a currency reform bill through Congress that established a Federal Reserve System through which interest rates in regional banks could be regulated. The Clayton

Anti-Trust Bill enabled the government to exercise closer control over monopolies through a newly created Federal Trade Commission—all of which was legislated in spite of big business resistance. Only Wilson's attempt to invoke minimum wages for women and children in industry was declared unconstitutional by the Supreme Court.

Meanwhile, the American people got to know something, but not much, about this stranger in the White House. He carried his 179 pounds on a five-foot-eleven-inch frame well. Erect, with broad shoulders and a slim waist, he had what appeared to be a disproportionately large head, oversized ears, an extremely prominent chin and a sharp nose on which sat rimless professorial eyeglasses that enhanced a look of primness. It was said he had moved into the presidential residence needing to borrow $5,000 to bring his furniture from Princeton. His was a Spartan new look, totally devoid of ostentation. Frequently mentioned was his huge collection of walking canes.

His habits were equally plain. He rose at eight and breakfasted on orange juice and raw eggs as prescribed by his doctor, part of a strict regimen to preserve his uncertain health. He liked to work on an old portable typewriter, typing his own speeches, correspondence and state papers. He was known to take that typewriter everywhere. At ten, he received visitors, seldom for more than ten or fifteen minutes in keeping with his passion for exclusivity. At one, he lunched with his wife and those of his three daughters who happened to be home. He did not socialize with cabinet members or congressmen—or even the many intellectuals, artists and professionals who sought his attention. He did not care for stimulating talk. To a reporter, he confessed that he seldom read a serious, important book to its end. At two, he returned to his office for more appointments. At four, he quit work and donned his Scots cap for an automobile ride, always on familiar routes. Or he went golfing or for a ride on the presidential yacht down the Potomac. At seven, he dined with his family at home. Rarely, they went to the theatre; his preference was for levity, mostly for vaudeville. His favorite was Will Rogers, the cowboy wit who told jokes as he spun his rope. When at home, Wilson would read aloud to his family the uplifting verse of Keats, Wordsworth, Browning, Shelley, Tennyson—significantly, all British. On occasion, he became playful, but only with intimates; he would assume a clownlike personality, artfully mimicking and impersonating favorite characters such as drunks, movie villains, fatuous British gentlemen. His adoring and uncritical women always laughed.

Most people found him ungiving and cold. His face was a mask. He seemed tense at public gatherings, in appearances at affairs of state. When he returned to the privacy of his room, he would flex his facial muscles to ease the strain. His piety was legendary. It was said of him that he wore out more Bibles than shoes. As a Calvinist Presbyterian, he often said that man was innately depraved, a corrupt sinner whose only hope of salvation lay in God's grace in granting eternal life.

Aware that he was not a handsome man, he enjoyed reciting a limerick at his own expense:

> For beauty I am not a star
> There are others more handsome by far,
> But my face I don't mind it
> For I am behind it—
> It's the fellow in front that I jar.

He was an enigma to everyone, regardless of how highly they thought of him—and, as it turned out, to himself as well. He confessed this to the National Press Club in 1914: "I have sometimes thought of going to some costumers, some theatrical costumers, and buying an assortment of beards, rouge and coloring and all the known means of disguising myself if it were not against the law. . . . If I could disguise myself and not get caught, I would go out, be a free American citizen once more and have a jolly time." A curious supposition, to say the least, for he had never known what it meant to be free of imprisonment since it was always self-imposed.

Overall, he confessed to a longing to be loved. His intolerance of criticism drove him to equate flattery with love. His cabinet, for example, consisted mainly of southerners like himself, and occasionally, he would send for one or another of them, then treat them like the teacher he was. The writer Hutchins Hapgood described him as a "cold and concentrated personality." To the journalist William A. White, his handshake "felt like a ten-cent pickled mackerel in brown paper—unresponsive and lifeless [this was the result of a partial stroke that had affected his entire right side] . . . a spare, ascetic, repressed creature, a kind of frozen flame of righteous intelligence. . . ." Jo Davidson, the noted sculptor who did his bust "admired the man but found nothing to love . . . interested in no art . . . no music. He was a moralist . . . invoked fear and respect, like God, but no affection."

His secretary, Joseph Tumulty, a genial Irishman who revered and protected him, claimed that the president was quick to take suggestions and criticism, but no one believed that.

There was no question but that Wilson was completely honest, that he refused all temptations and permitted no corruption. This setting of a high moral tone was, at the time, a much-respected quality, a reflection of America's rigid Puritanical heritage.

In Paris, however, it was both his strength and his weakness. He was the legendary slave Androcles walking blithely into the arena to face, this time, the wrong lion.

3. Woodrow Wilson's Fight for a Just Peace

There must be a new order of things in which the only question will be "Is it right? Is it just? Is it in the interests of mankind?" . . . I sent these lads over here to die. Shall I—can I—ever speak a word of counsel which is inconsistent with the assurance I gave them when they came over?

—Woodrow Wilson in Paris

If Wilson represented the hopes of the people, to the leaders of state in Europe he posed a threat. One could summarize the history of the Paris Peace Conference in that dichotomy, for the same men who had created the war were about to create the peace. The people, meanwhile, were forever their victims, reduced to suffering the consequences of vague forces about which they had little understanding and over which they had even less control. The idolization of Woodrow Wilson was, in itself, a pathetic symbol of their helplessness. Even as he had ridden like a god through the capitols of Europe, the peacemakers (recently the war makers) were keeping him from those whose support he needed most. In Paris, Georges Clemenceau prevented an organized mass of workers from parading in celebration of the democratic policies Wilson represented. The Italian monarchy and its flunky, Premier Vittorio Orlando, alarmed at the new outspoken drift toward socialism, cancelled a publicly announced Wilson speech and sent regiments of armed soldiers to block the huge crowds who came in defiance of the order. Even in London there were official restrictions preventing Labor Party and Socialist demonstrations before him. Nor had it been reported that when Wilson had first landed at Brest, he was greeted by the Socialist mayor, or that the delegation who called on him in Paris was led by Jean Languet, a grandson of Karl Marx, or that there was a huge and successful meeting at Albert Hall in London in support of the Fourteen Points, organized by radicals.

Indeed, when Wilson declared that food rather than guns might well be the cure for the spread of Bolshevism in Europe, the press began to attack him—including the editor of the Milan *Popolo D'Italia,* a man named Benito Mussolini who had left the Socialist Party to run a postwar reactionary newspaper. Even in America, newspapers sneered at his idealism, twisting his phrases, ridiculing his speeches with distorted explanations. Nor was Wilson himself the best servant of his own cause: stiff, aloof, defensive, he lacked the warmth and garrulous personality that made for good press. The journalist George Seldes recounted this firsthand: "The people he seemed to like least were the several hundred newspapermen who came to tell the world of his plans to bring about eternal peace on earth."

When, at last, the great conference began, Paris was a seething mass of petitioners with myriad grievances. John Dos Passos described the scene as follows: "Around the edges of delegations hovered all sorts of adventurers peddling oil concessions or manganese mines, pretenders to dukedoms and thrones, cranks with shortcuts to Utopia in their briefcases, secret agents, art dealers, rug salesmen, procurers and pimps.... Restaurants and night clubs were packed. Taxis were forever at a premium. Business boomed." Perhaps, more to the nub of it, there were no representatives from the largest, most populated nation in Europe: Russia. The Bolsheviks were simply not invited.

First, there were the plenary sessions. Then came the Council of Ten, a Babel-like bedlam of Allied powers, large and small, presided over by the seventy-eight-year-old Clemenceau (El Tigre, as he was called), capriciously banging his gavel to curtail debate in the fury of his boredom—except, of course, when France was involved. The Tiger alone had a single sense of purpose and never wavered from it. To John Maynard Keynes, British economist, member of Lloyd George's delegation: "He had one illusion—

France; and one disillusion—mankind, including Frenchmen, and his colleagues not least. . . . He was foremost a believer . . . that the German understands and can understand nothing but intimidation, that there is no advantage he will not take of you, and no extent to which he will not demean himself for profit, that he is without honor, pride or mercy. Therefore you must never negotiate with a German; you must dictate to him. . . . European history is to be a perpetual prizefight, of which France had won this round . . . certainly not the last. . . . For a Peace of magnanimity or of fair and equal treatment could only have the effect of shortening the interval of Germany's recovery and hastening the day when she will again hurl at France her greater numbers and her superior resources and technical skills. . . ."

Clemenceau's demand for a Carthaginian peace was inevitable, especially after his recent thunderous reelection by a majority of four to one, without so much as a mention of the Fourteen Points.

Then there was David Lloyd George, also reelected prime minister of England, having campaigned on a program of Make-the-Hun-Pay-to-the-Last-Farthing, Hang-the-Kaiser, all the shibboleths of the jingoistic world. Once a radical, he had been converted by the war. As Keynes wrote: "[He] is rooted in nothing; he is void and without content; he lives and feeds in his immediate surroundings; he is an instrument and player and the same time . . . he is a prism, as I have heard him described, which collects light and distorts it and is most brilliant if the light comes from many quarters at once, a vampire and a medium in one."

It was typical of Lloyd George to promise Wilson his support, then run a jingoist "khaki campaign." When he and Arthur Balfour met with Wilson for preliminary discussions at Buckingham Palace, Lloyd George appeared to endorse Wilson's firm opposition to colonial acquisitions and excessive reparations. Later, however, reporting this at the Imperial War Cabinet meeting, he would be less conciliatory, submitting to the hard-boiled nationalist Australian premier, William Hughes, who became furious at Wilson, glorying in savage attacks on the American's New World Order. "The British Empire must not be permitted to be dragged behind the wheels of President Wilson's chariot. . . . He had no claim to speak even for his country!" Throughout the Paris conference, Hughes would remain a thorn in Wilson's side. And how Clemenceau loved him! "I hear you are a cannibal!" the old Frenchman would tease the irascible Australian.

Whatever Wilson had expected to accomplish in this titanic clash of values and interests, his high-minded aspirations were quickly and thoroughly trampled under the boots of old-world traditions. Clemenceau, who had twice seen the Boche camped on the doorsteps of Paris, was not going to jeopardize the security of France for the blandishments of Wilsonian idealism. "God gave us Ten Commandments," he would sneer, "but Wilson needs fourteen." And Lloyd George, representing the financially depleted British Empire, demanded an expansion of colonial possessions with absolutely no abridgment of their control of the seas. Orlando came to spell out Italy's need for loot as agreed upon in the secret Treaty of London, Italy's bait to enter the war as an Ally. All of them were like vultures around carrion; Wilson could but beseech them to reconsider such abominations. Were they not violating the very terms of the armistice itself? He believed only in his art of persuasion, embarrassing them with his moralisms like a missionary among cannibals. What could they do but seek to eat him alive? He was a man who loved principles, the more abstract the better. He would reason from principles rather than facts. How could they deal with such a mind? He had never been adept at one-on-one confrontations. Here, for the most part, it was two-on-one, a pair of unprincipled minds working in tandem, using and abusing facts at will, pummeling him with harsh demands based on admittedly immoral secret treaties that had brought on the war in the first place—but, they rationalized, would it not be just as immoral now to break them? Indeed, how could they? Were not the fruits of those treaties precisely why they had sacrificed so much?

Like boxers, bobbing and weaving through opening rounds to test the opponent's reflexes as they probed for the weakness, they soon found Wilson's. The League of Nations was Wilson's pet—the Wilsonian League as the world's hope for eternal peace. He played the league as an open hand, cards face up on the table, and the conferees chipped away at him, forcing devastating violations of his Fourteen Points in exchange for their support of the league. By tradition, they were masters of manipulation, flattering and cajoling as they bargained, attacking and retreating when necessary but never giving ground. It was always Wilson who gave ground, retreating while thinking he advanced. In time, then, it became evident that Wilson would get his League of Nations, but the Allies would get their treaty.

It was said that this need not have happened. Wilson could have stopped such madness in its tracks. America, after all, was the world's most powerful nation, far and away the richest, having emerged from the war totally unscathed, a creditor nation to whom the Allies owed billions. America was the dominant source of food and manufactured goods, and neither England nor France could begin to function without her continued aid. Wilson had but to lay down the terms of the treaty. He had but to spell out the nature of the peace. Like it or not, the Fourteen Points had been the genesis of the armistice agreed upon by the Allies as well as Germany, and thus must dominate the terms of the treaty. If not, Wilson might have declared that America would withhold all future credits, refuse to do any business, and the Allies would suffer the threat of shortages and starvation.

Wilson, however, was not one to deliver ultimatums. He saw his mission as messianic, above the sordid squalor of bargaining. He did not wish to be adversarial. They were, were they not, colleagues on a mutually motivated goal. If there were disagreements, he would guide them out of self-seeking determinations by the force of his purity. America was in Paris for purely selfless reasons, with no claims on any territories nor desire for reparations. The future of the world was at issue. How could anyone deny its salvation?

The trouble was, although Wilson had hundreds of expert advisors, he had not created a functioning organization with specific responsibilities. His advisors consisted of five mediocrities whose advice he took no heed of. Except for his dear friend, Colonel Edward House, who was beside him in all matters, he barely consulted with any of them. His secretary of state, Robert Lansing, a former State Department attorney, was reduced to doodling bizarre caricatures on notepads, for Wilson had no use for lawyers. His military expert, General Tasker Bliss, was a jovial old roly-poly way out of his depth—no doubt selected for that very reason. Henry White, Republican diplomat, was now an elder statesman without function or portfolio. As a team, they were more conspicuous for the absence of important Republicans (if not Lodge then perhaps Elihu Root, or ex-president William Howard Taft) or even prominent representatives of the Senate itself. As Will Rogers, the most popular master of whimsy in his time, described it: "I'll tell you what, we'll split this thing fifty-fifty. I will go and you can stay."

For such selections—and omissions—Wilson was severely criticized. So too was his decision to go to Paris. Ill-advised, everyone said—especially Colonel House: "The moment Woodrow Wilson sits at the council table with those prime ministers and foreign secretaries, he has lost all the power that comes from distance and detachment. . . . In Washington, Wilson has the ear of the whole world. . . . He can go before Congress and appeal to the conscience and hope of mankind. . . . This is a mighty weapon, but if the president were to participate in the proceedings, it would be as a broken stick."

Wilson had insisted on going. How could he resist? He saw himself as invulnerable, armed with the sword of God. Blessed with such power, he did not even bother to prepare a plan of action, not a single offering on which to state his claims. He came with a thousand silenced experts and a faith in divine providence. Keynes, who suffered through it all, described the tragic confusion:

"Never had a philosopher held such weapons wherewith to bind the princes of the world. [But] the president was not a hero or a prophet; he was not even a philosopher but a generously intentioned man . . . lacking that domination of intellectual equipment . . . in a game of which he had no experience at all. . . . His head and features were finely cut . . . and the muscles of his neck and the carriage of his head were distinguished. But, like Odysseus, the president looked wiser when he was seated. . . . He was not only insensitive to his surroundings in the external sense, he was not sensitive to his environment at all. What chance would such a man have against Lloyd George's unerring sensibility to everyone immediately around him? The president would be playing blind man's buff in that party. . . . The Old World was tough in wickedness anyhow; the Old World's heart of stone might blunt the sharpest blade of the bravest knight-errant. But this blind and deaf Don Quixote was entering a cavern where the swift and glittering blade was in the hands of the adversary.... There can seldom have been a statesman of the first rank more incompetent than the president in the agilities of the council chamber.... By pleasantness and an appearance of conciliation, the president would be maneuvered off his ground, would miss the moment for digging his toes in, and, before he knew where he had been got to, it was too late."

Wilson alone was no match against the group mind of the British—compact, articulate, shrewd, magnificently elastic, a mind of a hundred minds seasoned to rule over centuries of the empire. It never wavered as did the mind of an individual. The French too worked with a group mind, iron-willed in its quest for security. And behind them both was a formidable national will. Behind Wilson was a weak and fragile ideology that lacked even a mandate. Having been sorely beaten in the recent 1918 Congressional elections—in spite of his request that the American electorate support the Democratic candidates in this time of need—Wilson alone had come to Paris rejected by his constituency. And the outspoken ex-president Theodore Roosevelt, no fan of Wilson's, made sure that all of Europe was made aware of it:

"Our allies, and our enemies, and Woodrow Wilson himself should all understand that Mr. Wilson has no authority whatever to speak for the American people at this time. His leadership and the Fourteen Points and his four supplementary points and his five complimentary points and all his utterances every which way have ceased to have any shadow of right to be accepted as expressive of the will of the American people."

It was true: in no other free country in the world would Wilson still be in office.

An interview with the prestigious Nicholas Murray Butler, president of Columbia University, was published in Paris newspapers: "President Woodrow Wilson has not the slightest chance of getting any treaty ratified that is repugnant to the sentiments of the Republican Party... which are framed in unreserved support of Great Britain and France...."

How, then, could Europeans trust Woodrow Wilson, already discredited with his own electorate in its 1918 Congressional elections, to implement his proposals for peace?

Even with members of the American delegation, this disparity produced a sense of impotence. Wilson, meanwhile, maintained a cool evasion of all such considerations that might disturb the foundations of his somewhat mystic faith. He would have had to be a far more brilliant and determined leader to triumph over such a given.

From the beginning, the Wilsonian leadership had been slovenly. Hardly had the Council of Ten, consisting of the Allied nations, assembled in January when Wilson astonished the assemblage by conceding the Tyrol-Brenner region on Italy's northern border to the Italians. No matter that several hundred thousand people of purely German heritage lived there. What price self-determination, it was pondered? This was Wilson's opening gesture to gain Orlando's support for the league, and it would rock the conferees for its blatant abdication of Wilson's own conceptions. Harold Nicolson of the British delegation was distressed: "The impotence of the president immediately became clear, and they proceeded to tear him apart." Shortly thereafter came the attack on Point Four ("Impartial adjustment of all colonial claims based on interest of populations"). Lloyd George had opposed return of colonies to Germany—and Wilson startled everyone by a prompt agreement with what became known as the "mandate" system under League of Nations supervision—a feeble formula to disguise the old imperialist reality.

The result was the quickening demoralization of high-minded Wilsonian supporters. To other conferees intent on battling for spoils, the league would be a matter to be bargained with after the German carcass had been agreeably dismembered. It was the spoils they were after. The league meant nothing to them but a bargaining chip. Only Wilson was dedicated to the league, and cared little for the spoils.

Every evening, then, he assembled a small coterie of supporters to fashion a covenant. Others of the great conference were reveling in the pleasures of Parisian nightlife, but Wilson and his crew kept working. And he would be heard. In time, a trial covenant was written, and just before his temporary return to the States, in February 1919, he insisted on reading its noble articles before a plenary session.

"This covenant is definite in the one thing we are called upon to make definite," Wilson said. "It is a definite guarantee of peace. Many terrible things have come out of this war, but some very beautiful things have come out of it. Wrong has been defeated, but the rest of the world has been more conscious than it ever was before of the majesty of the right.... The miasma of distrust, of intrigue, is cleared away.... We are brothers and have a common purpose . . . and this is our covenant of fraternity and friendship."

Thus it was spoken after those weeks of incessant wrangling. All would be right with the world, and the conferees and their staffs responded with resounding applause. The ever-genial Colonel House made it clear to the president that he approved, quickly scribbling a note: "Dear Governor. Your speech was as great as the occasion—I am very happy." And the governor responded in kind: "Bless your heart. Thank you from the bottom of my heart."

How noble they were all made to feel. How glorious, suddenly, were the fruits of their inglorious negotiations. Wilson's genius for obfuscation was seldom more apparent. And when he embarked on the *George Washington* the following day for a month of mending political fences back at home, he carried the covenant in his coat pocket, significantly close to his heart as though it were his passport to immortality.

He could even believe in the adoration bestowed on his return. As he saw it, he had but to reveal the covenant's grandiloquent phrases and all potential opposition would melt away. When he landed in Boston, he spoke like one who held the future of the world in that pocket: "And these ideals have wrought new magic that all the peoples of Europe are buoyed up and confident in the spirit of hope, because they believe that we are at the eve of a new age in the world, when nations will understand one another; when nations will support one another in every just cause; when nations will unite every moral and every physical strength to see that right shall prevail."

There were comments that it was not America but Woodrow Wilson who was about to fail the world. Others remarked that Woodrow Wilson was about to fail America in his attempt to save the world. To many, however, his oratory maintained its impressive impact. *Literary Digest Magazine* would conduct a massive poll with a single query: Do you favor the proposed League of Nations?

The result showed 70 percent in favor. Democratic-affiliated newspapers with a circulation of five million were over 90 percent in favor. Even Republican newspapers with a circulation of seven million were 60 percent in favor. Independent papers with nine million circulation were also 60 percent in favor. Only the Hearst chain with 2,500,000 readers was opposed. A reflection of popular opinion—but it was nonetheless two-thirds of the Senate who would be responsible for ratification.

Wilson had taken House's advice and invited leading senators to a special White House dinner on his return, the better to brief them on his accomplishments in Paris. In the process, he was stung by the extraordinary Republican resistance to the very idea of his league. Led by Henry Cabot Lodge of Massachusetts, the Republican Party was determined to use whatever means necessary to return to power in 1920, the most obvious of which was to prevent the Wilson heroics from reaching fruition. Beat the league, beat Wilson, beat the Democratic administration. It seemed irrelevant that Republicans were unable to decide whether they objected to the league because this covenant was too strong or because it was too weak. Senator William Borah, for example, the Idaho isolationist, opposed the league because he believed it committed America to involvement in European affairs not legitimate to truly American interests. Senator Lodge opposed it because it restricted American expansionism.

The battle lines were drawn. Among others was the ever-present Wilsonian nemesis, ex-president Teddy Roosevelt, who spared no opportunity to lash at him with far more venom than sensibility: "To substitute internationalism for nationalism is to do away with patriotism. . . . The man who loves other countries as much as he loves his own stands on a level with the man who loves other women as much as he loves his own wife."

Or, to flip this on its head, one might suggest that the superpatriotic T.R. really believed a man should stand first by his own wife, but if he refused to leave her to go to war on behalf of the wives of France, Britain, Belgium, Serbia, et al., he is to be damned as a traitor to his family and his country.

Wilson ignored Roosevelt, concentrating his hostility against Lodge, who was successfully rallying senators to defeat him. Said Lodge: "It is the sense of the Senate that while it is their sincere desire that the nations of the world should unite to promote peace and general disarmament, the Constitution of the League of Nations in the form now proposed to the peace conference should not be accepted by the United States." That this resolution was not approved by the Senate was of infinitely less consequence than that thirty-nine senators signed it, more than enough to block ratification of the treaty. Let Woodrow Wilson go back to Paris, then. Let him simply negotiate a treaty with Germany to end the war, and they would ratify.

Republicans felt ample reason to show their hostility. They had demonstrated submissiveness throughout the war effort in spite of the president's imperious posture, but the war was now over and with it the need for patriotic unity. Peace permitted the return to the vagaries of the old political process. And the Senate, which had been denied its constitutional "advice and consent" to all treaty-making, was ready to take on the haughty president. The resolution of the thirty-nine was merely the opening declaration of that intent—"To give Mr. Wilson a crack in the shins . . ." According to one letter-writing wag, "They wanted to make him stop smiling in that irritating way of his." The entire treaty-making affair had been kept as secret and confusing to the senators as it had to the entire American public. Wilson had promised he would seek good council; then, quite deliberately, did no such thing. They saw him as something of a used-car salesman pointing to advertisements as to what a wonderful machine it was, running well, its trimmings still intact, *they had only to believe him.* Someone else dug into Wilson's own *History of the American People* for this significant passage: "In April 1844, Mr. Tyler sent to the Senate a treaty of annexations which he had negotiated with Texas. Secret negotiations, a piece of business privately carried to completion and made public only when finished, suited well with the president's temper and way of action. . . . The Senate rejected the treaty by the very decisive vote of sixteen to thirty-five, men of both parties alike deeply irritated that the president should spring this weighty matter upon the country in such a fashion, taking no counsel beforehand save such as he chose to take."

Through all this endless Sturm and Drang, Wilson was quick to demonstrate his fury. They were trying to take away his crown even before it could be placed on his head. On the day before he sailed back to Paris, at the New York Metropolitan Opera House, he openly spoke his defiance (thereby adding to the defiance of the defied). "When that treaty comes back, gentlemen [in the Senate] will find the covenant not only in it, but so many threads of that treaty tied to that covenant that you cannot dissect the covenant from the treaty without destroying the whole vital structure." In short, they would have to take the treaty with the League of Nations or get no treaty at all.

Wilson landed at Brest on the thirteenth of the month, exactly as he had arranged in December at his first arrival. (Numbers, it seemed, were one of his more bizarre passions, and thirteen was his favorite. Because of the thirteen original colonies and the stripes of the flag? Because of the thirteen letters in his name? Because others thought it to be unlucky?) On this thirteenth, however, Wilson took a far greater trouncing than he was prepared for. In his absence, his dear friend, Colonel Edward House, had permitted the detachment of the league from the preliminary treaty as a concession to the other conferees. The preliminary treaty dealt exclusively with economic and military matters. The resolution of the more complicated, and controversial league covenant was to be withheld for the final treaty that would be drafted later.

Wilson was stunned. When he emerged from his cabin after a meeting with House, his wife Edith reported that "he had aged ten years.... I look back on that moment as a crisis in his life... from it date the long years of illness." Said Wilson: "House has betrayed everything I have worked for...." That this was a gross overstatement became irrelevant to what Wilson saw as devastating implications: the Senate would doubtlessly ratify such a treaty, the war with Germany would be over and the league might very well be scuttled in elapsing time ("disLodged," as it were). House, unaware of Wilson's feelings, advised that this was a time of compromise; he was proud of his powers as a negotiator. Wilson, however, immediately indicated his lack of congeniality. Compromise? He had done nothing but compromise. Later, Wilson would snap at House: "I've learned that there is nothing you can win without fighting for it!"

For historians, the moment would go far beyond disagreement, or even the breach of Wilson's confidence in his friend. The significance of the scene lay in the fact that it could have happened, that the fate of nations lay in the neurotic complexities of such a relationship. What, one might ask, was House doing there in the first place? No one had elected him. He had never held political office. The Senate had not approved his appointment. What forces had arranged that such enormous power be placed in his hands? This, of course, was Wilson's doing, in many ways as strange as his numerology bent.

According to George Creel, who despised him, the colonel's growing arrogance was rooted in his diary writing. Creel believed that any man who, each night, recorded for posterity the events, thoughts, conversations of the day, was doomed to the sin of self-aggrandizement. Ray Stannard Baker, Wilson's friend and biographer, described House as "a dilettante, a lover of the game.... He stands in the midst of great events ... and plays at getting men together for the sheer joy of using his presumptive power." House once astonished Baker in Paris: "If he had it to do," House had told him, "he would make peace in an hour!" Bernard Baruch, one of Wilson's highly respected economic advisers, also believed House to be intoxicated by the power he exercised in Wilson's name, as he had once heard House ejaculating at the glories of his position: "Isn't it a thrilling thing to deal with the forces that affect the destiny of the world!"

All the while, however, House was aware of his transiency, a reaction, as he put it, "to the governor's cold gray eyes and rigid manner."

At Brest, then, on the fateful thirteenth of March, the relationship would begin to dissolve. The sycophancy of the colonel had brought him to the top of the diplomatic world, then dropped him off with nothing but his diary.

So it was that Wilson had been devastated by the same man who had fed Wilson's drive to play "the noblest part that has ever come to the son of man," as House had described the president's role in Paris. Suddenly, as well, Wilson remembered the gossip on board the *George Washington,* tidbits suggesting House's lack of loyalty, his overblown opinion of his abilities as negotiator, all derisive of "Little Woody," as House's own son-in-law was wont to label the president. And Wilson's wife Edith, no fan of House's influence over her husband to begin with, found other reasons to speak ill of him.

It was all of a piece, then, and more than Wilson cared to tolerate. He had never been a forgiving person. Accustomed to martyrdom, he would now stand alone if he had to, the stalwart fighter in a den of thieves. Whether or not he said anything to House of this startling change of heart, inevitably the colonel became aware of it. Nothing, in fact, was ever said.

Wilson arrived back in Paris prepared to put up a fight. His indignation at the news of a preliminary treaty translated to a statement released through Ray Stannard Baker that became a bombshell at the conference:

"March 15, 1919. The president said today that the decision made at the peace conference at its plenary session, January 25, to the effect that the establishment of a League of Nations should be an integral part of the Treaty of Peace is of final force and that there is no basis whatsoever for the reports that a change in this decision was contemplated."

The result was there would be no preliminary treaty. Everything would be postponed until all terms had been agreed upon. Throughout Europe, the blockade of Germany would be extended, chaos and starvation would escalate, the threat of revolution become more imminent.

To expedite negotiations, the Council of Ten was reduced to the Council of Four (Great Britain, France, Italy and the United States), a group that would meet in private session. All covenants would now be secretly arrived at. Only in due time would the world press be informed as to what the Big Four chose to tell them. To worsen a distressing situation, Wilson himself persisted in maintaining his normal aloofness, avoiding press conferences and refusing all interviews. William A. White, the great journalist from Topeka, Kansas, became indignant at this violation of Wilson's own Fourteen Points: "That settles it. That finishes the conference and Wilson. Lloyd George and Clemenceau will now take him into a private bedroom and f- - - him to death," he wrote in a locution not typical of the great journalist.

Secretary of State Robert Lansing wrote: "The result has been to destroy faith and arouse resentment. They [the conferees] now looked on the president as in favor of a world ruled by the Great Powers and international despotism of the strong.... Secret diplomacy, the bane of the past, is a menace from which man believed himself to be rid."

The new structure suggested the turning point in the conference history. The truth was, after four months since armistice, everyone had become tired and tense. As Harold Nicolson reported it: "Apart from the actual strain... there is the moral exhaustion of realizing one's own fallibility and the impossibility of extracting from the lies with which we are all surrounded any real impression as to what the various countries and nationalities honestly desire."

According to Herbert Hoover, "The whole air had suddenly become charged with currents of indescribable malignity."

Wilson was now facing the slings of overt animosity. The Paris press, under Clemenceau's thumb, was sharp with the barbs of insidious lampoons. If Wilson could tolerate adversarial positions, the daily ridicule would chop him up. To be put in a constantly ridiculous light was intolerable. He had arrived in Paris as a giant with more prestige than any man in history, but the Paris newspapers now made him out to be a comic and irritating academic.

As Lloyd George wrote, "Clemenceau [was following Wilson's] movements like an old watchdog keeping an eye on a strange and unwelcome dog who has visited the farmyard and of whose intentions he was more than doubtful." The prime minister himself was losing patience. "I really think that the idealistic president regarded himself as a missionary whose function it was to rescue the poor European heathen from their age-long worship of false and fiery gods. He was apt to address us in that vein, beginning with a few simple and elementary truths about right being more important than might, justice being more eternal than force."

Even Wilson's staff had become disenchanted with his isolation. Lansing wrote: "[We are] like a lot of skilled workmen who are ordered to build a house. We have the materials and the tools, but there are no plans and specifications, and no master-workman in charge.... We putter around in an aimless sort of way and get nowhere.... With all his natural capacity, the president seems to lack the facility of employing teamwork and of adopting a system to utilize the brains of other men."

Wilson, as noted, believed he could dominate all by his power of persuasion, especially now, when determined to fight. The result became a comparable resistance on the part of the other three. Clemenceau, for example, sat like a diminutive menace in his large brocaded chair, his oversized head with its white walrus moustache, eyes blazing in perpetual anger. He was coughing too, for he had been the victim of an assassin's bullet close to a lung just weeks before. "My enemies never could shoot straight," he had declared in defiance, them promptly refused to press charges. His recovery during the conference suggested the enormity of his determination. To the French, at any rate, he had replaced Wilson as the hero of Paris. As it was summed up: "Clemenceau was shot, but Wilson was wounded."

When Clemenceau confronted the new Wilson determination, it fired up his own. He did not really believe what he saw; Wilson was not capable of sustaining a fight; Clemenceau need simply taunt him, bait him, challenge him. According to Lincoln Steffens, the Old Tiger once interrupted a Wilsonian sermon with a gloved hand-slap on the table and the long-suffering look of a much-put-upon man.

"Well, gentlemen," he said, "we can make this a permanent peace; we can remove all the causes of war and set up no new causes of war. It is very, very important what you say, what you have been so long saying, Mr. President. We here now have the opportunity to make a peace that shall last forever, and the French people will be safe. And you are sure you propose to seize this opportunity?"

The others agreed, and Clemenceau, tapping his gray silk gloves gently now, asked if they were ready to pay the price.

The price?

"Yes, the price must be that you, Lloyd George, you English will have to come out of India, for example; we French shall have to come out of North Africa; and you Americans, Mr. President, will have to get out of the Philippines and Puerto Rico, and leave Cuba alone, and Mexico.... It is very expensive, this peace. We French are willing, but are you willing to pay the price, all these costs of no more war in the world?"

No, they didn't mean exactly that, it seemed.

"Then," said Clemenceau, "then you don't mean peace. You

mean war. And the time for the French to make war is now, when we have got Germany down; we shall finish them—and get ready for the next war."

The conference could hardly be expected to cope with such talk, the sort of words that would lay festering behind all the negotiations. That Clemenceau directed such an attack on Wilson was the meat of it—anything to take the winds of virtue out of the American's holy sails. They would all have to suffer from the truth as much as they suffered from the lies.

Harold Nicolson of the British delegation was expert at nailing down these hypocrisies: "The Anglo-Saxon is gifted with a limitless capacity for excluding his own practical requirements from the application of the idealistic theories which he seeks to impose on others. . . . The United States, for example, in the course of its short but highly imperialistic history, had constantly proclaimed the highest virtue while as constantly violating their professions and resorting to the grossest materialism. Such American principles as the equality of man did not apply to the yellow man or the black—or even the immigrant. The doctrine of self-determination had not been extended to the Red Indians or even to the Southern states. The Mexican War was a violation of every 'noble' American conception. Treaties with Indians were shamelessly violated even as the ink was drying. The great expansionist American empire had been gained by ruthless force—as had the great fortunes of its so-called Robber Barons."

Or, as Clemenceau himself would put it, "America is the only nation in history which miraculously has gone directly from barbarism to degeneration without the usual interval of civilization."

Wilson's inevitable breakdown appeared early in those secret sessions. The first "violation," to purify William A. White's vigorous obscenity, came when Clemenceau got him to commit to an agreement wherein the United States would defend France in the event of a German invasion. For Wilson to believe that such a commitment would stand the slightest chance at ratification by the United States Senate was preposterous. For Wilson, it offered assurance of France's security as the rest of the negotiations proceeded. For Clemenceau, it was another plum to take back to the Chamber of Deputies. It was also an indication of concessions to come—the demand for a thirty-year occupation of the Rhineland, for example, in spite of the fact that the area was populated exclusively by Germans. Or Clemenceau's insistence on French occupation of the Saar Valley, that critical coal and industrial area, also German. Wilson protested: Clemenceau was bringing up questions of territorial acquisitions that were in complete violation of the armistice agreement. He was making mockery of the basic conception of self-determination about which he cared little. The security of France was at stake, and he roared at Wilson for daring to compromise that.

"You are pro-German!" he shouted in a remarkable challenge to the president's equanimity. "You are seeking to destroy France!"

"That is untrue and you know it is untrue!" Wilson cried out, stunned by such a preposterous charge.

Clemenceau insisted that if France did not receive these territories, he would not be able to sign the treaty. He was, in effect, a schoolboy threatening to take home the only baseball if his teammates did not let him pitch.

"Then if France does not get what she wishes, she will refuse to act with us in conference?" Wilson asked. "In that event, do you wish me to return home?"

"I do not wish you to go home," The Tiger replied, "but I intend to do so myself." He then left in such a huff that Wilson wondered if he would ever see him again. He did, as it turned out, that very afternoon, whereupon Wilson delivered still another sermon on the need for higher purpose: "Why has Jesus Christ so far not succeeded in inducing the world to follow his teachings? It is because he taught the ideal without devising any practical means of attaining it. That is the reason why I am proposing a practical scheme to carry out his aims."

Whatever Clemenceau thought of this notion, he saw fit to congratulate Wilson. Later, he would himself declare, "How can I talk to a fellow who thinks himself the first man for two thousand years who has known anything about peace on earth?"

The question of the Rhineland remained temporarily unresolved. Orlando, meanwhile, took advantage of the turmoil to make his own demands for the annexation of Fiume, yet another violation of the Fourteen Points. The Italians, furious that the other Allies were chopping them up at will, insisted on using an axe of their own. Lloyd George, master of playing one side off against another, was reveling in his own successes: "[I]f you had told the British people twelve months ago that they would have secured what we have, they would have laughed you to scorn. The German Navy has been handed over to us, the German mercantile shipping and the German colonies. . . . Our chief trade competitor has been seriously crippled and our allies are about to become her biggest creditors."

Kcynes had a few choice reflections on the equities of such solutions. "The war has ended with everyone owing everyone else immense sums of money. Germany owes a large sum to the Allies. The Allies owe a large sum to Great Britain. Great Britain owes a large sum to the United States. The holders of war loans in every country are owed a large sum by their respective states. The states, in [their] turn, are owed a large sum by taxpayers. The whole position is in the highest degree artificial, misleading and vexatious. We shall never be able to move again unless we can be free of these paper shackles." Then, in a chilling prediction, he summarized the coming history of the world: "If we aim deliberately at the impoverishment of Central Europe, vengeance . . . will not limp. Nothing can delay for very long that final civil war between the forces of Reaction and the despairing convulsions of Revolution before which the horror of the late German war will fade into nothing."

By this time, Wilson was stuck in the muddle he had permitted of his principles. From the godlike figure he'd been at his arrival at Christmastime, he had been reduced by Easter to a fool. The Just Peace was being snatched from his hands, and his head reeled with myriad problems that seemed hopelessly without solutions. Unless he could reform his allies, to force them to abandon their imperialistic war aims, the war itself would be based on a lie. That too had become part of his delusion. Repeatedly, he sought to console himself with a spate of ennobling speeches, hoping that his message would somehow catch fire and burn out the evils that motivated them. There was, of course, no real chance of that, and the great quandary persisted. It was Colonel House who spelled out the compelling irony: "If the president should exert his influence among the liberal and laboring classes [who had the most at stake for a sensible peace] he might possibly [cause] the overthrow of governments in England, France and Italy—but if he did, he would still have to reckon with our own people and he might bring down the whole world into chaos . . . a grave responsibility for any man to take at this time."

Wilson, then, was possibly less afraid of failure in implementing his goals than of success—even though it meant betraying the mass of working people who had been his greatest supporters.

Enter William C. Bullitt, a young graduate of Yale from a distinguished moneyed family from Philadelphia, a member of the American delegation. Colonel House and Lloyd George had dispatched him to Russia in hopes of finding some modus operandi with Lenin. Together with Lincoln Steffens, he managed to gain an audience. "A quiet figure in old clothes," Steffens wrote of Lenin, "with an open inquiring mind, a slight droop in one eye that suggested irony or humor." When queried about the numerous executions the Bolsheviks had carried out, however, Lenin's humor segued quickly into anger. "Do you mean to tell me that those who have just generated the slaughter of seventeen million of men in a purposeless war are concerned over the few thousand who have been killed in a revolution with a conscious aim—to get out of the necessity of war?"

It was a statement with a hundred years of tsarist tyranny behind it, of countless brutalities and corruptions, of the recent warring conspiracies of counterrevolutionary forces to restore the aristocracy that could not function without the support of the Allies.

"If we have to have a revolution," Lenin said, "we have to pay the price."

Nonetheless, he advised them of his wish to accommodate. If the Allied armies would be withdrawn, along with all support for the White armies—if the blockade of Russian ports could be lifted that they might buy food for the people, the Bolsheviks would permit the White Russians to retain whatever territory they held, announce a general amnesty for all political prisoners and make good on the debts of the old regime. These terms, Lenin insisted, must be offered *by the Allies* no later than April tenth.

Bullitt and Steffens returned with what they considered to be a dramatic opportunity for peace with Russia. Steffens also became newly aware of what was taking place in Paris. "There I got a true perspective on the peacemaking and the crumbling civilization of Europe." Doubtless, enthusiasm for what they had seen in Russia was of no help to their cause, for it cast them as dupes rather than diplomats. Said Steffens to Bernard Baruch, "I have been over into the future and it works." In Paris, Bullitt glowed with the prospects of changing the course of the entire conference. A fruitless episode, as it turned out. Lloyd George, whom they saw immediately after their return, subsequently refused to acknowledge even the existence of the mission. Wilson, in his turn, refused to see Bullitt at all. According to House, who did see him, the president was simply too involved with Germany. Others were convinced that any conciliation to Lenin by Lloyd George had been smothered by Lord Northcliffe, the reactionary press baron with enormous power in England. Bullitt blamed all these rejections on the news that Admiral Aleksandr Kolchak, leading the counterrevolutionary forces, had made a substantial hundred-mile advance against the Reds and was allegedly threatening the Bolsheviks at the gates of Moscow. If so, there was no reason to deal with Lenin for he was about to be unseated.

The Bullitt report, then, was not even released at the conference. Months later, Bullitt testified before the Senate Foreign Relations Committee: "I prepared a statement for the press based on my report, giving the facts, which I submitted to be given out. The report was given to the president. The president received it and decided that he did not want it given out. He thought he would rather keep it secret in spite of the urging of others. . . ."

Thus Lenin's April tenth deadline would pass without comment, typical of Wilson's refusal to deal with the entire Russian question. One might sympathize with his dilemma, so rich with contradictions and misinformation as to befuddle all Allied conferees in the seats of power. As far as Russia was concerned, anything was indeed possible. The accepted wisdom of the time had the revolution doomed to failure, for it did not represent the Russian people, who were, as Wilson had pontificated, "traditionally, and by nature, democratic." Besides, Lenin and Trotsky were German agents, and the entire revolution had been executed through German influence in order to clear the Eastern front— or postwar Germany was likely to go Communist—or postwar

Germany was going to crush the Bolshevik Revolution and dominate all Europe—or the Bolshevik Revolution was going to sweep across the continent, then leap the Atlantic Ocean and take over the United States.

For Woodrow Wilson, all this was so alien to his expertise, he preferred to rely on the speculations of Colonel House than to deal with any of it. There had been no Russians in his life, no sense of revolution. He knew nothing of Karl Marx. He showed no inclination to so much as examine the persona of Lenin. The aggressively razor-sharp mind of Trotsky would have offended him. He would meet with Lloyd George, Clemenceau and Orlando but never with the Russians. He was, above all, a Christian capitalist who saw only God at the end of the tunnel. He had come to Paris against the advice and blandishments of all his advisors, too intent on satisfying the demands of his ambitiousness in the service of the Lord and refusing to sacrifice his chance at immortality. He had repeatedly accomplished the impossible in his sixty-three years on earth, but he was not about to risk it all with any confrontations with the Bolsheviks.

It was one of the many contradictions of the Paris Conference that the armies of the celebrated Prince of Peace, two months after armistice, were still in combat in Russia, with whom we were not, nor ever had been, at war. English troops were also there, and French, and Japanese, all tacitly dedicated to the overthrow of the Bolshevik Revolution. It was another contradiction that the delegations would be distinguished by the absence of the one man whose presence was essential for its resolution. This was Vladimir Ilyich Lenin. One might speculate on the enormity of the reception he too might have received from other millions in the many starving cities of Europe. In the great scheme of things, however, the only Russians who were welcomed in Paris were the representatives of the old Romanov tyranny.

For Wilson, the crises inherent in his position inevitably escalated after his return to Paris. In matters of ideology alone he was walking a tightrope in high winds. A few weeks before, he was shaken by a challenging letter from an old New Jersey friend and political adviser, George Record, who pleaded with Wilson to concern himself with "securing to men the full fruits of their labor. You cannot stand for the principles of political democracy any more than the Ten Commandments. The league, like all your other policies, does not go to the root of the problem. Viz . . . war is caused by privilege. Every modern state is governed by the privileged—those who control industry by owning the railroads, lands, mines, banks, credit. These men thus obtain enormous and unearned capital, for which there is no use in the country where it is produced because the poverty of the workers limits the home market. Those who control this surplus capital must seek new countries and new people to exploit, and this clash of selfish interests leads to war."

Wilson could not deal with this. No matter that his friend's ideas had led to gubernatorial successes, indeed, all the way to the White House itself. Wilson was fully aware that the postwar conflict of rich versus poor, capital versus labor, peasant versus landowner was deeply rooted in all societies. The masters of 1914 Germany undoubtedly brought on the war in order to escape the civil conflicts that would have unseated them. So too in France with its ever-threatening socialist movement. War was forever an inhibitor of class conflict, forestalling protest and revolution under a banner of patriotism. Now, in 1919, because of the Russian Revolution, these conflicts threatened to overwhelm the peace. Wars had always ended with peace terms made in the interests of the same ruling elite who had initiated the wars to protect those interests. But was this still possible? Where could Wilson make his stand? If he submitted to the old imperialist traditions, would it not negate the democratic promise of the war itself? Would it not break the back of his pledge to the world?

In desperation, on April second, he summoned House to his suite to discuss the diminishing prospects—hardly an easy confrontation for Wilson in light of his recent disenchantment with his old friend. House was sympathetic and full of his usual acuity. Seeing the president's new determined look, House tilted accordingly. Yes, he offered, resistance to Clemenceau was definitely in order. But even then, Wilson's confusions appeared to be overwhelming. As quickly as he spoke his defiance, he retreated. If the president insisted on holding the line on reparations, for example, he argued to give way on the occupation of the Saar. For all Wilson's combativeness, combat did not come easily to him. In the end, House simply retreated. Nothing was decided. The meeting had succeeded only in fueling Wilson's confusion.

Then, on the following night, came the breakdown that very nearly killed him. Wilson was wracked by spasms of such violent coughing he was barely able to breathe. His stomach erupted in a siege of vomiting, his bowels in uncontrollable diarrhea. His urine showed blood, his swollen prostate acted up painfully. His neuritic right shoulder felt as though needles were being jabbed into him. In the first flush of a threatening stroke, the left side of his face began to twitch, his eye reacting with a frightening tic. His head ached, temples throbbing unmercifully, as his temperature soared to 103 degrees. In the frantic crisis-ridden ambience of the conference, there was reason to suspect that he had been poisoned.

More likely, the poison was in the politics, not the potion. For the last three months, he had been boxed into the corner with his fellow conferees' persistent violations of agreed-on pledges. They had combined to deceive and manipulate him, turning the fulfillment of the peoples' will for peace into a cutthroat scramble for the spoils. They had stripped him of his inspirational leadership and threatened to turn him into a fool for his idealism. His great crusade appeared to be collapsing.

Woodrow Wilson's tenuous pathology had always been vulnerable in times of stress. Since childhood he had been an incurable victim of dyspepsia, keeping him close to his protective mother. His fragility dominated his young life, then imposed frequent nervous and physical breakdowns, always at tormented periods in his young adulthood. No explanation of this terrifying night can ignore the possibilities of its psychosomatic origin. There is no question but that his health was severely damaged—perhaps sufficiently enough to cause the stroke that would incapacitate him six months later.

There was, in fact, seldom an extended period in his life during which he did not suffer peptic disorders, severe headaches, nervous breakdowns. Many of such incidents occurred during career crises or periods of emotional distress. They became almost predictable. "Turmoil in Central America," he would say of his stomachaches to make light of the burden, but the turmoil kept mingling with emotional instabilities in a perpetually vicious cycle.

To Sigmund Freud, Wilson became a test case of psychosomatic disability.

On the night of April 3, 1919, all the myriad fragilities in his crumbling pathology appeared at once. It was as if he had pulled out all the stops. To his doctor, Admiral Grayson, and his wife, Edith, who attended him, he had never seemed worse, from his bloodless lack of color to the total breakdown of body functions.

In his psychological study of Wilson on that particular fateful night, Sigmund Freud offered other insights. It was not flu but failure that oppressed him: "He faced alternatives, both of which were horrible to him." He felt trapped without a viable course of action, and because of his recent emotional break with his friend House, there was no one to consult for whom he had trust. Whichever way he turned, he saw the disastrous consequences. His negotiations with Clemenceau and Lloyd George had all but collapsed in a deadlock of unresolved issues. What was Wilson to do about the Rhineland, the Saar, the British demand for indemnities and reparations, the Italian irredentist demand for Fiume, the Japanese demand for Shantung? And how was Wilson to contend with any of those conundrums in light of the devilish political consequences? If he held to his pledge to be the Prince of Peace, to demand adherence to what was left of the Fourteen Points as agreed upon at armistice, he would have to fight with the last weapon in his arsenal: the withdrawal of the financial and material support of the United States, a termination of credit. He would have to publicly denounce both Clemenceau and Lloyd George, whose betrayals had forced him to this position. To activate the threat, he would be obliged to leave Paris and return home.

All this on the hope they would give in to his will—for if they refused (as he believed they would), he would have no recourse but to carry out the threat and go home.

And if so, what then? As Wilson saw it, there would be chaos in Europe. Marshal Foch, backed by the militarist-reactionary groups, would take over and march an embittered French Army through starving Germany, into Eastern Europe, and destroy every last remnant of a civilized peace. Or worse, if Foch should fail to accomplish this, Wilson saw the spread of Bolshevism across Europe as a rampant plague.

Like other Allied leaders, Wilson hated and feared Communism far more deeply than he hated and feared militarists. He had no radicalism in his nature. He was the Christian statesman sent to bring light to the capitalist world by paraphrases of the Sermon on the Mount.

"Europe is on fire and I cannot add fuel to the flames!" he had repeatedly said.

The consequences of such a decision devastated him. To be condemned (and not loved) was unbearable to him. The attacks from the London press had been exceedingly painful, then, even more, the ridicule of Parisian papers through the barbs of Clemenceau himself. To be called pro-German, to be accused of "wanting to let the Hun off lightly" was the kiss of death. And would he not be labeled pro-Bolshevik as well, to be despised by the entire Western world? In America, his disgrace would be consummate. He would be pilloried by all but a handful of radicals whom he had long since abandoned as allies anyway.

And his precious League of Nations. What would happen to the league?

On the other hand, Wilson could give in. He could let Clemenceau have his way in Germany and Lloyd George his demand for reparations, and Orlando his claims in the Adriatic. He could compromise the guts of the treaty in order to save the league. If so, would he not be responsible for what certainly would be condemned as an unjust treaty? Would he not be vilified for leading his country into war, then abandoning its purpose at the conference table? Would he not be forced to stand before the world, not as the son of God who had gone forth to war to gain a kingly crown, but one who had quit when he saw the cross?

Either way, then, Wilson saw failure and ignominy. Whichever course he took, he would be doomed. This was the stuff of panic that fed the neurosis that induced the breakdown.

On the morning of April fifth, Wilson was still confined to his bed. The Big Four met in his suite, the bedroom separated by a huge bookcase with a door built into it. Through this door, Colonel House would pass to transfer messages. On this morning, the deadlock on the agenda dealt with reparations to be paid by Germany. How much and how quickly? The demands of greedy and punitive powers could not but add another layer of outrage to the ethics of the Fourteen Points, thoroughly brutalizing the terms of the armistice. As France demanded extensive payments for the devastation of its land and its homes, England, unscarred, insisted that Germany pay pensions for British soldiers—a whole new wrinkle, as it were. Wilson demurred. In an astonishing show of defiance, on the sixth of April, Wilson had Admiral Grayson cable to America that the *George Washington* should be readied to return to Brest as quickly as possible. Should Lloyd George and Clemenceau refuse to give way, he would leave.

Paris was unnerved at such an unprecedented act. Would he actually leave?

"He's bluffing, *non?*" Clemenceau asked Admiral Grayson.

"He hasn't a bluffing corpuscle in his body," the doctor replied.

In such madness, the fate of the treaty came down to its concluding sessions. Wilson climbed feebly out of bed on the seventh, dressed, but sent House to the conference at Lloyd George's apartment. The persistent Allied demands for reparations became outrageous, even to House. When Wilson heard, still in a fighting mood, he agreed. In fact, he told Ray Stannard Baker he would make no further concessions. Italy would not get Fiume, for all its contentiousness. Nor France the Saar or the Rhineland. "The time has come to bring this thing to a head," Wilson declared. "I will not discuss anything with them anymore. We agreed among ourselves, and we agreed with Germany on certain general principles. The whole course of the conference has been made up of attempts, especially by France, to break down the agreement, to get territory and to impose crushing indemnities." The duplicity of Lloyd George, most recently indicated by a statement that blamed Wilson for the delays, was especially irritating to him. Then there were constant and bothersome references to the report from Russia by young Bullitt that Wilson had deflected.

But Wilson was now defying them all. Let them see the prominent jawline, the tight-lipped challenge, let them hear the stern and adamant sound of his voice. He would hold the line, by God.

Then on April ninth, Wilson received a cable from the White House from his secretary, Joe Tumulty: "The ordering of the *George Washington* . . . looked upon here as an act of petulance on the president's part...a withdrawal at this time would be a desertion." Another cable from the secretary of the treasury, William McAdoo, reported that credits to the Allies could not be immediately stopped, for they had been previously granted through July.

Wilson's gun had suddenly been stripped of ammo, though a more determined fighter might have found other weapons. The two cables were all he needed to justify his change of heart. He really did not want to fight. What amazed everyone, especially House, was the change in personality as well. No longer defiant, he was, at first, conciliatory, then pathetic. Almost sheepishly, he requested of his conferees that an exemption for the Monroe Doctrine be included in the league covenant (the United States Senate, he explained, would not ratify without it). Oddly enough, this was the first request he had made in deference to United States interests, a request that they recognize the sanctity of an American position that contradicted the very principles Wilson had continually insisted that others be made to recognize. America, reserving for itself the right to interfere in the affairs of Europe, was now insisting that Europeans be permitted no rights to interfere in the American Atlantic. This was so blatantly hypocritical that Wilson was quite obviously embarrassed, dissembling like a child with his hand caught in the cookie jar. "Well, my friends," he would say with a helpless little smile, "and we are all friends here"—his voice so oily with pain that Clemenceau could not but attack: "Every time you say that you send a cold shudder down my spine!"

It was all they needed and they moved in for the kill. If they deferred to Wilson's request, they immediately demanded something far greater in return. For the British, whose fleet for a century had secured that same Monroe Doctrine from European intervention, Wilson agreed to limit the sea power of the United States so that Britain could continue to rule the Atlantic waves. For France, he agreed to turn over the industrially rich Saar Basin. A few days later, he even conceded to Clemenceau's demands for a thirty-year occupation of the East Bank of the Rhine with its ten thousand square miles of territory vital to Germany's industrial survival, and its 5,500,540 Germans. When a special article in the covenant for equal treatment of all "religious" minorities was discussed, the Japanese proposed the addition of two words: "and racial."

The tempestuous prime minister of Australia, William Hughes, would have none of it, for equality of race suggested the opening of his continent to "a yellow tide of immigration." Guilefully, Hughes released this threat to American reporters from Western states: How would *they* appreciate such a prospect? Wilson dropped it like a hot potato. The Japanese, feigning indignation at this insult, threatened refusal to endorse the league—unless, of course, Wilson agreed to *their* occupation of the Chinese province of Shantung. Then, at last, came Italy's demand for Fiume on the Adriatic Coast, which all but Italians believed totally unjustified. Here Wilson made his last stand—especially significant after so foolishly promising the Tyrol-Brenner region with its 250,000 German-speaking Austrians in January. With typical bravado, he appealed directly to the Italian people to support him against their own premier, Orlando—with disastrous results for Wilson. Where his picture had hung reverently in the huts of peasants, it now appeared in cartoons, insidiously wearing a German helmet. France and England then conceded, whereupon Fiume was granted to Italian exploitation, and Wilson suffered one last violation of his image.

And when the spoils had been finally divided, the mandates validated for league supervision, the British Empire grew by 1,607,053 square miles and over thirty-three million inhabitants; France acquired 420,000 square miles and four million inhabitants; Japan got Shantung and twenty million Chinese; Italy added 680,000 square miles of North Africa with 880,000 Africans. They were called "mandates," but were in actuality old-fashioned imperialistic takeovers. Purported to protect the natives' freedom of conscience and religion, banning trade in slaves, drugs, liquor and gunrunning, the mother countries blessed themselves with a halo of benevolence to sanctify their exploitations.

Said Prince Faisal, friend of T. E. Lawrence of Arabia: "Mandated people are apparently peoples with oil, gold, natural resources—but no guns to protect them."

Germany, meanwhile, lost whatever territories that might have reduced her financial debts to the Allies—while the Allies gained colonial possessions without losing any claims for German indemnities. To the German loss of the Saar to France, with its rich mines and industrial capacity, was added the annual supplying of seven million tons of coal to France, eight million tons to Belgium, 4,500,000 tons to Italy. Germany would have to export twenty-five million tons a year, over a third of its total production. To Poland, meanwhile, Germany ceded Upper Silesia, from which it had extracted nearly a quarter of its annual tonnage.

The demands for reparations turned out to be equally crushing. How much could Germany pay? Lloyd George ("We'll squeeze the orange until the pips squeak!") had called for $120 billion over a period of forty years. The French would top even that, demanding $200 billion. Bernard Baruch was appalled: "If Germany were left economically prostrate, all Europe would suffer." John Maynard Keynes rebelled: "It was the task of the peace conference to honor engagements and to satisfy justice; but not less to reestablish life and to heal wounds." In the end, he resigned in protest at "this scene of nightmare."

Last, but hardly the least, came the ultimate insult, the final violation of the spirit of the armistice, a newly laid-in premise of the treaty itself: Germany must bear the sole responsibility for starting the war and suffer, thereupon, the consequences of her defeat.

So it was that the Fourteen Points of Woodrow Wilson had become no less than "a scrap of paper," precisely what Germany's minister Theobald von Bethmann-Hollweg had called Germany's agreement respecting Belgium's territorial integrity. It was but one of many jokes on the same morbid theme.

Wilson, however, had made his peace with the treaty. The great interior debate that accompanied his feverishly tormented night a few weeks earlier had been resolved with classic Wilsonian rationale. As he now chose to see it, he had done his utmost within the limitations of the needs of fellow conferees. Since they were, after all, substantial men of good Christian character, the resulting agreement was doubtlessly the best that could be achieved. If there were flaws and inequities and excessive punishment in the articles of its treaty, the League of Nations would serve as an ameliorating force. All disputation would be resolved by the league. The league was now locked into the treaty, Wilson's testament to the peace of the world for all time to come, the justification for America's participation in the bloodshed.

Not merely the best possible treaty, but a just and equitable best. Since he had come to Paris in God's good name, how could it have turned out otherwise? ("I believe in divine providence. If I did not, I would go crazy.") Wilson's idealism could hardly permit him to believe in anything less. His sense of the pragmatic now demanded his faith, for he was fully aware of the battle he was about to face on his return to Washington.

From that moment until his death in 1924, he would not waver from this conviction.

The treaty was concluded in the final week of April. There had been seventy-two sessions of the Council of Ten, thirty-nine of the foreign ministers and 145 of the Council of Four. The fifty-odd special commissions held over one thousand meetings. The result was a document that went on for eighty thousand words now readable in its entirety for the first time.

Herbert Hoover, who read it in his hotel room the night of its release, was so upset he could not sleep. At daybreak, he went for a walk and ran into General Jan C. Smuts and John Maynard Keynes, both of whom had suffered the same reaction. Others responded with shock sufficient to speculate that Germany would not sign it, whatever the consequences.

To the Germans, the treaty was catastrophic. Summoned to receive it officially, a delegation arrived in Paris on April thirtieth, 160 of them with barely enough time to digest their fate. Without being consulted on any of its terms, they were now handed a treaty that violated the promises of the armistice at a time when starvation and the pounding threat of revolution made it impossible for them not to sign. As if chosen deliberately out of a Hollywood casting cliché, they were led by Count Ulrich von Brockdorff-Rantzau, the personification of the despised Prussian Junkers with his imperious manner, replete with a monocle and face scarred from dueling. The French held court at the Trianon Palace in Versailles, the site of a comparable reverse humiliation in 1871, another ornate room with crystal chandeliers and tall glittering mirrors. Several hundred Allied delegates were in attendance at this presentation. Prime Minister Georges Clemenceau, still in command, made his opening remarks with typical acidity: "Gentlemen, plenipotentiaries of the German Empire, it is neither the time nor the place for superfluous words. . . . The time has come to settle accounts. You have asked for peace. We are ready to give you peace."

Von Brockdorff-Rantzau was either unable or unwilling to rise. In barely audible tones, his throat choked with suppressed fury, he made his statement. "We know the power of hatred which we encounter here. . . . It is demanded of us that we shall confess ourselves to be the only ones guilty of the war. Such a confession in my mouth would be a lie. We are far from declining our responsibility for this great war having come to pass, and for its having been made in the way in which it was made . . . but energetically we deny that Germany and its people, who were convinced that they were making a way of defense, were alone guilty." He spoke of the Allied blockade that was causing untold death and starvation, of hundreds of thousands of malnourished children "killed by cold deliberation after our adversaries had conquered. . . . Think of them when you speak of guilt and punishment."

Lloyd George listened and inadvertently snapped an ivory letter opener. Woodrow Wilson was appalled at this German lack of humility. "The Germans are really a stupid people," he would say. "They always do the wrong thing. . . . This is the most tactless speech I have ever heard."

Back in Berlin, at the Reichstag, a German Socialist commented: "This is not a peace but a continuation of war by other means."

A day or two later, May Day, a mass of French workers, labor organizers and Socialists turned out for the annual parade. As if in a last gasp of promise for the future, they chanted: "À Bas Clemenceau! Vive Wilson!" For that they were savagely mauled by police and soldiers.

On May seventeenth, William C. Bullitt publicly declared his resignation from the American delegation in a letter to the president: "I am one of millions who trusted implicitly in your leadership and believed you would take nothing less than 'a permanent peace based on unselfish, unbiased justice.' But the government has consented now to delivering the suffering peoples of the world to new oppressions, subjugations and dismemberments—a new century of war.... I am sorry you did not fight to a finish and that you had so little faith in the millions of men like myself in every nation who had faith in you."

In the United States, the treaty was denounced. Some newspapers declared it to be pro-German, some pro-Bolshevik and some even pro-both. Wilson responded to none of it.

There was, however, more to come, for questions continued to arise as to whether Germany would, indeed, sign it. Lloyd George came back from a trip home where the treaty had been attacked from all sides. From Labor and the Socialists came the opinion that his treatment of Germany had been excessively harsh. From the Tories, the feeling that he had given away too much to France. The old British standby, the balance of power, had simply shifted from Germany to France. When back in Paris, Lloyd George went to work on Wilson, seeking to modify the terms— at the expense of Poland and France, without sacrificing any of England's booty, hoping to amend the treaty by reopening old controversies. Wilson responded with indignation, "Mr. Prime Minister, you make me sick! For months we have been struggling to make the terms... exactly along the lines you now speak of, and never got the support of the English. Now, after we have finally come to an agreement, and when we have to face the Germans and need unanimity, you want to rewrite the treaty."

Clemenceau also refused to discuss this, especially since Lloyd George would not make concessions of his own. "The Welsh Shylock," he was called, his British pound of flesh securely in his pocket as he went about preaching unselfish concessions from others.

In London, Winston Churchill described the peace conference as a turbulent collision of embarrassed demagogues—while totally without embarrassment himself, he scurried around the seats of British power pushing for an invasion of Russia that they might wipe out the Bolsheviks, whatever the cost in money and men—insisting as well on a continuing blockade of Germany to force them to sign, whatever the resulting deaths by starvation.

Harold Nicolson pondered all the follies as the inevitable consequence of capitalist statesmanship. "Human nature, like a glacier, moves but an inch or two every thousand years."

On June twentieth, in the British harbor of Scapa Flow, the German Navy, detained there since the armistice, scuttled the remains of the fleet—nine battleships, five heavy cruisers, over fifty destroyers. One last gesture of Germanic defiance before ending six months of suspended agonies. The German government had agreed to sign.

On June 28, representatives of the new Weimar Republic returned to Versailles on the fifth anniversary of the assassination at Sarajevo. That day, Wilson consented to a rare press conference.

"All things considered, the treaty adheres more nearly to the Fourteen Points than I had a right to expect," he said. "Never forget that Germany did an irreparable wrong and must suffer for it. . . . Think of the positive achievements of the peace—the newly liberated peoples who had not dared to dream of freedom, the Poles, the Czechoslovaks, the Slavs, the people of Turkey. The peace has given a new charter to labor, has provided for economic equality among the nations and gone far toward the protection of racial and religious minorities, and finally, and the greatest of all, it has banded the peoples of the world in a new League of Nations."

A reporter was heard in cryptic comment: "Oh? What treaty is that?"

The signing was pageantry for a thousand in attendance. Guns began to fire in the distance, shouts of exultation were heard from crowds outside the palace. The fountains of Versailles, not operative since the outbreak of the war, were suddenly turned on. Airplanes buzzed overhead, and the setting sun made the windows sparkle like a jeweled treasure.

Paris went berserk with joy. There was dancing in the streets. It was impossible not to be kissed and almost impossible not to be drunk. It was said that more Parisian babies were conceived on this day than any other date in history. In cafés, overwhelmed by throngs, the singing never stopped. The city quivered with love and laughter.

What the people wanted was peace. Whatever the former

demonstrations for Woodrow Wilson, there was no longer a demand for a generous, idealistic peace; no one seemed to care anymore. As soon as the adulation for Wilson had had a chance to subside, there was only vengeance toward Germany that could make the victory satisfying and profitable. Only the Socialists found little to rejoice at.

In Berlin, the newspaper *Vorwartz* made this editorial comment: "We must never forget it was only a scrap of paper. [That phrase again!] Treaties based on violence can keep their validity only so long as force exists. Do not lose hope. The resurrection day comes." German bitterness seemed concentrated on Wilson, the so-called noble American president who had promised so much—and betrayed them.

In London, M. P. Conservative Andrew Bonar Law told the House of Commons on the very day of the signing that twenty-three different wars were raging in various parts of the world.

Meanwhile, in Munich, a young German corporal named Adolf Hitler, wounded in a French gas attack at Ypres in 1918, returned to Austria, where he watched with loathing the rise and fall of the Bavarian Soviets. Hitler met with a small, viciously anti-Semitic group called the German Labor Party. Intrigued by its passion, Hitler joined. His membership card read Number Seven. He became a dedicated ideologue with a gift for oratory as convincing as Wilson's, soon attracting a following of other disgruntled veterans who soaked up his vicious diatribes against Jews, Marxists and other betrayers of the beloved Fatherland.

It is not known if Woodrow Wilson ever heard of him.

4. WOODROW WILSON'S BATTLE FOR THE LEAGUE OF NATIONS

It was America that saved the world, and those who oppose the treaty propose that we should desert the world.

—WOODROW WILSON

Woodrow Wilson returned from Paris in June 1919, steaming into New York Harbor on the *George Washington,* still the hero returning from the wars with an escort of battleships, airplanes and dirigibles, and hundreds of small boats. As whistles and horns blew, guns roared, while the president stood on the deck, smiling and waving at his welcomers. Those closest to him could also sense his fear.

In Washington, D.C., everything was different. The political structure of Congress itself reflected the change. The Republicans who had sat out the war mouthing the requisite superpatriotic blabber now saw the chance to upset the Wilsonian power structure and everything Wilson pretended to represent. The Wilson war, albeit successfully fought, was now too high-minded for the new American ethic. Those who had made money from the sacrifices of others, Democrats and Republicans alike, were not inclined toward idealistic solutions in a demobilizing world, much preferring the political patterns by which they could best hang on to their new-found wealth. Congress could not but reflect such trends.

Besides, America had been caught short by the suddenness of the armistice. The administration had made no plans for it.

The entire demobilization process was as bewildering to the government as the transition to war had been in 1917. Trains carrying new conscripts to training camps, for example, were reversed en route. When soldiers returned from Europe, no one knew how to take care of their needs. They were at once both war heroes and peace pests. With the gradual termination of the war industry, the women and overaged men who had held jobs were not about to give them up. Organized labor, which had struggled to unionize and increase wages for its war efforts, would not abandon its new power in the industrial world. Nearly 4,500,000 shed khaki and found nothing to come home to—not even a legal beer at a friendly tavern. In the vast agricultural community, legendary Cincinnatus, that classic citizen-soldier returning to the plow, reached home to find the plow was gone, replaced by complicated farm machinery that did not need him, and a large surplus of food.

That Americans did not demobilize well was a matter of psychology as well as socioeconomics. It had always been a truism that demobilized soldiers would immediately seek their pleasures. Now everyone else did too. Whatever money had been saved now entered the new age of consumption. In 1919, a spate of new gadgets appeared like magic in stores: pink bathtubs, the first radio sets, electric refrigerators, the four-wheeled progeny of Henry Ford. Even more magical were the rising hemlines of urban women and the accompanying new sounds of popular jazz.

Meanwhile, in Congress, the results of the 1918 election were about to bear fruit. Wilson's ill-advised October plea to the electorate to support only Democratic representatives that he might continue to control Congress had proved embarrassing. Change horses in midstream? Why not? Armistice was clearly close at hand; the water was calm and not at all deep. The Republicans offered far easier panaceas than Wilson. There was no need for sacrifice. Americans could live again for themselves. And as for the peace conference, the philosophy of "unconditional surrender" seemed a lot more American than "peace without victory."

The new Senate was especially testy with the president. The old group had served loyally for two warring years, suppressing any voluble opinions of its own. In deference to Wilson's leadership, its legislation had been predictable out of fear of antagonizing its patriotic constituents. Even as citizens' rights were brutally abused, and the essence of the Bill of Rights subverted, Congress submitted to the emotionalism of the essentially dishonest administration. It was said that Congress had spent the war "like an amiable fat man all puffed up with loyalty and good cheer." Now, however, it was ready and eager to be its old contentious self, angry at times, assertive and definitely independent. No more would the president be able to dictate or usurp legislative power.

The result was a curious realignment of American thinking. The same intellectuals who had always ridiculed Congress had led the country into war, supporting a Bourbon administration that did more to destroy basic American freedoms than any Congress would have normally permitted. For all its shortcomings, its clumsiness, its numerous Yahoos and Know-Nothings, Congress now represented a responsible middle-class American consensus.

When Wilson returned from Paris with his treaty, they were far more ready for him than he for them.

There was no doubt but that the president had fallen from grace. Liberal senators saw his performance in Paris as an outright surrender to reaction, a betrayal of his own idealism. The debate on the treaty created a style of dissent that amazed Senate-watchers for its vigorous amalgam of radicals and reactionaries. Even Old Guard Republicans, shocked at the imperialisms of Paris, rebelled against the cynical ruthlessness of its terms: the injustice of Shantung mandated to Japan, the cruel overburdening of reparations, the unworkable tyranny of territorial and colonial spoils. They feared the resulting threat of war. They saw the League of Nations as a meaningless bureaucracy superimposed on a bad treaty to perpetuate unworkable peace terms with no provisions to prevent chaos and revolution on the continent. The much discussed Article Ten in which league members declared for mutual defense against all external aggression was, to some critics, little more than a protector of governments in power no matter what the people wanted. Indeed, the article suggested contradictory implications. Had not American independence, for instance, been achieved with the help of "external aggression" by France against Britain? Some claimed that Article Ten was a surrender to the same imperial traditions that had brought on the war, a preservation of every territorial inequity that emerged from the division of spoils, a sentence of death on any liberal self-determining attempt at the future. Nor was it extraordinary that its most articulate defender was the Republican McCumber of North Dakota who was also openly advocating invasion of Russia to "protect the innocent people of the world from another revolution."

Then there were those who believed that the League of Nations was little more than a device to benefit international bankers to whom it was a manageable bureaucracy, much preferable to deal with than people at large. Wilson himself had appealed to them for support. As one senator put it: "This League of Nations is the most dangerous piece of machinery in the interests of financial imperialism that the world ever saw!"

It was a bizarre demonstration of conflicting ideologies. Reactionary Republicans became far more progressive than Southern Democrats—and more liberal, in effect, than the president, who preached idealistic liberalism but failed to keep his word. As the isolationist Senator Borah put it: "There is just as much of an understanding between the president of the United States and myself as there is between the senator from Massachusetts [Lodge] and myself." What the new Senate demanded was an abridgement of rhetoric and a return to facts. The president, it seemed, had left a legacy of distortions.

It followed that the Democrats would suffer at the debate. Their leader had failed them. They had nothing to fall back on except the league itself. If they could get it through ratification, perhaps they could use their triumph to retain power in the coming 1920 presidential election. This was indeed Wilson's treaty, but its ideology became less than its political significance. Curiously, for all the debating, the treaty and its league were not really partisan. In its terms there were no basic intrusions on old party differences such as high tariffs, armament controls, labor relations. It could even be called more Republican than Democrat. If Wilson had presented to the Senate a draft with only a vague conception of a league, the Republican opposition would have protested that a treaty without a strong league to give it validity would be useless. Since Wilson purported to do the opposite, the Republicans called it a surrender to our sovereignty, like lawyers seeking adversarial positions to win a case; all else was irrelevant except the fate of Wilson.

Behind it all sat Henry Cabot Lodge, who knew when to jump in and knock heads—which he did with consummate glee. As Wilson proceeded to deny compromise, Lodge was quick to justify his opposition. Wilson's first important meeting on his return was with Nebraska Democrat Gilbert Hitchcock (retiring chairman of the Foreign Relations Committee). The president insisted that the Senate take immediate and uncompromising action to pass the treaty. Time, he claimed, was critical; any delay "would prove disastrous . . . bring upon Europe conditions even more terrible than those wrought by the war itself." If the Senate refused, it would have to take responsibility.

Wilson formally presented the treaty on July 10, with a message that called the League of Nations "the only hope for mankind. . . . The light shines on the path ahead and nowhere else . . . America in truth shall show the way." Then, with typical Wilsonian piety, he demanded immediate ratification since "it has come about by no plan of our conceiving but by the hand of God who led us into war."

More senators saw his sickly pallor than paid attention to his words. And he paid no attention to theirs. When Senator Frank Kellogg of Minnesota came as spokesman for thirty-two Republicans who, with supporting Democrats, would be enough to assure ratification, if Wilson would approve of certain innocuous modifications to the treaty, Wilson replied that he would consider them. He would let the senator know of his decision. But he didn't. Against all advice, he simply declined to respond. Other compromise offers would follow, but Wilson rejected them all. As the debate became increasingly strident, only Lodge and his irreconcilables found pleasure in the prospects.

Into this maelstrom came William C. Bullitt, this time to testify before the Senate Foreign Relations Committee. Coming barely a few months after his resignation from the American delegation, his testimony was a stinging attack on Wilson's compromises in Paris. The treaty was a sellout to the same forces that had brought on the war. The peace would never work. The League of Nations was useless. He cited Robert Lansing, secretary of state, who said,

"The league can do nothing to alter the unjust clauses of the treaty except by unanimous consent." The treaty had been created "by an oligarchy of five great powers" and thereby created an oligarchy to sustain itself. (Lansing was the second Wilson secretary of state to resign over ideological differences with the president.) Above all, Bullitt railed against Wilson's abdication to the old seats of power by consenting to the seating of state diplomats on the league's council rather than representatives of the people themselves.

The Senate debate continued to be rich with metaphor. To Borah, the treaty was a keg of dynamite waiting to explode into a far more dreadful war than the one just ended. Lawrence Sherman, Republican of Illinois, said: "History would forget the reign of Caligula in the excesses . . . [of] the President Woodrow Wilson and Colonel House." To James Reed, the League of Nations would permit the black races to rule the world. Another warned of papal supremacy as a result of the treaty. Then there were the German-American and Irish-American constituencies and their hundreds of thousands of voters, and why didn't Britain concede to the liberation of Ireland?

Throughout the debate, the president remained indifferent to its substance. He cared neither for the political implications nor the legitimacy of the critics. He saw himself as father to a perfect baby and would suffer no compromises to its perfection, preferring to permit its destruction before its alteration. He stood almost alone in this regard. Those of his friends who had his ear, even his wife, urged him to compromise. Colonel House, who had told him, "The history of civilization had been built on compromise," had long since been abandoned. For all his opportunism, Wilson had never been a pliable man. The voices he heard were within him as if God himself had so stated. He cared little for either facts or opinions. In one astounding moment in his meeting with a body of senators at the White House, he denied knowing anything of secret treaties while in Paris. Even their existence had somehow eluded him. The more his opposition grew, the more the hated Lodge mounted his attack, the more Wilson refused to give way. For one who had so completely compromised in Paris to Clemenceau and Lloyd George, his intransigence in Washington was inexplicable. Was it the result of a fixation on Lodge as Sigmund Freud would suggest? Wilson would never submit to Lodge. Let Lodge do the compromising, he repeatedly told others.

All this suggested doom for the treaty. At the end of August, it seemed inevitable. Wilson then reverted to one last demonstration of magical thinking: he would go to the people. By the power of oratory, he would convince them of God's and his mission to save the world through this treaty and its sacred league. No matter that it was not even the people's will but the Senate's that would determine its fate. There would be no referendum of the league just as there was no referendum on our entrance into the war. In Wilson's vision, the glory of his words would create a tidal wave of public support that no senator would dare to oppose. To best express his defiance, he would go west, where the opposition was strongest. His triumph, then, would be the final justification for the war itself.

That his physician, Dr. Grayson, and his wife, Edith, opposed the trip for the strain on his fragile health, or his secretary, Joe Tumulty, for its political futility was all the more reason for him to go. In potential martyrdom was the greatest glory of all. He could sacrifice himself to justify the sacrifice of others. ("Even though, in my condition, it might mean giving up my life, I will gladly make the sacrifice to save the treaty.") He would be the statesman of his boyhood dreams, mounting the people's podium to deliver the word for all mankind. In his lifetime, had he not climbed the ladder speech by speech from school debates to the presidency of Princeton, from the governorship of New Jersey to the White House itself? Was this not the very meat of his talent, the fullest measure of what he was put on earth to do?

So he entrained for the western states with his wife, doctor, secretary and little typewriter. He made over a hundred speeches in thirty cities, travelled eleven thousand miles in twenty-seven days. Huge crowds came to see him and hear his golden words in stifling auditoriums, before small crowds at the back of whistlestop railroad stations.

In Columbus, Ohio, he said, "The League of Nations is the only safeguard against more war. . . . If we do not do this thing, we have neglected the central covenant we made to our people." In Indianapolis: "This league is the only conceivable arrangement

which will prevent our sending our men abroad again very soon.
... It is a case of put up or shut up." In St. Louis, to please his
audience, he changed his style to attack his political enemies. They
were small-minded men incapable of altruism—"absolute con-
temptible quitters." He added to that in Kansas City: Those who
fought the league for private political purposes should "be gib-
beted ... little groups of selfish men must not plot the future of
America." In Omaha: "This [peace treaty] is the work of honest
men ... I would be glad to die that it might be consummated." In
St. Paul, Minnesota; Bismarck, North Dakota; Helena, Montana
... he kept insisting on the justification of everything that tran-
spired in Paris. The treaty was perfect. The Allied conferees were
great and noble souls. The Germans got only what they deserved.

In Coeur d'Alene, Idaho, he said that Germany was combin-
ing with the Bolsheviks for a new campaign to conquer Europe
and that "Germany wants us to stay out of the treaty," adding that
Lodge was therefore playing directly into Germany's hands. In
Seattle, Wilson's procession drove slowly through town, and suddenly there were block after block of denim-clad IWW workers,
arms folded across their chests in an awesome, silent protest. In
Portland, he told his audiences he had no respect whatever for
his opponents and their pro-German propaganda. In San Francisco, then Los Angeles he began to speak in elemental pieties.
He rambled, his words began to sound meaningless, he made
preposterous assumptions long since disregarded or abandoned
even by his most ardent supporters. He made contradictory statements from city to city, sometimes even within the same speech.
In Reno, Nevada: "This treaty was not written ... in Paris—it was
written at Château-Thierry, in Belleau Wood.... Our men did
not fight with the purpose of coming back and having the same
thing happen again...." He was bathing in absolutes to make his
point. In Denver: "There is no question of reservations or amendments to the treaty. The issue is flatly acceptance or rejection."
He offered incredible scenarios of eternal peace. He guaranteed
it. If only the Senate would ratify.

Then, at last, came the end. In Pueblo, Colorado, he sank
deeply into bathos, his worn voice choked with emotion like an
actor playing a tear-jerking role. "Again and again ... mothers
who lost their sons in France have come to me, and taking my

hand, have not only shed tears upon it but they have added 'God bless you, Mister President!' Why should they pray God to bless me? I advised the Congress of the United States to create the situation that led to the death of their sons. I ordered their sons overseas. I consented to their sons being out in the most difficult parts of the battle line, where death was certain.... Why should they weep upon my hand and call down the blessings of God upon me?

"Because they believe that their boys died for something that vastly transcends any of the immediate and palpable objectives of the war. They believe, and rightly believe, that their sons saved the liberty of the world."

It was his last speech. That night, he collapsed in his railroad car. Dr. Grayson immediately terminated the ill-advised tour and sent the train, shades down, back to Washington. Now partially paralyzed, the left side of his face immobilized, his nervous system shot, Wilson was all but completely helpless. Three days after his return to the White House, he was found prostrate on the bathroom floor, after suffering another stroke that almost killed him.

Bedridden now, he remained totally isolated through the late autumn months. In the Senate, his precious league went through a continuing crisis, all compromise plans from both sides of the aisle meeting with the same fate from his sick intransigent mind.

On November 19, 1919, a year after the armistice, the United States Senate voted at the president's bidding and defeated the treaty with Lodge's reservations by a vote of fifty-five to thirty-nine.

It neither startled nor dismayed the American people. Indeed, one might summarize the entire World War experience by the magnitude of this indifference. The war, then, had all been for nothing. All the hate-ridden, superpatriotic dedication to save the world, all the death and deprivation came down to a few worn-out meaningless debates that no one believed in anymore.

"The war to end all wars", "fighting to make the world safe for democracy" turned out to be empty phrases to justify the bloodbath and the profiteering, like grandstand cheers at a football game, the necessary adjuncts to all combat. Woodrow Wilson had been the apotheosis of this deception, pretending at idealism with God in his pocket. America had, at first, swallowed the message, bathed self-righteously under the light of his leadership, succored by the ennobling claims of how glorious was our democracy. Under Wilson, how could our cause not be noble? How could the war not be holy? Or the peace he negotiated not be pure and just?

This had been America's lie of the soul, this insidious pretension at nobility of purpose, this false faith in a glorious destiny. Wilson's fall from grace had, in the end, exposed the lie and demeaned us all. It was all of a rotten piece—the war, the peace, Christian faith, American democracy—we had lost them all. International peace could never be achieved by covenants outlawing war any more than revolutions could be prevented by declaring them illegal. Peace and security could not be legislated, nor were they, in themselves, implicit in the democratic process. The good fight, whatever that might be, would be conceded as lost to the inadequacies of unchangeable human nature.

So it was that the whole house of cards could now come tumbling down. Indeed, had it not been inevitable from the outset? The duplicity of our neutrality, the deviousness of our purpose, the out-and-out profiteering, the shabbiness of our patriotic conformity, it was all so futile. America had been taken in by itself, made a patsy by its own leadership, a nation gorging on its self-deception. We had raced heroically off to save the alleged virgin from bestial rape only to discover what we already knew, that she was not a virgin at all but a willing whore. This was our sickness, this willing submission to the lie. It was a feel-good lie, the more moral and sacrificial and noble the better. War *was* the health of the state. America came alive with the war. It took Wilson's pathetic peace to make mockery of it.

This, then, was the ultimate message of 1919. When it invaded the American psyche, its impact could not be contained. It shamed and angered and frustrated us all. 1919 was made for the cynic.

Wilson, however, never abandoned the fight, demanding an uncompromised victory. From his sickbed, with preposterous haughtiness, he proposed his own third term for the presidency as a form of referendum on the league. He even prepared himself for the Democratic Party convention on the assumption that a groundswell of delegates would vote to draft him. It was never seriously considered. The country wanted no more of him or his League of Nations, or anything that suggested that America assume a responsible position in an ideal world. The new ism, once shifting from socialism to patriotism, now shifted to cynicism.

In cigar smoke-filled rooms at the Chicago Republican convention, a small-town Ohio kingmaker named Harry Daugherty succeeded in creating a presidential candidate named Warren Harding solely because "he looked like a president," perhaps the first such judgment—three decades before the advent of television. The choice was inspiring for the total blandness of his image, the absolute antithesis of Wilson's high-minded professorial ethic. Indeed, the genial Harding's sole campaign contribution was the phrase "return to normalcy," a euphemism for the abandonment of all principle. It is noteworthy that this smiling, simplistic, hard-drinking philanderer tried hard to avoid running at all. It took the strident demands of his ambitious wife to force him to it after a crucial hour she spent with a crystal gazer. He was elected by an overwhelming majority over the Democrat, James M. Cox, who campaigned on a League of Nations ticket. On Inauguration Day, Wilson donned the formal clothes of state and rode to the Capitol with Harding. He made no mention of the league or the fact that the new president also had thirteen letters in his name. In his abbreviated term as president, with his mentor Harry Daugherty as attorney general, Harding turned the White House over to his poker-playing cronies, who proceeded to steal the country blind. (The Republicans also made noises about the Wilson administration's conduct of the war, no doubt to prove that corruption was really an American two-party inevitability.) When Harding died a mysterious death while on a tour out west, the nation mourned even as it suffered his hollowness, then turned the distinguished office over to the vice-president, the vapid Calvin Coolidge, a sphinx without a secret who, in turn, was reelected on another Republican know-nothing ticket.

Meanwhile, in Europe, Kaiser Wilhelm was neither tried nor hung, for all the vengeful threats, but retired to a huge estate in Holland after fleeing Germany with the Hohenzollern family jewels. . . . In America, William Jennings Bryan continued to preach gospel solutions to world crises on the Chautauqua circuit until he attempted to take on Clarence Darrow at the trial of John Scopes, a schoolteacher in Tennessee who dared to teach Darwin's theory of evolution. Humiliated by the great lawyer, Bryan died shortly thereafter.... Colonel Edward House, who never saw Wilson again, collected his diaries and reminisced for posterity.

Woodrow Wilson lingered in relative solitude through his extended illness with his wife in Washington, a reclusive and bitter man. He made few political comments and refused to submit to interviews. In 1924, just before he died, his last known comments on the colossal events that had created such controversy seemed an appropriate summary: "Perhaps it all worked out for the best. This too was God's will."

THE RED SCARE

This alien element dominated domestic radicalism, directly controlled by Lenin and Trotsky.... Each and every adherent of this movement is a potential murderer or thief.... Out of the sly and crafty eyes of many of them leap cupidity, cruelty, insanity and crime; from their lopsided faces, sloping brows and misshapen features may be recognized the unmistakable criminal type.

—A. MITCHELL PALMER, attorney-general (Democratic Pres
  idential aspirant)

I believe we should place them all [radicals] on ships of stone, with sails of lead, and that their first stopping place should be hell.

—GENERAL LEONARD WOOD (Republican presidential aspirant)

Woodrow Wilson,
Governor of New Jersey.
(Library of Congress) Wilson
(below) with his first wife,
Ellen, and daughter
at Princeton.
(Library of Congress)

Wilson and Theodore Roosevelt *(above)*
squaring off for the presidency, 1912.
(Library of Congress) Colonel Edward
House and "The Governor" *(left)*.
(AP/Wide World Photos) President Woodrow
Wilson and his first cabinet *(below)*, with
William Jennings Bryan, his Secretary
of State, to his right. *(Library of Congress)*

Wilson *(left)* with his secretary, Joe Tumulty. *(Library of Congress)* President Wilson with his second wife *(below)*, Edith Bolling Gault. *(Library of Congress)*

President Wilson *(right)* delivering the speech in which he declared war against Germany. *(Library of Congress)* Wilson *(above)* addressing the joint session of Congress to declare war. *(Library of Congress)* The Big Four at the Paris Peace Conference *(below, left to right):* Vittorio Orlando, David Lloyd George, Georges Clemenceau, Woodrow Wilson. *(AP/Wide World Photo)*

WHO IS THIS WILSON?

Not even Napoleon
received such acclaim.
(Library of Congress)

President Wilson with General John
J. Pershing in Paris, reviewing troops.
(Library of Congress)

Wilson with King
George of England,
December 1918.
(Library of Congress)

Wilson's staff at Paris *(left to
right):* Colonel House, Secre-
tary of State Robert Lansing,
Wilson, Henry White, and
General Tasker Bliss.
(Library of Congress)

Wilson's return to the States on the
George Washington, July 9, 1919.
(AP/Wide World Photos)

Ex-President Wilson near death.
(Library of Congress)

John Dos Passos. (Library of Congress)

Robert LaFollette U.S. Senator,
Wisconsin. (Culver Pictures Inc.)

Ole Hanson, Mayor of Seattle, and his All-American family. *(Library of Congress)*

William Z. Foster, organizer of the great U.S. Steel strike. *(Library of Congress)*

Samuel Gompers, first president of the American Federation of Labor. *(Library of Congress)*

Judge Elbert Gary, Chairman of the Board, U.S. Steel. *(Library of Congress)*

Governor Calvin Coolidge of Massachusetts *(above)* and Boston Police Commissioner Curtis. *(Library of Congress)* A. Mitchell Palmer, *(below)* U.S. Attorney General 1919–1921. *(Culver Pictures Inc.)*

1. The Trashing of the Seattle General Strike or How Mayor Ole Hanson Red-baited His Way to Fame and Fortune

Let the United States stop pandering to and conciliating those who talk against it . . . call it what they may, this was the first American skirmish with Bolshevism.

—Ole Hanson

It was said of Ole Hanson, mayor of Seattle in 1919, that his political opinions were no more durable than a fart in a hurricane. In his history, he ran roughshod over constantly shifting ideologies like a man standing on a revolving seesaw. He named his three sons Theodore Roosevelt Hanson, William Taft Hanson and Robert LaFollette Hanson, thus covering the entire spectrum of Republican Party opinion. Some said his political popularity had sprung from his physical similarity to Uncle Sam, though he wore no whiskers, and from his talent for oratory, though no one seemed to remember much of anything he said.

Yet he sounded convincing, having succeeded in convincing himself. Emotional, emphatically tub-thumping, his voice would rise and fall like a well-oiled yo-yo. "I have never heard anything like Old Ole until Hitler came along," said one Washingtonian in reminiscence. Others called him a "poor man's Woodrow Wilson."

He had come to Seattle in 1902, moving west from Racine,

129

Wisconsin, where he was bored as a lawyer. He arrived on a buck-board with vague notions of an ambitious life. He bought a grocery store, became a realtor, worked as an advertising writer and an investment banker. His political career began in 1908 when he became a representative to the state legislature, where he sponsored progressive legislation for labor in the most labor-progressive state in the union.

Ole, it appeared, was anything but a leader. Shrewd he was, opportunistic and devious, a case study in how far a man could go in American politics by skillfully going with the flow. At first he idolized Teddy Roosevelt, but when T. R. bolted from the Republican Party, with classic western antiwar prejudices, Ole campaigned for Wilson, then quickly shifted into being a super-jingo patriot in 1917 when the bugle called. He convinced work-ingmen to vote him into the mayoralty in 1918, then swung neatly to the side of the conservatives in 1919.

With this talent for political adjustment, he was at least partly responsible for a political gift that became the opening gun in the longest-running, native, all-American drama of the year.

It was called the Red Scare. And Ole Hanson was its first official manipulator.

Seattle was the Queen City of the Northwest. The end of the Trans-Continental Railroad line, it was proud of its superb harbor for shipping to the Pacific. And it was a gateway city to the Alaskan gold rush, heart city of the lumber industry, giant of wartime shipbuilding. Because of the war, production of everything had leaped 300 percent between 1914 and 1919.

Seattle also became the strongest labor-union city in America. Fifteen thousand union workers in 1914 multiplied to sixty thousand in 1918. Over 50 percent of eligible workers were organized. Seattle was that nemesis to industrial management exploitation: a closed shop town. There were over 110 craft unions affiliated with the American Federation of Labor, solidly organized by a Central Labor Council with three delegates from each union, all cooperating in mutual support. The Seattle AFL was distinctive in that it proudly went to national AFL conventions and cast the one dissenting vote in opposition to the reelection of the conservative Samuel Gompers. Gompers, they believed, was government-controlled, a conformist without sufficient militancy, a tool of Wall Street.

The basic debate was over individual craft unions versus industrial unions. In Seattle, craft unionism was considered to be obsolete in large production industries where employers would play off one complementary trade against another. Divide and conquer. To prevent this, union leaders argued, why not establish a combination of unions to counter the force of management-controlled industry?

The One Big Union was the driving force of the Industrial Workers of the World, its goal to unite all workers for the purpose of overthrowing the capitalist system and rebuilding for a socialist society. "The working class and the employing class have nothing in common," said the IWW's statement of principles, "There can be no peace as long as hunger and want are found among millions of working people, and the few who make up the employing class have all the good things of life." Its founders, led by Big Bill Haywood, were of American stock, so individualist in spirit, their organization was less structured than philosophical. Their goal was not simply better wages and working conditions in one mine or another mill, but workers' control of their own destiny, a better life for all. To a Wobbly, as an IWW member was called, the eye was always on the future. As one Seattle Wobbly put it: "We wanted a new society. Educate the workers to be more than wage slaves ... to be a full human being, not just a bored worker doing the same job week after week. The Wobblies saw the so-called American dream that any man could become a success as a fraud. Those who made it did so on the backs of others. The IWW tried to be uplifting, a spiritual force. It welcomed peoples of all races and religions. It actually lived as it preached the brotherhood of man."

The Seattle Central Labor Council showed the IWW influence. Unions involved themselves in co-op business ventures. The Boilermakers Union, for example, put $12,000 in a co-op food store, $15,000 in the *Daily Union Record* (circulation 112,000 and the only union newspaper on the West Coast), $3,100 in a labor-owned laundry. All were successful operations. A workers' college was activated to counter Washington State's reactionary anti-labor educational leanings. The unions also ran a bank and a film company, had their own political candidates and local school board officials. It was their hope to send a labor representative to Congress rather than the usual businessman or corporate lawyer.

It was axiomatic, then, that the IWW offices would be raided, their meetings broken up. Police invaded IWW printing establishments to prevent publication of their literature. Vigilantes wrecked a plant that printed their weekly newspaper. Hundreds of government and local spies, infiltrators, provocateurs operated in and around Seattle. Private "patriotic" organizations were dedicated to the destruction of the IWW and the American Protective League, that national superpatriotic organization left over from the war, hounded them.

Ole Hanson had always hated the IWW.

In Seattle, all the forces endemic in the great all-American battle of unions and employers were thus concentrated. After the armistice, the restraints with which they had conducted themselves during the war were now abandoned. Both sides had made huge gains, labor by wage increases through union organization, and management by huge profits via cost-plus contracts, where wage increases were just another part of the cost paid by government. In a peacetime economy, wages would be the first item to be reduced. And to accomplish this, management dedicated itself to crushing the unions that had implemented those gains. The magic of collective bargaining implied an equality of give-and-take that management had no intention of honoring. The closed shop of all-union workers, the symbol of that equality, had to be broken. For the first time in American history, the nationwide battle of organized capital versus organized labor would be clearly joined.

In 1919, management in Seattle was well-organized and empowered through an Employers Businessmen's Association with all the usual accompanying servants: newspapers, city hall, courts, police department. The association had long since declared its intentions: "When the war is over, we will get the unions!"—a cry of battle heard all across the country. To this the Central Labor Council replied: "We will not give up any concession in organization that we have won during the war!"

This was the conflict waiting for an inevitable eruption.

In January 1919, the Metal Workers Union at the shipyards,

in dispute over a wage increase, had been granted permission by the Federal Emergency Fleet Corporation, a wartime agency of the United States government, to renegotiate its contract with management. The head of that agency, however, sent a telegram to the employers' Metal Trades Association ordering it to resist any union demands under a threat of losing its steel allotment, thus undermining the collective bargaining process it had just endorsed. Like the assassination at Sarajevo, the triggering incident was touched with madness: the Western Union messenger, a teenager whose bicycle had just been stolen, mistakenly delivered the telegram to the Metal Trades *Council*. Read by union members instead of the intended management executives, the result was fury at such duplicity, at the subsequent confrontation with an intransigent employer, the union members, twenty-five thousand strong, voted to strike. They immediately appealed to the Central Labor Council for support.

What followed was an unprecedented demonstration in labor solidarity. The 110 union delegations went back to poll their memberships, and with astonishing majorities, sixty thousand union men fully discussed, debated, then voted to join the strike. It was a mass expression of their own grievances as well, for all had complaints about the high cost of living, their own wages and working conditions. Above all, they sensed their own fear of powerlessness as individual craft unions. The Meat Cutters Union, for example, had lost its closed shop after a lockout. Longshoremen were bitter after an unfair mediation award. Less than a week later, then, the Central Labor Council called the first general strike in American labor history.

Seattle was stunned. *The Seattle Times* headlines began what proved to be the inevitable distortion that would dominate the year: "A General Strike at What? The Government of the United States? Bosh! Not 15 percent of Seattle laborites would consider such a proposition!" *The Seattle Post-Intelligencer* ran a cartoon on the front page showing a red banner flying above the stars and stripes. "NOT IN A THOUSAND YEARS!" ran the caption. The Employers Association declared that this was nothing but the work of the radical IWW union leaders intent on the disruption of American society. *The Seattle Star* cried out: "STOP BEFORE IT IS TOO LATE! This is America, not Russia!" Every Seattle newspaper printed the IWW credo: "Every strike is a small revolution and a dress rehearsal for the big one." Full-page ads were placed in all Seattle papers demanding that labor leaders "be hanged on the nearest telephone pole," advocating that employers fight to turn the city into a bastion of open-shop Americans lest "red flag agitators in the guise of labor leaders" make Seattle "the most labor-tyrannized city in America." The tone was so inflammatory, in fact, that union typesetters refused to set it. There was no mention that the real basis for the strike was not revolution at all, but the preservation of the status quo. Nor was what had caused the strike in the first place ever mentioned. Nor did anyone appear to wonder why sixty thousand workers from 110 unions had actually voted to go out. Indeed, the press devoted itself to linking unions and the closed shop with the Russian Revolution. After all, had not unions held a meeting to protest the United States intervention in Russia? Was this not treason? Why else did police invade, beat up people, arrest the leaders in a so-called legitimate patriotic curtailment of free speech? (Significantly, Ole Hanson was there to observe this raid.) The Seattle newspapers had endorsed the raid as it had endorsed the intervention.

Meanwhile, all attempts by the union to renegotiate the contract—the source of the problem—were frustrated by the disappearance of the employers. Gone for vacation, went the response. It was as if they actually wanted to let the strike happen.

It was accepted, almost without question, that this titanic event would be the start of a revolution in America in the image of the Bolsheviks at Petrograd, instigated by German propaganda and German gold by representatives of the Soviet government and their trained agents in the IWW. The good people of Seattle immediately stocked up on food and supplies, reinforced the locks of their homes, bought every weapon in town and oiled their hunting rifles in fear of civil war. Those who could leave town did so. There were endless rumors of blown water mains, of poisoned water systems, of the arrival of IWW radicals imported to head the revolution, of tons of tacks to be strewn across roads to frustrate the police, of two hundred Bolshevik gunmen brought by train from Chicago, of the assassination of Ole Hanson, of property confiscation in wealthy neighborhoods. When a car backfired in downtown, many thought it was the opening shot of the revolution itself.

The hour of the strike call, 10:00 A.M., February 6, 1919, arrived and suddenly all was quiet. One striking ship worker stood at the window of the vigorously anti-union *Seattle Post-Intelligencer* and watched the presses come to a halt. "It was the most beautiful thing I ever seen!" he said. For the citizens of Seattle, there was water and power, milk stations for children, gasoline for doctors. There was laundry and cooking gas for hospitals. Thousands of union men of the War Veterans Guard patrolled the streets with white armbands to prevent chaos. Everything possible had been organized in preparation for this day. This was not revolution but order.

The people of Seattle were astonished. The unions had taken over the city and all was peaceful. What became apparent was that the object of the general strike was not to provoke anarchy but to show solidarity for the sole purpose of redressing grievances. The Strike Committee functioned in continuous session to alleviate whatever conditions demanded its attention. Business representatives were forced to seek approval for their actions and they did so courteously, as did the mayor himself; they were dealt with accordingly.

But Ole Hanson was not one to let power slip away. Besides, he knew the potential resentment of his middle-class constituents; the sparks were everywhere, he had but to fan the flames. With considerable fanfare, he deputized an army of 2,500 additional police, fully armed them for no other purpose than to create alarm. With the threat of violence carefully laid in, he would use force to break the strike, thereby endearing himself once and for all to the powerful business community. He would make himself into a hero by saving his beloved city from revolution.

Quietly, without knowledge of the local press, he released to the wire services a preposterous statement that totally belied the reality of the strike: "The sympathetic revolution was called in the exact manner as was the revolution in Petrograd.... We refuse to treat with these revolutionists.... I issued a proclamation that all life and property would be protected—shoot on sight anyone causing disorder.... Let us clean up the United States of America. Unconditional surrender are our only terms."

In Seattle, however, he did not "refuse to treat with these revolutionists" but called for negotiations through a citizens' committee—labor, civic, management—a testimonial to his fair-mindedness. Management, however, had no intention of negotiating anything, a fact that Ole was fully aware of. Ole immediately took the bit in his teeth and issued a public proclamation to stop the strike by the sheer power of his words. The Seattle press leaped to his side, excoriating the strikers: "There can be no compromise on Americanism!" Suddenly the workers were "muddle-headed foreigners . . . scum of the melting pot of hell . . . riffraff from Europe intent on terrorizing the community."

Ole called for the state militia, United States Army troops from Ft. Lewis. He appeared in the streets in a large automobile draped in the American flag. His declaration was stunning: "End the strike or suffer the consequences," and suddenly there were machine guns in the streets of Seattle. How else can a patriotic mayor stop a Bolshevist threat? Business groups approved, the more militant the tactics the better. There was no concern for the issues or any appreciation for the sympathetic and orderly way in which the strike was being conducted. The people of Seattle observed—but believed what the newspapers told them.

In the meantime, Ole was big news on the front pages of every major newspaper in the country. They printed his releases as if they were gospel. They quoted his warnings and his diatribes in headlines. Ole put Seattle on the map and himself on a pedestal: "Reds directing Seattle strike—to test chance for Revolution. . . ." "The Seattle Strike is Marxian . . . a Bolshevist beast comes into the open." Said Senator Knute Neilson of Minnesota: "The strike posed greater danger to the nation than the war against Germany." And, said Senator William King of Utah, "From Russia they came and to Russia they should be made to go!"

The AFL leadership cringed; this is what Samuel Gompers had spent his life in fear of. The *New York Times* called Ole Hanson "a man of force, direct and democratic in his methods."

Though the Seattle community was more bored than terrorized, pressure on the unions began to mount with a growing public disquietude. Because of insufficient planning by the strike committee for the achievement of specific goals, many of the workers began returning to work, and with that, solidarity diminished.

The national AFL, forever in conflict with the Central Labor Council, publicly opposed the general strike, imposing on striking locals cause for second thoughts. After two days, streetcars were seen in operation and stores began to open. Life was returning to normal.

The Committee of Fifteen of the Central Labor Council was faced with impossible odds and unfortunate alternatives: to submit to the radical extremists who would turn the city to chaos—or capitulate with whatever face-saving tactic they could devise. They voted thirteen to one to capitulate.

Not without pride, however. For five days, the unions had run the city. If they had failed to gain better wages for the Metal Workers Union (now left on their own), they had shown to themselves and the city an astonishing power. With even greater solidarity, they might have gone further. Editor Anna Louise Strong of the *Union Record* had written at the start of the strike: "We are undertaking the most tremendous move ever made by labor in this country, a move which will lead NO ONE KNOWS WHERE!" It was enough of a victory to have gotten as far as they did.

"We went out to demonstrate the solidarity of labor," Strong said later, "and having accomplished that, there is no longer any reason for continuing the strike."

For management, let it be said that the demands of the Metal Workers Union were never even negotiated.

Unquestionably, Ole was the real victor. Though it was the Committee of Fifteen that had called off the strike, Ole claimed victory for crushing them. He never did care for details. Having tasted the sweet juice of national fame, he was eager to capitalize on it. Basking in the glow of what everyone called his triumph, he reverted to his old oratorical talents. He began to create dire scenarios of Bolshevik power in America, blaming the threat on Washington's failure to deal with it.

Having conquered it in Seattle, Ole would offer himself to the rest of the country. With an eye on bigger prizes, he abandoned the mayoralty for a cross-country speaking tour. His message had no reason to vary—or to suggest any truths. It was the Red Menace, pure and simple. He was the first of the new professional Red-baiters who would exploit the new great lie that would come to dominate the national psyche. From earning the mayor's annual salary of $7,500, he cleared $38,000 in his first seven months on the lecture circuit. His message for the future of America was not only in its content but in his capacity to get away with it.

So the Red Scare was off and running, ready to feed like maggots in rot. When Premier Georges Clemenceau was shot in Paris in the midst of the peace conference, American newspapers immediately reported the would-be assassin to be "a Bolshevik." To allay American fears, the United States Secret Service arrested fourteen leading Wobblies to prevent a worldwide assassination plot against Allied and American officials. No other country in the world had such a reaction.

2. THE SPREADING WILDFIRE OR HOW TO LIE WHILE SINGING "THE STAR-SPANGLED BANNER"

We must bring home to the people the truth that a compromise with Bolshevism is to barter away our inheritance.

—LEE OVERMAN, United States senator, North Carolina

Wars accumulate statistics. Casualty figures take strange forms, the most significant of which need not derive from the battlefields. Take the cost of living, for example. In 1919, it had risen 104 percent over 1914. Food was up 84 percent. Clothing, 114 percent. Furniture, 125 percent. There was no essential product that did not similarly rise in price. No statistic had a greater impact on American postwar life nor was there any that better illustrated the plight of the workingman. If he had made good money during the war, in 1919 he realized that he had made no financial progress, no steps toward his security. Wherever he lived—city, town or country—the conditions were similar. He had spent the years working hard, bought defense bonds out of loyalty to the war effort, denied himself and his family all unnecessary acquisitions. Now that the war was over, his savings had been all but eroded by inflation. The promises of his loyalty were not fulfilled.

It was not difficult to understand the reasons. Rising prices were inevitable from the moment Congress rejected the imposing of drastic war taxes on those who would profit the most. A mere 30 percent excess profits tax was a guarantee of inflation, a figure considerably less than in any other neutral or belligerent nation in the world. In the United States, the demand for pay-as-you-go tax schemes (as vigorously proposed by Senator Robert La Follette) was considered akin to a treasonable violation of the free enterprise system. To the workingman, however, it was an admission that business would not function in wartime unless promised its profits.

It followed, then, that costs of living would rise more rapidly than wages but seldom as high as profits. To accept this simple fact was also to accept a condition of spiraling distress for wage earners.

In 1919, the news was leaked that fifty million eggs had been secretly stored in warehouses by food speculators in order to create the scarcity that would raise their price. This was also true of sugar, rice, tons of beef. The Department of Justice was said to be hunting them down in a special war on profiteers, but the prices continued to rise. This was a year for unbridled free enterprise. Control the supply, increase the demand. The higher the price, the greater the profit.

Labor reacted to such basic economic laws in the only way it could: by striking. In March, there were 175 strikes. In New York City alone, twenty thousand harbor workers went out, fifty thousand garment workers, forty thousand cigar makers, fifteen thousand streetcar employees and thousands more. It was much the same all across the country, a growing wave of strikes. There had never been so many, with so many thousands participating. Before the year ended, there were 3,600 strikes involving over four million workers. The workingman, having become unionized during the war, demonstrated his recently organized strength.

And so, of course, did the employers, resisting the very idea of a militant labor movement no matter how fat their profits. What had happened in Seattle was a warning to them all. If strikes became the workers' device to right their grievances, they became management's excuse for breaking the unions through the creation of a colossal fraud. The workers were portrayed as victims, not of alleged grievances such as wages or working conditions— and certainly not the high cost of living, which, it was claimed, made victims of everyone—but of their union leaders who were "radicals," one and all. They were Bolsheviks who forced the membership to strike in order to destroy the fabric of American society. The truth was quite the contrary: it was the union leaders who were almost universally conservative, certainly more so than the rank and file. The membership who worked the factories and mills were the militants, driving their leaders into action. The leadership was repeatedly trying to restrain the workers.

Newspapers accepted the premise of the owners. The lie proliferated. The public readily swallowed it. It was far more convincing to picture a few bad apples in the barrel than a whole barrelful. As a result, the public could then feel sympathy for the oppressed workers who were duped by the Reds into a self-destructive action. Beat the strike, save the nation from Bolshevism and the workers from their leaders. The pattern repeated itself endlessly. There was no such thing as a strike that was not labeled Bolshevik.

Congress was quick to sense which way the winds were blowing. The result was a well-publicized Senate Judiciary Sub-Committee hearing to determine the extent of radical influence over American society, and particularly American labor. (Not accidentally, this was the same committee that had recently investigated German propaganda, now segueing into Russian.) A recent speech by the distinguished churchman Albert Rhys Williams at a radical meeting a few blocks from the Capitol actually suggesting recognition of the Soviet government became a cause célèbre. What followed was a month of sometimes hair-raising anti-Bolshevik testimony: The Soviets were nationalizing women, establishing free love bureaus. According to United States ambassador David Francis, they were "killing everyone who wears a white collar or who is educated and who is not a Bolshevik." The Bolshevik government had slaughtered twice as many Russians as had been killed in the war. An entire nation was being held captive under a terror more savage than anything in recorded history.

The press thrived on the gore of the testimony. Stories were spread of atrocities that made the German troops in Belgium seem like benevolent missionaries. Editors referred to Russians as "madmen . . . human scum . . . crime-mad . . . beasts." Russia was a place of maniacs roving in the streets, where starving people fought with dogs for carrion. When the final report was released, detailing 1,200 pages of atrocities, newspaper headlines could hardly contain their enthusiasm: "RED PERIL HERE," "PLAN BLOODY REVOLUTION," "WANT WASHINGTON GOVERNMENT OVERTURNED."

New York State, long the center of America's radicals, proceeded to exploit this distinction with an investigation of its own. An earlier report by Archibald Stevenson, a prominent New York attorney distinguished as "the only man in the country truly feared by all radicals," was its inspiration, for Stevenson had concluded that Bolsheviks were exceedingly prominent among working people in the state, and that strong remedial action was called for. Backed by prominent conservatives of the prestigious Union League Club, the New York State Legislature appropriated $30,000 for its own committee to investigate all such seditiousness with Senator Clayton R. Lusk in charge.

This investigation began with a massive raid on the offices of the Russian Soviet Bureau in New York City. Two tons of Russian propaganda were confiscated, and the bureau's spokesman, L. C. Martens, subpoenaed to testify. Martens was labeled the American Lenin with huge allotments of Moscow gold at his disposal, his bureau the clearinghouse for all radical activity in the United States. Through Martens, labor was to be Bolshevized, the country propagandized through the distribution of over fifty radical publications reaching five hundred thousand readers in New York City alone. Then, as quickly as this flurry over the so-called Russian connection subsided, the Lusk Committee followed up with another raid, this time on the Rand School in New York City. Here, more literature was confiscated, more incriminating documents, and above all, mailing lists. "Names!" Lusk had cried out in triumph to justify his actions. "Names of all parlor Bolsheviks, IWW members, Socialists. They will be a real help to us later on." There were, in fact, six thousand names in the files. A second raid gained access to the Rand School safe, and Lusk had a field day with fresh accusations. Radicals, it seemed, dominated over a hundred trade unions. L. C. Martens and the Soviet Bureau were working directly with them. The Rand School was training others to radicalize Negroes, subsidizing Negro speakers to use exaggerated accounts of injustice, establishing radical Negro publications. Lusk, having accused the Rand School of being the headquarters for the fomenting of revolution, then attempted to initiate legal action to close this radical "haven of refuge."

The Lusk Committee's report to the citizens of New York and the rest of America ran 4,456 pages, replete with thousands of "captured" radical documents, hundreds of footnotes, transcriptions of expert testimony, vast bibliographies of seditious literature. Its conclusion was another statement that the country was under the gun of European Communists, that strong sedition legislation was called for, careful screening of all immigrants, deportation of undesirables, nationwide programs of Americanism, loyalty oaths for teachers, censorship of textbooks.

The massive size of the report appeared to justify these conclusions and its weight alone lent it the dignity of investigatory scholarship, the outgrowth of impeccably pursued sources and intense research. No matter that the case was presented exclusively by the prosecution; the defense, as it were, had been denied any rebuttal. This was argument by sheer bulk, nothing challenged, no substantiation. Not one word had been directed toward the root causes of the American radical movement. The inequities of an economic system that bred poverty, slums, child labor went unmentioned. One could find no reference to the astonishing fact that there were more American casualties at the workplace than American soldiers suffered in combat. Blacks were not exploited by American whites but by alien radicals. Everything that was wrong in America was, in fact, brought about by radicals.

A new expression emerged from the Lusk Committee: the Parlor Pink, a pejorative reference to the middle- and upper-class American whose political preferences did not jibe with the established norm. It became a sly, insidious term that suggested all manner of devious thought. The soft effeminate coloration exuded an odor of degeneracy. It tainted liberals with faint damnation. All in all, it proved to be far more damaging to free expression than the police cudgels on May Day.

It followed, then, that the American people had no real understanding of the Russian Revolution. Official explanations, commonly accepted, assumed that Lenin and Trotsky had taken power by guile backed by German gold. The notion that the tsars had created the revolution by their cruelties and corruptions was ignored. It was as if the American Revolution of 1776 had had nothing to do with the oppressions of George III. It was another link to the notion that radical labor leaders were the cause of strikes, not the inequities suffered by the workers.

This became the accepted dogma of 1919. In strike after strike, management bombarded the public with full-page ads. They made no distinction between labor leaders: AFL's conservative Samuel Gompers was no different from IWW's Bill Haywood. The union was the enemy in the forefront of the revolution. The strike was the union's weapon to achieve it.

Woodrow Wilson's secretary of labor, William B. Wilson, offered a typical statement: "...strikes...are not industrial economic disputes in their origin, but are the results of a deliberate, organized attempt at a social and political movement to establish soviet government in the United States." No one, it seemed, made note of the fact that strikes were frequently settled, wages increased, better working conditions either won or lost, and workers returned to work—without a single American soviet having been established.

The bomb scares began. First, there was a small brown package mailed to the office of Ole Hanson. Unopened in his absence (he was away on the speaking tour), it leaked acid on his papers. Cautiously opened, it revealed a homemade bomb. Said Ole with customary defiance: "If they have the courage, why don't they attack me like men instead of playing the part of cowardly assassins?" With this came the picture of the "Bolshevik" with wide eyes and unkempt hair, always holding a bomb in his hand, the new symbol of force and violence. *The Chicago Tribune* headlined the uncovering of a radical plan for bombing the Loop, but no details were exposed. Then the Department of Justice discovered an anarchist conspiracy in Pittsburgh to capture a government arsenal, steal the explosives and "lay the city in ruins." To lend evidence to the discovery, eleven anarchists were arrested, but nothing specific was ever revealed.

As it turned out, however, seventeen more bombs were rescued from delivery by a perceptive New York postal clerk named Charles Kaplan, who remembered storing brown-paper packages that resembled the one delivered to Ole Hanson. The "Bomb

Honor List" included an inexplicably clashing selection—from the enlightened liberal Frederick Howe, commissioner of immigration at Ellis Island, to John D. Rockefeller and J. P. Morgan. Then another eighteen packages, for a total of thirty-six, were found.

The press and public immediately clamored for reprisals. "Dynamitards," "human vermin" (the latter word would appear frequently in this context). Every anarchist ought to be deported, all bomb-makers hung. The vituperous Ole went out into deep right field to blame the administration as "weak, vacillating and chargeable.... If the government doesn't clean them up, I will." Unless some action was taken, others said that "we may as well invite Lenin and Trotsky to come here and set up business at once." And forever there was the evangelist Billy Sunday: "If I had my way, I'd fill the jails so full of them that their feet would stick out the windows."

But what action was possible? Against exactly whom? The New York City police worked around the clock, bomb experts from all over the East congregated over those brown-paper parcels amassing clues, promising to "run down the persons responsible," but no one was ever arrested. Even the staid *New York Times* was frustrated: "Has the gift of skill and genius in ferreting out criminals been denied to our present-day detectives?" The radical journal *Liberator* had a different explanation for the failure. "Some important person does not want to discover them."

Then there was May first, the traditional international celebration day for workers with parades and demonstrations—not with military bands or soldiers marching in uniform, but men, women and children carrying banners and red flags. In 1919, American radicals liberated from the ultrapatriotic constraints of the war went all out to reestablish the dignity of their beliefs in a show of strength against the new breed of Ole Hansons.

But Ole, it seemed, was everywhere. In Boston, for example, a Socialist parade of 1,500, denied a permit, was attacked by police with a resulting riot. Anti-Red mobs joined in, posses were formed to chase down marchers fleeing from the melee and Socialist headquarters were demolished as dozens of heads were bashed. In New York, there were more riots as soldiers and sailors attempted to break up parades and raided rallies, the most vicious of which was the storming of the Russian People's House on East Fifteenth Street, where the occupants were forced to sing "The Star-Spangled Banner" while their literature was being confiscated. The new offices of the Socialist newspaper, *The Call,* were also raided by hundreds of veterans who broke up a reception of seven hundred people, then destroyed the furniture and literature, savagely driving the guests into the streets. In Cleveland, a parade was stopped by an organized band of Victory Loan workers led by an Army lieutenant who was inflamed by a red flag. Again, the riot was savage, and twenty Socialists were injured, an action that was repeated several times in the city causing one killing and numerous hospitalizations.

A letter to *The Nation* magazine was loaded with appropriate implications:

> ... My sociological training is sadly limited and my sympathies toward any form of radicalism are nil. The *New York Call* as a newspaper scarcely existed for me, until the occurrence of May Day. My business office is in the Bible House. I was on my way down Fourth Avenue when my attention was attracted by cries and shrieks of women. I turned in the direction of the uproar and was met by a scene which it is difficult to describe. About two hundred men in soldiers and sailors uniform, armed with clubs, sticks and jacks were lined up in front of the building in two-line formation; from the building men and women were being driven; and as the men passed this line they were being beaten in a most savage and brutal manner ... eyes were blackened, heads broken, shoulder-blades crippled. I saw a man jump from the first story, preferring to risk this mode of injury to the prospect of walking the gauntlet. I am sure he must have broken a leg.... I think of America and its traditions of freedom, peace and patriotism. I think of the millions of our boys sent abroad to fight for democracy—and then I see this savage mob ... doing infinitely more to foster discontent than the worst forms of Tsarism.... An outcry of righteous indignation should be heard all over our land against this organized brutality.

The outcry, however, was against the victims. Newspapers approved of the vigilante action, made no comment that the police had done nothing to prevent it and endorsed the arrest of the radicals. It was like blaming an automobile for its drunken driver. The menace became free speech itself. "An unrestrained menace," the *St. Louis Tribune* called it in a headline. "Silence the incendiary advocates of force," advised the *Washington [D.C.] Post*. "Bring the law's hand down upon the...inciter of violence. Do it now!"

The American war against the Huns had turned into the war against the Reds.

(In Munich on May first, Adolf Hitler marched with the Friedkorps in a savage attempt to rid the city of Communists.)

In June the bombs exploded, the most celebrated of which hit the Washington home of the new attorney general, A. Mitchell Palmer. Only the perpetrator was killed, apparently stumbling as he left the scene and blowing himself to bits. It was determined from the fragments of his clothing and a pamphlet found near the scene that he was an Italian anarchist from Philadelphia. The text of the pamphlet was reprinted in the *Washington Post*, a statement of radical theory and revenge:

> "...We have been dreaming of freedom, we have talked of liberty, we have aspired to a better world, and you jailed us, you clubbed us, you deported us, you murdered us whenever you could. Now that the great war, waged to replenish your purses and build a pedestal to your saints, is over nothing better can you do [sic] to protect your stolen millions, and your usurped fame, than to direct all the power of the murderous institutions you created for your exclusive defense, against the working multitudes rising to a more human conception of life. ...Do not expect us to sit down and pray and cry. We accept your challenge and mean to stick to our war duties. ..."

It was signed: "The Anarchist Fighters."

Palmer, however, chose to summarize the statement as follows: "There will have to be bloodshed, we will not dodge. There will have to be murder, we will kill...there will have to be destruction; we will destroy....We are ready to do anything and everything to suppress the capitalist class...."

America was thoroughly alarmed and prepared to believe only the worst-case scenario. Palmer, once a liberal, insisted that the bombs were but the first demonstrations of Bolshevik revolution in America. No matter that all such bombings had the opposite effect, that they served only to strengthen the repression. The celebrated radical John Reed suggested that they were actually planted by reactionaries to accomplish this. In the *Liberator,* Max Eastman postulated that the capitalist press shouted "Bolshevism whenever an explosion occurs, but their shouting only strengthens the plausible hypothesis that it was for the purpose of this shouting that the explosion occurred."

Again, for all the fragments, not one bomber was arrested.

Nonetheless, the bombs and the shouting were grist for a rejuvenated patriotic mill. Organizations created to stir loyalty for the war effort now multiplied for the war against Bolshevism. The National Security League, founded in 1914, began an extensive campaign to spread the message, propagandizing teachers, church leaders, businessmen, congressmen, seasoned now in the techniques of George Creel and his Committee for Public Information. Hundreds of speakers were commissioned to deliver the messages of "False Idealism," "Parlor Bolshevism," "The Enemy Within our Gates." Anything critical of the government was labeled subversive. The American Defense Society was even more rabid, organizing patriotic functions in local school systems, enacting censorship proceedings in state legislatures, endorsing boycotts of such "radical" journals as *The Nation* and *The New Republic,* circulating millions of pamphlets warning of imminent Red takeovers, offering employers literature to be inserted in pay envelopes. Its conservatism went so far as to attack the recall, whereby a public official might be removed from office by a public vote or petition, and the referendum, whereby the electorate has the right to pass on an important piece of legislation, and the income tax, as Bolshevist. The National Civic Foundation, another patriotic wartime propaganda group, added to the respectability of the Red Scare by disseminating exposés on communism that led to more censorship of textbooks, radical leanings of churchmen, suspected associations of government officials. Its leading spokesman, Ralph Easley, made himself heard across the country, constantly alerting everyone to the dangers of indifference to the Red threat. Significantly, Samuel Gompers and his AFL leadership endorsed the Easley message with the same fervor he used to oppose the big business executives at the bargaining table. All these organizations were backed and financed by big money: August Belmont, Judge Elbert Gary, the Du Ponts, Henry Frick, J. P. Morgan, John D. Rockefeller. The National Security League spent over $100,000 in 1919, the first known political action committee intent on defeating congressmen who opposed its position. With such funds—and power—behind it, the political connections led into the White House itself. The Department of Justice allowed access to those confidential files as devised by J. Edgar Hoover.

The Army and the Navy, its highest officers in the War Department, endorsed the Red Scare, linking radicals with pacifism since the most hated enemy of armament appropriations were "those paid agitators and sentimental sob sisters, Reds seeking to undermine our form of government." In the *Army and Navy Register*, an article reported that "Three million dollars in gold had been sent to the United States by the Communist International for a campaign to eliminate the United States Army and Navy so that when the Red uprising came the country would be at its mercy."

It was the reductio ad absurdum of the Red Scare that anti-Prohibition Wets claimed that Drys were Bolsheviks; whereupon the patriotic Drys could hardly contain their indignation and made the same claim against the Wets.

Then there was the American Legion, organized at the beginning of the year out of fear that returning soldiers might respond cynically to their war experience with a less-than-ardent patriotic attitude. To resist any threat that the war had radicalized them, the Legion credo called for the need "to foster and perpetuate 100 percent Americanism." The press was overjoyed. Veterans against Bolshevism was the ultimate safeguard. The Legion was "one of the greatest forces for good this country has ever known." It would "keep all postwar changes safe and sane." At its first convention, it openly dedicated itself to the war against radicals and urged immediate deportation of all citizens and aliens who denigrated the American way. *The American Legion Weekly* pounded this thesis repeatedly. Ole Hanson became its star advocate in a series of patriotic articles. As a consequence, Legionnaires frequently took the law into their own hands with vigilante raids on Reds and brawls with socialists. "Leave the Reds to the Legion" went the popular battle cry.

H. L. Mencken despised them with savage candor "for supporting the most destructive institutions in our society. . . . Its officers ... like profiteers in search of jobs as chamber of commerce witch-hunters ... wholly devoid of patriotism, courage or sense. ... Nothing quite like it existed ... before the war, not even in the South. There is nothing like it anywhere on earth."

Nineteen nineteen was a great year for the Legion. A million veterans joined.

It was also the year of the Ku Klux Klan, suddenly rejuvenated into a powerful organization of Genii, Grand Dragons, Cyclops, Furies—the mumbo jumbo of white-sheeted beknighted spooks who fed on the brutal bigotries of those who hated Catholics, Jews, aliens and above all, "niggers." In one of the greatest manipulations of words and meanings, the KKK constitution stated its intent was to "cultivate and promote patriotism toward our Civil Government ... and conserve ideals of a pure Americanism," in what turned out to be a reign of terror that dominated many communities, and not only in the South. First intended as a purifying moral, religious and racial force, in 1919 it rode the new political wave of the Red Menace as well. A Jew was not just a Jew but a Red Jew. Even "niggers" were uppity because they were Red-tainted. Anyone, in fact, who was not a Klan supporter became suspect. Perhaps the most significant statistic of the year was that the Socialist Party, against which all this hatred was generated, had 109,000 members, while the American Legion and the KKK, but two of its many tormentors, each had ten times that many.

The impact of all this was a plunge into the grotesque, an orgy of self-deception built on the proliferation of preposterous lies. The result was an endlessly unstoppable spiraling of fantasy so far removed from reality as to seem inexplicable. With hindsight, it became clear that America loved it, loving the same wartime zealotry, the joys of sharing a continuing patriotic hatred for an enemy. There was a satisfying convenience in seeing the radicals as part of a worldwide revolutionary conspiracy financed by Prussian Junkers. And how devilish was that conspiracy to include a few masterful and wily conscienceless Jews from New York's Lower East Side. There was never a more perfect combination designed to attack our nativist faith in America's goodness. Our love affair with America, so brilliantly manipulated during the war by George Creel and his Committee for Public Information, was now being violated by alien vermin. No country in the world took to patriotism so naively. Not even in Prussian Germany had the individual German been so enchanted with his alleged traditions.

Since there were only a few radicals in America, and no revolutionary activities or acts, the Red Scare was forced to concentrate on using the radicals' words. To quote the words was enough to support the scare. The sporadic use of bombs could justify the exploitation of words. So the words made the news. The Department of Justice had nothing else to work on but "the largest collection of radical literature in the world." "Captured documents," the Intelligence Division called them. "Red Radicalism as described by its own leaders," was one of many releases to the press.

The department claimed that there were 471 radical newspapers in 1919. William J. Burns, the "heroic" private detective, claimed there were 422,000 United States Communists. The National Security League said six hundred thousand. The Allied Patriotic Society offered that there were ten thousand Communist Party meetings a week, and 350 radical papers. Radical words and superpatriotic words were, in a crazy way, mutually supportive. Each fortified the self-fulfilling prophesies of the other. If superpatriots argued that a revolutionary plot was stirring, radicals would agree and call for that very thing to happen. The superpatriots would then cite radical words as proof of the conspiracy, and radicals would then cite such rhetoric as the onset of repression. If the national patriotic press claimed a strike was "Red led," the radical press would then boast of how powerful they were. The patriotic press would then quote the radical press as proof of their claims. And when the radicals denied involvement in an alleged plot, the Justice Department would argue that secrecy and denial were typical tactics of radical conspirators.

To the Red Scarer, radical words became deeds, criminal deeds. Since there were no deeds, radicals were arrested solely for words. Radical words, then, had to be censored and suppressed—even as they were fabricated and repeated by the patriots to illustrate the menace.

Hysteria was encouraged, as more and more groups came to see the benefits. With it, a new bureaucracy formed, setting in motion numerous subbureaucracies representing one special interest or another. Each had a life of its own. They began to exchange information, personnel, membership lists, names. They financed each other's operations, anything to keep the action going. They testified in behalf of each other's groups, quoted each other's spokesmen, cited each other in pamphlets to spread the word. They maintained the status of each other's secrets. The success of one nourished the motivation of others. It escalated into an ever-growing bureaucracy that created what it predicted. A big business came out of it involving major moneyed interests, and then it became part of the government itself. Federal officials endorsed it, sanctified it, thus reflecting the groundswell and fortifying it. Assisting the private effort was the government bureaucracy: The General Intelligence Division of the Department of Justice, the Immigration Bureau, Army Intelligence, the attorney general's Office, congressional committees and their staffs. Then there were detective agencies concentrating on radicals, private armies of Pinkertons, employers' associations, special cadres of police, agents provocateurs, publishers of large newspapers, the American Legion, the Ku Klux Klan. The greater the hysteria, the more people joined up. To the inner circle, the name of the game was to sell the product. Labor spies, hired to infiltrate and report on radical activities, would just as readily lie about them. Or if there was no action to report, they'd provoke it, then report it, submitting new names in each report, even if they were created out of thin air. The American Legion thrived on the business of new members. The KKK had salesmen on a commission basis. Detective agencies created the very havoc at strikes that got them hired to suppress them. Exploitable events were staged, carefully orchestrated for maximum propaganda. The creation of such pseudo-events was a major enterprise of the Justice Department for the purpose of glorifying itself. As for the press, no reporter dared to check the evidence, certainly not when the Department of Justice was involved. If the goal of all this was allegedly a last-ditch patriotic stand against the coming revolution, there was a lot of easy money to be made in the process.

Meanwhile, the mind of America was being warped. Education was turned into propaganda. Recent aliens learned quickly how to use it to prove their loyalty. Politicians loved it for the simplicity of appealing to bigotry. Churchmen could excoriate this Antichrist. Liberals joined in to gain their own respectability. The press thrived on it, selling ads, multiplying circulation with scare headlines. Yellow journalism went along with the Yellow Dog Contract, amalgamating the world of business with news. It made J. Edgar Hoover one of the most powerful men in America. It made Calvin Coolidge president. It made Ole Hanson rich and heroic. It almost put A. Mitchell Palmer in the White House. The State Department used it to generate support for its anti-Russian policy, another justification for American intervention in Archangel and Siberia.

In the spring of 1919, Winnipeg, a small Canadian city in the western reaches of Saskatchewan, suddenly made the headlines of every major American newspaper. Aside from an earthquake, only one occurrence could bring this about: a general strike.

Actually, it seemed too small a matter to deserve more than a passing mention. A few thousand members of the metal and building trades went out, the Winnipeg Trades and Labor Council called a strike in sympathy, and hardly thirty thousand workers were involved. A small version of what had happened in Seattle, as it were. But America was treated to the same abject failure to understand the issues, its causes and intent. To the Winnipeg strikers, revolution was never in question, but Canadian officials, taking a dip of Ole Hanson's brew, cried Bolshevism. Indeed, it was said in Canada that the same strike leaders who had failed to bring revolution in Seattle had come to Winnipeg to try again, and with the same Red-labor financing.

Americans, most of whom had never so much as heard of Winnipeg, were treated to huge daily headlines of rampant Bolshevik plots north of the border. Again, babies were suffering from lack of milk. People were living in garbage and slime. Winnipeg was under the heel of radicalism at its worst. Even the official American labor press endorsed the anti-Red orientation. The "One Big Union" was denounced. Gompers called the strike "evil . . . ill-advised . . . a complete fiasco." And, as in Seattle, the power of the employers' group and its subject press defeated it. After two weeks, during which the unions took over the management of the city, the strike collapsed. Winnipeg, after a strident fortnight in the red heat of the American sun, returned to anonymity.

But the flames had been fed and a lot more minds were seared, another victory for the Red Scarers.

It was the year of the continuing nightmare.

At a Victory Loan pageant in Washington, D.C., a man refused to stand for "The Star-Spangled Banner." At its end, a sailor standing behind him fired three shots into his back. The man slumped over, dead—and the crowd cheered.

An alien in Hammond, Indiana, shouted "To hell with the United States!" and was killed in the streets. The murderers were acquitted by a jury after two minutes of deliberation.

A clothing-store clerk in Waterbury, Connecticut, was sentenced to six months in jail for remarking to a customer that Lenin was an extremely smart man.

A truck driver in Brooklyn, hating the obligatory red flag at the end of a lumber pile, replaced it with the stars and stripes. He was arrested and fined for insulting the American flag.

A United Mine Workers organizer named Fannie Sellins tried to prevent violence at a picket line outside the Allegheny Steel Company when drunken deputies attacked the line. She was clubbed to the ground, her skull crushed, then she was flung into the back of a truck along with the dead picketer she had been trying to help. There was no prosecution of the murder. Businessmen and the law were solidly behind the company. Customers of Allegheny Steel assured the company they would wait for deliveries; there must be no concessions to the union.

In Guthrie, Oklahoma, a man heard reading the Declaration of Independence aloud was arrested by two policemen. The man protested, insisting that Thomas Jefferson had written it. At this, one policeman wrenched him around, his nightstick menacing the man's face: "Okay, where is this Jefferson? We want him too!"

In Chicago, several black families' homes were bombed to drive them out of a white neighborhood. (There were no accusations of Bolshevism at these bombings.)

In a Massachusetts village newspaper, Senator Henry Cabot Lodge was called a Bolshevik for advocating compromise instead of irreconcilability to the League of Nations covenant.

The American Legion Weekly demanded a one-language nation, the language to be called "American," not English. Even in Mexico, the article said, they do not stand for calling their language "Spanish."

On a hot July afternoon, a Chicago black boy swimming in Lake Michigan was drawn by the current across an unspecified dividing line that separated white from colored. Whites stoned him, and he drowned. The result was a murderous race riot that tore the city apart. Another in Washington, D.C., was almost as destructive, rooted both in the rage and resentment of the hot ghettoes and the racism of white bigots. Both were blamed on the radicals. The *New York Times* postulated that there was "no use shutting our eyes to facts . . . Bolshevik agitation has been extended among the Negroes." Any radical sentiments expressed by black leaders were immediately trumpeted by the white press as validation of the thesis. The KKK ate this sort of thing up: they could proceed to terrorize and lynch, then blame the rioting on the Reds.

When the government took over the railroads during the war, it turned chaos into order. The lines were made to serve the interests of the nation rather than the profits of their owners. Since the vast, complex interconnected systems that spanned the continent with their wasteful overlapping, uncontrollable tie-ups and discriminatory rates had proved to be a disaster, the brotherhoods had no desire to see them returned to the pre-war system. A remarkable new plan, drafted by Glenn T. Plumb, counsel for the unions, proposed that the government now purchase America's railroads, whereupon a corporation of fifteen men (five from the general public, five from management and five from labor) would run the system. The railroads, after all, were the be-all and end-all of transportation. Industry and agriculture relied on them. Here, then, was a program designed to service to the needs of the public. The Plumb Plan offered service at cost, ridding the nation of monopoly charges for an efficient, controlled system designed to reduce costs at all levels, not for profiteering purpose but for the public welfare.

Its theme was rooted in the philosophical premise that industrial crisis was created by the struggle for excess, business controlled by management solely for profits to its investors. When profits were large, labor inevitably reacted with demands for a share of the pie. Hence, endless industrial wars and strikes, not to mention a continuing breakdown of morale in the workplace, slowdowns, inefficiency and poor service. This was the reality of industrial relations worldwide. Wherever industry was run for profit, labor was forced to fight for itself. All attempts to control the worst of this fight, or compromise it with profit-sharing schemes, benefits and bonuses, solved nothing as long as the system of private ownership was left intact. Why not, then, work out a plan for service rather than a nonplan for profits, to run the railroads by experts motivated solely by the desire for efficiency and the reduction of costs, not by a private millionaire's monopoly designed for profits. With the Plumb Plan, there would be no profits to fight over.

To the liberal press, the brotherhoods had "stuck in their thumb and pulled out a Plumb."

To the conservatives, the plan was "'Plumb' Bolshevism."

And so the battle was joined. The brotherhoods, of course, were for it. Glenn Plumb was a tireless spokesman in its behalf, working through the Plumb Plan League with an estimated three million supporters. Again, the conservative AFL leadership, with Samuel Gompers in the forefront, resisted, fearing the Red smear. At the AFL convention in June, however, the will of the rank and file dominated and the AFL platform endorsed the plan.

This, of course, redoubled the efforts of the opposition. Congress, at first pressured by both sides, moved cautiously, torn between returning the railroads to their previous owners, regardless of their history of mismanagement, and the virtues of Plumb. Compromise proposals kept reappearing with emphatic safeguards to private ownership. As for the Plumb Plan, it was gradually smothered by the forces of free enterprise capitalism. Though the battle would extend through the turbulent American summer, the Red Scarers became the dominant force: "A bold, bald, naked attempt to sovietize the railroads of this country," "A plan that might have been formulated by a Lenin or a Trotsky." It was said that if a potion were invented to achieve immortality, the American Association of Morticians would damn it as Bolshevik.

*   *   *

The spring of 1919 was also a time of agitation for the release of Tom Mooney, a labor leader convicted for murder in a San Francisco Preparedness Day Parade in 1916. Often referred to as one of the great miscarriages of class justice, and the trial as a framed-up conspiracy to discredit radical unionism, the Mooney life imprisonment created a vast wellspring of mass protest that escalated to a plan for a general strike on July fourth to pressure for a pardon. As the weeks of June went by, the movement generated as much opposition as support. The AFL convention refused to support it, but individual unions were free to do so. Liberal and radical groups became all the more insistent at every newspaper condemnation of the planned strike. The public press railed against it, Mooney's guilt or innocence notwithstanding. The people were warned of chaos, of mobs running wild in the streets if such an event took place. More bombs, more Bolshevism. "Reign of terror planned" went the headlines. "Stolen explosives to be used." "Plans for widespread violence and murder." In San Francisco, radicals were rounded up and jailed in preventive arrest. In New York City, eleven thousand police and detectives went on twenty-four-hour duty guarding all public buildings, the stock exchange, homes of prominent citizens. All socialist meetings were suspended by law. Thousands were sworn in as deputies. So great was the anticipated danger, city authorities forced the American Defense Society to cancel its proposed Independence Day rally at Carnegie Hall lest it serve as a provocation to radical violence. Chicago brought two companies of infantry into the city on patrol duty. In Boston, armed soldiers stood guard at the Federal Building. In Philadelphia, the streets were "filled with policemen." In Oakland, known radicals were arrested in another preventive action. The entire northwest was alerted against Wobbly uprising by federal agents sent to meet the anticipated revolutionary threat.

July fourth came and all was still. There was no general strike. Throughout the country, the great day was totally without incident. The press trumpeted that the forces of law and order had prevented the seditious demonstrations by their vigilance. By this time, the American people had become so intimidated by the fear of Reds, the charade perpetuated itself.

Twenty years passed before Tom Mooney was pardoned.

3. THE TRASHING OF THE BOSTON POLICE STRIKE OR HOW TO BECOME PRESIDENT OF THE UNITED STATES BY LEAVING TOWN DURING A CRISIS

Never go out to meet trouble. If you will just sit still, nine cases out of ten someone will intercept it before it reaches you.

—CALVIN COOLIDGE
Governor of Massachusetts

In the summer of 1919, Calvin Coolidge was governor of Massachusetts, a strange, tense, tight-lipped New Englander from a long line of Vermonters. His vital statistics were twice noteworthy: his birthplace was Plymouth, and the date was July fourth (1872). His background was hard-bitten Yankee "from too many cold winters," it was said, despite the fact that the Coolidges were sufficiently well-to-do to be of a much-respected status. Like Woodrow Wilson, Calvin dropped his given first name (John), was nonathletic but adept at debating, his style reclusive and socially shy, his personality dour and forbidding. Throughout his life, his silences were legion, often appallingly so. In his drive for political power, he assumed that the unspoken word was worth far more than a hundred articulated. The Republican Party bosses admired his diligence and his responsiveness. In politics, there was always room for an unobtrusive man who does well what he is told and has nothing to say—except what he is told to say. Unlike Wilson, however, from the outset, Coolidge never crossed swords with his

158

political mentors. His credo spelled this out: "While I have differed with my subordinates, I have always loyally supported my superiors." A classical example of a company man. Or, in contemporary parlance, "You get along by going along." As for the parsimoniousness of his spirit, Dorothy Parker's famous quip at the announcement of his death said it all: "How could they tell?"

Indeed, his incredible ascendancy to the White House was based on his ability to avoid doing anything at any time but especially in time of crisis. His biographer, the astute Kansan William A. White, described Coolidge's talent for appraising the flow of automobile traffic at an intersection, then crossing the street at a normal gait leaving just enough time to prevent a passing fender from grazing his rear. Out of that talent, wrote White, there arose a political philosophy.

It was perhaps even more significant that when Coolidge first rode in a horseless carriage, he enjoyed the ride but totally failed to appreciate its potential. "It won't amount to much," he said. But then Henry Ford once said the same thing about Coolidge's political potential.

The occasion of Coolidge's meteoric rise to prominence was, in many ways, the history of 1919 in infinite microcosm, representing so much of its essence as to be foreboding. History records the incident as the Boston Police Strike, its subtitle "How Pusillanimity Pays Off."

It is axiomatic that the origin of strikes dates back to causes rooted long before the walkout. Accumulated grievances mutually shared become aggravated by time. To the Boston police force, by tradition all strikes were a national anathema, and all unions a sacrilege. They had faced enough of them, generally cracking heads with dutiful abandon to protect the property of respected taxpayers. Their resentments against other workingmen were no secret, especially the foreign-born factory workers who were wont to drunkenness and unruly behavior on Saturday nights, flashing substantial bankrolls in local saloons that left poorly paid policemen sour with envy. Everyone in Boston, it seemed, made more money than the police did. So the police organized, over a thousand strong, and to avoid any stigma of union, they called themselves the Boston Social Club.

Enter the first leg of the Boston tripod, the recently appointed police commissioner, Edwin U. Curtis. He was a scion of seven generations of Bostonian respectability, prematurely old at fifty-seven from a political career distinguished mostly by repeated frustrations.

As William White wrote of him in his Coolidge biography entitled *A Puritan in Babylon:* "...one of those solemn self-sufficient Bostonian heroes who apparently are waiting in the flesh to walk up the steps to a pedestal and be cast into monumental bronze.... He embodied the spirit of traditional inherited wealth, traditional inherited Republicanism, traditional inherited skepticism about the capacity of Democracy for self-government and a profound faith in the propertied classes' ultimate right to rule."

Above all, Curtis hated the newly rising political force of the Irish who had unseated his mayoralty twenty-five years before. And now, as commissioner of police in the twilight of his undistinguished career, he felt the Irish were at him again—twelve hundred of them in police uniform, protesting their skimpy $1,100-per-year base pay, with uniforms to be bought and maintained by each officer. At the precincts, the sanitary conditions were exceptionally distasteful. It was reported that even Governor Coolidge had commented on overcrowded station houses where men had to sleep two to a bed and share the same locker. In addition, when Prohibition became the law, the normal perks from Saloon keepers had suddenly been wiped out. The police, meanwhile, cited other departments where salaries and conditions were remarkably better. And then, since they made no progress with Commissioner Curtis, they went so far as to request a charter from the national A F of L—exactly as other police departments had done, as well as Boston firemen and other civil servants.

To the policemen, Commissioner Curtis was, by reputation, an extremely difficult man. His predecessor, Stephen O'Meara, had left a proud, highly efficient, graft-free organization of loyal, if underpaid, men. Curtis, a pompous martinet, was not inclined to perpetuate such useful traditions. Nor did his appointment appear to be any more than a sop to his diminished ego.

Predictably, then, he chose to ignore the actions of his men, allowing their grievances to fester through the long hot summer. In August, in the face of an oncoming crisis, he left for vacation. Not until the men voted to sign up with the AFL, and the charter was validated, did he confront them with his edict: "No members of the force shall join or belong to any organization, club or body outside the department," thus himself violating a Massachusetts law "by compelling a person *not* to become a member of a labor organization." According to Curtis's order, a policeman could not even be a member of the Methodist Church.

The AFL connection represented the danger, posing a problem as to how the police might act when detailed to maintain law and order at the scene of a strike. If the strikers were AFL brothers, for example, would the police not refrain from bashing heads? Would that not rob them of their official "impartiality"? To Boston's conservative press, such was the consensus: "Impartiality" was equated with strikebreaking.

To the Boston police, the AFL meant only support for a redress of grievances. And immediately, the Boston Council of Labor indicated its solidarity, welcoming the police into the four-million-member-strong national brotherhood.

His authority thus threatened, Commissioner Curtis took action. On August twenty-sixth, he held trial for nineteen police officers (seventeen union leaders plus two others wrongly accused on evidence of a stool pigeon) whom he accused of organizing the union in breach of his edict. The commissioner, however, came to no stated conclusion. He would render a decision at a later date, preferring to see which way the political winds would blow.

Enter the second leg of the tripod, the mayor of Boston, Andrew J. Peters, a Democrat whose party affiliations belied his Puritan New England heritage and his inherited wealth. As a politician, he was far more intrigued by the social blessings of his Harvard College and Law School education than by any sense of responsibility to his function. He belonged to all the right clubs and hobnobbed with the elite crowd while the old bagmen and grafters took over City Hall, openly rifling the city treasury. As Francis Russell wrote in *A City in Terror,* "Under the rule of [former mayor] Honey Fitz contractors had had a habit of charging the city for each side of a granite paving block. Under Peters, they sold the foundations of City Hall. His administration became the most graft-ridden in Boston's graft-ridden history."

Peters was a nervous man with a high-pitched voice and a recently acquired penchant for glad-handing. He lacked depth and resolution, and worked harder to please than to resolve problems. He was also something of a pervert. Though allegedly a happily married family man, he developed an overweening passion for an eleven-year-old girl named Starr Wynan, whom he finally managed to seduce by administering ether—a process she found addicting, as she later revealed in memoirs, much to the mayor's joy.

As with Governor Coolidge, the problems of the police department were being dumped on Peters. Unlike the governor, however, he found it best to deal with them. Sensing the potential of political controversy that would certainly reflect on his administration, he jumped directly into the breach with the obligatory option: the appointment of a citizens' advisory committee. Thirty-four Bostonians were to find a way out of the oncoming dilemma. For all the mixed-bag quality of its membership, the committee was not without class and political bias, certainly not in favor of the policemen's union. Nor did the mayor proceed without first obtaining the commissioner's approval. And so they met, mostly substantial, well-connected businessmen with a chairman, James J. Storrow, who had already publicly declared his opposition to the union affiliation with the AFL. And, as it was agreed, no decision was to be arrived at without friendly conference with the commissioner himself.

Meanwhile, Commissioner Curtis found important personal counsel, one Herbert Parker, corporation lawyer, former Massachusetts attorney general, currently allied with such lofty corporate power as the beef trusts, Standard Oil and U.S. Steel. Parker's political preferences were decidedly conservative. He actively opposed such democratic processes as referendum and recall, favored such restrictive legislation as the "Secret Police" bill (rejected) and an anti-anarchy bill (passed). Parker was, in fact, so prejudiced in favor of corporate power, the Boston Chamber of Commerce sent a special delegation to Curtis advising him to change counsel. On Parker's advice, then, Commissioner Curtis announced he would render his decision on the nineteen policemen on September fourth, ten days after he had tried them. On September third, the Storrow Committee sent a letter to Curtis requesting postponement—which letter was intercepted and read by attorney Parker, who saw fit *not* to show it to the commissioner.

Enter now the third leading figure in the drama, our hero, Governor Calvin Coolidge, who was quite positively even more Republican than Republicans are wont to be. Having returned from his summer vacation, he was immediately appealed to by the Storrow Committee on the fateful evening of September third. Would not the governor serve as intermediary in the pending crisis? Coolidge refused, claiming it was not his duty to make any communication with Commissioner Curtis in this matter.

Only a letter from Mayor Peters restrained the commissioner: his decision on the nineteen would be postponed for four days, until Monday, September eighth. Meanwhile, the Storrow Committee completed its work, reporting a plan acceptable to its members and the counsel for the policemen's union. The union was to surrender its charter with the AFL, and the nineteen organizers would be protected from punishment or dismissal. Arbitrators would be called to consider the policemen's grievances and wage demands. All that was necessary, then, was the commissioner's agreement. This plan was submitted to Commissioner Curtis on Sunday morning, September seventh, the day before his announced decision was scheduled. (It was also submitted to the newspapers, who editorialized almost unanimous approval.) It was also the wish of the committee that Governor Coolidge be consulted and a special Sunday conference was requested to avoid a crisis.

The governor, however, chose to be out of town that weekend. So, indeed, did the commissioner. The two endorsements of the Storrow Committee's plan necessary to stay the crisis were nowhere to be found. Coolidge, it seemed, had left a full day before, guardedly not revealing to reporters where he would be. Only his secretary, the state adjutant general and the attorney general knew. Coolidge had in fact driven to Northampton, remaining overnight Sunday in advance of a speaking commitment before the state convention of the AFL itself! (It was not known if Coolidge appreciated the macabre nature of the ironies collecting here. It *was* known, however, that he made no mention in his speech of the union troubles he was there to evade.)

On Monday, September 8, Police Commissioner Curtis returned to declare himself. He rejected the Storrow Committee recommendations and summarily dismissed the nineteen policemen from the force. Immediately, the policemen's union met, their Irish tempers at a boil, and in an amazing show of solidarity, voted 1,134 to two to strike at evening roll call, 5:45, on the following day, Tuesday, September 9. It was, then, a walkout without selfish motives, without a call for wage increases or improved working conditions, but solidly out of concern for their dismissed colleagues who had done only what they themselves had endorsed.

The fat was finally in the fire. Too late, Governor Coolidge returned to Boston and much too late, he finally agreed to join in conference with all of the principals—*except* the police and their attorneys. Commissioner Curtis advised his friend the governor that there would be no strike, for the policemen would not dare to walk out, whatever their vote indicated. Mayor Peters, however, assured the governor that they would. He begged Coolidge to prevent the strike by letting the suspended nineteen return to their jobs. Behind him stood the distinguished members of the committee, the newspapers of the city, the merchants and businessmen, the majority of the people. To the waiting reporters, came this official statement: "Governor Coolidge has taken under advisement what action he can take." How to translate that? In a casual repartee with reporters, he waffled masterfully: "Understand that I do not approve of any strike. But can you blame the police for feeling as they do when they get less than a streetcar conductor?" Was it ignorance that bid Coolidge to blame the strike on money when it wasn't so intended at all? Or was it guile? William A. White wrote: "Smart as chain lightning was the gaunt little Vermonter," then reported how Coolidge confessed to a friend that he had no intention of either pressuring Commissioner Curtis to change his position or interceding in any way. Nor did the governor respond to the mayor's desperate plea to have state troops ready to patrol the streets of Boston at the hour of anticipated walkout. In point of fact, Coolidge did absolutely nothing but remain solidly behind Commissioner Curtis, fellow Republican, patriotic maven of law and order.

Meanwhile, the newspapers spread the words of panic. The same editorial pages that had decried unionization and then endorsed compromise now cried Bolshevism. They declared any such strike was doomed to failure because "behind Boston in this skirmish with Bolshevism stands Massachusetts, and behind Massachusetts stands America." To the *Boston Herald,* it was the more shameful that Bolshevism should appear in the very city that had given the American Revolution its birth. There was even the greater fear of a general strike, that ultimate manifestation of Bolshevism. One policeman laid bare the utter preposterousness of the accompanying hysteria by asking, "What's a Bolshevik?"

As in Seattle six month before, and dozens of cities on July fourth, indeed like all Red-Scared Americans everywhere, the good people of Boston took frantic steps to protect themselves and safeguard their homes. All manner of weaponry was suddenly at a premium. Banks and businesses hired security guards. A volunteer police force was organized. The president of Harvard University, Abbott Lowell, assured the students that their contribution to the public welfare as deputy policemen would not damage their collegiate status. Ex-soldiers and sailors showed up in the numbers. Policemen on strike became fair game.

Said Commissioner Curtis on the eve of the anticipated walkout: "I am ready for anything!" He was, in fact, ready for nothing. As if by design, no plans had been made, no organization of emergency forces was activated. He kept insisting that his men would not dare to strike against the public. No patriot would even consider doing such a thing. And the governor, who knew better, threw the weight of his office with the commissioner, opting to put the burden of responsibility for the welfare of the Bostonians on the Democratic mayor, calling attention to the fact that the mayor had sufficient authority to get the help he needed from the military stationed in the city. "The mayor should exhaust all agencies at his hand before appealing to me for assistance," Coolidge said.

At 5:45 P.M. on the appointed day, the policemen went out.

What happened that night was glowingly described by White:

"...The mob rose. The forces of civilization weakened. The devil was loose in Boston.... Little knots of boys and young men began wandering through the streets. The old policemen were gone. Groups joined groups, at first hilarious, but acutely realizing that no one would bother them. Under the street lamps, scores of crap games began to operate on the Common.

... It was evident that the new police were not interested in crap games. This emboldened the gamblers. The mob grew noisy, also offensive. Its voice changed from a mumble to a high-keyed nervous falsetto. Sporadically, little mobs broke apart and gravitated toward the larger mob instinctively.... By midnight, the coagulating crowds had formed one raging mob, a drunken, noisy, irresponsible mob, without grievance, without objective; an aimless idiot mad with its own sense of unrestrained power. Someone threw a loose paving stone through a store window about one o'clock. The tension snapped. The mob was crystalized. It found its courage. Its desire took hazy form—loot! Sticks and bricks went whizzing into offices on second and third floors. By two o'clock, looting had begun."

So it was that damage was done, property stolen, fruit stands overturned, citizens molested (hats were knocked off passersby), volunteer police jeered and pelted with mud. It wasn't until morning that the mayor, acting under a law that empowered him to call out the guard only after rioting had begun, did so, and order was established.

The immediate, and most volatile, result was to blame the police and their union. The newspapers could hardly restrain their revulsion. Prominent citizens were quoted, branding the striking police as "deserters," "agents of Lenin," "Bolsheviks," all the while grossly exaggerating the lawlessness to indicate a continuing cause for panic. As they had with the Seattle general strike, the national press jumped on the story, responding with preposterous tales that the entire city was in the hands of a Bolshevik mob. "Worse than on Nevsky Prospect, Petrograd," "A Bolshevik nightmare." No matter that the police had not struck for money but out of loyalty, not one newspaper reported that fact, or that the action was less a police walkout than a commissioner's lockout. Such matters of fact were irrelevant to the greater scheme of things in this year of the lie.

And through it all, Calvin Coolidge continued to do nothing—to bide his time, as it were, watchfully waiting, totally incommunicado. If little else, he was, as William A. White had written, a master of timing. Even as a firemens' strike in sympathy was declared in the offing, when the streetcar union made noises about joining them, when there was talk of a revival of the telephone strike, Coolidge said nothing. All this menace was developing on Wednesday along with more threatening mobs at night and greater potential chaos. Coolidge refused to take a stand.

When he awoke on Thursday morning, he was greeted by headlines from the conservative *Boston Herald,* his favorite newspaper. "RIOTS AND BLOODSHED IN CITY AS STATE GUARD QUELLS MOB." The story described another night of disorder, finally suppressed by gunfire, leaving two dead and nine wounded, the crowd scattered by a cavalry charge with drawn sabres. "The city is not under martial law," the story went on. "Mayor Peters is in control of the entire machinery of law enforcement." Not the commissioner of police, but the mayor.

Included was a report on the death of one, a man named Geist, shot by a state guardsman. It appeared that Geist had been in an argument with a soldier during which he was first seen pushing or tugging the soldier's rifle, then running across Tremont Street to the Common. Here, another soldier took aim and shot him clear through the back, the bullet finally lodging in the knee of an elderly woman who happened to be passing by.

What was not reported, however, was the feeling among those present that the unarmed Geist could have been easily captured by the dozens of guardsmen in the area, at which considerable indignation was provoked at such an unnecessary killing. Then, on the following day, it was revealed that "socialistic and anarchistic literature had been found in the possession of Geist," as duly reported in the daily press. Immediately, all indignation quickly dissolved. Everything, then, was satisfactorily explained, the shooting thereby justified, the entire episode put to rest. No complaint would be made against the guardsman, and no one would complain about that either.

(With hindsight, what fascinates was the entire postshooting scenario. Geist was not accused of radicalism until *after* he was dead. Red papers were not found on him to cause the shooting. Apparently, the legal—and psychic—process had reached a whole new level: any punitive action could now be justified by calling the victim a Red even though he be so labeled after the action. It did not matter whether he was, indeed, a Red: suffice that he be *called* a Red for the perpetrator to be exonerated. The Red had become a person of distinct legal inferiority. He could no longer walk the streets, carry flags, read or write what he chose, possess books or journals of his choosing, maintain the privacy of his home or speak words except at the sufferance of others. He had no right to leave his work or, in other instances, to be hired. He had lost the right to charge others with offenses against known laws, for his Redness disqualified his testimony.)

It would later be known, but only to a few, that Geist actually had no radical affiliations, nor any socialist literature on his person, nor had he entertained any interest in such matters. He was, in point of fact, an honorably discharged veteran, a volunteer at that, in the American Expeditionary Forces, recently returned from France.

On that Thursday morning, however, Calvin Coolidge was at his best in typical silence. Then he received a communication from Washington in which his old political mentor, Senator Murray Crane, indicated his distress with the news as he'd read it. By one o'clock, the senator's vicegerent, William M. Butler, a prominent Bostonian textile manufacturer, was lunching with Coolidge and Commissioner Curtis's lawyer, Herbert Parker. Here Coolidge sat quietly, prepared to do what he was trained to do: wait for instructions. Now he was told to take over the entire situation by calling out the militia and declaring the implementation of the state power.

Back in his office, Coolidge issued a special order restoring Commissioner Curtis to his authorized power, thus discrediting the strike and the resulting chaos. He called for all citizens to assist the state in preserving order and directed all police officers to obey their commissioner. Then he called out the National Guard to secure the city from further disturbances.

Meanwhile, the entire nation was responding to the very concept of a strike by policemen. To many, it was made to seem like the next step in the sequence that began in Seattle and evolved into bombs. Senator Henry Myers of Montana, a classically antiradical spokesman, warned that unless proper action was taken, "the nation will see a Soviet government set up within two years." Newspapers fed on such wild talk. Woodrow Wilson himself, on his westward train tour for the League of Nations, stopped to comment that what the Boston police had done was a "crime against civilization."

Samuel Gompers, having returned from an international labor conference in Europe, saw the blunder of the Boston police and urged them to return to their posts in anticipation of mediation. When the policemen voted unanimously to do so, realizing that they had made a serious error in judgment, Coolidge was informed in anticipation of immediate arbitration. Curtis, however, again refused to comply. And again Coolidge backed him. "The action of the police in leaving their posts is not a strike, it is desertion," he told the press. "There is nothing to arbitrate, nothing to compromise." Gompers telegrammed the mayor and the governor, critical of the commissioner's intransigence, requesting reinstatement and arbitration "to honorably adjust a mutually unsatisfactory situation." At this point, Coolidge made the statement that would change the course of history. He wired Gompers in reply, releasing the contents to the press: "Your assertion that the commissioner was wrong cannot justify the wrong of leaving the city unguarded. . . . There is no right to strike against the public safety by anybody, anywhere, at any time." And because of these words, suddenly Calvin Coolidge became famous through the land.

Even Ole Hanson had never said it better.

So it was that this mediocre politician with no history of any distinction whatsoever, a relatively spineless man lacking in creative drive, a dull, pedestrian, uninspired yes-man became a hero. Newspapers made him so. Seventy thousand letters and telegrams poured into the state capitol from all over the country. Coolidge's picture made the front page of a thousand daily papers. Editorials extolled his courage and his leadership. Calvin Coolidge was our savior. This, apparently, was what the people of America needed, a symbol for reassurance that the drift toward anarchy and Bolshevism was being stopped. Americans could breathe more easily with a man like Calvin Coolidge in control. "At last a universal issue was defined," one commentator declared. "Either you stand for public safety or you stand against it." That Coolidge had stood as a coward, cringing silently in fear of commitment, that the entire affair was preventable through any simple decisive action on his part, that he had instead actually fled town rather than face what had to be his responsibility was either unknown at the time or irrelevant to the creation of a hero, nor was it properly attributed to his history, even with hindsight.

It was just another lie of the Red Scare.

When the final version of the Storrow Committee report was released, many of the governor's above-mentioned deficiencies were suggested. ("By Thursday morning order had been generally restored in the city. On Thursday afternoon, the governor assumed control of the situation.")

By such ludicrous contradictions are United States presidents made.

Like Ole Hanson, another creature of the Red Scare was born. As in Seattle, the strike was quickly over. The entire striking police force, not just the nineteen, was summarily dismissed. The union, such as it was, or wasn't, was crushed. As if to crown the bad joke, their replacements were quickly granted the higher wages and improved conditions that were the root cause of the entire disaster. Because of the Red Scare, the unions of the Central Labor Council did not strike in sympathy. The victory of the conservative anti-union forces was so complete, so overwhelming, a fund of $500,000 was raised among appreciative citizens to compensate members of the state guard for preventing further rioting—and to help the few loyal policemen who had not joined the strike.

Those who had, over a thousand of them, suffered the consequences of their dismissal and were left to shift for themselves under a blacklisting cloud. Prospective employers saw them as pariahs. William A. White claimed that Coolidge tried to help a number of them get jobs, a demonstration of his noble spirit. Failing, the policemen actually brought suit for reinstatement, but the Massachusetts Supreme Court upheld the decisions of the police commissioner.

The Boston Police Strike was of importance primarily for what it symbolized. A nonentity was catapulted into the White House because of it; another strike was made to escalate into a show of Red-baiting and Bolshevik hysteria; another union was crushed under the wheels. There were some inside informants who went further in questioning the way the chips fell, the better to explain the subsequent mayhem: a conspiracy, they believed, though not altogether planned and executed as such, was part of the national employers' larger effort to destroy the power of organized labor, actually encouraging a policemen's strike that would have to be the most unpopular of any that unions could undertake. A police commissioner created all the necessary ingredients while under the advice and counsel of his highly placed corporate attorney. A governor hid and waffled in support of these machinations, compliantly implementing the entire program. Above all, the police were exploited at their jobs, then doubly exploited when they protested, driven by the combined power of the state to their destruction. Thus, the result was another notch in the battle over organized labor.

4. The Rolling Snowball or How the Closed Mind Brought on the Open Shop

I congratulate you on your election as a victory for law and order. When that is the issue, all Americans stand together.

—Telegram from President Woodrow Wilson
to Governor Calvin Coolidge

There was little in America that remained untouched by the run of the Red Menace. In sophisticated urban centers where tastes and trends originated, "radicalism" was an inescapable topic of conversation, since many middle-class people were labeled Parlor Pinks. According to the Justice Department, there were between four and five million Red sympathizers and supporters. Many were distinguished political figures such as Senators George Norris and Robert La Follette. Even Woodrow Wilson was often referred to as a suspected pinko as were celebrated writers such as Theodore Dreiser and Walter Lippmann, movie star Charlie Chaplin, the great lawyer, Clarence Darrow. Reputations were forever subject to the slash of red paint, a warning to others who might wish to emulate them in this self-perpetuating war. It was a year of easy labeling. Nothing more subversive than a sympathetic word to a poor man was enough to create suspicion. Any dissent from a given norm was cause for accusation. Every profession suffered these indignities. Insinuation, character assassination, smears became extremely effective in stifling debate and creating a bland all-American conformity.

172

   The Red Scarers went after the schools with the same intensity
they went after unions. Patriotic journals such as the *Manufacturers
Record* and the *National Civic Federation Review* cried out at the
threat of Bolshevism spreading through the school system. A number of great colleges and universities were referred to as "hotbeds
of Bolshevism," a particularly erotic combination of words. Celebrated educators were denounced as Reds: John Dewey, James
Harvey Robinson, Felix Frankfurter, Zechariah Chafee, Jr. Such
professors were all over the country—but mostly in the Northeast.
   The attack on public schools was relentless, for what could
be more insidious than the poisoning of a child's mind? The class-
room was a shrine for patriotic devotion, and nothing less was to
be tolerated. In Baltimore, a teacher lost her job for comparing
the philosophy of Bolshevism with that of democracy. In Cam-
bridge, a Radcliffe teacher was fired for having been a member
of the Liberal Club, which saw fit merely to study Bolshevism. In
New York City, the superintendent of schools rooted out any
teacher whose personal convictions failed to be in accord with 100
percent patriots. A Brooklyn high school teacher, Benjamin Glassberg, who dared to quote Lenin and Trotsky as to their innocence
of ties with Germany, was obviously doomed to suspension. (In a
telling moment of his interrogation by a committee investigating
radicalism, Glassberg was asked, "Do you believe in the economic
interpretation of history?" as the inquisitor flashed a triumphant
grin like a prosecutor about to catch a defendant with smoking
gun in hand. In his classes, Glassberg had quoted Daniel Webster
on this very subject: "It seems to me plain that in the absence of
military force, political power naturally and necessarily goes into
the hands which hold the property." Glassberg had apparently
made the mistake of reading the fathers of the American republic
instead of simply praising them.)
   It was fitting, then, that when New York City high school
students were tested as to their reactions and attitudes toward the
Russian Revolution, they were also asked to include the name of
their teacher in the answer. It was also fitting that the board of
education would then withhold diplomas from all public school
children who did not sign a pledge agreeing that when they
reached adulthood they would "respect" the president of the
United States, and "oppose all revolutionary movements such as

Bolshevism, anarchism, IWWism or any movement antagonistic to the laws of the United States or tending to subvert the Constitution." It was left to future educators to interpret the phrase "or any movement."

In the course of this witch hunt, *Literary Digest Magazine* revealed that the income of public school teachers was among the lowest of all American professionals. A teacher of farm children was found to be paid less than a farmer paid a hired hand to swill his hogs. An Illinois coal miner's average income was four times that of the teacher who taught his children. In the city of New York, the majority of its 23,000 teachers (mostly women) received salaries from $900 a year, barely half of what the War Trade Board had estimated to be the cost of "minimum comfort" for a family of five. To the Red Scarers, this was made to appear as proof of Bolshevism in the school, for who else would submit to such economic deprivation but radicals? Wasn't poor pay the primary cause for protest? The implications of this circuitous thinking seemed not to bother them.

Then came the clergy. If the church, like the schools, had long been bastions of patriotic dogma as well as ardent supporters of the status quo on all controversial fronts, there were always a few who found reason for dissent. The Red Scarers attacked all religions: Dr. Harry F. Ward of the Union Theological Seminary, Reverend S. Parks Cadman of the Federal Council of Churches, Rabbi Stephen Wise. Religious radicalism was denounced as another part of the great conspiracy to foment revolution. In countless communities, the pressure on clergymen to suppress any such tendencies was decisive. Americans were of a mind only to seek comfort and conformity, not challenge and criticism. With few exceptions, organized religion submitted to the temper of the times.

Like a giant snowball rolling down a mountain, the Red Scare created an avalanche of thundering 100 percent Americanism that tolerated no equivocation or dissent.

Congress, meanwhile, was pushing the snowball. The Graham-Sterling Bill, one of seventy sedition bills introduced in 1919, asked for twenty years' imprisonment and/or $60,000 in fines for anyone who sought to overthrow the federal government, or prevent or delay the execution of federal law, or harm or terrorize any officer or employee. The Senate version was even more repressive.

Victor Berger, a stalwart among moderate Socialists, was duly elected to Congress from Wisconsin, but was unseated by the House of Representatives with only one dissenting vote. In the debate he was labeled "Hun...Dutchman...UnAmerican... Traitor...Bolshevik." In the subsequent election to fill the vacant seat, Berger was reelected...then unseated again, 330 to six.

In New York, three Socialists were elected to the state assembly but, as with Berger, were expelled 116 to twenty-eight. The *New York Times* extolled this: "It was an American vote, a patriotic and conservative vote. An immense majority of the American people would approve." Then, as with Berger, they too were expelled, then reelected—and again expelled, thus disenfranchising an entire electoral district of New York City. The state assembly then legislated the illegality of the Socialist Party, thus barring its candidates from the ballot. It then instigated the loyalty oath for teachers, thus insuring that the educational process be made secure against all dissent. So it was that New York, the most enlightened state in the union, the heart of the so-called melting pot of ideas and political thought, the seat of culture, came to represent the most degenerating forces it was celebrated for resisting. By denying the right of radicals to hold office, its legislature condemned them to a choice between revolution and impotence, thus destroying the essence of the democratic process and rendering the system worthless. The state established rules for autocracy that demanded the total compliance of its electorate, then preached a defense of democracy as a reason for violating democratic principles. That the legislature succeeded in getting away with such violations was rooted in the alleged threats of force and violence, those awesome bugaboos of the witch-hunt. The established order actually feared such methods so little—and were so ready to use them—that they did, in effect, instigate violence whenever possible, the better to bring about its suppression.

In Massachusetts, Coolidge was reelected governor by an overwhelming plurality of 125,000. For the first time in history, a Massachusetts gubernatorial election was national news. "WHOLE NATION HAILS MASSACHUSETTS." "A DEFEAT

FOR THE SOVIETS," headlined the *New York Times*. "MASSA-
CHUSETTS—GOD BLESS HER—AGAIN AND AGAIN!"

The president, meanwhile, suffered his illness in the White
House, incommunicado to all but a few intimates. When informed
of these events, he reacted with benign indifference. Whatever
he felt about such obviously high-handed violations of civil liberty,
he issued no statements to curtail them, thereby showing more
contempt for radicals than fealty to the First Amendment. Executive preferences can often be demonstrated as much by silence
as by action. Besides, had not Justice Oliver Wendell Holmes so
advocated in the event of "a clear and present danger"? In the
end, Wilson actively endorsed his attorney general's dedication to
the security of America, even supporting the new antisedition
legislation. Had he not also claimed that opponents of the League
of Nations were Bolshevik?

Through all this madness and mayhem, through all the bom-
bast and bluster, the sounds and the furies, one significant and
lasting issue lay at the heart of the battle: the open shop, a euphemism for the destruction of unions and the organized power
of working people. To the elite of the industrial world, this was
all that really mattered. If the Russian Revolution had never happened . . . if there were no such thing as Bolshevism . . . the war
against closed-shop unionism would have been just as virulent.
To paraphrase Voltaire, if Bolshevism did not exist, it would have
been necessary to invent it. The Red Scare of 1919 had many
psychic causes that flourished in postwar unrest, but the witches
to be burned had a union label on their brooms. The rest was
chimera.

The closed-shop union, then, was the real Bolshevism. That
was the main message and the Red Scarers hit it hard. Employers
combined in groups to counter labor councils of local unions,
which, in turn, had formed to counter entrenched employer
power over the community. In one industry after another, wherever and whenever possible, union demands for wage increases
in the face of skyrocketing costs of living were denied. Many
employers refused even to negotiate, deliberately provoking
strikes by denying the very existence of the union. And when the
strike was called, employers labeled it Bolshevik, and with their

power over the press, convinced the community that it was so. There were always enough radicals, socialists, aliens, Wobblies around to make the wildest claims believable. Anything to distract from the real issues was fair game. Don't consider the workers' grievances, they're Reds. Their union is a Bolshevik institution, their strike is part of a plot to sovietize the country. Destroy the union and save America. Only the open shop is basic to 100 percent Americanism, where a man is free to work as he chooses, unchained by the dictates of radical union leaders.

By the summer of 1919, this campaign was openly, declaratively, stridently in operation. Such employer organizations as the National Metal Trades Association, the National Founders Association and the National Association of Manufacturers had long since dedicated themselves to this function. Periodical journals, books, news releases were widely distributed, openly dedicated to the open shop. Their executives became directors of patriotic societies, interlocking in ever-expanding forces to spread the word. With almost unlimited funds to back them, they could spread it well. Publications such as the *Iron Trade Review,* the *Manufacturers Record* and the *Open Shop Review* were typical, flooding the industrial community with anti-union dogma. The more organized labor acted in defiance, the stronger became the resistance. Daily newspapers fed the flames, reprinting open shop arguments, equating unions with Bolsheviks, strikes with revolution. Distinguished clergymen went along with this conception of industrial relations and the defense of the open shop's godliness. Was not Bolshevism akin to atheism? Even the Bible was used to prove that the closed shop was unchristian and unpatriotic. Ex-president William Howard Taft repeatedly declared that closed-shop unionism was really "embracing soviet methods."

So it was that the open shop came to be known as the "American Plan," thus challenging the patriotism of all unionism. The closed shop was a violation of the individual's right to free choice. And if the workers themselves were not sufficiently patriotic to see this (primarily, no doubt, because of the intimidation of their radical leaders), they must be saved from themselves. This was management's function, to save the workers' freedom by crushing the unions.

The American Bankers Association (23,000 tightly organized

financiers) proclaimed the workers' right to work out their own solutions without being forced into any organization.

The National Grange defended the right of any individual "to work where his industry is needed at any time and at any wage which is satisfactory to him."

The Indiana Manufacturers Association: "We will not employ an individual . . . who does not sign an individual contract [agreeing that] he is not and will not become a member of a labor organization while in our employ." Thus began a new age of the Yellow Dog Contract.

United States Steel refused to sell steel to any contractor who hired union labor.

The National Open Shop Association offered spies and strikebreakers to suppress any attempt at militant unionizing.

By the fall of 1919, America was ready for Judge Elbert Gary, chairman of the board of U.S. Steel.

5. THE TRASHING OF THE STEEL STRIKE OR HOW THE HUNKY LEARNED THE TRUTH ABOUT THE AMERICAN DREAM

We are not obliged to contract with unions if we do not choose to do so.

—ELBERT H. GARY

Elbert H. Gary was known as a devout Methodist, a pillar of the church, a moralist and teetotaler. Without question, he was a handsome man of impeccable style and taste and unassailable dignity. As a young man, he was an outstanding corporation lawyer in his native Illinois, then made his reputation as a stalwart defender of law and order when a judge, having presided at the trial of the Haymarket bombers in 1886. Here, Judge Gary sentenced seven anarchists to death and one to the penitentiary although none had anything whatsoever to do with the actual bombing, finding, "The conviction proceeds [solely] on the ground that they had generally by speech and print advised large classes to commit murder." The defendants, then, were put to death as a consequence of their "advice, in pursuance of that advice, and influenced by that advice somebody, not known, did throw the bomb that caused the death." This extraordinary decision of guilt by words gained him the admiration of all patriots, not the least of whom was J. P. Morgan. To bring order to the steel industry, he made Judge Gary chairman of the board of directors of the newly created United States Steel Corporation.

The judge became the first salaried executive in America to make $100,000 a year, which led H. L. Mencken to call him the "Christian Hired Man."

To J. P. Morgan, Gary was worth every dollar of it. The United States Steel Corporation was the largest in America, an empire, a state within a state. It controlled over 60 percent of the nation's greatest industry. Its very name symbolized the enormity of its power. In the world of business, large and small, it was looked up to as the last bastion of unbridled capitalism.

Judge Gary boasted of a benevolent philosophy toward his hundreds of thousands of employees, having instigated what he called "a community of interest" between employers and workers through profit-sharing plans, company loans to loyal workers, bonuses for long and faithful service. In January 1919, he declared that management must "make the Steel Corporation a good place for [workers] to work and live. Don't let families go hungry or cold; give them playgrounds and parks and schools and churches, pure water to drink, every opportunity to keep clean ... to enjoy rest and recreation."

At the same time, his company was forcing over three hundred thousand unskilled workers to work twelve hours a day, seven days a week, at an annual pay of $1,466, considerably below the poverty level for a family of five. It was, apparently, more Christian to keep business costs low than to allow a majority of his workers the opportunity to attend church. How he reconciled that with "rest and recreation" was not known.

He was also irreconcilably against unions. He believed that his employees did not need any other benefits than those he chose to bestow upon them. Enlightened, benevolent management alone knew what was best for them. In his experience, any recognition or negotiation with a union was a concession to the devil himself.

On the other side of the tracks was a man less prepossessing but possessed with equal determination. William Z. Foster was born into a family of Massachusetts Yankees. To his heritage of shrewdness and practicality, he added an intellectual idealism. He lived his boyhood years in the slums of Philadelphia, surrounded by poverty and filth, where he learned the necessities of organization and agitation. He was only thirteen when he became in-

volved in his first strike, that of streetcar workers. He became a
sailor, worked stateside in fertilizing plants, construction, mining,
lumber mills and then, for a longer stretch, on the railroads.
Through all his experiences, he saw the gross inequities suffered
by workingmen. As a result, he joined up with the IWW while
working in the West, but found its theories and practices im-
practical. He also dabbled in socialism. During the war, however,
he did patriotic service as an organizer for Liberty Bond drives.
He was one of the better Four-Minute Men under George Creel's
CPI. By the war's end, Foster had abandoned all syndicalist ideas
and concentrated on what he called "pure and simple trade unionism." He saw life as it was. To accomplish results, one had to use
the tools that existed in society, to work for reasonable goals with
appropriate methods. This was not "boring from within," as his
critics would later refer to his methods, but practical organizing.
For years, he worked hard to get IWW leaders to adopt his approach and rejoin the trade union movement. He believed in social
progress through the evolution of progressive forces. His was not
a doctrine of compromise or intrigue but the creation of industrial
unions by the massive organization of the unorganized. By 1919,
he was highly regarded by trade union men throughout the country, even such conservatives as Samuel Gompers himself.

In the autumn of 1919, Judge Gary and Bill Foster would
lead America into the most titanic battle of the year. Never would
the lines of power be so clearly drawn, the struggle between capital
and labor so bluntly defined.

The National Committee for Organizing Iron and Steel
Workers had been formed, with Samuel Gompers as honorary
chairman, John Fitzpatrick as acting chairman and William Foster,
the secretary-treasurer. Its function was to make big steel a union
industry. It was tantamount to a declaration of war.

To organize steel workers in Pennsylvania mill towns, for
example, was like running a patrol behind enemy lines. Local
police and company thugs would meet incoming trains and lean
on all suspects in no uncertain terms. To hire a meeting hall was
often impossible. Open-air meetings were broken up by club-
wielding mounted police, "Black Cossacks," they were called. Permits for parades were seldom granted and no flags, Red or Amer-

ican, or marching bands allowed. Ministers and newspaper editors would denounce their missions. If a gathering was secretly arranged, there were always spies to give names to company officials, and those attending were summarily fired. When Rabbi Stephen Wise from New York offered to come to Duquesne, Pennsylvania, to speak on behalf of the union, the mayor refused to allow it: "Jesus Christ himself could not speak in Duquesne for the A.F. of L." When a union-organizing meeting was called in Bethlehem, the police chief told the owner of the hall to cancel the contract, return the deposit and keep the agitators out. The union organizers appealed to the mayor, but the mayor backed the police chief: he was, after all, a vice president in the steel company. The newspapers who reported the refusal made no mention of that.

Foster defied all this with a "Flying Squadron" of eight militant organizers whose incredible success indicated the enormity of the popular will. For all the threats and oppression, over one hundred thousand joined the drive by midsummer, most of whom were uneducated immigrants representing all the countries of Europe. They were living in wretched company-owned shacks without plumbing, beholden to the company for all purchases and services. As the legendary eighty-nine-year-old Mother Jones (Mary Harris) told them in Homestead, Pennsylvania, "We are going to see whether Pennsylvania belongs to Kaiser Gary or Uncle Sam. . . . Our kaisers smoke seventy-five-cent cigars and have lackeys with knee pants bring them champagne while you starve, while you grow old at forty. . . . If Gary wants to work twelve hours a day, let him go in the blooming mill and work. What *we* need is a little leisure, time for music, playgrounds, a decent home, books and the things that make life worth living."

One man in the audience cried out: "I been in America twenty-five years; no get chance to learn English yet!" A life of struggle was thus capsulized in one pathetic flash. And when the police broke up the meeting and marched Mother Jones off to jail, the crowd followed her, gathering outside the jail with sufficient menace that the sheriff thought better about holding her.

In Homestead, Lackawanna, Youngstown, Wheeling, Johnstown, Cleveland, Milwaukee and even Gary (a city named after the judge himself), the Flying Squadron persisted in spreading the word.

It would seem to have been an impossible mission. The steel companies owned not only the mills but the towns in which the workers lived, their stores, homes, churches. They ran the schools, the courts, the police departments. They controlled the newspapers, the legislatures. They bought spies and informers to infiltrate the workers' lives; the Pinkertons were worse than police. They insisted on Yellow Dog Contracts to create a legal enslavement to the open shop. Their control was as tyrannical as that of the tsars; it was logical, then, that any attempts at protest would be labeled Bolshevik—one of the more cutting ironies of the Red Scare.

Meanwhile, the company played its paternal role, preaching loyalty for its benefits, forever setting one class of workers against another. The skilled were mostly American stock who made more than twice that of the unskilled, the latter immigrant Poles, Croats, Serbs, Slovaks, Hungarians, Italians, a polyglot force that made up two-thirds of steel's employees. These were the "Hunkies," as Americans called them, the theory being that no decent American would have anything to do with them, that the workers had their class divisions the same as other people. So, indeed, were they instructed in Sunday sermons, in the press, in the very mores of American life. Such social tensions helped link skilled workers to the company; since they were made to feel elite, the union would have little appeal.

The recent war had added tensions to this disparity. When the companies lost over 130,000 workers to the army (in itself a comment on the preferences of steel workers), and since immigration had been cut off, they brought blacks from southern states, five hundred thousand by the end of the war, to comprise 12 percent of the work force. (Judge Gary, alarmed at such shortages, had suggested it might even be necessary to import Asians.) Wartime turnover of labor in the steel industry had been extremely high, largely the result of the company's nonunion policy and its resistance to alleviating grievances. At a time of spiraling cost of living, wages had risen a bare 10 percent while United States Steel amassed over $300 million in profits in 1916 alone. By the end of the war, dividends for stockholders had risen three times higher than the increase in wages. All the while, strikes for a larger piece of the pie were beaten back by gunfire. Said Judge Gary: "There are agitators prowling about the mills . . . spreading German propaganda for the conversion of foreigners especially.... These IWW and socialist vermin, working under the guise of AFL organizers, teach that the war is bad. These strangers are liars and German propagandists, some of them probably in the Kaiser's pay." Four-Minute Men repeated this message linking union organizers with the Hun.

At the armistice, however, labor was prepared to make its stand: "If the war was waged for the destruction of autocracy, we demand...the elimination of industrial autocracy in this country." The War Industries Labor Board in Washington had given its authorization for the right to unionize. Immediately the National Committee for Organizing Iron and Steel Workers was formed. And so, it followed, the companies were organizing to fight them and huge sums of money were appropriated by the National Patriotic League under the auspices of J. P. Morgan, Du Pont and Rockefeller, and millions of dollars were raised to preserve the open shop. In defiance of the WILB order, the companies persisted in firing union men, some with over thirty-five years with their companies.

Note the following testimony before a congressional committee on industrial relations: Joseph Mayer of Homestead had joined the union on August 5, 1919 and was fired on August fifteenth.

Superintendent: "Somebody turned your name in."

Mayer: "What I do, rob company of couple of dollars?"

Superintendent: "I don't want union men to work for me."

The superintendent had asked him about a meeting Mayer had attended, wanting him to name names. Mayer was a United States citizen, married, a steel worker for fourteen years, but when he refused to talk, he was fired, then blacklisted in steel. He changed his name, moved and finally got a job elsewhere.

The repression was pervasive, but especially in the state of Pennsylvania. The entire city of Pittsburgh was closed to union organizers, a delegation of whom went to Washington to protest: "Does the United States Constitution apply to Pennsylvania?" The delegation was denied access to the White House, its protests pigeonholed in Congress, a dubious treatment of representatives of the organization their most worthy president lauded for its contribution to winning the war.

In Donora, permits to hold union meetings were granted only because workers organized boycotts of local stores.

More congressional testimony was illuminating:

Chairman: "What happened to the [proposed union] meeting?"

Superintendent: "Well, we simply prohibited it."

Chairman: "You denied a permit?"

Superintendent: "Yes."

Chairman: "The authorities prohibited the meeting?"

Superintendent: "On the ground that they [the union] said they were going to hold a meeting without having a permit."

For all the opposition, the organizing of steel workers became an unstoppable force. By the end of spring, the union grew to hundreds of thousands, but U.S. Steel refused to recognize it.

The crisis was inevitable. The workers' frustration inspired their militancy; promises of back pay, for instance, were broken, even though such pay was authorized by the War Industries Labor Board, and nothing was done to resolve the dispute. To the workers, the sacrifices in support of the war effort, the responses to patriotic appeals for higher production goals while the company executives became millionaires, added to their grievances. They did not need government statistics to tell them that prices had become far greater than whatever increases in wages they had won. Nor was the great Wilsonian promise of American democracy ever a small thing.

In May, the National Committee met in Pittsburgh. Union leaders came from Chicago, Birmingham, Youngstown, Bethlehem, all of them brimming with reports of defiant workers with a deep wellspring of rank-and-file resentment that was growing by the day. Never before had it been so blatant. Never had they sensed such anger. Workers were demanding better wages, shorter hours, better working conditions. Above all, they were demanding union recognition for collective bargaining. Even the skilled workers were getting on board.

Samuel Gompers finally wrote to Judge Gary, requesting that a meeting be arranged with the committee. Three weeks later, Gompers reported to Foster that there had been no reply. The union response was to redouble its organizing drive, and thousands more joined, in spite of the repressive forces of the police.

The public, sharing the workers' anger at Gary's intransigence, became increasingly sympathetic. When the union membership was polled, an astonishing 98 percent endorsed strike action if the steel companies refused to negotiate. Steel workers were finally standing up to the company.

On July twentieth, a month after Gompers' letter to Judge Gary, the National Committee adopted the union's demands. The right of collective bargaining . . . reinstatement of union members . . . eight-hour days . . . six-day weeks . . . abolition of the twenty-four-hour work shift . . . increased wages to meet rising cost of living. The membership's agreement to strike was backed by the committee in support of its negotiation.

The critical confrontation was at hand. The three top representatives of the committee arrived at the executive offices of United States Steel, 71 Broadway, in New York City, and requested an audience with Judge Elbert Gary, chairman of the board. He refused to see them. Instead, he requested they state their business in a letter. Their response, in writing, was another request for a conference. Again, he rejected them, claiming that union leaders were not authorized to speak for the employees, *his* employees. He refused to recognize the existence of a union. He believed only in an open shop. The National Committee then did the only thing that was left for them to do. An ultimatum was issued to the United States Steel Company: confer or we strike!

At this point, Samuel Gompers wired President Wilson requesting his intervention, hoping that he might use his high office to persuade Judge Gary to meet with the union. The president sent Bernard Baruch as his emissary, but again, Gary refused to alter his stand. There was no union, he insisted—and even if there were, he would not talk to them. Besides, he told Baruch, he knew for a fact that 85 percent of his employees would refuse to go out if a strike were called.

To his intimates in the White House, Woodrow Wilson spoke of his opposition to Gary's stand, but he refused to press the issue, his energies concentrated on the fight for the League of Nations. Nor was he eager to get involved in labor battles, whatever his preferences. There were no White House telegrams of indignation to Judge Gary, no public statements of any kind. The president simply backed away from the greatest domestic crisis of his administration. Instead, on Labor Day, he announced the calling of an industrial conference in the near future "to discuss fundamental means of bettering the relationship of capital and labor."

The National Committee, meanwhile, having waited in vain for presidential action to compel Judge Gary's compromise, finally declared a strike date for September twenty-second on the same day that Wilson publicly announced his request that the union postpone any action pending the outcome of his industrial conference on October sixth. This, the first presidential declaration relating to the crisis, was a perfect development for U.S. Steel. The country immediately assumed that the union would comply, indeed, they would have to comply, if only as a conciliating tactic for good public relations. Why, however, had the union not been notified of this proposal by a telegram from the White House? The committee might have at least considered the delay before issuing its strike date. Surely the president knew of their meeting. Gompers, meanwhile, sensing the public aversion to the strike, immediately urged the National Committee to comply.

This, as it turned out, was like asking a geologist to turn off an eruption of Mount Vesuvius. The workers had been stewing for too long. The company had persistently brutalized them and too many men had been killed. There was persistent fear that the company was hell-bent on destroying the union in order to cut wages. Indeed, the list was endless. Foster and Fitzpatrick informed the president that they could not possibly delay: "Delay here means surrender of all hopes." They explained that even the terms of the delay were too vague to begin with, and therefore demoralizing. Telegrams were pouring in to committee headquarters from locals demanding that the strike take place as scheduled. To agree to postpone would validate all the old suspicions that AFL unions were docile in the face of big steel's power.

The committee reconsidered and voted twelve to three to strike.

Foster, who approved, was nonetheless fully aware of the dangers, sensing that the strike was precisely what United States Steel wanted. Rich as Croesus, bloated with war profits, never was an industrial power so mighty, so dominant. The company would use the strike for its own purposes. Indeed, all American industry would rally behind it. The union, meanwhile, was still in its infancy. For all their passions, the workers were still too green, too dispersed, too unaccustomed to the strike process and all its complexities. This would be a major war with an untested guerrilla force taking on an undefeated, all-powerful army.

If United States Steel under Elbert Gary was the dominant company in the industry, others such as Bethlehem, Carnegie and Republic, were at least as anti-union. Buyers of steel, also opposed to unions, immediately pledged their support, anything to stop concessions. The National Council for Industrial Democracy (an employers' association for industrial oligarchy) declared for the maintenance of the open shop. Charles Pirez (who had led the Emergency Fleet Corporation and provoked the Seattle general strike) stated that the steel industry "was the last barrier against the complete and final unionization of American industry." Judge Gary released an open letter to his subsidiary companies: "It is the settled determination of the United States Steel Company that the wages and working conditions of employees shall compare favorably with the highest standards of propriety and justice.... A conference with these men would have been treated by them as a recognition of the 'Closed Shop' method of employment.... The principle of the 'Open Shop' is vital to the greatest industrial progress and prosperity. It is of equal benefit to employer and employee." From London, J. P. Morgan telegrammed Gary: "Heartiest congratulations on your stand for the Open Shop.... I believe American principle of liberty deeply involved and must win out if we all stand firm."

The National Committee for Organizing Iron and Steel Workers sent out two hundred thousand strike announcements in seven different languages. "The workers in the iron and steel mills and blast furnaces ... are requested not to go to work on September twenty-second and to refuse to resume their employment until such time as the demands of the organization have been conceded by the steel corporations.... If we will but stand together as men, our demands will soon be granted. But if we falter and fail, we will sink back into our miserable helpless serfdom."

And so it was. Backed by a strike fund of $400,000, on September twenty-second, 250,000 steel workers went out, over half the industry's work force. Where unions were well organized, some companies were forced to shut down completely. Others tried to operate on a partial basis. To Foster, the walkout was highly exhilarating, exceeding anything he had anticipated, a magnificent demonstration of rank-and-file solidarity. "The past obedient slaves of the United States Steel Company are fighting for a share in the profits of reconstruction and . . . democracy," he announced. The strike was necessary because the companies "still persist in their un-American efforts to impose the iron will of the autocrat on their employees."

Never had so many men struck at one time with such an impact, totally demolishing Judge Gary's claim that the union had no support. Before the week was over, the numbers swelled to 365,000. According to Foster, the strike became almost 90 percent effective. Even in the most company town of all, Pittsburgh, over three-quarters of the plants had to shut down. But the *New York Times* headlines referred to "THE DYING STEEL STRIKE." And so went the company press releases, downplaying the impact of the walkout. The American people, having found themselves bemused by the president's call for industrial peace through conference, were jolted by the union's defiance. Directly on the heels of the Boston police strike barely two weeks before, the popular reaction to the steel strike was hostile. The *New York Times* called its leaders "radicals, social and industrial revolutionaries." The *New York Tribune:* ". . . another experiment in the way of Bolshevizing American industry. Its motive is political; its leaders have mobilized industrial alienism for a disruptive purpose; and its purpose is un-American." The *Chicago Tribune:* ". . . the decision means a choice between the American system and the Russian— individual liberty or the dictatorship of the proletariat." Said Judge Gary at a businessmen's dinner in New York: "If the strike succeeds it might and probably would be the beginning of an upheaval which might bring on all of us grave and serious consequences."

A prominent West Virginia businessman wrote A. Mitchell Palmer: "There is hardly a respectable citizen of my acquaintance who does not believe that we are on the verge of armed conflict in this country," a consummate illustration of a man believing his own fabrications.

The *Boston Evening Transcript* editorialized that the union's primary goal was to change the character of government.

Since the main body of strikers was alleged to be from Eastern Europe, what better proof was needed that this was all part of a radical European conspiracy? With appropriate guile, the United States Steel Corporation assembled a body of American-born skilled workers and sent them to Washington to testify: "Only the foreign element went out." Wrote the *New York Times:* "The foreign element... stupid in the doctrine of the class struggle and social overthrow [is] ignorant and easily misled." The strike was nothing more than a manifestation of the Bolshevik conspiracy, an attempt at revolution, Russian financed, alien and un-American, not a legitimate strike at all.

Let the poet Edgar Guest, pride of conservatives, set the scene in U.S. Steel's publication, *Gary Works Circle:*

> Said Dan McGann to a foreign man who worked at the selfsame bench,
> 'Let me tell you this,' and for emphasis, he flourished a monkey wrench,
> 'Don't talk to me of this bourgeoisie, don't open your mouth to speak
> Of your Socialists and Anarchists, don't mention the Bolshevik.
> For I've had enough of this foreign stuff, I'm sick as a man can be
> Of the speech of hate, and I'm telling you straight that this is the land for me.'

Then, out of this miasma, it was discovered that William Z. Foster had once written a syndicalist pamphlet, long since out of print. Immediately, it was reproduced a thousandfold. As Foster had written: "The syndicalist considers the state a middling capitalist institution.... He recognizes no rights of the capitalists to their property, and is going to strip them of it, law or no law.... With him, the end justifies the means." And this, went the propaganda, was the man who was leading the great steel strike.

Congress immediately responded with fury. Senator Henry L. Myers of Montana called Foster "a notorious syndicalist, revolutionist and enemy of organized government." Senator Charles

S. Thomas of Colorado said Foster was a radical working for economic chaos. Representative John Cooper of Ohio said he was not fit for the protection of the American flag. Newspapers echoed with all the usual fulminations. The strike was now labeled full-fledged Red radical Bolshevism.

This propaganda was all U.S. Steel needed to start its repression, to begin breaking the strike; it was a turning point for the rationale to justify whatever means it deemed necessary. Sermonized the Reverend P. Molyneux in Braddock, Pa.: "This strike is not being brought about by intelligent or English-speaking workmen.... You can't reason with these people. Don't reason with them. You can't anymore than you can with a cow or a horse.... Knock them down!" Governor Sproul of Pennsylvania commended the sermon, which was then reproduced in newspapers across the country. Full-page advertisements appeared to declare Bolshevik plots. The very sound of the name United States Steel was made to bear out this patriotic position against the IWW syndicalism of W. Z. Foster.

So the official violence began. In western Pennsylvania's Allegheny City, the sheriff deputized five thousand men, paid and armed by the steel companies of Pittsburgh. At Homestead, mounted troops of state policemen rode brutally through a union picket line, swinging clubs at everyone, women and children included. Strikers were beaten and jailed without formal charges, and when tried, sentences were stiff beyond reason. In Lackawanna, strikers were beaten when refusing to disperse. Between Pittsburgh and Clairton, there were twenty-five thousand deputies bearing arms, all company bought and paid for. In Duquesne, men were given the choice of returning to work or going to jail. Law enforcement officials condoned any act of violence, and refused to deal with union complaints of official brutality. In Clairton, the union was unable to get a permit to hire a hall for a meeting, and so resorted to a vacant lot where a permit was finally granted. Here, state police rode down the crowd of men, women and children, which was immediately dispersed to avoid them. Then a trooper pulled down an American flag, no doubt intending to provoke a riot, and trampled it under his horse's hoof. At this, the union men, some of them ex-soldiers, became incensed and rushed at the troopers, only to be beaten down with clubs. The resulting riot was headlined throughout the state, but no mention of the flag was included.

A letter from a pastor in Duquesne to William Z. Foster described the extent to which the conflicts were made to escalate:

> "...[M]y congregation leaving church was suddenly, without any cause whatever, attacked on the very steps of the Temple of God, by the Constables, and dispersed by these iron-hoofed Huns. Whilst dispersing, indignation and a flood of frenzy swayed them, being lifted by some invisible force, thrown into the flux of raging...against the Cossacks of this State. Nevertheless, it was the most magnificent display of self-control manifested by the attacked ever shown anywhere. They moved on, with heads lowered, jaws firmly set, to submit. Oh, it was great; it was magnificent....Oh, only for one wink from someone, would there be a puddle of red horse-blood mixed with the human kind. But no, we want to win the strike. We want to win the confidence of the public....[The next day] the little babies of No. 1 were going to school. They loitered for the school bell to summon. And here come the Cossacks. They see the little innocents standing on the steps of the school house; their parents on the opposite side of the street. What splendid occasion to start the 'Hunkeys' ire, let us charge the babies. That will fetch them to attack upon us. They did. But the 'Hunkeys,' even at the supreme test of his coolheadedness, refused to flash his knife to save his babies from the onrush of the cruel horses' hoofs...."

Another incident involving the flag occurred in Weirton, West Virginia, where 150 Finnish steel workers picketing outside a mill were attacked by police, then forced to kiss the American flag before being loaded on trucks and driven out of town—leaving their women and children destitute. This unlawful action by the police was not denied by civil authorities—but the official story referred to the men as members of the IWW. That, presumably, was sufficient to justify their arrest and deportation. Other than their comrades and families, no one appeared to object.

For it all, the American people were not without sympathy for workingmen taking on such giants as U.S. Steel, a factor recognized by company propagandists. But public opinion was there

Wayne Wheeler, "Mr. Dry Boss," driving force of the Anti-Saloon League. *(Library of Congress)*

THE RABID PROHIBITIONIST WHO HAS JUST HAD A BOTTLE OF OLD CROW FORCED UPON HIM BECAUSE HE COULDN'T BEAR TO OFFEND BY SAYING "NO" REGISTERING EXTREME GRIEF —

Cartoonist Herbert Johnson's portrait of hypocrisy. *(Library of Congress)*

Cartoonist Berryman's comment *(above)* on the failure to enforce the Volstead Act. *(Library of Congress)*

Cartoonist W.A. Rogers on the new menace after Prohibition. *(Library of Congress)*

Al Capone, the principal beneficiary of the 18th Amendment until the I.R.S. took over. *(AP/Wide World Photos)*

The heritage of Prohibition. *(Library of Congress)*

"Shoeless" Joe Jackson *(right)* in 1915 with Ty Cobb. *(Library of Congress)*

Charles Comiskey, Chicago White Sox owner, "The Old Roman." *(Library of Congress)*

Kenesaw Mountain Landis, first commissioner of baseball. *(AP/Wide World Photos)*

"Shoeless" Joe Jackson
(George Brace Photos)

Every major American
newspaper headlined
the great scandal.
(New York Times)

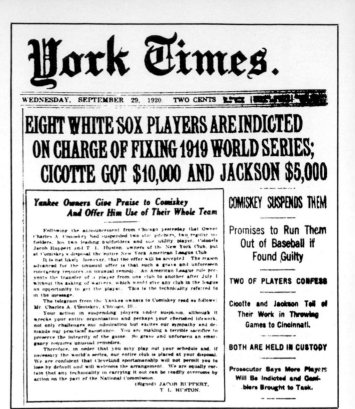

York Times.

WEDNESDAY, SEPTEMBER 29, 1920.   TWO CENTS

EIGHT WHITE SOX PLAYERS ARE INDICTED ON CHARGE OF FIXING 1919 WORLD SERIES; CICOTTE GOT $10,000 AND JACKSON $5,000

Yankee Owners Give Praise to Comiskey And Offer Him Use of Their Whole Team

Following the announcement from Chicago yesterday that Owner Charles A. Comiskey had suspended two star pitchers, two regular infielders, his two leading outfielders and one utility player, Colonels Jacob Ruppert and T. L. Huston, owners of the New York Club, put at Comiskey's disposal the entire New York American League Club.

It is not likely, however, that the offer will be accepted. The reason advanced for the unusual offer is that such a grave and unforeseen emergency requires an unusual remedy. An American League rule prevents the transfer of a player from one club to another after July 1 without the asking of waivers, which would give any club in the league an opportunity to get the player. This is the technicality referred to in the message.

The telegram from the Yankee owners to Comiskey read as follows: Mr. Charles A. Comiskey, Chicago, Ill.:

Your action in suspending players under suspicion, although it wrecks your entire organization and perhaps your cherished lifework, not only challenges our admiration but excites our sympathy and demands our practical assistance. You are making a terrible sacrifice to preserve the integrity of the game. So grave and unforseen an emergency requires unusual remedies.

Therefore, in order that you may play out your schedule and, if necessary the world's series, our entire club is placed at your disposal. We are confident that Cleveland sportsmanship will not permit you to lose by default and will welcome the arrangement. We are equally certain that any technicality in carrying it out can be readily overcome by action on the part of the National Commission.
    (Signed) JACOB RUPPERT,
                T. L. HUSTON.

COMISKEY SUSPENDS THEM

Promises to Run Them Out of Baseball if Found Guilty

TWO OF PLAYERS CONFESS

Cicotte and Jackson Tell of Their Work in Throwing Games to Cincinnati.

BOTH ARE HELD IN CUSTODY

Prosecutor Says More Players Will Be Indicted and Gamblers Brought to Task.

Oscar "Happy" Felsch
(George Brace Photos)

George "Buck" Weaver
(George Brace Photos)

Eddie Cicotte
(George Brace Photos)

Arnold "Chick" Gandil
(George Brace Photos)

William "Kid" Gleason
(United Press International Photo)

Claude "Lefty" Williams
(George Brace Photos)

Abe Attell *(left)*, Featherweight Champion of the World, 1909. *(Culver Pictures, Inc.)* Attell *(above, center)* fifty years later with Jack Dempsey *(left)* and Max Baer.

Ring Lardner, 1924.
(Culver Pictures, Inc.)

to be molded, and the resources to do so were unlimited. All of a sudden, there were press reports that steel workers had made up to $70 a day, that the more luxurious hotels in New York were preparing for an influx of vacationing strikers. How many showed up for this indulgence was not revealed. Other reports kept harping on the failure of the men to maintain the walkout. "Strike Crumbling," ran the Pittsburgh press and "Conditions Almost Normal in All Steel Plants," "Workers Flock Back to Jobs." Someone estimated that these news stories printed back-to-work figures totalling 4,800,000, although only five hundred thousand had ever been employed. Between September 27 and October 8, thirty full-page ads in Pittsburgh newspapers damned the strike and urged steel workers to return to their jobs. "Stand By America." "Show up the Red agitator for what he is." In Gary, Indiana, thirty thousand black strikebreakers were brought in as deliberate provocations to rioting. Labor spies and provocateurs were all over the striking communities. Company spies infiltrated the National Committee itself. There were police-provoked riots in Donora, Braddock, Homestead. Because of the black strikebreakers, the riots in Gary, Indiana, became so threatening, the state militia was called out to stop (then participate in) the attacks, and finally federal troops under the celebrated general Leonard Wood placed the city under martial law to protect the scabs. (Only when scabbing, it seemed, were blacks protected by federal troops—this in a year of unprecedented racist rioting and lynching.) Once again, "documents" were discovered by Army Intelligence purporting to use the strike to "capture the power of the state" in order to "establish the dictatorship of the workers." Then too there were the inevitable bomb scares directed against the homes of prominent Gary citizens—no doubt by the same elusive anarchists who had been so dramatically active in the spring. And again, the radicals in the forefront of all this action were termed neither workers nor organizers but an advanced "Red Guard" planning to destroy American industry.

Meanwhile, the president's National Industrial Conference, designed to produce peace and cooperation between capital and labor got under way on the very day General Wood declared martial law in Gary to protect the thirty thousand black strikebreakers. Woodrow Wilson disobeyed his doctor's orders to dictate his message of faith in the Christian ethic as a panacea for these conflicts: "At a time when the nations of the world are endeavoring to find a way of avoiding war, are we to confess that there is no method to be found for carrying on industry except in the spirit of, and with the very method of, war? Must suspicion and hatred and force rule us in civil life? Are our industrial leaders and our industrial workers to live together without faith in each other, constantly struggling for advantage over each other, doing naught but what is compelled? My friends, this would be an intolerable outlook ... an invitation to national disaster. From such a possibility my mind turns away, for my confidence is abiding that in this land we have learned how to accept the general judgment upon matters that affect the public weal."

Unfortunately, the "general judgment" of the National Industrial Conference was too heavily weighted on the side of the boys of big business, namely, John D. Rockefeller and Judge Elbert Gary himself. The steel strike was excluded from the agenda as too controversial. So too, as it turned out, was anything that referred to the rights of organized labor.

In these meetings, Samuel Gompers saw himself being backed into a do-nothing corner until he was forced by his title alone, president of the AFL, to declare for a resolution that would guarantee to labor the right to organize and bargain collectively with management (the obvious but unspoken issue behind the steel strike). He was promptly voted down. For all his hunger to cooperate, Gompers was then forced to retire from the conference; he simply had no choice; he was being denied the very essence of his function.

For his departure, Gompers was viciously condemned as a quitter while the factors that had driven him to it went unmentioned. This, of course, represented the prevailing attitude of state power toward all matters relating to organized labor. What Gompers finally recognized was the sine qua non of the new capitalist position: the workingman was being denied the right to challenge the existing distribution of economic power. There would be no discussion as to whether that power made for productive efficiency or stripped millions of wage earners of legitimate motives and morale at the workplace. Any challenge by labor would be denounced as a show of enmity to the public security and would bring down upon it the full authority of the state. All this to the end that it would not be for labor to decide whether or not it wished to work or under what terms it preferred; labor must work under the terms that the employers, in combination with the state, decided were just.

Samuel Gompers, then, had been declared a nonperson, the AF of L a nonexisting union. It was as if the Republicans in the Senate had voted a resolution stipulating the nonrecognition of Democratic credentials. There would then be no Senate. Likewise, when the employers denied Gompers's claim for recognition of labor, there was no conference. He might have remained at the table, but he had actually been voted out of existence.

Nonetheless, for his departure from the conference, Gompers was labeled a Red. Did it not link him with all radicals? As the *Wall Street Journal* put it: "Organized labor was succumbing to the IWWs and Russian Bolsheviks." The same Samuel Gompers who had forever shunned revolution with as much ardor as his accusers, with hardly an unkind glance at the God-given industrial order, now was heard to warn the steel magnates that if they succeeded in breaking the steel strike, men would go about "preaching the tyranny which they experience and the injustices which have been meted out to them—then, whatever betide, you will have sown the seed and will bear the consequence."

This statement did not appear to frighten them at all.

It was said later that the strike was doomed by Foster's 1911 pamphlet. Or by the riots in Gary after which the United States Army was called out. Or by Samuel Gompers's walking out of the president's industrial conference. The inference was that public opinion was turned against it and the Bolshevik label was made to stick. Unless something was done, Senator Miles Poindexter said, "there is real danger that the government will fall." What finally was done was a combination of force, lies and intimidation. So vast was the deluge of the Red Menace, even the AFL leadership turned openly against the strike. Gradually, by attrition, the ranks of the union began to break. First, as might have been predicted, the native skilled workers went back. For a while, the unskilled aliens remained loyal to the cause, all the while seeing their jobs going to scabs, and then they too started to go back.

Over three months after the strike was called, on January 8, 1920, there were still one hundred thousand men out, but production was returning to near normal. The National Committee finally voted to end the walkout.

In the end, the strike gained not one concession for the men. Twenty lives had been lost to thugs, strikebreakers and police violence. Some $112 million had been lost in wages. Above all, the union had been crushed and the open shop remained triumphant.

The Senate Committee on Education and Labor reported its findings that the union was mostly at fault, first for refusing to postpone the strike at the president's request, then for its folly in having William Z. Foster as its leader, citing its own evidence to show he had not renounced his earlier radical views. The committee found that a "considerable element of IWW anarchists, revolutionists and Russian socialists" had massed behind the strike and were using it to gain power. The Reds had instigated the strike, and the Reds had caused its defeat.

There was also a special commission of inquiry conducted under the auspices of the liberal Interchurch World Movement that came to completely different conclusions. It attacked the steel companies for its strikebreakers, spies and provocateurs. It cited numerous "violations of personal rights and liberties, men arrested without warrants and imprisoned without charges, homes invaded without legal process, magistrates' verdicts rendered on the basis of whether the striker would go back to work or not." It claimed that the grievances of the men were just, and repressions against the strike were not. It found the conduct of the union leaders was orthodox and conformed to AFL regulations. It had no criticism of Foster, clearly indicating that his syndicalist background was irrelevant. It concluded that the Red Menace charges that had finally broken the strike were without substance, forcing the American people to lose sight of the real issues.

6. INCIDENT AT CENTRALIA OR HOW THE AMERICAN LEGION SAVED THE COUNTRY FROM BOLSHEVISM BY EMASCULATING A VETERAN

This detestable outrage is the fearful penalty which Centralia has paid for the over lenient policy of the national government toward anarchists and murderous communists.

—MILES POINDEXTER, U.S. senator, Washington

It has been duly noted in these pages that an endless spate of violations to American civil liberties was violently perpetrated. Grossly destructive though they were, what seemed infinitely more significant was the acceptance, if not outright approval, with which the citizenry responded. America appeared to need this violation of itself. It was as if it wished to gorge on its own destruction, the more vicious the better. It saw no danger to its heritage, but condemned those who dared to give warnings.

What had brought it on? What unseen forces had driven it? Where was it heading?

Was it because of the war that was, in effect, an apparent love affair of Americans for America or, more erotically, of Americans for war itself, for the exquisite satisfactions of hating and killing Huns, for feeling noble in the process and then for being rewarded by a far greater prosperity than we had ever known? Was this highly emotional splurge then stopped too suddenly at the

197

very height of its passionate pursuit, a veritable coitus interruptus? Were we not, indeed, copulating with the greatest whore of all?

From armistice in 1918 came celebration, but the victory brought no real satisfaction. There were no Huns to hang from all those lampposts we had boasted of, nor was the Kaiser available to oblige our need for vengeance. What sort of victory was this anyway? Was there anyone left in America who could find satisfaction in the now-discredited idealism of the presidency? Who cared about such things but politicians in their pursuit of political games? Americans sought outlets not for the mind to reason but for the throbbing libido to exploit.

There was, as well, an enormous wellspring of guilt in the American psyche. The madness of the war made it inevitable. Righteousness and inequities. Slaughter and profits. Sacrifice and pleasure. How could a nation so blessed, so rich, so regionally secure not have felt guilt at its incredibly good fortune? And when that guilt turned to frustration, what then? Where would the anger go? Above all, at whom?

All the Red Menacing, though it thrived from coast to coast, almost from day to day, seemed infinitely less than satiating. Like the account of the Braddock constabulary attacking "babies" to provoke the fathers, the bloodbath did not happen; there was little in the incident to sink your teeth into (and hence it was never reported in the newspapers). The Seattle general strike had been devoid of confrontation. The Boston police had simply capitulated. The steel strike was an endlessly plodding drawn-out battle of attrition, with no more casualties than a routine mine cave-in. America still needed its orgasm.

Came then the celebration of Armistice Day, November 11, 1919. A day to commemorate the making of a truce, a day of suspension of conflict, a day to celebrate peace. There were four communities in the United States named Centralia, but only one, in Washington, south of Seattle, that left its mark on history. A smallish town of a few thousand people and a railroad line to service its agriculture and lumber business, a town prosperous enough to enjoy its security. As in the great steel industry, the price of lumber had risen during the war from $16 to over $120 per thousand feet for huge profits to the lumber companies. Typically, the companies saw the postwar loosening of controls as an opportunity to do whatever they wished.

But Centralia was also one of the last strongholds of IWW militancy, waging small wars on the "slave camps" of the lumber trusts. They were active all over the northwest, but only two of its halls had survived the repressions of local patriots. The hall in Centralia had been shut down in 1918 by Legionnaires paid to sack the place, burn its literature under the approving eyes of the chamber of commerce and sell its fixtures to the Red Cross during a patriotic parade. But a new hall had been hired, a much-needed refuge for itinerant radicals. The IWW, in fact, had even increased its membership in defiance.

Finding this intolerable, a group of local businessmen, calling themselves the Centralia Protective Association, organized to save their community from Bolshevik influences. A few weeks before Armistice Day, rumors began to circulate that the IWW hall was to be attacked again, quite possibly during the parade on November eleventh. In its inimitable provocative style, the IWW appealed for tolerance of its right to exist, charging that "the profiteering class of Centralia have of late been waving the flag of our country in an endeavor to incite the lawless of our city to raid our hall and club us out of town." And, quite obviously, its members were not about to permit that.

On Armistice Day, at two in the afternoon, the people of Centralia gathered for the parade. There marched the Elks, a band played behind them, the Boy Scouts followed, and then the American Legion contingent led by its post commander who was also a leading figure in the Centralia Protective Association. The IWW had prepared for the event, especially since the line of march was to proceed directly by the new IWW hall. Several were positioned inside the hall, others deployed directly across the street in the Avalon Hotel, still others several hundred yards off on a height known as Seminary Hill. All were armed with rifles and/or revolvers, among them Wesley Everest, an ex-Army sharpshooter who had put on his uniform for the occasion. "I fought for democracy in France, and I'm going to fight for it here," he said. "First man that comes in here, why he's going to get it!"

At first, the parade passed the hall peacefully enough, although a number of ropes with dangling nooses suddenly appeared among the marchers (later described as merely "a joke"). But then the Legionnaires suddenly, inexplicably, retraced their steps, not without the confusion of an improper line of march, and once again passed the IWW hall.

This time, it was not a joke. A cry from the Legionnaires was clearly heard: "Let's go get 'em!" and a number of them moved toward the hall. Immediately, shots rang out, from the street and from the IWW vantage points. Legionnaire bullet holes riddled the front door. One Legionnaire was shot through the head as he broke into the hall. Another was killed as he reached the curb. Still another was shot in the middle of the street.

When the shooting stopped, three Legionnaires were dead. The Wobblies were arrested, but Wesley Everest refused to be taken, escaping through the melee for the Skookumchunk River. There, waist deep in water, he was overcome by a posse. But he was unwilling to surrender and stood his ground in a gun battle, killing another Legionnaire as he emptied his revolver. At this point, he was seized, beaten badly, his teeth knocked out by a rifle butt, then taken back to town to be jailed with the others.

What followed was beyond horror. That night, as Wesley Everest lay suffering on the floor of his cell, the lights of Centralia went out, a mob broke into the jail, seized Everest, then beat him unmercifully in the street. In a car, en route to the Chehalis River, an all-American avenger tore open Everest's pants and cut off his genitals with a straight razor brought for the occasion. At the river, he was hung by a rope from the girders of the bridge as he cried out, "Shoot me, for God's sake, shoot me!" Instead, they pulled him to the ground to substitute a longer rope, then again, and only then, they pushed him to hang over the side. Still alive, he clung to the edge until they stamped on his fingers, and when he hung, dying, they riddled his dangling body with bullets.

Not for several days was the corpse cut down and the body (with a distortedly long neck) presented to the Wobblies as an omen. When the undertaker refused to handle it, four of Everest's comrades were forced to dig his grave. As to the cause of death, the Centralia coroner was said to comment: "Everest broke out of jail, went to the Chehalis River and committed suicide. He jumped off with a rope around his neck and then shot himself full of holes."

Meanwhile, it was the news of the dead Legionnaires so savagely murdered by the Bolshevik Wobblies that spread across the country to provoke a horrendous rage. The first Associated Press dispatches gave no hint that the IWW hall had been attacked, that there was cause for the IWW shootings or even that the hall had been destroyed a year before during a similar parade. When a more accurate report was made a day later, it was too late to stay the damage; the American public was inflamed. One of the more demonstrative scenes was a single address delivered simultaneously in thirty-one Minneapolis churches by their pastors and eighteen members of the Legion. This sermon contrived to liken the antagonism of the American Legion to the IWW with that of Christianity to all forms of Bolshevism. Every newspaper in the country headlined the killings in a continuing orgy of cries for vengeance. There was no contrition for the lynching; quite the contrary, it inspired a new wave of justifiable repression, a declaration of "war to the death" on all radicals. November twelfth brought official action in a series of raids on West Coast cities to rid the area of the Bolshevik menace. In Tacoma, thirty-four Wobblies were seized. In Spokane, American Legionnaires, acting as deputy sheriffs, seized seventy-four more. In Oakland, a mob literally demolished radical meeting halls in a rampaging demonstration to show that "law and order shall prevail." In Seattle, home of ex-mayor Ole Hanson, thirty-eight Reds were rounded up, the *Union Record* labor newspaper suspended, its staff arrested after an editorial dared to suggest that the IWW be permitted to present its case.

Nor was it different in the halls of Congress. There were no condemnations of the lynching. No one dared to mention that Wesley Everest was an ex-soldier who had served overseas. When Representative Albert Johnson (from Centralia's district) read a spate of telegrams from legion posts condemning the murders of their patriotic comrades by "IWW draft dodgers and traitors," singing their praises as "victims of a long premeditated conspiracy to bring about an armed revolution in the United States," the House resounded with applause and cries of support. In the Senate, another Washingtonian, Senator Wesley Jones, provoked another enthusiastic response: "The shots that killed those boys were really aimed at the heart of this nation by those who oppose law and seek the overthrow of government." To Republicans involved in the coming presidential election, the Red Scare was a continuing godsend.

So it went everywhere. "RETURNED HEROES SLAIN BY IWW...WAR TO THE DEATH IS DECLARED AGAINST IWW...RADICALISM RUN MAD," declared the *New York Times*. "AN ACT OF WAR AGAINST THE U.S.," headlined the *Boston Evening Transcript*, "TIME FOR A SHOWDOWN." Newspapers editorialized that all radicals "active or philosophical, parlor or outhouse," be suppressed.

The counterclaims by radical journals seemed almost pathetically feeble.

Months later, the trial was held in the Washington town of Montesano, which the judge admitted was less than a fair impartial place in which to hold it, yet he refused to change the venue. A delegation of Legionnaires attended the sessions in full uniform. To offset them, a "labor jury" bravely sat to watch and to judge for themselves. A lawyer who had defended the IWW in previous trials had himself been indicted with the others in the murder charge—a bizarre legal ploy to tarnish the entire defense. There were no indictments against those who had savagely tortured and lynched Everest.

Still, the trial was not without fascination for the contradictory testimony that emerged, much from the Legionnaires themselves. Had the Legionnaires charged the hall with intent to destroy it? Had the IWW simply reacted to the shots fired against them? In the end, seven of the ten Wobblies were found guilty of but second-degree murder and sentenced to twenty-five to forty years, a decision unanimously upheld by the state Supreme Court. From this, however, it could be assumed that the prosecution had been unable to prove its case, that there was no evidence of an IWW plan to attack the Legionnaires, that the state had to settle for a judgment based upon pure prejudice.

The verdict and sentencing were denounced, both by 100 percent American patriots as not sufficiently punitive and radicals, who called it "one of the greatest judicial outrages of modern times."

Again, it seemed not to matter that one juror admitted in a sworn affidavit: "I verily believe . . . that if these men had not been affiliated with the IWW organization they would never have been convicted." Indeed, it was so obvious that no one called the juror a traitor.

It was left for A. Mitchell Palmer to make the best use of such an ethic. The man who came to be known as "the Fighting Quaker" would take over from the "Christian Hired Man."

7. THE PINCH OF THE PALMER RAIDS OR HOW, IN THE END, ONLY THE REDS WERE SCARED

Too many people had free speech in this country.

—A. MITCHELL PALMER, U.S. attorney general

In 1912, A. Mitchell Palmer was vice-chairman of the Democratic National Committee. He was also chairman of the Pennsylvania delegation to the Democratic Convention, where he swung his state to Woodrow Wilson. In deference to such services, the new president offered Palmer the Cabinet post of secretary of war—a strange proffering to a religious Quaker. Palmer gratefully declined.

His Pennsylvania Quaker background had dominated his life, taking him through Swarthmore College, a distinguished Quaker institution, from which he graduated at the age of nineteen with the highest honors. Two years later, he was admitted to the Pennsylvania Bar, then became active in politics as a successful reform candidate for Congress, where he served three terms.

Woodrow Wilson thought highly of him, appointed him to a judgeship on the United States Court of Claims, the alien property custodian, then finally, in March 1919, to the Cabinet as attorney general. Palmer's reputation as an administrator was exceptionally good—A diligent, competent, incorruptible public servant. He was also a devoted supporter of Wilson's policies, especially the League of Nations. As attorney general, he was believed to be an excellent liberal choice, which he was, in fact, until June when his home was bombed. (Here, one might predate a recent joke in paraphrase: "A conservative is a liberal who has just been bombed.")

Shortly after that frightening experience, he induced Congress to appropriate $500,000 to establish within the Department of Justice and its new Bureau of Investigation, a General Intelligence Division, to which he appointed a young Washington attorney named J. Edgar Hoover as head. Hoover was twenty-four years old, an ex-librarian with the Library of Congress, possessor of a filing-cabinet mind. Under Hoover's genius, an elaborate card index system was created, over two hundred thousand cards with detailed information on American radicals and radical organizations and publications, membership rolls, names of officers, times and locations of meetings. Included were complete histories of sixty thousand "dangerous radicals." Palmer could boast that nothing comparable existed anywhere in the world.

With this data at hand, the General Intelligence Division took to disseminating antiradical propaganda. The 1919 foundation of two rival Communist Parties in the United States gave this an added respectability. All major newspapers, for example, received a letter signed by the attorney general with the latest information. "My one desire is to acquaint people like you with the real menace of evil-thinking which is the foundation of the Red Movement," Palmer wrote. The division created its own news stories, supplying "documents" along with appropriate editorial comment. Newspapers would print these releases as news. "Warns Nation of Red Peril; the U.S. Department of Justice Urges Americans to Guard Against Bolshevik Menace, Calls Red Plans Criminal." "Manifesto of Communist International Seized in U.S. Dept. of Justice Raids. Tells Reds' Own Story of Plans for World Wide Plunder." Even as strikes and riots took place, they were analyzed and interpreted by the division to fuel carefully orchestrated antiradical response. The department had, however, acted prematurely in May when it rounded up fifty-four Reds for deportation, for only three were shipped out. It would not make this mistake again.

A sensible and ambitious politician, A. Mitchell Palmer then bided his time. It was never out of his mind that 1920 was a presidential election year. Since Woodrow Wilson, obviously incapacitated in the White House, had left no one minding the store, Palmer would make whatever moves he thought best for himself.

Besides, he had the secretary of state, Robert Lansing, in his ideological camp, and the president's secretary, Joseph Tumulty, a
kindred spirit and friend. As Palmer invisioned the scenario, he
would use the office of attorney general to overwhelm the entire
radical movement, take the Red Scare away from the Republicans
and catapult himself into leadership of the Democratic Party.

Up to this point, the administration had not taken the Red
bull by the horns. Whatever moves the Department of Justice had
made were carefully orchestrated to stay within the limits of public
criticism, for there were too many prominent liberals who had
supported Woodrow Wilson. For all the strident accusations of
reactionary Republicans in Congress, this was still a government
that pretended to be legal, respecting the people's Constitutional
guarantees to civil rights. If such guarantees had been repeatedly
violated by random actions, so be it, but the Department of Justice
found it politically convenient to maintain a hands-off policy. It
confined itself to propaganda, to the furtive collecting of information, to the shadowy world of infiltration and spying, to the
quiet manipulation of covert pressures. Its voluminous files from
the genius of J. Edgar Hoover had never been idle.

By the fall, however, there was an appreciable change in
American opinion. Where there had been continuing verbal opposition to Red Scaring and a desperate defense of civil rights,
there were now strong signs of withering. The effects of relentless
anti-Red pummeling on the American psyche could not but overwhelm the few who resisted it. The big lie of oncoming revolution
that had once seemed too preposterous to be taken seriously had
achieved a new respectability. Those who knew it for the lie it was
had become helpless to resist it. And therein lay the difference.

A woman named Katherine Gerould had written in *Harper's
Magazine:* "America is no longer a free country in the old sense.
Liberty is, increasingly, a merely rhetorical figure. . . . No thinking
citizen . . . can express in freedom more than a part of his honest
convictions. . . . The only way in which an American citizen who is
really interested in the social and political problems of his country
can preserve any freedom of expression is to choose a mob that
is most sympathetic to him, and abide under the shadow of that
mob."

As though to prove which mob was dominant, she was overwhelmed with letters calling her a Bolshevik—then terrorized by a mob who threatened to destroy her home.

Then there were the comments of writer Walter Lippmann: "So thoroughly confused are [American liberals] that the universities, the United States Congress, the government departments, every newspaper office is stocked with men who are in mortal terror.... They tiptoe by day and quake by night, because they know that at this moment any man who in domestic policy stands about where Theodore Roosevelt stood in 1912, and in foreign affairs where Woodrow Wilson stood when he first landed in Paris ... is absolutely certain to be called pacifist, pro-German and Bolshevist."

This had created a wasteland of nonpolitical action, of deferring to one's enemies without daring to contest their atrocities. One did not readily take on the presumably thankless task of protecting someone else's right of free speech, especially since it would almost certainly mean the loss of one's own. Nor was it advisable to protest such unfortunate United States government actions as the blatantly illegal invasion of Russian territory, or the cruel blockade obviously intended to starve out and destroy the Russian government. To react to such heresies in any social circumstance had become neither entertaining nor safe. To pursue an active public protest had become suicidal.

The gradual acceptance of this reality was, in the end, stupefying. The independent American mind simply gave way to a know-nothing majority, preferring submission rather than controversy until, soon enough, submission had drifted into agreement. One could hear the granting of concessions in polite conversation with such phrases as "You can't really blame them [the Legionnaires]" or "Where there's smoke there's fire [the Bolsheviks]." Those who continued to read critical journals such as *The Nation, The New Republic* and *The Call* did so with increasing furtiveness. There were fewer meetings, speeches, demonstrations, not only out of fear of violence but for lack of ideological support. Seldom were there protests from the pulpit, for the clergy, even in the liberal cities, gave way to passivity. Nor were students prepared to speak out, even at great universities known as "hotbeds of radicalism." The treading was light, the manner cautious. In school systems throughout the country, the most repressive minds were dominant. This was no longer drift, this was now stifling conformity.

It was what A. Mitchell Palmer had been waiting and working for. Bolshevism was the enemy, the Red Scare was the device and the alien was the patsy. Meanwhile, Congress was the weather vane. Congress was groomed to gauge the public mood or, at least, those pressure groups to which its members were beholden. The Department of Justice was made aware of every petition from state legislatures, business associations, American Legion posts that poured into Congress demanding anti-Red action. And Congress responded by demanding that action. In the Senate rose Miles Poindexter with yet another cry for patriotic zealotry, denouncing the Department of Justice for its failure to take action. The Senate then dutifully resolved that the attorney general "advise and inform the Senate whether or not the Department of Justice has taken legal proceedings . . . for the arrest and punishment . . . of the various persons within the United States who . . . have attempted to bring about the forceable overthrow of the government."

But what proceedings were, indeed, legal? Palmer saw the difficulties of taking on radicals (especially those who were United States citizens) on the grounds of espionage or even sedition, now that the war was over. Whatever action was taken, therefore, had to be directed against aliens, subject to deportation under the Alien Law of 1918. Since J. Edgar Hoover had already concluded that 90 percent of all radicals were aliens, why not hit them again, and this time with full force?

So began the great Palmer raids, beginning with an assault on a nationwide organization called the Union of Russian Workers, some four thousand strong, its headquarters in the Russian People's House, 133 East Fifteenth Street, New York City. There (as in eleven other cities), agents of the Bureau of Investigation parked in dark sedans to await the given signal in simulated military fashion, then closed in to take the establishment by surprise. Several hundred men and women were driven out of the building by riot squads. As the *New York Times* reported, "victims had been badly beaten by the police . . . heads wrapped in bandages. Doors were taken off, desks were ripped open and even a few rugs were torn up." Although there had been no resistance, the place "looked as if a tornado had struck it.... blood was everywhere on the walls." Hundreds were taken to Justice Department offices for questioning; many were thrown in jail without hearings. Some who spoke no English and had no awareness of revolutionary dogma were held for months.

During the raids, truckloads of literature were confiscated with much subsequent fanfare about the seditiousness of their content. In essence, however, absolutely nothing was found beyond the usual pamphlets whose revolutionary verbiage was already familiar to all. There was an almost pathetic quality to the raids due to the assumption that these allegedly guileful intrigue-trained revolutionaries, seasoned by years of surviving the ultimate tyranny of the tsars, should be so stupidly careless as to expose whatever devilish plans they might be hatching to such obviously hostile forces as the raiding bureau.

Not to be outdone by the feds, state and local officials themselves jumped all over suspected groups of aliens. The Lusk Committee, with the help of seven hundred New York City policemen, raided seventy-three suspected radical centers, arrested five hundred people, seized tons of literature. Radical groups, apparently, never stopped proliferating.

The American people rejoiced. Having acted "in the nick of time," the Department of Justice had stopped what everyone believed to be a "gigantic plot" to overthrow the established order. Once again, America had been saved. A. Mitchell Palmer became the new national hero, precisely as he had planned it. The newspapers acclaimed him a "lion-hearted man [who] had brought order out of chaos" and "a tower of strength." "The Fighting Quaker," he came to be called. First Ole, then Cal, now Mitch.

Palmer sent his report to the Senate as he had been ordered to do, advising them of the vastness of radical and seditious propaganda that was threatening to undermine the state. He proposed the enactment of a new sedition bill that would make it unlawful to commit "any act of terrorism, *hate,* revenge or injury against the person or property" of any United States officer "with intent to... cause the *change,* overthrow or destruction of the government, or of any of the laws or authority thereof," imposing a penalty of ten years' imprisonment on anyone who "makes, displays, writes, prints or circulates any sign, word, speech, picture, argument or teaching" that might justify such an act.

Such legislation, so far beyond the limitations imposed by the Bill of Rights as to be extremely unlikely of passage even in the 1919 Congress, was the attorney general's vision of America during the Red Scare. Meanwhile, his public speeches were endlessly devoted to civil liberties, the embodiment of every principle of freedom as guaranteed by the Constitution he had pledged to uphold. No one was better able to so dignify with words the terrorism he directed. Low acts and high ideals. The spy-defender of free speech. To quote Palmer: "We cannot be less willing now than we have always been that the oppressed of every clime shall find here a refuge from trouble, disorder and distress; those who remain shall stay with the intent to become Americans in every sense."

John Dos Passos wrote about the steel baron and public benefactor Andrew Carnegie as a great man of peace—except in time of war. A. Mitchell Palmer was a great advocate of free speech—except in time of repression.

Meanwhile, in the White House, there was an ominous silence. Washington, which had always thrived on rumors, now bathed in them. How sick was the president? Paralyzed? In a coma? Or, as some suggested, was he dead? There were reports that the president's wife was in charge, the regent who decided who and what got to the president's attention. As Senator Albert Fall put it: "We have no president. We have a petticoat government."

What Palmer knew was what he wanted to know: he had the president's support. Others in the Cabinet like Josephus Daniels (Navy), James Houston (Agriculture), Franklin Lane (Interior) may have opposed him, but there were no cabinet meetings to give vent to their objections, for the incapacitated Woodrow Wilson had vigorously objected to their sitting without him. Only William Wilson (Labor) dared protest what Palmer was doing, brazenly charging that the raids were creating more Reds than eliminating them, and that Palmer (and the president), by not pardoning Eugene Debs, still in prison for sedition, were cruelly and stupidly making a martyr of him.

But Palmer had his Tumulty, who could not do enough for him. Tumulty, the true-blue anti-Bolshevist and an ardent Catholic, believed the Reds were the Antichrist and Palmer the great crusader. Tumulty was the man most wise to the ebb and flow of public opinion, the master of gauging which way the political winds would blow. If he saw that Palmer's eye was on the 1920 election, he also saw the potential for himself as a continuing presidential secretary. Meanwhile, he would serve Palmer well with this president.

As for the purpose of the raids, the scenario called for mass deportation. Unfortunately for Palmer, however, it was discovered that any such deportations could not legally be ordered by the Department of Justice; they were, instead, the function of the Department of Labor. Not only was Secretary of Labor William Wilson hostile to the attorney general, there was his assistant secretary, Louis Post, who persisted in open opposition to the Red Scare—and both men opposed the excessiveness of the Palmer plans for deportation.

The attorney general, it appeared, would be stuck with his raids, unable to enjoy the fruits of them.

Then, as if by magic, two events occurred that turned the tide for him. The first related to the liberal Frederick Howe, ex-commissioner of immigration, and his administration of Ellis Island. Howe had been an outspoken critic of the exploitation of immigrants, the inadequacy of the facilities, the callousness of immigration officials, the bribery and corruption and extortions of the entire immigration process. Before that, in earlier days, he had spoken out against the war, protested the profiteering, the severity of repressive laws. An intellectual gadfly to bureaucracy, Howe was now fair game at the high time of the Red Menace. No doubt J. Edgar Hoover had a massive dossier on such an obvious suspect, and no doubt it was replete with cross-indexed names and organizations. And no doubt all this was forthcoming at precisely the moment when an attack was needed. Indeed, the House Committee on Immigration jumped into the breach, investigating the conduct and methods of Ellis Island. It revealed that between 1918 and 1919 over six hundred aliens had been arrested by federal authorities as anarchists, but only sixty had been deported.

Howe, it appeared, had not found the vast majority of them guilty as charged. He had also resigned as commissioner rather than compromise his views.

Even as this contentiousness was being exposed, Palmer suddenly instigated another raid on the celebrated Russian People's House, and this time, for reasons that can only be guessed at, his agents found "a secret chamber in which was deposited material for one hundred bombs"! The convenience of its timing was, to say the least, exquisite. The press from coast to coast made hay of the story. Fifty small bottles of nondescript chemicals made the headlines: "RED BOMB LABORATORY FOUND," "FIND REDS' BOMB SHOP." An inspector of the Federal Bureau of Combustibles claimed this was "the most deadly and most dangerous assortment of explosives and bomb ingredients . . . seen in my years."

So there they were, the anarchist Bolshevist Red vermin who were going to kill us all, but the liberal Frederick Howe could send only sixty of six hundred away. Came then the inevitable deluge of protests from every patriotic organization in America, demanding that "Americans should . . . drive from these shores all disloyal aliens." Bills were proposed to take the deportation process away from the Department of Labor and give it to the attorney general. Nationalized citizens were to be equally subject to cancellation of their certificates if they too espoused radicalism. Senator Kenneth McKellar of Tennessee proposed that even native-born Americans be subject to deportation to a special penal colony for Reds on the island of Guam.

The massive display of public indignation was all Palmer needed. A group of selected radicals was assembled on Ellis Island and held incommunicado until the logistics of deportation could be arranged. Then, amid great enthusiastic publicity, 249 deportees, including three women, were placed aboard an old steamer, the *Buford,* which had first been a troop transport in the Spanish-American War "to save Cuba for democracy," then used across the Atlantic to France "to save the world for democracy." Then arrived the celebrated Reds Emma Goldman and her lover, Alexander Berkman, who had been arrested for interference in the draft. The *Buford* was laughingly rechristened the "Soviet Ark," stacked with provisions for a voyage of six weeks and equipped with a special crew of 250 American soldiers for security, one for each alien Red. The irrepressible Emma Goldman described her quarters at Ellis Island "the worst dump I ever stayed in." Among the spectators at the crowded sailing was J. Edgar Hoover, available to be photographed and interviewed. Also were the wives and children of a dozen men, desperately trying to join them, thus inspiring a typically warped report in the morning press: "REDS STORM FERRY GATES TO FREE PALS."

Not reported was the fact that most of the 250 were not violent at all, had never participated in terrorism and had no criminal record. They were being deported solely for their beliefs after an arbitrary decision totally devoid of review. Regardless of how peaceable and law-abiding an alien may have been, he could be summoned before an inquisitor of the Bureau of Immigration. He might prove that he had never advocated and did not believe in violence or disobedience to the law, or active opposition to the government. He might believe in passive resistance as a philosophical anarchist such as Tolstoy; he might never have taken a single active step toward bringing on the dissolution of the state. But if the bureau so chose, he could be deported.

There was, for example, one David Horwath, a Wobbly who had never so much as violated a police ordinance. He admitted to believing in the organization of the working class to take over the industries of the country. He believed in the efficacy of the general strike, but never in the use of force or violence. "Don't you think a strike is force?" he was asked. He replied that he didn't know. He did not believe in bombs or bomb plots. "Do you believe in God?" He replied that he did not. For that he was on the *Buford.*

Kalman Pantek, also a member of the IWW, had once studied to be a priest. "I learned from this priest [that] God made man free," he said. He believed in the Bible. He also believed that "if you do not work you do not eat." He did not believe in anarchism, but the philosophy of anarchism "is good for a dream, maybe four thousand years from now." He did not approve of the Bolsheviks because they had established a dictatorship. Nonetheless, he too was deported.

Louis Gyori believed that workers should control industries, either through the IWW or the AFL—there would be local and national councils. "Who would belong?" he was asked. "Workers." "What would become of other people?" "There would be no other people; *everyone* would work." He did not know when the revolution would come but thought it would be only when the majority wanted it, he hoped without violence. He thought killing officials "would be madness." Gyori was also on the *Buford.*

Of them all, however, only Emma Goldman was quoted. "This is the end for the United States. I shall be back....We shall all be back. I am proud to be among the first to be deported."

If her predictions (of revolution) were overblown, the reactions of the press made her words seem pallid. Wrote the *New York Evening Mail:* "Just as the sailing of the Ark that Noah built was a pledge for the preservation of the human race, so the sailing of the Ark of the Soviet is a pledge for the preservation of America." "As epoch-making as the immortal voyage of Columbus," wrote the *Boston Evening Transcript.* "The *Mayflower* brought the first of the builders to this country; the *Buford* has taken away the first destroyers," read the *Saturday Evening Post.*

The Department of State released its own explanation:

> These persons, while enjoying the hospitality of this country, have conducted themselves in a most obnoxious manner; and while enjoying the benefits and living under the protection of this government, have plotted its overthrow. They are a menace to law and order. They hold theories which are antagonistic to the orderly process of modern civilization....They are arrayed in opposition to government, to decency, to justice. They plan to apply their destructive theories by violence in derogation of law. They are anarchists. They are persons of such character as to be undesirable in the United States of America and are being sent whence they came.

The *Buford* docked at Finland, and the 249 were taken across the border. In Russia, they were greeted with a warm welcome.

All things considered, the November raids had been so successful that Palmer wasted no time preparing for another. Having found a good horse, he would be a fool not to ride it again—all the way to the Democratic Convention, he hoped. The targets, this time, were two spanking-new superradical organizations: the

Communist Party and the Communist Labor Party. And this time, he made certain of support—from the Department of Labor, through its new solicitor, one John W. Abercrombie, who was conveniently also a member of the Department of Justice.

The legal premise for the raids was substantially the same: both Communist parties contained aliens subject to the deportation laws under the 1918 Alien Act. Abercrombie, then assistant secretary of labor, signed over three thousand warrants for their arrests and turned them over to the Department of Justice for execution. Since no crime was to be charged, no trial would be impending; no judge or jury involved. Deportation, the province of the Department of Labor and implemented through the Bureau of Immigration, was not even considered as punishment. It was, then, strictly an administrative procedure, all normal legal procedures and due process of criminals circumvented. Radicals would not be arrested for crimes; they need merely be thought of as criminals.

In the background of this preparation was the evolution of a sophisticated technique of undercover agentry wherein an untold number of Palmer's men had joined the two Communist parties and achieved important positions within their executive staffs. These agents not only informed on activities but were trained to provoke them. Many had become known as vigorous Communist agitators. For these new raids, Palmer instructed the spies to arrange that meetings be held on the night of January 2, 1920. Herein, part of the testimony of federal agent William J. West:

Q: And presumably you acted upon instructions that came to you from your chief in Washington, did you not?

A: I, in each instance, carried out all instructions issued to me, to the best of my knowledge.

Q: And do you recall there were specific instructions to hold meetings that night?

A: I recall yes, sir.

Q Were Communist meetings actually held that night?

A: Yes, sir.

Q: In large numbers?

A: On the night of January 2 there were Communist meetings held in Worcester, there was a meeting at the city headquarters in Boston, there was a meeting at Nashua, New Hampshire; I believe there was a meeting in Lynn, I believe a meeting in Springfield.

The agents were also ordered to adhere to a coordinated plan that all documentary evidence be available (charters, membership books, minutes of meetings, correspondence), that no member be allowed to communicate with any outside person, that on arrest, American citizens must produce documentary evidence as proof of their citizenship, that aliens be lined up against the wall and searched immediately.

The raid results were, indeed, stunning. Four thousand radicals were rounded up in over thirty cities in twenty-three states. Every Communist cell was raided, practically every leader was arrested, many without warrants. Agents entered known popular hangouts such as pool halls, cafés, bowling alleys, even private homes to dig out their prey. Again, families were separated, prisoners held incommunicado. American radicals were carefully separated from aliens and turned over to state jurisdiction for prosecution, while aliens went through the abominations of the federal deportation process.

Again, it was brutal, even more so than in November. In New England, the eight hundred seized in Boston, Chelsea, Brockton, Nashua, Manchester and Portsmouth were taken to atrocious holding pens at immigration stations, or shipped to Deer Island in Boston Harbor, many of them forced to proceed in chains. Let one, Mrs. Stanislas Vasiliewska of Chelsea, a married mother of three young children, tell (under oath) of the experience of that night:

"I went with my little girl . . . to do the shopping for the next morning, and I stepped in the hall to the mailman to give a letter I had, and when I went there I meet quite a few people there . . . so there comes a civilian man . . . and there comes some police in uniforms and they make every man 'Hands up!' So every man just stand like that and they fish all the pockets in the men and they get to me, they look all over the bag but there is nothing in it because I didn't buy anything yet. So they looked all over the hall; they broke the platform, move every chair; of course, they take every picture from the wall, the sign 'No Smoking' in Russian language—take the signs and everything and put into their patrol wagon, and they put every man two by two handcuffed and put those men and another lady and the child in a patrol wagon with those pictures. . . . Well, I wasn't care for it because I was thinking about the two children waiting for me. . . . They bring me to Chelsea police station; they closed me and my little girl and another lady in one cell, the other lady she was in the family way, and she was kind of nervous. There was one bed there, very narrow . . . and I make her lay down for a while, and she kick one sheet off and I find under a very dirty mattress, and I couldn't sit down or lay down, I had to stand there all one night. About twelve o'clock at night they take my little girl and send her home all alone— about fifteen or twenty minutes' walk from the police station. . . . Half-past eight or nine o'clock in the morning I was put in an automobile . . . and I has a ride to the boat . . . but three of us, two men was handcuffed on, and me and two policemen and one man of justice in the machine . . . but the boat was gone and we had to wait until the afternoon boat. . . . So, of course, they don't get no room for me. They put the men in a separate room so one man take me . . . and he pushed me into the toilet . . . on the wharf where I was waiting for the boat . . . and I stayed in the toilet about, I don't know, there wasn't no clock there, I could not tell the time, but it seemed very long. I was feeling cold; and after I stayed there long, they push another woman in. She was pushed into the same toilet. It was more than dirty . . . a lot of cigars and spitting on the floor, and everything, and I wait until the afternoon boat, and when the boat come we went and so we got to Deer Island."

It was many days before this woman could communicate with outsiders or obtain a lawyer to help her or make contact with her family. Her story was significant because it was multiplied by thousands on that day.

On Deer Island, others were brutally beaten. One went insane. Two died of pneumonia, still another leaped to his death from a fifth-floor window. Of the eight hundred, those who had not been sent to Deer Island were, in the main, released for lack of evidence. Thirty-nine bakers in Lynn, Massachusetts, for example, had been arrested for suspicious assemblage but managed to prove that they were only planning to form a cooperative.

Over four hundred arrested in New York City at Communist Party headquarters and the Rand School suffered more violent treatment. Excessive verbal abuse was followed by beatings, black-jacking. "I was struck on the head . . . knocked down, one detective sat on my back, pressing me down to the floor with one knee and bending my body until blood flowed out of my mouth and nose. . . . I was questioned and released," said one arrestee.

In Philadelphia, over one hundred were given third-degree interrogation. In Pittsburgh, 115 were seized, although only twenty warrants had been issued. One man disappeared for almost a month before friends discovered he was in jail, arrested without a warrant, then held incommunicado.

In New Jersey cities, five hundred were arrested, almost all of whom were released for insufficient evidence. One was pulled in because "he looked like a radical," another because he stopped to ask what the commotion was all about. In New Brunswick, when a socialist club was raided, agents discovered mysterious drawings that were sent to demolition experts as "the internal mechanism of various types of bombs," only to discover they were designs for a phonograph.

In the Midwest, the Detroit and Chicago raids were exception-ally savage. Eight hundred in Detroit were put into a dark, win-dowless corridor of the Federal Building, forced to sleep on the bare floor for three to six days with only one toilet available and denied all food until their families could supply them. Once again, they included a mixed bag of "citizens and aliens, college gradu-ates and laborers, skilled mechanics making $15 a day and boys not yet out of short trousers." Only 140 of the eight hundred were held, transferred to the Detroit Municipal Building and photo-graphed after a week of unspeakable conditions. The press used them as illustrations of filthy Bolshevik terrorists that Palmer had finally captured. Their new space, a single room called the Bull Pen, was even worse, and afforded another week of abominable existence.

The Chicago raids were complicated by a bizarre mix-up, for the state and city had long planned their own raids on January first. In those, 150 to two hundred radicals were arrested, eighty-five of whom were Communists, among them Big Bill Haywood and Rose Pastor Stokes. Palmer's federal raids on the second nabbed 225 more, of whom eighty were held for deportation. When they were jailed, the prisoners already in residence rioted at the prospect of sharing cells with Reds. Wrote that paragon of Americanism, the *Seattle Times:* "There are some things at which even a Chicago crook draws the line."

In the far west, there was little action, for the states had already done the job after Centralia.

All in all, the raids were impressive more for their numbers than for results. The American people remained thoroughly bedazzled by them. As the *Washington Evening Star* put it: "This is no mere scare, no phantom of heated imagination—it is a cold, hard, plain fact." Or, from the *Washington Post:* "[There] is not time to waste on hairsplitting over infringement of liberty." A. Mitchell Palmer could not have written it any better.

"All Aboard For the Next Soviet Ark," ran the headlines.

Said the attorney general: "We have halted the advance of Red radicalism in the United States."

There was no question but that the Communist Parties were dealt a devastating blow. Their leaders were in jail, a large part of their memberships decimated by anticipated deportations, their records and membership lists confiscated. It was, indeed, a "cold, hard, plain fact."

And again, Palmer tried to ride with his triumphs. This time there would be at least 2,720 deportations, he declared. And after that, there would be more. In raids to come, he pledged to purge the country of all alien agitators. What he needed was the legal authorization of Congress to proceed; Congress must pass a more stringent sedition law. Only when all Bolsheviks were rooted out could speech be truly free and civil liberties be secured. Palmer, eager to accomplish this, would burn down the barn to kill the rats. He cared little about the cost, only what he could accomplish. Any determined tactician could tell you that you can't make ketchup without busting the tomatoes. Did not the righteousness of the ends justify the means? Palmer read his congratulatory telegrams and spoke endlessly eloquent phrases at press conferences. He did not have to face Mrs. Stanislas Vasiliewska of Chelsea, Massachusetts. It is doubtful that he ever heard of her.

The recently resigned commissioner of immigration, Frederick C. Howe, bemoaned this travesty of American principles. He asked how our newspapers would react if American citizens, legally in Mexico, were deported under similar procedures. "There is little to justify the assumption that the alien is a dangerous 'Red.' . . . Reread the records of Liberty Bond sales. In community after community where aliens predominated, Liberty Bonds issues were oversubscribed. There were fifteen thousand Russians in the American Army and the subscriptions of Russians totalled $40 million. . . . Many alien groups went over the top in shorter time than did similar communities of native born. . . . Reread the records of the doughboys. The alien did not wait to be conscripted. He volunteered. The casualty lists that came back from France read like a census of foreign countries. . . . There was no disloyalty in France; there was little disloyalty in this country. Yet for two years, tens of thousands of Secret Service agents were filling the press with scare stories of treason, of spies, of munitions plots, of burnings, of poisoned water supplies, of conspiracies." He saw the effect of the Palmer Raids as more devastating than the deportations themselves. Aliens "are living in perpetual fear . . . a fear that they are likely to be seized and torn from their homes, and that all America is eager to be rid of them. . . . We have made Americanization impossible."

As it turned out, there were no more raids. Only 591 aliens were eventually deported (thirty-five of whom were left over from the days of the *Buford*), a far cry from the promised 2,720 and the thousands more to be gathered on subsequent arks. The Red Scare had reached its zenith. No sooner had the sensational impact of the January second raids subsided than Americans suddenly began to nurse second thoughts on the meaning of all this. It was as if the start of the new decade spawned a whole new way of thinking. After all, the strikes had ended with a total rout of radicals. Unions had been crushed. Bolshevism had been beaten back, not only in America, but in Europe as well. Suddenly, there was something terribly disturbing about the New York State Legislature's vote (not once but twice!) to unseat the duly elected members of the Socialist Party. Suddenly, it became legitimate to criticize this gross violation of representative government and the established electoral process. Suddenly, even the conservative press was asking where such procedures might lead. All over the country, eyes were on the New York Assembly with mounting protests at its high-handedness, no doubt inspired as much by all prejudices against the hated eastern metropolis as by democratic political principles. No matter, the impact was salutary. Men of such diverse opinions as Senator Warren Harding and Dean Roscoe Pound were making the same critical statements. Even A. Mitchell Palmer would defend the right of Socialists to sit (but not Communists). William A. White called New York "preposterous." Fiorello La Guardia of the Board of New York Aldermen warned: "If we keep on at this rate, we shall build up a radical party in this country." Charles Evans Hughes, Wilson's Republican adversary in 1916, representing the New York Bar Association, offered his services to defend the Socialist electees. And suddenly too there was a rising criticism of the new peacetime sedition bills before the United States Congress, especially as proposed by A. Mitchell Palmer. Even the *New York Times* finally saw the threat to the First Amendment and the limitations to the right of free press. Supreme Court Justice Oliver Wendell Holmes condemned the bills. Samuel Gompers reacted to their threat to organized labor in every clause. A distinguished body of American clergymen signed an appeal to "return to the old faith in the fundamental principles of our civil liberty." It was finally considered no longer necessary to destroy American liberties in order to preserve them.

A. Mitchell Palmer tried hard to go on, but his horse was all played out. He took one last ride with a preposterous claim that the last Reds left in America were going to use the coming May Day for a great radical takeover. Once again, major cities were primed for red flags and Bolshevik exhortations, bombs and riots and the stench of gas. In San Francisco, Chicago and New York, every available Red was jailed in preventive arrest. Thousands of police lined the streets, surrounded government buildings and public utilities. State militias were summoned to emergency alert. The public could not help but react with tension and fear. Then, nothing happened, absolutely nothing. Palmer took credit for being the force that saved the day, but no one believed him. He had fired one too many blanks.

So it was that the "Fighting Quaker" became the "Quaking Fighter," or even the "Fighting Faker," and once he became a joke, his political career was ruined.

Nonetheless, he would not be forgotten or his message ignored, for he had laid in the fear of any identification with dissent. In the wake of the Red Scare, it remained far more convenient to adopt safe positions; for over a decade, there would be no significant revivals of radical thought. The Red Scare was a marvelous horse to ride, and both parties rode it, or, as Sean Dennis Cashman put it, "like two stagecoaches running side by side in the same direction, splattering mud on each other." No matter that the fears were bogus, the issue was made to seem so overwhelming, the two rival parties became as one.

It is axiomatic that American politicians would cling to any winning formula, that the best vote-getting techniques are often the basest. In our history, the tragedy of the preposterous witch-hunters of 1919 lay in the inspiration they offered to the future. The Red Scare became embedded in the American political system to be hauled out like an old cannon and fired whenever anyone needed to make a big noise. Americans loved or hated its thunder but no one would ever deny its impact. It would remain a dominant factor in foreign policy that brought on numerous international crises, wars great and small. It was the driving force behind the Cold War and the ever-present threat of nuclear holocaust. On the domestic scene, it would repeatedly make a mockery of the Bill of Rights, send dissenters to jail as traitors and cause random firings and loss of careers through blacklisting. It forced the political center into extremely conservative positions. It inhibited young minds from embracing unpopular ideas. It polluted the political atmosphere by sewing dissension and disunity through irresponsible accusations of disloyalty. It made civil rights an issue to fight over rather than to exercise. It eroded truth in journalism and the dissemination of information. It befouled the meaning of patriotism.

In time, the Red Scare became a ritual. We were warned of Reds under every political bed, domestic or foreign. They were the objects of such hate and fear that opportunistic politicians could use that to move into positions of incredible power. It was bewildering how readily this could be accomplished. Ole Hanson, who abandoned politics to become a real estate developer—the most successful of his ventures being a new community in California called San Clemente—would have envied the career of his leading resident, Richard Nixon. A. Mitchell Palmer, who retired to his law practice, would doubtlessly have been awed by the effective fulminations of Senator Joe McCarthy. Calvin Coolidge might even have smiled (!) at the revered presumptions of another president named Ronald Reagan. Seventy years after Seattle and Boston and Centralia, George Bush would gain the presidency by tagging his opponent with the despised "L" word: not a Red but an unmentionable liberal, no doubt the reductio ad absurdum of all Red Scaring.

3
PROHIBITION

If you think this country ain't dry, you just watch 'em vote, and if you think this country ain't wet, you just watch 'em drink. . . . You see, when they vote, it's counted, but when they drink, it ain't.

—WILL ROGERS

Prohibition is an awful flop.
We like it.
It can't stop what it's meant to stop.
We like it.
It's left a trail of graft and slime,
It don't prohibit worth a dime,
It's filled our land with vice and crime,
Nevertheless, we're for it.

—FRANKLIN P. ADAMS

1. RUM, RELIGION AND RURAL RIGHTEOUSNESS

Oh they say that drink's a sin
In Kansas
Oh they say that drink's a sin
In Kansas.
Oh they say that drink's a sin
So they guzzle all they kin
And they throw it up ag'in
In Kansas.

—OLD FOLK SONG

At approximately 3:15 on the afternoon of October 27, 1919, Wayne B. Wheeler sat in the gallery of the United States Senate and, not without some justification, saw himself as one of the most powerful men in America. The austere body of legislators below him, all eyes on him, had risen as one man in a thunderous ovation. To what ordinary citizen had such honors ever been bestowed? Largely through his efforts, a hundred million Americans had just been "liberated from the evils of alcohol." The Volstead Act implementing the Eighteenth Amendment to the Constitution, at least partly his composition, had just been passed, overriding President Wilson's veto barely two hours before.

This natty little man had moved the mountain. Or, as he preferred to see it, "the Biblical David had slain the giant." Like him or hate him (hardly any were in between), no one denied the extraordinary energy of the man. "A locomotive in trousers," he was called. Later he could boast (and often did) of having controlled six Congresses, dictated to two presidents (Harding and Coolidge) and deeply impressed a third (Wilson), directed legislation in countless states, directly influenced the election of numerous candidates for a variety of governmental offices, held the balance of power in both political parties, distributed a vast amount of patronage and run a federal bureau without even holding office.

The Anti-Saloon League, of which he was general counsel, had more than a few distinguished leaders—from Howard Hyde Russell to Bishop James J. Cannon—but Wheeler had become its driving force, its single-minded tireless true believer, its ever-in-the-limelight champion. This five foot, six inch human dynamo was the terror of the liquor trust. "Mr. Dry Boss," everyone called him.

He was born on November 10, 1869, in Brookfield, Ohio, of New England stock and an American Revolutionary heritage. Even as a boy, he never stopped to rest. Work, work, work. Since there was little money in the family, his boyhood was a continuing series of chores. (Once, when he was pitching hay, an experienced farmhand accidentally jabbed a prong into Wheeler's thigh because he had been drinking. Wheeler, who never forgot anything, could even remember the man's alcoholic smell—then again, that same smell when a drunken visitor to his home made suggestive remarks to his mother.) He was brighter than his peers. "You're too smart to go to school," his work-oriented father told him. Self-educated even in his teens, he taught school when he seemed barely older than his students. When he faced disciplinary problems with them, he learned how to maintain what he called a "smiling exterior under fire." His poker face would become legendary. At Oberlin College, he was self-supporting, paying all his expenses by working at several jobs almost at the same time. Like Woodrow Wilson and Ole Hanson, debate was his passion. His first literary society address was titled "Rum in the Congo," in which he criticized a Massachusetts brewery company for sending eight million gallons a year to besot the unfortunate natives. He was all over the campus all the time. The music teacher told him: "We wouldn't mind having you in the Glee Club, Wheeler, if you didn't try to sing all the parts yourself."

Howard Hyde Russell, another Oberlin graduate, heard of

Wheeler's extraordinary talents and induced him to join the new Anti-Saloon League of Ohio. Immediately, Wheeler astonished everyone by getting a dry candidate elected to the state Senate through relentlessly campaigning on his bicycle. "Wheeler on his wheel" did it, everyone said. Whatever they said, he loved it as long as they said it about him. He spent his life heaven-bent for notoriety, forever on his wheel (real or symbolic), obsessed by a passion for making himself not only "Mr. Dry Boss" but the world's greatest achiever. Like Ole Hanson (whom he was said to admire), he was blessed with a mastery of opportunism and the gall of a safecracker. There was no lie he would not employ for his cause nor tactic so devious as to be outside his scruple. Like A. Mitchell Palmer (whom he helped get into the president's cabinet), he obliterated his opposition without concern for their rights and liberties. Like Calvin Coolidge (whom he succored but quietly despised), he was blessed with an impeccable sense of timing. Like all three, he was unalterably ambitious for power. He would use the cause of Prohibition the way a skilled gambler uses a deck of marked cards. Had Wheeler been seduced by John D. Rockefeller before Howard Hyde Russell got to him, Wheeler would have made Horatio Alger seem but a flea on a mangy dog. It was his unrelenting policy to care nothing about any political candidate but the potential of his wet/dry vote. He used whatever power he had to threaten, sway or even blackmail an officeholder. He would see no difficulty in backing a submissive governor though he owned two saloons in the state capital, in order to punish a tee-totaler rival of independent spirit—just as a threat to all.

He became so famous as to have a term associated with his very name: "Wheelerism" stood for forcefulness, redbloodedness, intestinal fortitude. It suggested power and persistence and punishment. And how he loved the sight and sound of its usage! His religiosity served to justify his deviousness as a tactician on a crusade of Christian virtue. Indeed, he enjoyed that enormously. It enabled him to sit with the devil, to play the devil's game. Even more, it inspired him to play it better than the devil himself. And if, in the end, he succeeded in corrupting the entire governmental process, it was a necessary part of his ego that this would never so much as occur to him. It was, after all, in pursuit of God's will.

Sigmund Freud, who deplored Woodrow Wilson's excessive

identification with Christ, would surely have laughed at Wayne Wheeler's comparable affinity for Satan.

In 1898, when Wheeler joined the Anti-Saloon League, a gambler could have gotten one thousand to one odds that national prohibition was an impossible goal. Wayne Wheeler would always claim that there was never any doubt of it.

Americans had always been a drinking people as well as a God-fearing one. As John Kobler recorded in *Ardent Spirits* from the early days of the colonialists, alcohol was conveniently considered "one of the good creatures of God," to be received with thanksgiving. The "dram" before breakfast was a fixture in the American home somewhat comparable to a modern drink of orange juice, designed to ward off New England chills and to kick the sleepy body into the actions of the day. The proverbial "eye-opener," as it were. Since New England did not lend itself by soil or by climate to the cultivation of the grape, nor did the early colonists have the industrial capacity to produce good beer, their trading enterprise brought them molasses from the West Indies, the raw material for rum. Rum became the hard liquor that turned them into heavy drinkers. It was traditional to set a bottle of rum with a cornerstone of a public building, even a church. Harvard University had its own brewery, George Washington his own distillery. Doctors prescribed alcoholic drink for a variety of afflictions from teething in infancy to the rheumatism of old age. The clergy appeared to thrive on it. Early drinking was also associated with snobbish references to a family's status. It was customary to serve the best available alcohol to guests. Water was not considered to be a proper libation, sometimes out of fear of polluted streams. It was often treated with molasses to dignify the affluence of the donor. (A century later, the great wet philosopher/comedian W. C. Fields refused to drink water "because fish copulated in it.") The absence of booze at social gatherings signified "meanness or parsimony." In 1792, there were already 2,579 registered distilleries to service a population of four million, their annual production amounting to two and one-half gallons per person. The figure quickly doubled at the turn of the century. Apple cider was de rigueur throughout New York and New England, most of it fermented to be stronger than wine. In New Jersey, cider was allowed to freeze in the keg, whereupon a hole was bored into the liquid core for the alcohol to drain into a jug. "Jersey Lightning," it was called.

And so it had been throughout the history of the world. Had not civilization and the use of alcohol developed at the same time? Why else did the Book of Genesis describe mankind as engulfed in wickedness before Noah "began as a husbandman and planted a vineyard"?

At the same time, temperance was a counterforce right from the start. George Washington was quoted accordingly: "The sure means to avoid evil is first to refrain from drink which is . . . the ruin of half the workmen in the country." Nevertheless, he paid off his gardener not only in wages but with a generous allotment of rum. During his presidency, it was estimated that almost a fourth of all household expenses went for liquor. President John Adams would preach abstemiousness but drank a large tankard of hard cider every morning before breakfast.

The eighteenth-century fur trade depended on rum as barter to Indians in exchange for furs. No matter that Indian chiefs foresaw the ruin of their people because of the tragic effects of drink, and requested that white fur traders abandon the practice; the whites saw not only profits but an easy way of conquest. Puritan Massachusetts refused to oblige the chiefs, "the court apprehending that it is not fair to deprive the Indians of any lawful comfort which God alloweth to all men by the use of wine." The Indians, in fact, were to be denied all rights except the right to get drunk.

To illustrate the hypocrisy of our nation's attitude toward drinking, witness this comment in the Congressional Record: "Mr. Speaker, rum has more enemies in public and more friends in private than any other substance the world has ever known." Nor was there any lack of rebelliousness at the early attempts to tax it. In the very first administration under George Washington, the secretary of the treasury, Alexander Hamilton, imposed an excise tax on whiskey. The settlers in western Pennsylvania, mostly Scotch-Irish, for whom whiskey was the dominant commodity, protested the tax's discriminatory impact on their liberties and economic well-being. When the government attempted to collect the taxes, rioting had to be crushed by government troops in this first significant challenge to governmental power in United States history.

* * *

The history of the Temperance movement offers a fascinating thematic symmetry, for both its origin and conclusion were rooted in a crusade to preserve the moral leadership of the Protestant church. In its origin, the Puritan New England Federalists, that old aristocracy of sedate, virtuous, upstanding people, were losing their moral and political dominance to the expanding frontier ethic. The new Western Americans were uneducated, adventurous, roughly hewn free spirits. And they drank. They built saloons before they built churches. They bought whiskey even as they bought firearms. Temperance, then, became a crusade to restore the morality of the Puritan Protestant East. Early in the nineteenth century, the American Temperance Society, led by the Reverend Lyman Beecher of Boston, started the first drive for total abstinence, its ultimate aim a law to abolish hard liquor from the nation. Its credo: "Everything that rests my body or mind, improves my health and elevates my soul is commendable. Everything that stimulates my nervous system until I become a walking maniac; everything that debauches my body, weakens my conscience; excites impure thoughts and makes my soul a terrible house of imagery; and everything that makes me forget God and eternity is dangerous, and in the last, damnable."

From the start of Temperance, the drinker was neither foolish or sick, he was sinful.

A hundred years later, only the geography of the crusade had reversed itself. The rural West (and South) became the Drys and the urban culture of the East became the drinkers. But the sedate, virtuous, upstanding people of the Protestant church remained as crusaders for Temperance.

At the base of the conflict lay the age-old antipathy of country people for the libertine nature of cities. Even in colonial years, cities were seen as sinful. There were grog shops, saloons, drunks, prostitutes in cities. The money people were there, the snobs of old European "aristocratic" class lines. The United States Constitution reflected the hegemony of the farm, favoring rural conceptions over urban. Not accidentally, state capitols were set distant from the big cities: Albany, Harrisburg, Trenton. Agrarianism was the first dominant force in America, farmers its leading citizens. "God made the country; man made the city," it was said. Thomas Jefferson wrote: "Those who labor in the earth are the chosen people of God.... Corruption of morals in the mass of cultivators is a phenomenon of which no age or nation has furnished an example."

A conspiracy of exaggerations had been used to implement the expansion of the West. Throughout the nineteenth century, many thousands struggled and suffered more hardships than they had bargained for, and when they survived they were left with less than what pleased them. The alleged desirability of farming, for example, became dissipated by its perennial starkness. The writer Hamlin Garland exposed this grotesque truth in 1891 in *Main-Travelled Roads,* wherein farm life was shown as endless drudgery, despised by farm families in their slavery to milking cows and swilling hogs, in a setting of worms, flies, bugs, heat and an endless stench. Despite this, the lore of its dignity persisted. It could not be attacked with impunity, so much so that Garland was forced to recant. Meanwhile, other distortions of the truth rode with it, especially the serenity of the small town, the purity of rural life, the majesty of the expanding western frontier so brashly trumpeted by the railroad lines, the shipping lines from Europe, the land speculators, the touters of easy profits from easy harvests, the self-serving promoters of local newspapers. As Andrew Sinclair described in his exceptional history, *Prohibition, The Era of Excess,* it was a continuing myth. Towns were built, then quickly deserted. In Iowa, for example, there were over two thousand settlements abandoned, but "never a discouraging word," as the great song had it. The myth had to be gilded. The basis of the preposterous glorification of Texas by Texans emanates from this cult; hyperboles in the interest of promotion were considered more essential than truth.

Meanwhile, there was continuing hardship exacerbated by the exploitations of the new trusts, discriminatory rates of railroads, banking consortiums, all of which were centered in Eastern cities. The farmers' religion reflected the deprivations of their lives. It dealt with simple truths of good and evil, God and the devil, right and wrong. Methodist and Baptist missionaries fed them a Manichean conception of heaven and hell to dignify their endless labors. The sinners were said to be in the cities; the Catholics with their ritualistic absolutions in glorious cathedrals, Jews with alien Hebraic tongues, Episcopalians in lofty ceremonies. Out of this clash of ideology and religion, of hardship versus easy affluence, of victim against exploiter, of rural American goodness as distinct from urban alien sin came the roots of Prohibition.

As Sinclair suggests, it had little to do with drink. The West, and then the South, were notoriously hard and heavy drinkers. They were the first to build the dingy saloons, the filthy, vice-ridden purveyors of rotten whiskey. In small towns, saloons were the obvious enemy and were wiped out years before the coming of Prohibition. Prohibition, then, was the struggle of the rural middle class to assert its moral and ethical superiority over the city, not a fight for the removal of drink.

"T for total" abolition, the origin of the word "teetotaler" made a mockery of this struggle, a hundred years of warfare that moved constantly into expanding territories, ever-changing populations and waves of immigration. Some saw it as the greatest war ever fought, for it challenged the very nature of man and his capacity to cope with his weakness. Could there be human progress in a society of drinkers? The fledgling American theatre came alive with Temperance plays, the most famous of which was *Ten Nights in a Barroom*. The great showman P. T. Barnum had considered himself a temperate drinker because he drank only champagne at dinner after the tumult of his workday. Then he heard a sermon against all drink that so inspired him, he went home and smashed every bottle in his well-stocked wine closet and became a teetotaler. The reward was his new production of *The Drunkard* at his Philadelphia and New York theatres—the first modern superhit of the American theatre.

Nothing was easy in this war, no battles went according to plan, no victory proved decisive. In the mid-nineteenth century, there had been several waves of temperance battles: at one time, thirteen states voted to go dry, or partially so, then abandoned the legislation at their inability to enforce. Every force provoked a counterforce. Saloon keepers would actually join the Temperance Society in order to seduce ex-drinkers to return to the fold, thus dismembering the organization, a form of "boring from within." The society grew, but so did consumption, a pattern that seemed eternal. Warned Abraham Lincoln when a young attorney: "Prohibition will work great injury to the cause of temperance—for it goes beyond the bounds of reason in that it attempts to control a man's appetite by legislation and makes a crime out of things that are not crimes. A prohibition law strikes at the very principle upon which our government was founded." Indeed, in 1850, the heavy-drinking state of Maine became celebrated for the reforms of its deeply committed prohibitionist leader, Neal Dow, the high-handed mayor of Portland: for all his efforts, however, there was just as much drinking as ever. Nor did this change with the advent of the Women's Christian Temperance Union in 1874, under the inspiring leadership of Frances Willard. The Protestant church gave the cause power and prayer, but for all its ever-rising impact throughout the country, per capita consumption rose from from 4.08 gallons in 1850 to 13.21 by 1880. Frances Willard became the most celebrated woman of her time, but bootlegging and illegal pubs proliferated even as communities were voting themselves dry.

There was the great Utopian novelist, Edward Bellamy (*Looking Backward*), who proposed a plan for the nationalization of liquor whereby the federal government would become the sole dispenser of all alcoholic drink through government stores. The Populists of the 1890s at first approved, for it promised the elimination of the profit motive that brought on debasing saloon life, impure liquor, a corrupt and corrupting liquor industry. Prohibitionists, however, saw Bellamy's plan as another conciliating gesture toward the immoral habit of drinking itself. And since the Populists were seeking the broadest possible national coalition, the proposal became too controversial. The Prohibition Party, meanwhile, was becoming a force of its own, with its own presidential candidate, the foremost single-issue political entity in American history. Yet for all its doggedness, it never made much of an impact.

Then, in 1893, the Anti-Saloon League was "born of God" at Oberlin, Ohio, in the midwest heartland of temperance. The name, so brilliantly conceived, made a huge difference in the movement, for it fixed on what many believed to be the foremost blight on our noble ethic. Cautiously the league declined to advocate prohibition in the broad sense, preferring to work for the widest possible acceptance. Although intensely political, it would be nonpartisan, working to unite people of all persuasions to support its program. Its structure would be a federation of strong state organizations over local temperance groups, mostly under church auspices. The motto that gave it energy was "The Saloon Must Go!"

The saloon was many things to many people, but to the God-fearing middle class it was a sleazy, beery, spitoon-filthy iniquitous gathering place where bartenders sold diluted whiskey to illiterate immigrants and shortchanged drunks, where whores and gamblers congregated to ply their degenerate trades, where local police were paid off to permit whatever transgressions might be committed under its tacky roof, where public officials and party hacks came to bribe and swindle for immigrant votes, while behind and above it all were the liquor distillers and breweries whose enormous resources were devoted to preserving the liquor-lined status quo. After all, everyone knew of the corruption of the cities, those sprawling, violent, chaotic centers of polyglot populations dominated by political bosses who bought power through bribes and deals and favors, where nothing was done on the square, no streetcar line franchised or street paved or building constructed without dirty business being done. Indeed, city people admitted all that, even boasted of it.

No doubt this sordid perception of saloons came from good country folk who feared and despised cities they had never seen. The image of God himself could not be more grossly violated than through the existence of this sinful creation of man. And no more ardent apostle of its destructiveness could be found than the woman named Carry A. Nation. She was the ultimate strange one. As described by J. C. Furnas in his book *The Late Demon Rum,* she was "always corny, usually vulgar and intermittently psychotic." Many of her family members were institutionalized, including her own daughter, whose father had drunk himself to death within six months of his wedding. When married again, Carry moved from Texas to Kansas, a dry state typically loaded with saloons.

Her rage at their evil presence was forever stirred by their unlawfulness. She took to invading saloons, singing hymns of virtue while smashing bottles and back-of-the-bar mirrors. She gathered a hard core of disciples, all women, and stoned saloons in a hurricane of screaming virtues. "It is very significant that the paintings of naked women are in saloons," she wrote. "Women are stripped of everything by them. Her husband is torn from her, she is robbed of her sons, her home, her food and her virtue, and then they strip her clothes off and hang her bare in these dens of robbery and murder." Carry and her followers were arrested but so disrupted jails with the fury of their cause that the prisons could not hold them. Late in the winter of 1890, she gathered the militants of the Wichita WCTU and went on a spree. While others carried iron rods and stones wrapped in newspapers, Carry Nation hid a hatchet under her coat, "which she used so devastatingly in the joint's stock and fixtures that it became her mascot symbol, like Arthur's Excalibur." She cried out: "God gave Samson the jawbone! He gave David the sling, and he has given Carry Nation the hatchet!"

2.   AN IDEA WHOSE TIME WAS COMING

Kaiserism abroad and booze at home must go!

—WAYNE B. WHEELER

And thus America moved into the twentieth century, a time of tumultuous transitions. The Western frontier was closing. The industrial revolution was changing the face of the country in myriad ways. Factories and mills created great centers of industry. The growth of cities was so vast that by 1910 almost as many people were living in cities as in rural areas, not only because European immigrants were arriving by the millions, but because Americans from the farms and small towns were leaving the desolate prairies for the factories and mills. It was as if the essence of life was being stripped from the farmer.

Country preachers never left this trend's sinful implications alone: the city was an alien's place. Foreign money owned the breweries that poured an endless flow of beer into sinister saloons, debasing the city people, corrupting their politicians. Foreign agitators infiltrated the American mind with radical ideas that shook the foundations of American faith. The numbers were so great as to be stupefying. Millions were crowded into filthy ghettos, speaking dozens of languages, the flotsam and jetsam of decadent Europe, refugees from the dregs of civilization. And they drank. It was the rotten core of their heritage. They had to have their beer and their wine. They drank and they sinned and then found absolution in their foreign churches.

The cities were, in fact, many things. Because they were also the seats of power, they were linked to all the injustices that brought on the Progressive Movement, dominating American politics and thought for several decades around the turn of the century. Never had the demand for reform been so strident.

To the Evangelical Church, the solution to all problems lay in the removal of the temptation of alcohol, after which reform was possible. It was believed that man, by his very nature, was a sinner and must be denied the source of his sinning. The Progressives, however, brought a different conception to the Temperance crusade: temperance meant self-control. It accompanied man's capacity for industriousness, impulse-renunciation, resistance to sin. The new Progressive middle-class reformer believed that man was ever in control of his own destiny. Any lapse in self-control was but a weak link in the chain, a threat to the way of life itself. Sobriety, then, was a necessary virtue without which all else tended to unravel. To achieve this, political action was necessary. Only by legislation could the drinker be impelled to abandon his weakness. To legislate was to dignify, for law was another form of Christian rectitude. As for the problem of enforcement, the reformer would not fall into the trap of opening it up for debate. Weren't laws against theft and murder no less necessary even though criminals frequently got away with both? The passage of reform laws would, by its very essence, enhance the self-esteem of a society and degrade the culture of its transgressors.

This was the issue most closely allied to the rural and small-town middle classes—even more than the Red Scare with its sanctimonious passion and patriotism. It was also the first major expression of organized women through the WCTU, and its impact went far beyond anything in the evolution of the new women's movement—it was infinitely more powerful than suffrage itself. Since drinking had always been a male-oriented evil associated with the subjugation of women, temperance was the perfect feminist cause. Nonetheless, the WCTU urged reforms that transcended it. Since Frances Willard was a Socialist, the organization also advocated the federal income tax, direct election of senators, an advanced free system of public schooling—all of which put them two generations ahead of their time. (Nor were the women free of that old irony of the Temperance movement, for as the

WCTU advanced the feminist cause, so did it lead to a corresponding increase in drinking among women.) Willard hated that men saw fit to indulge in the vices of the flesh that they so despised in women. But it was the image of the drunk staggering down the street, or the six-year-old girl working for pennies because her father was besotted in a saloon, or the worker who came home drunk and beat up his protesting wife that inspired her work. How could any decent person resist such a cause? By 1912, Jack London, at the peak of his fame, came into town from his California ranch to vote for women's suffrage in order "to drive the nails into the coffin of John Barleycorn." As he saw it, the women's vote would bring it about.

To the middle class, temperance was touted as a stabilizing force in the labor-management turmoil, a preventative of violence in strikes, a moderator of excessively emotional responses that beclouded reason. Whiskey exacerbated class tensions. The middle class, squeezed by its struggle for identity between its envy of the wealthy owners and its distrust of hardworking laborers, found an agreeable cause around which to rally. The drunkenness of the American Indian demonstrated how alcohol could debase an entire race, and the superiority of the abstemious whites became the more apparent by this comparison. Did it not also tend to purge white of the guilt of genocide? Now it was the immigrants who were vulnerable, and the movement merely sought their salvation through sobriety. Temperance was designed for the dignity of all.

Meanwhile, urban saloons were proliferating in phenomenal progression. In 1909, there were more saloons than schools, libraries, hospitals, theatres and parks combined. Cities were overwhelmed by their numbers. In the city of Chicago alone there were more saloons than in all the southern states. The urban saloon had become the center of all the evils inherent in the industrial revolution.

The ultimate enemy, however, was the liquor industry itself, a perfect symbol of capitalist greed, notorious for its corruptive power over officials, unscrupulous dispensers of an all-but-poisonous product out of which it made millions. (As early as 1874, the administration of U. S. Grant was almost destroyed by the corruptions of the St. Louis Whiskey Ring, which succeeded in defrauding the government of millions in taxes in collusion with high officials. Nor was it a secret that the president himself suffered a strong affinity for alcohol.)

Three national organizations dominated the liquor interests: the United States Brewers Association, the National Wholesale Liquor Dealers Association (of distillers, importers, vintners) and the National Retail Liquor Dealers Association. Each maintained a lobby in Washington with huge sums financed through annual assessments of its members. As the influence of the Anti-Saloon League grew, so did the funding of these lobbies. The brewers' association, the most powerful of the three, created subsidiary agencies to protect its needs, at times under "fronts" to mask its identify. Eagerly, it joined with the National German-American Alliance, a German propaganda group to preserve the efficacy of German-American culture and the popularity of German beer. A newly created Protective Bureau became the brewers' agency for a vast propaganda drive of their own. It mailed millions of pieces of literature directly to voters, and induced local newspapers to publish columns written by its own propagandists.

Liquor interests paid off editors to print only anti-Prohibitionist articles and editorials and hired well-known writers to plant sympathetic articles in distinguished national magazines without attribution. Above all, liquor money was always available for the nomination and election of wet congressmen, then for controlling their votes. The liquor interests were, in fact, bold about such solicitations. From the Pabst Brewing Company in 1900, for example, came this communication to others in the trade: "Dubois will surely be the next senator from Idaho. I think it would be for the interest of the brewers to have his cooperation—he is aggressive and able—send me $1,000 to $5,000. I think it will be the best investment you ever made."

When corporations in various industries supported Prohibition for reasons of accident-prevention and increased efficiency at the workplace, the liquor industry sought reprisals. Thus, when the Sante Fe Railroad promoted Drys, thousands of liquor industry circulars called on its associates to ship freight by rival lines. When a New York packing company announced its support for drys, it was so threatened with boycotts, it reversed its stand. Nowhere was the power of the brewery industry more evident than in the violation of New York's Sunday Blue Laws, that standby of Protestant mores. Since the Irish and the Germans wanted their Sunday beers, the saloons chose to remain open (five thousand out of 5,820 did so), an obvious demonstration of their control over the city constabulary.

Then came an astonishingly brazen statement by a liquor dealer at an Ohio brewers' convention: "We must create the appetite for liquor in growing boys. Men who drink...will die, and if there is no new appetite created, our coffers will be empty.... Nickels expended in treats to boys now will return in dollars to your tills after the appetite has been formed."

There were ploys involving state excise departments that would revoke saloon licenses, then allow saloon keepers to buy new licenses and operate until they recouped their losses, then repeat the procedure. Working-class saloons were choice targets for graft since through them politicians could deliver the vote. Any attempt by reformers to stop such devious practices would be easily countered with police intervention, sometimes including violence. In New York, both Democrats and Republicans used saloons for neighborhood party conventions. Since the saloon keeper was friend and mentor to the workingmen who frequented his place, he became a political leader as well. In Milwaukee, for example, thirteen of forty-six city councilmen were saloon keepers. Lincoln Steffens related the story of a boy rushing into the St. Louis Municipal Assembly and hollering out: "Mister, your saloon is on fire!" whereupon the house was nearly emptied. In New Orleans, a saloon politician also ran a chain of bordellos, a directory to which his bartenders sold for a quarter (including ads for Anheuser-Busch beer and Harper's Rye Whiskey).

And always there were images of drunken violence. Take note, temperance advocates would warn: John Wilkes Booth was a celebrated drinker, having taken his last shot of whiskey at a saloon near Ford's Theatre on the night he shot Lincoln. Charles J. Quiteau, another drunk, shot James A. Garfield. Leon Czolgasz, a saloon keeper's son, was living in a saloon when he assassinated William McKinley. John Shrank, the failed assassin who shot Theodore Roosevelt, had been a saloon keeper and bartender for years.

The Methodist Episcopal Church had this comment on the liquor industry: "There is no law it will keep, no pledge it will honor, no child it will not taint, no woman it will not befoul, no man it will not degrade. It feeds upon dishonesties of conduct and on the shame of brothels. It stimulated all revenges and makes the murderer dance upon the body he has killed. It falsely claims to be a great public interest because it employs thousands and pays heavy taxes. But no ... profits, however real or immense, can compensate for the corruption of our politics, the emptiness of a drunkard's home or the fullness of prisons or graves."

There was no question that the liquor industry paid heavy taxes, bringing federal revenues of $262 million in 1914, 35 percent of the annual total, plus an equivalent percentage to municipal, county and state treasuries. Indeed, no other industry could account for as much. Would any government choose to vote out its own vested interest? The liquor trust was so well entrenched, its overthrow seemed virtually impossible to accomplish.

By 1910, there were over thirty million immigrants in America, representing a third of the population, over half of whom lived in cities. Most were peasants with an age-old devotion to a tightly knit community, where their social status was fixed through all of history, beholden to the feudal lord who was the source of all blessings. They had no heritage of freedom, no training in individualism or the competitive drive for social mobility. They had no understanding of democracy or personal participation in government. That they had been abused and exploited from the day they left Europe, packed into the filthy holds of abominable ships for a dangerous and subhuman passage, was never astonishing to them. To be then herded into ghettos in unspeakable conditions, to be victimized by cruel and low-paying jobs, to be left to live in squalor without surcease or even hope—that was their lot prescribed by history itself. It was no wonder they failed to learn English or become Americanized.

To the immigrant, the saloon was escape from squalor and provider of warmth and companionship, the occasional free lunch, billiards and backyard bocce, club rooms for card tables, letter-writing and reading matter. One could get hired out of a saloon or find help when in trouble. How could they understand the nativist notion that drink was a sin? Wasn't this just another crazy American idea? To take away their saloon and their drink on the grounds that it was for their own good was like drilling a hole in the bottom of a boat to bail out the excess water. The biggest opponent of the Drys was the man they called "Hunky."

The Committee of Fifty, a group of scholars and businessmen concerned with the truth about temperance, had this to report: "The saloon is the most democratic of institutions. It appeals at once to the common humanity of a man. There is nothing to repel. No questions are asked.... The door swings open before any man who chooses to enter. Once within, he finds the atmosphere one in which he can allow his social nature freely to expand. The welcome from the keeper is a personal one. The environment is congenial. It may be that the appeal is to what is base in him. He may find his satisfaction because he can give vent to those lower desires which seek expression. The place may be attractive just because it is so little elevating. Man is taken as he is, and is given what he wants, be that want good or bad. The only standard is the demand."

Andrew Sinclair then compared it with the Protestant church. "There was human fellowship and equality in the saloon . . . a center of tradition, the spirit of community, a place of recreation. It could be said that they were rivals in the same general business: consolation." The church and the saloon, battling for the soul of the city. To condemn the saloon as a place of corruption was to miss the point. To banish saloons for the presence of lowlifes was akin to banishing automobiles because drunken drivers killed people.

The church and the saloon, wrote Finley Peter Dunne, "They kind iv offset each other, like the Supreem Coort an' Congress. Dhrink is a nicissry evil, nicissry to th' clergy. If they iver admit it's nicissry to th' consumers they might as well close up th' churches."

The Evangelical Church was prepared to see this battle to the end. At stake was the restoration of rural superiority. The church was afraid of the city, especially after the proliferation of automobiles. Suddenly the city folk were appearing in their cars and their libertine ways, and were twice as threatening as before. The automobile was like a chariot for the devil himself. The church felt helpless before its impact, for it could not even inveigh against the automobile's swelling popularity.

But it could make Prohibition the issue.

The first region to go dry was comprised of the eleven states of the South, less for the rural hostility toward the cities than the white man's need to keep the blacks under control. Substitute "niggers" for "Hunkies," "dram shops" for "saloons," and the similarities became clear. While there were virtually no immigrants in the South, eight million of America's ten million blacks were scattered throughout southern states. "Dram shops" were dingy saloons where liquor was measured in drams. Since whites were perpetually on edge over anything relating to the race problem, drinking was said to be the cause of those troubles. Liquor, it was believed, simply could not be handled by the lower classes in general and colored people in particular. Drink supposedly made blacks unmanageable; it was the instigator of crime, vice, immorality and most of all, racial confrontations. The ever-explosive problem of black-white rape *had* to be the result of drink. There was a popular bottled gin, for example, on which salacious labels showed obscene pictures of naked white women, its copy claiming increased potency with every sip. "Nigger gin," they called it, for such bottling was not found in white saloons. On top of such corruptions, the liquor interests became adept at buying black votes with whiskey, sometimes in sufficient numbers as to swing elections. The black vote, in fact, had become so controlled by them that reformers worked to disenfranchise blacks as the only means of getting legislation enacted.

So too was it a reflection of the South's continuing battle with the North. The North had beaten the South in the Civil War, freed their slaves, forced through the Fifteenth Amendment to enfranchise blacks. To Southerners, the Northern wets only wanted to keep the black man drinking in order that he might continue to rape the saintly Southern women. And Southern politicians, needing an issue around which they could rally to cement their hold on the Democratic Party, clung to Prohibition. One could picture them on plantation porches, discussing tactics with an ever-present bottle of good Bourbon at hand.

The pattern was typical of all dry strategists. Whatever restrictions might be placed on minority groups or individual liberties was considered worth the sacrifice for the common good. The conception of personal liberty ended where public injury began. Did a man have the right to fire a gun in a crowded hall, or sell rotten meat, or drive an automobile on a sidewalk?

The weak had to be protected against themselves and their weakness, not only for their own good, but out of fear that they would eventually corrupt the strong. The plague syndrome, as it were. It made no difference if only a few were so severely affected, or that their capacity to affect others was questionable. To safeguard the common good, the liberties of the many would be abrogated. In this context, the moderate, temperate drinker frightened the Dry because he showed that man could drink without destroying himself and his family. The Dry preferred the real drunk. He even claimed that the temperate drinker had to give it up lest he convince the potentially intemperate drinker that he too could imbibe so sensibly. Or, to put it savagely: "Temperate drinkers are the parents of all drunkards." They were likened to a man in a barrel approaching Niagara Falls crying out not to worry, "I am only taking a lovely ride!" It was all too often repeated that, like the poor, the drunks would always be with us. They were, in fact, interchangeable with the poor, the chicken and the egg, one the cause and/or the result of the other.

Although such legislated action appeared to violate basic American rights, the Anti-Saloon League crusaders assumed that the end justified whatever means, or sacrifices, had to be employed. Wayne Wheeler, that "Fearless Fighter," "the Bane of the Brewers," was the arch-exponent of this dubious ideology. He was master of the pragmatic approach. In his endless manipulations of elections, nothing mattered but the battle for Anti-Saloon League dominance.

Wheeler, the crusader, was but a symbol of the excesses of the Drys. The Ku Klux Klan rode on the backs of the Prohibitionists, and vice versa. The Anti-Saloon League unleashed a host of Carry Nations with proposals of extraordinary solutions to bring about the end of drink. Deport them, hang them, poison them. Exclude drinkers from church (or force them into church), forbid them to marry, torture bootleggers as a threat to all, restore the stocks to cage drinkers in the public square. The Anti-Saloon

League was said to send drunks into churches, the better to infuriate the congregation before a fund-raising sermon. Middle-class children would be dressed in filthy rags to beg in the streets outside of saloons because their fathers were drunk inside. ("Father, dear father, come home with me now," went the popular lyric.) Mothers, also in rags, would weep in the streets that their drunken husbands had beaten them and deserted them for saloon prostitutes.

It was justified for the ultimate salvation of all, the eternal battle of conscience versus lust. There could be no moderation. All rights had to be abrogated. When the war came, beer was, above all, German, and therefore treasonable—wine too, for country people had no tradition in wine. The movement smothered all logic, all sensibility, and as such was akin to the xenophobia of the Red Scare.

The tragedy was that it need not have been this way. There might have been true temperance. There might have been moderate restrictions, the permission of wines and beers, and the entire movement would have found virtue.

After the turn of the century, temperance was an idea whose time had finally come. The Progressive Movement was an indignant cry for reform that put Theodore Roosevelt in the White House and even split the Republican Party. The Anti-Saloon League quickly became a part of it, using the Progressive thrust to enhance its own. Wheeler, who would share a bed with anyone, kept organizing his primary source of power: Protestant churches. By 1913, the Anti-Saloon League had developed into a federation of state organizations in a system of highly centralized control. It could reach down into forty thousand churches within its membership and, at a moment's notice, mobilize millions of Protestant voters to take action. With power in the hands of a few men, it moved quickly and effectively with one mind. It raised huge sums from small donors, mostly through subscriptions in the churches, but also through wealthy benefactors, not the least of whom were the Rockefellers, father and son, who contributed over $350,000 to the cause. By 1919, the league was taking in $2.5 million annually.

In 1900, only five states had enacted laws curtailing the manufacturing and sale of liquor, but by 1913, local option laws had dried out vast areas of the country, in counties as well as states— so much so, in fact, that Congress passed the Webb-Kenyon Act to protect dry states from neighboring wet incursions, thus making Prohibition a matter of national politics. Although the act was vetoed by President William Howard Taft on the presumption of its unconstitutionality, Congress immediately overturned the veto.

By 1913, strengthened by its merger with the WCTU and the Prohibition Party, the Anti-Saloon League decided to make its big move. After a march of ten thousand conventioneers down Pennsylvania Avenue to the Capitol dome, the league presented Congress with its unanimous resolution: "We declare for [alcohol's] national annihilation by an amendment to the federal Constitution which shall forever prohibit throughout the territory of the United States, the sale, manufacture for sale, importation for sale of all beverages containing alcohol." Not use, it must be noted, but "sale," for the target was to destroy commercial liquor traffic on a national scale and thereby, once and for all, remove the saloon. The appeal was so artfully conceived that anyone except real Wets and the liquor industry could support it. Although it gathered a majority of votes in the House of Representatives (197 to 190), it lacked the required two-thirds.

It was followed by an incredible demonstration of nationwide electoral campaigning. As Wheeler put it: In the 1916 congressional elections, the Anti-Saloon League "boiled and bubbled with hotter fire.... We laid down such a barrage as candidates for Congress had never seen before.... [In the 1916 campaign] there were double the number of trained speakers (fifty thousand)... directing their fire upon the Wets in every village and town." The Anti-Saloon League publication, *The American Issue,* turned out five hundred thousand copies a month. Speakers and agents circulated in the field like ants, churches were informed of preferred, sympathetic candidates, and congregations thus instructed as to how to vote, all of which was supplemented by direct mail and door-to-door canvassing.

And they won. "On election night, the lights burned late in our Washington office," Wheeler wrote of that 1916 campaign. "Many hours before the country knew whether [Charles Evans] Hughes or Wilson had triumphed, the dry workers throughout the nation were celebrating our victory. We knew the prohibition amendment would be submitted to the states by the Congress just elected."

Curiously, it was a strange, almost silent, victory, for neither party platform had so much as mentioned Prohibition.

It was typical that Calvin Coolidge would begin his political career in 1910, a mayoral candidate in Northampton, Massachusetts, a teetotaler who happened to be the lawyer for a brewery. That should have destroyed him with the Anti-Saloon League, but Wheeler saw the man's pliability behind the chilling mask. Besides, the opposing Democratic candidate had once dared to cross swords with Wheeler, an action that would never occur with Coolidge. In this town of eighteen thousand, with eighteen churches and eighteen saloons, evenly divided Protestant and Catholic, old stock and immigrants, wet and dry, Coolidge learned his silence on the four R's: race and religion, rum and reform. He was elected largely because Wheeler was on his side. Curiously, even the Boston police strike that would propel Coolidge to the White House was inspired by Prohibition, since the saloons were closed and the gratuities to policemen that supplemented their low pay had been cut off.

Wheeler was like a squirrel leaping from tree to tree, gathering and saving nuts. No one in America wrote more letters than Wheeler. No government office from the White House to the halls of Congress was exempt from his solicitation. Leaders of business and labor unions, churchmen, educators, professional societies were fair game for his efforts. One of his bulletins to the public was typical Wheelerism: "Start a saloon in your own home. Be the only customer. You'll have no license to pay. Go to your wife and give her two dollars to buy a gallon of whiskey, and remember there are sixty-nine drinks in a gallon of whiskey. Buy your drinks from no one but your wife. . . . Should you live ten years and continue to buy booze from her, and then die with snakes in your boots, she will have enough money to bury you decently, educate your children, buy a house and lot, marry a decent man and quit thinking about you entirely."

Meanwhile, opinions seemed to be coming around almost universally to Wheeler's viewpoint. Medical science, for example, was issuing new reports decidedly opposed to drink. The use of alcohol was declared to be not a stimulant but a depressant. It did not induce bodily warmth as formerly believed. Nor was it a source of energy, but more likely a source of disease—cirrhosis of the liver, birth defects, stomach ulcers. All the great myths of the beneficence of alcohol were suddenly shattered. A study of New York schoolchildren found that over half with drinking parents were mentally retarded as distinct from only 10 percent with temperate parents. Dr. Charles Mayo, president of the American Medical Association, stated categorically that he would welcome Prohibition as a boon to the nation's health. In dry states, social workers discovered a substantial decline in welfare cases. One survey of large cities concluded that in dry areas, bank deposits increased, retail trade was stimulated, debt collections improved and attendance was way up at amusement and entertainment spectacles. In professional baseball, Connie Mack, manager of the Philadelphia Athletics, attributed four championships in five years to his insistence on total abstinence during the playing season.

Convicted criminals petitioned state legislatures to enact Prohibition on the grounds that a large percentage of crime was due to the excessive use of liquor. A survey of prostitutes revealed that saloons were favored for soliciting. Another report offered that 70 percent of all venereal infection in men under twenty-five was contracted while drunk. Either directly or indirectly, new statistics showed that liquor caused an estimated sixty thousand to one hundred thousand deaths a year, much of which took place at work. In industry, safety experts constantly reminded workers of the dangers of drink. When Congress and the states passed workmen's compensation laws, companies and their insurers immediately saw the economic gains of greater sobriety. Railroads, responsible for the lives of their passengers as well as expensive rolling stock, insisted on abstinence, and even hired detectives to spy on their employees and keep them sober. Workers would find Anti-Saloon League printed slips included in their pay envelopes, picturing a sack of flour and a barrel of beer and the caption, "Which one will you buy?"

Meanwhile, the arrogance of the liquor industry continued to play eloquently into Wheeler's hands as its endless corruptions kept tumbling into the public eye. Incredibly, the industry had not contested the thrust of the Prohibition drive. There were no organized campaigns to stem the tide, no public meetings of consequence, no furious fund drives to keep the country aware of the Prohibition threat. Never, in fact, had the rights of millions (and the profits of a few) been so threatened with such little resistance. It was as if the liquor trust believed it could not lose; that even when it appeared to lose an election or a new piece of dry legislation, the consumption of liquor was always increasing. And when the breweries finally went about trying to clean up their tawdry image, they came through with too little and too late.

As it turned out, their old pigeons suddenly came home to roost, smothering the coop with sordid droppings. A federal Grand Jury in Pittsburgh indicted the United States Brewery Association for conspiracy to corrupt federal officials in Pennsylvania. In the spring, the German-American Alliance, in association with the United States Brewers Association, was exposed as directly engaging in pro-German activities since the beginning of the war in 1914. Said Wheeler: "The Anti-Saloon League couldn't buy such publicity for a million dollars!"

Then, on April 6, 1917, the biggest bonanza of all: war!

Immediately, Wheeler saw the potential, his shrewd action-oriented mind conjuring up slogans and causes to wrap Prohibition in the American flag. For greater wartime production efficiency, alcohol must go. With the lives of American soldiers going on the line, how could drunkenness at the workplace be tolerated? The Lever Act with its food control provisions was a golden opportunity for dry legislation. Since liquor used quantities of grain, sugar and yeast, drinking could now be deemed unpatriotic as well as sinful. Banning liquor would free yeast for an estimated eleven million loaves of bread a day. If America was to continue to feed its desperate Allies and its troops as well, how could we afford to waste precious grain to distill whiskey? And who, above all, was the greatest enemy of Prohibition but the Germans of the brewery industry? Had not the Kaiser himself declared: "If ever a man was worthy of high decoration at my hand, it is Herr Doktor Hexamer," who was head of the German-American Alliance. Wheeler called it "a menace to patriotism because it puts beer before country. . . . Kaiserism abroad and booze at home must go!"

"Shall the many have food or the few have drink?" went the new cry. Then too it was Wheeler who pressured the secretary of war to order dry areas in and around military camps, forbidding the sale (or gift) of liquor to any member of the military. Intoxication made servicemen liable to disciplinary action. Within days after the declaration of war, Congress legislated the presidential limitations of alcoholic content in the making of beer and wine.

The matter of the proposed Eighteenth Amendment—Prohibition—was too big an issue to attempt to resolve in time of war. It had become another tiresome thorn in America's side. Not only tiresome but uneconomical. If war was to be fought, money became a paramount problem. Since the liquor industry had supplied 35 percent of federal revenues, what foolishness could demand its termination? Besides, everyone knew that a majority of Americans wanted access to drink however their state legislatures might have voted on the matter. Would it really be wise to deny them, even (or especially) in time of war? Who knew how the country was going to react to any of these new and catastrophic developments? The Selective Service Draft was enough to pose threatening consequences. Patriotism was suddenly loaded with a variety of implications. Who could tell what the public would swallow and what it would not? Would they not insist on their beer and their booze (exactly as congressmen would)? Would not the great liquor trusts fight like tigers to preserve their multibillion-dollar industry with vested interests in every state in the union, dozens of allied industries with millions of employees, hundreds of thousands of saloons and bartenders, stockholders and properties and plants and suppliers that could never be eliminated without a devastating effect on morale as well as the economy?

Wheeler's concentration was directed to two-thirds of the Congress. Since the Democratic majority was beholden to the president, it worried him that Wilson was anything but a Prohibitionist. He needed Wilson on his side—or at least not in opposition. Cautiously, Wheeler tried to impress upon him the wisdom of neutrality, advising him on the practical course of watchful waiting: If the Eighteenth Amendment was adopted, as it was likely to be, and proven beneficial, would it not work to the administration's credit? And if it failed to be ratified, no one would hold the president to blame since he had not been an active supporter.

William Jennings Bryan, the secretary of state, endorsed such a stratagem. The president considered it and, for a time, agreed.

So it was that the resolution for the Eighteenth Amendment, adopted by the Anti-Saloon League with all its great guns firing, proposed to go one big step closer to Prohibition itself. Wheeler, the little David who would hurl his missile at the giant Bacchus, was the dominant force behind the new league decision: we were to be no longer a society merely in favor of temperance; the League no longer merely the scourge of the saloon or even destroyer of the liquor traffic. Section 1 of the amendment was to read, in part: "After one year from the ratification of this article, the manufacture, sale or transportation of intoxicating liquors... is hereby prohibited," not as it previously had been written, "manufacture *for* sale." The only thing that would not be prohibited was the drinking of it.

There were, of course, deals to be made and numerous compromises adjusted. To make the measure acceptable to Congress, Wheeler conferred with Senator Warren Harding, a hardy drinker but a compliant politician. Harding, it seemed, insisted that a limitation of time be allowed for ratification. Wheeler, though doubting the constitutionality of such a proposal, nonetheless agreed to a six-year limitation. If thirty-six states, the required three-quarters, had not ratified by then, the article would be ruled inoperable. (The House later adjusted the limitation to seven years.)

The league then inundated Congress with its message. As Wheeler described the action: "The word went out...to send letters, telegrams, petitions to Congress.... They rallied by the tens of thousands...like an avalanche." The issue was put to Congress in Wheeler's own special way: "The Anti-Saloon League is not asking any member of Congress to declare that he is in favor of national prohibition, but simply that he shall not become an avowed exponent and protector of the liquor traffic by refusing to allow the people of the nation, by states, through their representatives, to determine the question in the manner provided therefor by the framers of the Constitution."

In short, only a congressional dry vote would uphold the democratic process.

Or as one critic put it: "Dry Nevada (population one hundred thousand) finally gets to be the equal of wet New York (population ten million) and both states are, at last, the same."

With less than truly committed enthusiasm—it might even be called perfunctory—Congress went about its debate, taking barely thirteen hours over a period of three days in the Senate and just seven hours in a single day in the House. To the contention that the amendment removed a substantial source of revenue, it was argued that national prosperity, the new federal income tax and new war business revenues would more than offset the loss. Then there was the question of all those property rights: how could the vast holdings of the liquor industry and its stockholders be confiscated without compensation? Here the Drys argued that property considered harmful to the health of the people had long been subject to confiscation. Had not the twenty-six states that had already abolished the liquor traffic done so without compensation? Then it was also contended that the whole proposition was unworkable, that it would never actually prohibit; indeed, it never had. To this came the regular dry argument that laws did not stop murder or theft or rape, but who would dispute the necessity of such laws? Besides, the sentiment for prohibition was so powerful, so rooted in the great new evangelical spirit of America, so highly endorsed through the Progressive Movement, was it not well worth the try? And what of the dubious wisdom of increasing federal power in the enforcement process? Would that not constitute a new threat to individual freedoms? And what of the threat to the sanctity of states' rights? Even though the article clearly stated that "Congress and the several states shall have concurrent power to enforce . . . by appropriate legislation," it was generally believed that the states would leave it to the feds to carry the brunt of it—which, to crown this great doublethink, was precisely the way the states wanted it to be.

Lobbying was as old as Congress, but the Anti-Saloon League gave it a special stamp. If corporations persuaded by bribes and special favors, Wayne Wheeler came at Congressmen with the ultimate fear—that of losing their seats in the next election. Here, for the first time, it was shown that a man could use the electoral process in order to subvert it, a flaw that was built into the system itself.

When the Eighteenth Amendment came for enactment, the

league had compiled a list of thirteen thousand prominent businessmen. All Drys, of course. The great chain-store magnate S. S. Kresge had financed this operation. "We blocked the telegraph wires in Washington for three days," Wheeler wrote. "One of our friends sent seventy-five telegrams, each signed differently with the name of one of his subordinates. The campaign was successful. Congress succumbed. The first to bear the white flag was Senator Warren Harding of Ohio. He told us frankly he was opposed to the amendment, but since it was apparent from the telegrams that the business world was demanding it, he would submerge his own opinion and vote for submission."

In the field, fifty thousand Anti-Saloon League workers went after the five hundred thousand American leaders and opinion-makers they deemed important, stating, "As we hold these five hundred thousand, so we shall hold the law." Apparently, the other ninety-nine million citizens could be counted on as apathetic.

And the liquor industry, meanwhile, totally failed to rally. The greatest irony about the liquor trust was that it was accused of meddling in politics when, in this awesome crisis, it did little or nothing of the sort. Only the league did. In each of the 435 congressional districts of the United States, the league had a functioning organization. The brewers had none. They thought only to rely on the old trusty methods of the robber baron days— bribery and buying elections and votes. But times had changed through the pressure of Progressive reformers. There were public elections of senators now, and the Anti-Saloon League had grown up with them.

Congress, meanwhile, could hardly cope with the issue, much less the vote. As H. L. Mencken put it: "A congressman is a man who prepares for a speech on prohibition by taking three stiff drinks." Wrote Dallas Lou Sharp of the amphibious Sixty-fifth Congress: "No caterpillar ever crawled into its cocoon and came out so changed as came this drink question out of Congress. It went in temperance and came out prohibition. It went in license and came out enforcement. It went in personal choice and came out national mandate; it went in individual right and came out bootlegger and a kitchen still. It went in local option and came out the Eighteenth Amendment."

Through the seemingly endless battle, only one side appeared to be fighting. As Charles Merz wrote: "The opposition remained scattered, ineffective and perpetually out of breath." A mass meeting in Madison Square Garden denounced Prohibition, and everyone cheered the demand for repeal—then it ended and everyone went home. Twenty thousand paraded in Baltimore on a hot June day—then scattered. A press campaign set aside a day of protest wherein everyone opposed to Prohibition would wear a daisy in his buttonhole. The only genuine threat finally came from the workers in the American Federation of Labor; at their convention in June 1919, they demanded modification of the law. "No beer, no work," they cried out in a threatened strike, ten thousand marching to the steps of the Capitol. But that too petered out. There were too few daisies, and no strikers.

When the matter finally came to a vote, the House approved 282 to 128, while the Senate voted sixty-five to twenty. On December 22, 1917, the resolution was submitted to the states for ratification. They had until 1924 to do so. As Wheeler's guidelines had reassured them, this was not a monumental action on their part. More pusillanimous, in fact, than bold. Hardly any of Prohibition's supporters actually believed that three-fourths of the states would ratify, certainly not in the prescribed time period, and definitely not in wartime. After all, it took only thirteen wet states to hold firm. Besides, as someone observed, in all of United States history, over three thousand amendments had been proposed and only seventeen adopted. There were also a few wet critics who complained that the margin of sixteen votes in the House might well have swung to the Drys if the ballot had been a secret one. Congress, it seemed, did not always vote its conscience, a fact well known to Wheeler. No politician could afford to let himself be counted on the wrong side of a moral issue, no matter what he thought of its rectitude; moral memories in America were tenacious and Anti-Saloon League vengeance was known to be ruthless. And was there anyone in politics less forgiving than Wayne B. Wheeler?

This close to the finish line of the long marathon, Wheeler was indeed a "locomotive in trousers." By 1918, the Anti-Saloon League had tripled its staff, now functioning in high gear as the greatest crusading pressure group in American history. In Washington, he went to work on his favorite target, the brewers, having found yet another opening in which to lay his charges: the German-American Alliance again, this time cited as rabid anti-Prohibitionists in concert with the German government as well as the American Brewers Association, all part of a grandiose plan that would undermine the American war effort—or so he chose to interpret it. Wheeler implemented his patriotic concerns by securing the support of none other than the ex-president and superpatriot Theodore Roosevelt, who contributed a stingingly critical editorial to this cause. It was powerful enough to bring the German-American Alliance to its knees. The organization disbanded. Wheeler then wrote to A. Mitchell Palmer, then alien property custodian, to publicize the report "that the Anheuser-Busch Company and some of the Milwaukee companies are largely controlled by alien Germans," this at a time when you couldn't even listen to Beethoven for fear of treason. Palmer responded with a public address in which he publicly attacked the brewers as both corrupt and responsible for unpatriotic practices. And Wheeler then followed with a startling revelation that *The Washington Times* had been purchased by Arthur Brisbane, long a vigorous enemy of the Anti-Saloon League, with $500,000 financing from the United States Brewers Association. Wrote Wheeler to Brisbane: "We respectfully submit, however, that an alleged newspaper which prints only on the beer and liquor side should properly be designated as a brewery agent and not a newspaper." The Senate Judiciary Committee substantiated the charge, supplementing it with all manner of tie-ins that Wets propagandized the paper's readers. Wheeler's booklet exposing all this was brilliant propaganda for the Drys. To add insult to all these injuries inflicted on the brewers, Congress enacted the War Prohibition Act, forbidding the manufacturing of beer and wine after May 1, 1919, and outlawing the sale of all liquors after June 30, both provisions to remain in effect until the termination of the war and demobilization. America, then, would actually go dry on midnight July 1, 1919.

Except for these manipulations, there was surprisingly little attention paid to the problem. War was the news, not Prohibition or its ratification. Meanwhile, the Anti-Saloon League, which had urged congressional support because it would give three-fourths of the states the final right to decide, now tried to convince a simple majority of state legislators that they were obliged to ratify what two-thirds of congressmen had approved. There were, after all, twenty-six states that had been dry for years. There were also a few referendums, and they too went dry. To many, however, it seemed that the entire sequence had somehow happened without their being aware of it.

One southern pundit had this comment on the battle: "You can put this down for sure: when the women, the churches and business are united in any fight, as they are in this one, nothing can stand against them. A cause that opposes any one of them is in for a bad time, but a cause that has them all three for enemies hasn't got a chance on earth."

Ratification did not take seven years, but a mere thirteen months. Thirty-six states moved with astonishing swiftness, starting with Mississippi in January 1918, then four more within a month, until on January 29, 1919, the great state of Nebraska became the clincher, its upper house voting thirty-one to one to ratify. Ten others would follow. Prohibition would be the Constitutional law of the land one year from that date.

It was then the duty of Congress to enact an enforcement law, and again, the Anti-Saloon League stepped in to take the lead. Wheeler and company set the alcoholic limit at 0.5 percent, or one-half of one percent. Anything above would be illegal. The act forbade anyone "to manufacture, sell, barter, transport, import, deliver, furnish or possess any intoxicating liquor" though certain exemptions were allowed; in deference to farmers, for example, cider and fermenting of fruit juices were permitted, their intoxicating status to be determined by the courts. Drinkers were allowed to keep the whiskey they had stocked prior to July 1, 1919, as long as it was consumed solely at home. Industrial alcohol was, of necessity, a permissible product, with severe limitations placed on its use and distribution. Also, alcohol for medicinal and sacramental purposes was permitted. The enforcement of all this was placed in the hands of the Bureau of Internal Revenue of the Treasury Department, the only agency with experience in the field, having been responsible for collecting liquor taxes and apprehending the legions of violators.

In the end, the legislation came out of an artful bag of compromises, a caution against public antagonism over those restrictions considered to be too severe. It was not without significance that the only three groups who were allowed by the law to make, prescribe or sell beverage alcohol were the three groups who had been most committed to condemning the stuff: the ministry, the farmers and the medics. This was predominantly the handiwork of Wayne Wheeler, who then presented his draft to an obscure congressman from Minnesota, Andrew Volstead (it was never clear why), for whom the celebrated act was immediately named.

And there, in the Senate gallery on the afternoon of October 27, 1919, sat its true mentor, Wayne B. Wheeler, as the Senate honored him with the aforementioned standing ovation.

3. THE ENFORCEMENT MYTH

There's gold in them thar' mountains,
There's gold in them thar' hills;
The natives there are getting it
By operating stills.

—JOHN JUDGE, JR.
Noble Experiments

It was a strange law that seemed to change the very nature of the way a man spent his leisure. No saloons, no beer, no alcohol. It was like legislating away the automobile or banning the playing of baseball. When had there ever been such a personal law as Prohibition?

Nonetheless, for all the huffing and puffing, most Americans felt good about it. It was a remarkable victory for reform. The Progressive will had become the law of the land for the good of all, and Americans rejoiced at the glowing prospects of a life without intoxicants. To parents, their children could grow up without having to deal with its horrors. Even old drinkers were pleased at not having to drink any more—it was a habit they had always wanted to break. This would be a new beginning for everyone, whatever the limitations, and a great wave of hope washed over the land. Some called it "The American journey to Utopia." It would be difficult to measure the extraordinary power it generated. How could such a changing attitude be appraised, even in its own time? Let it simply be said that a lot of men stopped drinking, and as many families were the better for it.

Then, with astonishing suddenness, the new godlike serenity

was assaulted by a devilish counterforce that turned the great law into a farce. It was as if the armies that had fought for the Eighteenth Amendment abandoned the field at its passage, leaving no one to hold the fort.

At midnight, on the very hour when Prohibition became the law of the land, a half dozen trucks drove to the railroad yards in Chicago, their occupants emerged under the cover of darkness, then broke into the railroad cars on a siding to remove over $100,000 of imported whiskey specifically reserved for medicinal purposes, loaded the contraband into the trucks and disappeared unchallenged into the night. Another gang stole four barrels of grain alcohol from a government bonded warehouse. Still another hijacked a truck transporting whiskey.

So much for openers, as they say.

In California, a vintner who had spent his life in the cultivation of grapes for his vineyard committed suicide in despair over the future. Others of his industry, however, saw reason to be less pessimistic. It was, in fact, sufficiently apparent to many that Prohibition would become "the lie of the land."

The Treasury Department, responsible for enforcing the law, had barely two thousand agents, whose experience was strictly in revenue collecting. Now, however, there was no licensing, no legality and above all, no revenue. There was, then, no adequate motivation for a bureau not dedicated to law enforcement. The two thousand agents, at a paltry salary of $1,200 a year, were now assigned to patrol 18,700 miles of the United States borders of land, sea and river, plus countless millions of homes and farms in all states, and apprehend all violators of the manufacture, transportation, delivery and sale of all liquid products of 0.5 percent alcohol and over. "This was like trying to stop a German tank attack with a bow and arrow," one agent commented. Said Congressman Fiorello La Guardia: "In order to enforce Prohibition, it will require a police force of 250,000 men and another force of 250,000 men to police the police."

Said Wayne Wheeler to Congress et al.: "There will be no problem of enforcement because the American people approve of the law." To Wheeler, it wasn't really a war at all because there was no enemy. He prescribed an appropriation of a mere $5 million to assure its enforcement—like a sandbag or two to stop a flood. "There will be collected in fines, forfeited bonds and Prohibition taxes more than it costs to enforce the law," he said. He promised "returns to the government more than is paid out for enforcement." And Congress, reluctant to spend the taxpayers' money on anything so treacherous, immediately approved. Senator Morris Sheppard of Texas, author of the resolution that became the Eighteenth Amendment, stated categorically on the Senate floor that $5 million was sufficient, that there would be no problems. (Even as he spoke, however, a still producing 130 gallons of moonshine a day was functioning on his own property.) To Congress, the solution to this endlessly tiresome problem was to pretend that it simply did not exist.

As it turned out, the problem did not disappear. Liquor did not disappear. Only the law disappeared.

In time, the massiveness of this onslaught bewildered, then overwhelmed, the nation. There was no movement behind it, no conspiracy, no organization: quite simply, the American people wanted to drink, just as they had always wanted to drink. It was their natural right to drink. In this great free country, how could anyone deny such a God-given right? There was no talk of the law. No one cared about the law. The law was what anyone chose to make of it.

Besides, to avoid the law would quickly enough become a game, simple enough, like taking candy from a baby. Suddenly Americans were showing ingenious techniques at violation. The Canadian border, for one, was ideal for the ancient art of smuggling, over three thousand miles of virtually unguardable lands, lakes, rivers. There was, for example, the automobile: how better to transport the finest whiskey concealed in hollowed-out seats, or buried in secret compartments in trunks, or false compartments under the chassis that could hold as many as seven hundred bottles? A smuggler could drive from New York to Montreal, load up and return in one day, and make enormous profits for his simple effort. At the border, agents could not possibly search every car, and most did not bother to search any. Then there were upper New York state residents who rode trained horses across the border, loaded them with bottled whiskey, then turned them loose to find their way home. Others would empty ordinary eggs by puncturing the ends, then fill the shells with Scotch and seal them.

The Great Lakes were swarming with all manner of craft, loaded to the gunwales. In the first year of Prohibition, as much as $100 million worth of liquor came across the border, nine hundred thousand cases in the first seven months alone. The Caribbean Islands became known as Rum Row, the center of smugglers as they once had hosted pirates. An old seaman known as Big Bill McCoy turned smuggler, an expert at delivering fine imported whiskey from Nassau in the Bahamas, and was responsible for the origin of "the Real McCoy," named for its superior quality. Over a hundred ships operated along the East Coast, forty-seven more in the Gulf of Mexico. When threatened by the United States Coast Guard, smugglers had devised submarining barges that were cut loose to sink—salt bags dissolving in the deep, then releasing detectable buoys for the smugglers' return. Nor did the Rio Grande on the Mexican border offer any great difficulties. After 1919, Mexico's whiskey trade with Great Britain suddenly increased eightfold. The Bahamas multiplied one thousand gallons annually in 1918 to 386,000 in 1922. In the Midwest, Detroit, just across the border from Toronto, became the center of the Canadian trade. The most direct railroad route from Buffalo to Detroit was through Canada. Whatever the product listed on the manifest, in Windsor, Ontario, liquor was substituted, counterfeit seals secured it and a $200,000 load would arrive in Detroit. Fifty thousand new jobs were created in Detroit; the illegal importation of alcohol was a business that escalated to $215 million a year, second only to the manufacturing of automobiles.

It followed that, for the well-to-do, there was an adequate supply of fine whiskey available. In place of the liquor store was the personal supplier; the bootlegger, like the bookie, became a necessary supplement to the vagaries of the law.

Since the Volstead Act permitted doctors to prescribe alcoholic beverages to patients for medicinal purposes, it was less than startling that fifteen thousand M.D.'s and fifty-seven thousand pharmacists applied for licenses in the first six months after the law took effect. Thus began a whole new source of income for the medical profession that came to over $40 million with an average of ten million prescriptions a year. In Chicago, a bootlegger named George Remus bought up chains of drug stores so he could order truckloads of medicinal liquor, whereupon he hijacked his own trucks to sell at much higher bootleg prices. Doctors who had been active campaigners for the amendment were now getting rich from its passage. Sure enough, drugstores, with their own new booty, would take over the sites of former saloons and carry on the trade.

It was discovered that three-quarters of sacramental wine, legally delivered to churches for religious purposes, had been stolen and bootlegged.

It was also discovered that all the new restrictions on the illegality of alcoholic consumption had created a new interest in the use of hard drugs. Morphine, cocaine, heroin, opium, laudanum, paregoric and codeine were prescribed by medics as legal usage for addicts (for a fee of $4 per prescription). Doctors would write as many as two hundred prescriptions a day, whereupon thousands of users would pay a new high price of $60 to $70 an ounce for heroin. In the dry South, where good liquor was hardest to obtain, cities were overrun by a new wave of drug addicts, 11,690 under medical care in Atlanta alone—still another spinoff of the Eighteenth Amendment.

For the less well-to-do, there were other sources, foremost of which was the still. For $500 one could buy the basics to produce one hundred gallons a day at a cost of less than 50¢ a gallon, market value $3. Thus a still could pay for itself in a week or less. What made it all so beguiling was that the process had long since been published in United States government manuals still legally on sale. All one needed was a teakettle, a quart of cornmeal, a bath towel...

> "You may not have a fairy in your home
> Or a miss in your car—but feller!
> Everyone nowadays surely has
> A little maid in his cellar."

After a hundred-year history of contention with the problem in states that had gone dry, the manufacture of moonshine was as common as milking cows. In the first six months of Prohibition, 9,553 stills were seized (twenty times the number of any pre-1919 period), the most celebrated being the one on Senator Morris Sheppard's property in Austin, Texas.

Then there was industrial alcohol, approved for manufacture by the Volstead Act, and improved for consumption by its numerous violators—a simple matter to purify by distilling a second time, then seasoning and flavoring and bottling. The mixture was potable enough if not entirely palatable. Some ten million gallons of denatured alcohol produced for industrial use in 1918 became twenty-eight million in 1920. In colleges, chemistry was suddenly the most popular of sciences. For the most unscrupulous, there was wood alcohol that sometimes blinded, sometimes paralyzed and often killed. A "Coroner's Cocktail," it was called. As to this, Wayne Wheeler commented that poisoning of industrial alcohol was for the benefit of all since it would deter people from all drink, and those who defied this were merely committing suicide.

Then there was the monumental problem of beer. Breweries became "cereal beverage plants" to establish legitimacy, first manufacturing the required 3 percent to 4 percent brew for the dealcoholization process. The compromised product that emerged was called near beer, the butt of another Will Rogers quip: "After drinking a bottle of this weak beer, you have to take a glass of water as a stimulant." A more colorful and obscene wit posed the problem in a riddle: "Why is near beer like lovemaking in a canoe?" The answer, of course, was that they were both fucking close to water.

The solution, as with moonshine liquor, was home brew. As the sign read:

> Be it ever so humble
> There's no place like home
> for BREWING.

Over five hundred thousand families were brewing 8 percent beer in New York state alone. A number of beer-drinking states actually passed legislation that allowed the manufacture and sale of beer with 3.5 percent alcohol in direct violation of the Volstead Act. New Jersey even filed suit to have the Eighteenth Amendment declared null and void. New York initiated an investigation of Wayne Wheeler and his methods, especially as they related to his manipulation of Congress through control of patronage. Had not the Volstead Act removed the enforcement appointees from the civil service so that he could control them? And wasn't it common knowledge that Wheeler had been responsible for that article? Hadn't Wheeler, in fact, written the body of the act itself? Years later, the National Civil Service Reform League would call him on it: "Congress wanted the plunder and you let them have it. You bought the Volstead Act with congressional patronage and paid for it not with your own [Anti-Saloon League] money but, far worse, with offices paid out of taxes levied on the people!" Then the New York State Legislature defiantly voted the legitimacy of 2.75 percent beer.

In California, vintners suddenly began to thrive as never before. Production doubled. Andrew Volstead came to be known as "the Patron Saint of the San Joaquin Valley." The vintner who had committed suicide had died totally in vain.

It was declared as fact that more Americans were bottling their own booze than were canning applesauce or jam.

> "Mother makes brandy from cherries;
> Pop distills whisky and gin;
> Sister sells wine from the grapes on our vine,
> Good grief, how the money rolls in!"
>   Periscope Magazine

And never before were dandelions so welcomed on the suburban lawn.

So it was that the snowball of violation became an unstoppable avalanche. "When you talk about Prohibition, you're talking about something that doesn't exist," went another of the conventional quips. The Anti-Saloon Leaguers would not accept the vastness of the problem. Some would say it was merely a symptom of "growing pains." Wayne Wheeler declared it to be the result of "a vicious conspiracy of Wets to discredit the amendment." Official statements denied that any problems so much as existed. Congress continued to pay no attention to it. In Woodrow Wilson's final state of the union address in 1920 there was no mention of Prohibition or any suggestion of oncoming disasters. In the press, there were, at first, no special investigatory reports, no editorials, only one letter of comment was published in the *New York Times.* The country was being brought to its knees in dead silence.

Then it was postulated that the amendment to the Constitution was in itself of questionable constitutionality. Could the federal government be instructed by the amendment (and the Volstead Act that implemented it) to assume a power that was delegated to the states? How could the states delegate authority (for enforcement) that was already guaranteed exclusively to them? Was it not, in effect, establishing a precedent that could, if taken in extremis, destroy the entire structure of constitutional government? The question was posed, but never pursued. The passion and fervor of its moral backing stopped any congressional or legal attack, even though many distinguished legal opinions saw the necessity.

All the while it was claimed that the ratification process did not reflect the will of the people in the first place, and certainly not a majority of American voters. Some even argued that a giant swindle had been manipulated through the false impression that the Eighteenth Amendment was designed only to destroy the saloons, and that the people had not been properly advised that they would be denied beer and wine. Why wasn't there a universal resort to referendum? And since when did state legislatures represent anyone but the more powerful interest groups? The disenchantment began to feed on itself. Some confessed they had voted dry primarily because they were shamed into doing so, a moral community action not to be taken all that seriously, or so they had believed. It was merely a gesture to purge themselves of sin by the vote itself—like a momentary vow to be made without awareness of its consequences, a sort of New Year's resolution that would somehow be forgotten when convenient. Then there were others who approved of Prohibition because it would be good for others while they themselves would keep on drinking. And some who simply bubbled with sacrificial virtue, willing to give it all up for the good of all, then regretting that decision when tasting the pain of denial.

But the reality struck home, exposing all the old hypocrisies, and thus setting off the greatest hypocrisy of all: the ever-increasing inclination to ignore the law while, with sublime indifference, the public was advised that all was going perfectly well. Indeed, official statistics appeared in newspapers that 17,500,000 former drinkers had stopped imbibing. At the same time, so many violations of the Volstead Act were bringing in fines (exactly as

Wheeler had predicted) that their returns added up to more than the $5 million it was costing the taxpayers to enforce.

Prohibition, they said, was actually a money-maker.

Or, as most Americans came to realize, their government was lying.

Let the record show: In New York, James L. Shevlin, the first federal administrator, admitted at the end of seven unsuccessful months in office that liquor was being widely sold throughout the city, that his staff of two hundred agents could not possibly stop it. For that statement alone, Shevlin was transferred to El Paso, and succeeded by Frank L. Boyd, who declared a new line of attack designed "to make illegal traffickers sit up and take notice." Boyd lasted barely three months, then took leave of his job with a statement that it was "a thankless and hopeless task." He was succeeded by Daniel Chapin, who had new conceptions to enforce the law, but he too lasted only three months. Then came Ernest Langley, who immediately announced plans to rid Chapin's staff of its corruption, set new standards for his agents and give the city real enforcement.

Some said that the revolving door was invented by the Eighteenth Amendment.

Government on all levels was being rendered helpless by a law that everyone knew could not possibly be enforced but was continuously defended as being inviolable. Government policy itself was, in essence, as corrupt as the people who took advantage of it. The disaster began in the White House with presidents who had too many political irons in the fire to create enforcement procedures they had pledged their constitutional duty to enforce. It segued to Congress and its dry representatives who simply found it far more expedient to do nothing than to make fools of themselves. It followed that the state and local party bosses would further corrupt the Prohibition bureau with jobs for their ward heelers and protection for their friends.

Then, like the flu epidemic of 1919, it simply raged. With Prohibition, however, Americans found it less an atrocity than an entertainment.

The country was off on a tear. Dubuque had forty-one thousand citizens, one thousand bootleggers and an uncounted number of moonshiners. In Detroit, it was said to be "impossible to get a drink unless you walked at least a dozen feet and told a very busy bartender what you wanted in a voice loud enough to be heard above the uproar." Will Rogers put it this way: "I had a friend who wanted a drink awful bad when we were in Washington, but he couldn't borrow a [police] uniform from anybody." As reported by historian David Murphy, a visitor to a southern town asked a taxi driver who was taking him from the depot to his hotel: "Where do you get a drink in this town?" "Boss, see that there dress shop? . . . Well, that's the only place where you *can't* get it." Paul Gallico wrapped up the American scene with a quote from his bootlegger: "I couldn't exist if it weren't for the fact that I have the cooperation of the local police, the state constabulary, the municipal police and 85 percent of the citizens. . . . Tell the average person that you've got a load of liquor in your car and he'll hide you, lie for you and help you. It's a moral help as much as a physical one."

The mayor of Chicago declared that he would "make Chicago a dry city inside of thirty days if I have to dismiss every captain and lieutenant in the police department." It astonished no one that he did neither. The governor of Pennsylvania said that in one Philadelphia saloon, "Drinkers surrounded the illegal bar four deep . . . crowds walked in and out. A policeman stood at the very door." The celebrated Marine general Smedley Butler called his enforcement job "worse than any battle I was ever in. . . . The petty annoyances that are piled on me are worse than the Chinese drip torture."

As an experiment in voluntary enforcement in New York, the Federal Bureau called for the public to bring in their home distilling and brewing equipment—or be severely penalized if caught with them at home. When no one complied, 178 agents were supposed to search 1,278,431 residences.

In California, the feds padlocked a giant redwood tree in which a hollowed-out chamber concealed a fifty-gallon still.

Meanwhile, so many arrests were being made as to tie up the court system and overcrowd the jails. As a result, it was admitted that only a small fraction of violators were arrested, much less sentenced. Besides, judges were reluctant to sentence on Prohibition cases; it was simply not popular to do so. Pleas of guilty, eliminating the need for jury trials, accounted for 90 percent of convictions. Such adjudications were considered akin to traffic violations. It was not unusual for a judge to slap a fine on a guilty bootlegger, then retire to chambers to share a drink with him from the evidence itself.

From the euphoria of the Anti-Saloon League, it was claimed that "Industry, commerce, art, literature, music, learning, entertainment and benevolence all find their finest expression in this saloonless land."

From a congressional spokesman from Wisconsin: "Vice, crime, immorality, disease, insanity, corruption and a general disregard for the law directly traceable to the unenforceability of the Volstead Act are increasing with alarming rapidity."

From a drunken poet in a Greenwich Village blind pig: "Legislating prohibition to stop drinking is like legislating sexual abstinence to control the birthrate."

The trouble was all-inclusive since almost no one was committed to enforcement. It was believed neither possible nor, as drinking people testified, desirable. The various states, for example, having ratified the amendment that gave them "concurrent power" to enforce, abrogated all such responsibilities, dumping the load on Congress and the federal authorities. Thirty states contributed nothing. Other states allocated less than half of what they spent on maintenance of parks, one-eighth of expenditures on enforcement of fish and game laws. Fifteen police officers in Philadelphia had amassed over $800,000 in bribes—more than all the states of America had spent on enforcement. The Anti-Saloon League, with all its prodigious organization and propaganda resources, declined to deal with the problem. In one of the more dubious rationalizations of the day, Wayne Wheeler had this to say: "The very fact that the law is difficult to enforce is the clearest proof of the need of its existence."

Woodrow Wilson, who had never been an advocate of Prohibition, had been blocked by the war from preventing it. "Those miserable hypocrits in Congress—voting to override my veto—many with their cellars stocked with liquors and not believing in prohibition at all—jumping at the whip of the lobbyists...." He suggested that the Democratic platform in 1920 incorporate an alteration of the Volstead Act to legitimize beer and wine, but so great was the power of the Drys and "those miserable hypocrits in Congress" that he did not wish to risk challenging his far more critical fight for the League of Nations. Wheeler himself warned Wilson that the Democratic Party was in enough trouble already.

For Wheeler, the 1920 election was a critical test of his resourcefulness. Prohibition was already in such trouble, even Andrew Volstead's congressional seat was threatened. But this was Wheeler's passion, and he knew how to play all his cards. Here was his list of Drys, he declared for all of Capitol Hill to take note of, challenging the Wets to do the same so that the voters could then decide which way to vote. To Wheeler, all of politics was a single issue. And when the wet list did, finally appear, he pounced on them with a public questionnaire: Do you support the Constitution of the United States? Or, in translation: will you vote the precise enforcement provisions as the Anti-Saloon League prescribes them, refrain from making anti-Prohibitionist waves? Incredibly, he won again. Almost solely by Wheeler's efforts, Volstead regained his seat—for one more term. There were no calls for congressional investigations that might tarnish the dry image, no speeches from the floor that might threaten the status quo as Wheeler saw it. Warren Harding, the first president to be elected principally because he looked like one, was the perfect example of a wet politician who supported dry laws for the sake of keeping peace with the Anti-Saloon League. Said Harding to the great dry church: "My prime motive in going to the White House is to bring America back to God." (Wilson, the most pious of Christian politicians, who wore out more Bibles than shirt collars, must have gagged when he heard that.) Meanwhile, in the White House, Harding's Ohio Gang sold pardons to convicted bootleggers from a special list put together by the Department of Justice. Gaston B. Means, that celebrated special agent, claimed that he collected $7 million from bootleggers in a goldfish bowl and turned it over to the Department of Justice. The Ohio Gang actually sold whiskey brought to them by special agents of Justice after it had been confiscated by treasury men. George Remus, known as the King of Bootleggers (estimated to have made a profit of $40 million), testified that he paid more than $250,000 in bribes to a member of the Ohio Gang—but was prosecuted, not for bribery but for bootlegging, and jailed. "I tried to corner the graft market, only to find that there is not enough money in the world to buy up all the public officials who demand a share of the graft."

All the while, Wheeler did not concern himself with such hanky-panky, for he had Harding's endorsement.

None of this appeared to distract the American people from the pleasures of the postwar world. America became a whole new country in 1919, almost unrecognizable from the lofty idealism of the war years. For all the labor turmoil and the stridency of the Red Scare, there was an incipient lightheartedness that turned off the lights of anything that smacked of seriousness. Or so it appeared in the great cities that were becoming the dominant tastemakers for American society. The list of excesses was a long one: jazz, short skirts and bobbed hair, automobiles, the Charleston and other jubilant styles of dancing, much sex and open talk of sex, big-time sports and great heavyweight fights, the incredible invention of radio, the proliferation of movies. And the new speakeasies, always the speakeasies for those who had the funds, a new kind of private-public club where one drank new cocktails with assorted ingredients and exotic names. The appeal was rooted in exclusivity, the glamour in the appeal to snobbishness. Who's your bootlegger? Where did you get that fabulous silver flask? There were oh-so-smart quips about so-and-so "who still has a little [from his pre-Prohibition stock] and so-and-so who has a little still." Or the quips about all those women who were going to hate Prohibition because it would lead to their husbands having to stay home. And how does Wayne Wheeler celebrate? With dry toast, of course. Then there were all those serious stories about the new breed of students, clerks, ex-farm boys who turned to the liquor trade, first as a sideline to supplement income, then as an acceptable career. There were an unprecedented number of college dropouts in 1920. The middle class, sponsors of Prohibition, would become its principal violators. The younger generation, whom the Anti-Saloon League had claimed would be saved by the morality of a dry society, were actually being corrupted by it.

Everyone talked about Prohibition: take either side and any

position in between. There were strange wet arguments that revolution flourished on dry soil since it drove normal working people into radical action, the result of frustrations of no beer, for one thing. Sam Gompers claimed that Prohibition "wrecked the social and economic fabric of the nation. . . . Denied beer, men are forced into the streets to meet others as restless and unsettled as they— they rub together their mutual grievances and create sparks. . . . I believe Bolshevism in Russia began in prohibition [The tsar had initiated it to improve the war effort]. The apostles of Bolshevism in the United States are seizing Prohibition as a mighty weapon with the foreign born who are accustomed to beer and wine." One distiller had warned Wilson in a highly publicized letter: "The Eighteenth Amendment bids fair to start a landslide that will grow into an avalanche carrying private ownership of property over the brink of socialism and thence into the gulf of anarchy."

The Drys insisted that the opposite was so. Drink created the economic and political turmoil that had dominated the year. Strikes and violence were alcohol-inspired. Prohibition had terminated the worst of radicalism. The revolution no longer threatened.

Then there was the radical notion that big money had supported the tax-free religious institutions, then forced them to do something for these contributions. The churches had latched onto Prohibition and ridden it to enactment as a way of maintaining corporate support. For the corporate power, Prohibition had been a political bromide to conceal the results of their own greed. In 1919, America's anguish had to be blamed on something other than Bolshevism.

To the working stiff, 1919 was a total disaster to his faith and his liberties. "No more radical talk, or assembly in protest, or picketing or strikes without getting bashed. . . . And now you can't even take a drink!"

Historian Herbert Ashbury defined it: "The Drys lied to make Prohibition look good; the Wets lied to make it look bad; the government officials lied to make themselves look good and to frighten Congress into giving them money to spend; and the politicians lied through force of habit."

Sean Cashman wrote that Prohibition achieved four things

for politics (and a celebration for the much-maligned letter "p"): "increased pusillanimity of presidents, parsimony of politicians, particularism of parties and the perniciousness of the people."

H. L. Mencken complained: "I believe there is more bad whiskey consumed today than there was good whiskey before Prohibition."

Congress, all the while, did absolutely nothing about Prohibition. It simply refused to act. Occasionally, purely for the record, there was a fiery speech or two, but no legislation would follow, regardless of protest from prestigious Drys. After the first two years of $5 million appropriations, every sign was pointing to disastrous consequences. The so-called responsible officials in too many places were in collusion with the lawbreakers, or rendered helpless against the growing spread of the evil. Some demanded that the president call out the Army and Navy to stem the tide of smugglers. The only bill brought before the House proposed to attack the problem by the Palmer method of deporting aliens. Wheeler had suggested that too. "In many places, most of the offenders against the liquor laws are aliens," he explained. But Congress abandoned it, just as they had abandoned the law they did not really wish to pass. Obviously, it now made no sense to them. They themselves drank, as usual, and bootleggers were always welcome in the Capitol buildings. Several congressmen were discovered with cases of bootleg booze in their offices. But there was no prosecution for there was no law—not so anyone could prosecute it. It was simply ignored.

As for the president, be he the temperate Wilson or the extremely wet Harding or later the teetotaler Coolidge, there was seldom a word except perhaps an occasional platitude about the need for all good Americans to obey the law. And the president, as everyone knew, was constitutionally responsible for the execution of the law.

From the outset, the federal commissioners were distinguished by their optimistic rhetoric. The first was John Kramer, who assured America that the government would see that liquor was not manufactured "nor sold, nor given away, nor hauled in anything on the surface of the earth nor under the sea nor in the air." Somehow, this appeared to convince no one. Major Roy

Haynes, who succeeded him, insisted that the law under his regime was "rapidly approaching the highest point of efficiency," and that "the amendment is being enforced to an even greater extent than many of its devoted friends anticipated." During the previous year of 1921, "various fines, assessments and taxes amounted to nearly $63,000,000," this on an enforcement expenditure of only $9,500,000. Out of his offices came the glorious words: "Home brew is taking its final gasp. . . . Bootleg patronage has fallen off more than 50 percent. . . . Moonshine in cities [is] on the wane. . . . The death rattle [of bootlegging] has begun. . . . There is but little open and above-board drinking anywhere."

Although no one believed any of it, it was precisely what Congress wanted to hear. The Prohibition Bureau worked harder to convince the public than to enforce the law. Commissioners kept braying of successes to come, one more trial effort, one more idea on how to beat the violators. What emerged were highly publicized "drives," one after another, all of them accompanied by a deluge of public relations.

Meanwhile, in New York City, there were two agents who actually gave law enforcement a good name. They were Izzy (Einstein) and Moe (Smith), masters of the artful disguise and gifted with the guile of impostors. As gravediggers, they raided a speakeasy across from Woodlawn Cemetery. They were trombone players at a Yorkville casino, football players in Van Cortlandt Park, churchgoers in the Palm Sunday parade along Fifth Avenue. Everywhere they suspected that booze was being sold, they made arrests. There were no agents like them. In the end, their services were dispensed with, allegedly because their fame had robbed them of their usefulness. (It was also said that Izzy had set up his mother in a million-dollar townhouse on the East Side.)

There were, in fact, no shortages of arrests in every major city, far too many for the courts to handle. Attorney General A. Mitchell Palmer threw up his hands at the overload of cases pending. His successor, Harry Daugherty, had over ten thousand cases to deal with. By 1925, that number more than doubled—but for it all, there were too few enforcers to stop violations. "Bargain days" were instigated wherein defendants came in en masse and pleaded guilty in exchange for small fines and light sentences. Then, in a new twist, federal agents took to padlocking speakeasies, hotels, even private residences that served as blind pigs. But all this accomplished was the temporary inconvenience to their victims—who simply set up shop elsewhere.

And forever there was official corruption, mostly at the lower level of agents. Barely two months after the start of Prohibition, the first two agents were arrested in Baltimore for taking bribes. Warrants were issued in Philadelphia for the arrest of federal agents for conspiring to withdraw $15 million of liquor from distilleries by means of fraudulent permits. Indictments charging the illegal sale and transportation of alcohol were brought against seventy-five citizens of Gary, Indiana, including the mayor, a city court judge, a former prosecuting attorney and various police officers, fifty-five of whom were found guilty. Charges of extortion and conspiracy to violate the Volstead Act were brought against twenty-three justices, ex-justices, aldermen and sheriffs of Fayette County, Pennsylvania. One hundred agents in New York City were dismissed after an investigation into the abuse of permits for the use of intoxicating liquor and so on and so on, ad nauseam.

Over the years it was estimated that over 8 percent of Prohibition agents were found guilty of some form of corruption. As one senator pointed out in defense of the bureau, "One out of twelve of the disciples went wrong." Someone else pointed out that no other bureau in Washington had nearly as many.

Of course, Wayne Wheeler saw nothing but blue skies and rosy sunsets. "The saving of human life since Prohibition has reduced the death rate equivalent to a million lives," he said. He made no mention of new vaccines or serums, or health-care improvements or public hygiene. And certainly not the fact that death rates were also dropping in other countries where people drank without Prohibition. Then too: "The crime rate has so decreased that many jails are closed. Others are sold. Our penal population is below the average year's." He even credited Prohibition for the new prosperity. "Prohibition is responsible for gains in bank deposits, insurance, the building boom. It eliminated pauperism and slums that clustered around their creator, the saloon.... [It encouraged] vast expenditures on moving pictures, athletic equipment and other wholesome entertainment...." It was like crediting the covered wagon for the gold rush.

4. THE COMING OF THE SAWED-OFF SHOTGUN

I make my money by supplying a public demand. If I break the law, my customers, who number hundreds of the best people in Chicago, are as guilty as I am. Everybody calls me a racketeer. I call myself a businessman.

—ALPHONSE CAPONE

If Detroit was the centerpiece of the Prohibition business, Chicago was the showplace. In 1919, its mayor was William "Big Bill" Hale Thompson, Jr., hero to every pimp, whore, gambler, racketeer and bootlegger in the city. As a politician, he was a total fraud, his expertise going no further than saccharine oratorical charm dedicated to telling every ethnic or business interest what it wanted to hear. He was a liar and a thief without principle or intellect. When he took office in 1915, after winning by the largest plurality ever registered by a Republican in Chicago, there was a $3 million surplus in the city's finances. By the end of his first term, it was reduced to a $4,500,000 deficit. There were also more whorehouses and gambling dens and corrupt cops than ever before in the city's grotesque history. For this astonishing record, he was duly reelected for another term.

"Big Bill" opened the door for "Big Jim."

In the history of Chicago gangsters there is no more appropriate story than Big Jim Colosimo's. As told in John Kobler's biography of Capone, this son of a Calabrian immigrant grew up in the Levee, an area of Chicago known for its concentration of vice and crime. His boyhood adventures led him to pimping, at which he became masterful, and he rose to riches as a white slaver. By the time he was thirty-two, he was owner and impresario of the most glamorously successful cabaret in all of Chicago, a place of gaudy opulence, superb food, beautiful dancers and top-notch entertainers. Big Jim was host to celebrities from everywhere. Al Jolson, John Barrymore, George M. Cohan and Sophie Tucker all considered him a friend. Since he loved opera, he was proud of his friendship with Enrico Caruso. Other opera singers were always greeted with special warmth. He lived sumptuously with his wife and his father, two limousines with private chauffeurs, a treasured chamois sack of his favorite diamonds and countless other conspicuous manifestations of his affluence, the principal source of which came from his bordellos.

Like all such illicit potentates, he had the police in his pocket and the mayor at his choice table. He was inevitably subject to the never-ending threats of rivals to his power and prestige, not the least of which was a society called La Mano Nero. The Black Hand. To secure his widespread interests, he turned to his young nephew in New York, another Calabrian named John Torrio, whose reputation for being both resourceful and ruthless made him suitable for Big Jim's needs.

Torrio was at least as ruthless as he was resourceful. He was also exceedingly squeamish about violence, so much so that he wanted no part of it—except to give orders when necessary. In Brooklyn, he always had others to do his bidding as enforcers, one more competent than most, a young thug named Alphonse Capone, who was never known to be squeamish about anything. Torrio, meanwhile, lived an ascetic life without smoking or drinking or gambling. He was a devotee of classical music and deeply devoted to his wife, from whom he never strayed. As such, he was an ideal choice for a whoremaster. His uncle, Big Jim, was indeed made secure by him and wealthier than ever.

Enter a beautiful 19-year-old soprano named Dale Winter, by way of Ohio, New York, Australia and San Francisco, currently soloist in Chicago's South Park Avenue Methodist Church choir. She was presented to Big Jim for an audition—and the rest of the scenario could have been written by any reasonably competent Hollywood screenwriter. She was hired. She was lovely. She became a star in the café, singing light opera to everyone's delight, even Caruso's, and especially Big Jim's. With this as a showcase, she had several prestigious offers for New York shows, including Florenz Ziegfeld's, but she turned them all down. Big Jim had fallen madly in love with her, and she with him. To Dale it was tingling glamour and dangerous excitement. To Big Jim, it was the sweetness of idyllic love.

To John Torrio, however, it was bad news. A big-time gangster doesn't do things like that. If you want to stay healthy, that's what you don't do.

But Big Jim left his wife, no small thing for an Italian Catholic, with every intention of marrying Dale. Said the touchy denizens of Chicago's underworld: "Big Jim must be getting soft," and the next thing he knew, La Mano Nero was threatening again, demanding extortionary payments and preposterous quid pro quos.

John Torrio was far too cold-blooded to understand his uncle's passion, seeing only the potential for trouble that came inevitably from such romantic distractions. The "Big Jim is slipping" sort of talk cast a new light on things, and Torrio nursed his rising skepticism. Suddenly, then, the world changed. Suddenly, right under their noses, there was a new route to riches beyond their wildest dreams. It was called the Eighteenth Amendment.

Big Jim Colosimo, however, was not interested. He had enough to do with his wife-to-be and his numerous white slaves. He was, indeed, slipping. Torrio saw the handwriting on the wall. Or, perhaps more accurately, he wrote it there himself. If Big Jim was going to turn down the gold mines of bootlegging, then Torrio would proceed without him.

He too turned to Brooklyn for the security he needed.

And so Al Capone came to Chicago.

Thus, the scenario moved to its inevitable denouement. Torrio, with Capone, began to deal in big gang bootlegging. Big Jim didn't care, and as a result, he lost his control. Torrio saw the weakness as an excuse to assume the role as head man. When Big Jim came blissfully back from his honeymoon, he got a phone call from Torrio announcing a 4:00 P.M. delivery of two truckloads of whiskey to the café. At a few minutes to four, he kissed his bride and left in his limo. At the café, he waited for the delivery. The only delivery, however, was a bullet behind his right ear from a gunman who remained unidentified. At the Chicago railroad station, police picked up a renowned executioner named Frankie Uale (pronounced Yale), who just happened to own a place in Brooklyn called the Harvard Inn, where Al Capone just happened to have been bartender and bouncer. Uale, about to board a train to return to Brooklyn, claimed complete ignorance of Colosimo's death. Later, a stoolie reported an unimpeachable underworld rumor that Torrio had paid Uale $10,000 to do the job. But rumors, as every Hollywood screenwriter knows, are not evidence. The point was, Big Jim was dead and Torrio emerged as the beneficiary of the power vacuum.

As for Big Jim, he had the biggest funeral in the annals of the white slave–whoremaster crowd. It might also be identified as the first great execution of the Chicago bootlegger wars. One thousand First Ward Democrats preceded the cortege. Five thousand mourners followed. There were fifty-three pallbearers and honorary pallbearers including nine aldermen, three judges, two United States congressmen, an assistant state attorney and a state Republican leader—plus the heart of Chicago's criminal underworld.

Dale Colosimo went back to New York, starred in the musical comedy *Irene*, the longest-running Broadway musical of its time, married an actor in San Francisco, then disappeared.

John Torrio, with Capone, immediately began to expand into the Chicago suburbs with speakeasies and white slave whorehouses, opening up new properties in Burnham, Cicero and other points south and west of Chicago in deference to the new automobile age. Unlike Torrio, Capone enjoyed the pleasures of debauchery. At one of his own establishments, he contracted syphilis.

Around this time, a new listing appeared in the Chicago telephone directory: "Capone, A. Antique Dealer. 2220 S. Wabash Ave." It was a storefront stocked with old junk. In the rear, however, it was stocked with hundreds of cases of bootleg whiskey.

The Capones had emigrated from the slums of Naples to the slums of Brooklyn. As part of his heritage, Al learned that politicians and police were the enemies, that laws were meant to protect the rich and enslave the poor and that loyalty to family came before loyalty to country—especially in Brooklyn. There Italian immigrants were brutalized in the lowest-paying jobs—ditchdiggers, bricklayers, pipe-layers in sewer systems, fruit-wagon ped-dlers—and like Al's father, barbers. First-generation Italians were undernourished, sickly from slum life. Infant mortality among Italians was double that of other ethnics. Sixty percent were illit-erate, also the highest rate of all ethnic groups. Less than 1 percent went to high school, and young Alphonse was among the 99 per-cent who didn't. It was also remarkably true that a very small percentage of Italians turned to crime. Those who did, however, made an extraordinary impact.

Al was born in Brooklyn, January 17, 1899, one of nine sib-lings. His earliest memorable friend at P.S. 7 was a kid named Salvatore Lucania, later known as Lucky Luciano. Al's formal education ended after repeated truancy; when reproached by his teacher, he hit her; when thrashed by the principal, he quit school completely. He grew up in the streets and in its gangs. Irish, Sicilians, Neapolitans, Jews—all brutal, violent, endlessly in con-flict. Home was a crowded, filthy, stinking place; the streets rep-resented freedom and escape.

His first real job was at the Harvard Inn, a Coney Island dime-a-dance dive owned by Frankie Uale. There he got the chance to show his prowess with fists and guns. And there he was knifed across the face, leaving enormous scars, thus his nickname, Scarface. (He would later claim the scars came from wounds suf-fered while fighting in France.) Torrio's call from Chicago was doubly welcome, since Capone was a prime suspect in New York for murder.

In Chicago, the Torrio-Capone partnership immediately thrived. Capone took care of the dirty work of convincing saloon owners to buy their product. He bribed, strong-armed, murdered his way into control. Within three years, he had amassed an army of seven hundred men with sawed-off shotguns and the sensa-tional new Thompson submachine gun. Using the first wave of profits, he spent lavishly to bring the police under control. The civic process was so decadent, he didn't have to corrupt it; they wanted him to. His control went up the political ladder to include judges, then politicians. When he and Torrio took over Cicero, they put their own mayor in office. Capone had 161 bars under his control, plus the Hawthorne Hotel, which was their command post. By 1924, he was worth millions, primarily through the distribution of beer. He was called "the John D. Rockefeller of anti-Volstead filling stations."

But always there were rival gangs. O'Banions, Gennas, Aiellos—it was a competitive society, the ultimate fruition of free enterprise. Wars in the streets were fought in stolen cars. Machine-gun rivals would disappear in traffic and then abandon the car or induce another rival into the car on the promise of a deal, then "take him for a ride," kill him and dump the body; or lease an apartment overlooking a front door, station a lookout and wait, then slaughter him from behind gauze curtains. Survival of the fittest, it was called.

Dion O'Banion was Capone's leading rival, a bootlegger and a passionate florist, a wary gangster who always packed three weapons concealed in a specially tailored suit. One day, he was visited in his florist shop by three "friends." One shook hands and then held on while the other two put six bullets in him, walked out and left in a waiting sedan. At his garish funeral, among twenty-six truckloads of his beloved flowers was a huge bouquet basket "From Al." Soon enough, the other O'Banions came at Capone, in broad daylight, eight sedans in the streets of Cicero, raking Capone's headquarters at the Hawthorne Hotel and adjacent buildings with a steady spray of machine-gun fire, one gunman brazenly pouring over a hundred bullets into the lobby like a fireman with a hose. Capone hid under a table. Then, on St. Valentine's Day, 1929, at a garage on North Clark Street, seven O'Banions awaited the arrival of a hijacked truck. Three men dressed as policemen arrived to arrest them, stripped them of weapons and lined them up against the wall—whereupon two others in civilian clothes came in with submachine guns and slaughtered them all, then all five drove away in the most notorious of Chicago's Prohibition gang wars.

In Chicago alone, there were five hundred murders in the Prohibition decade, and no convictions. Capone organized the city to suit his needs. So enormous was the quantity of alcohol smuggled, shipped and delivered, and so huge were the profits, no force of government could contend with his power. Capone's revenue was estimated to be $60 million a year—while the officials of the bureau assigned to stop him were paid less than $2,000.

Capone became as great a celebrity as Jack Dempsey, Charlie Chaplin and Charles A. Lindbergh. Everyone knew that he controlled the bootlegging process in over ten thousand Chicago speakeasies; that he dominated supply routes from Canada to the coast of Florida; that he drove around in armored limousines, protected in front and back by other such cars; that he went to the theater with an eighteen-man armed bodyguard all dressed in tuxedos; that he loved his estate in Miami, where he lavishly entertained the rich and famous; that important people, including judges, took orders from him over the telephone; that, incredibly, at the height of his wealth and fame, he was only thirty-two years old.

It would follow that he had imitators, for Prohibition spawned gangsters like mushrooms in damp woodlands. Gangs prospered in many American cities: Toledo, Detroit, Cleveland, Boston, New York. But Chicago was Capone's creative prize. Capone had made Chicago into his own image, and Prohibition had made it possible. More than any other individual, Capone exposed to Americans the fraud and folly of the Eighteenth Amendment. The mores of an entire nation were assaulted by the depravity of what Capone came to symbolize. No matter what he had done to acquire his wealth and power, it was his success that gave him celebrity. "Give the devil his due," it was said. The poor son of an Italian immigrant had climbed out of a Brooklyn slum and taken the capitalist ethic to a convenient conclusion. American society, after decades of freewheeling robber barons, trust magnates and tyrannical banking consortiums, had achieved its economic purposes through corruption at top levels, and was no longer astonished to discover that it had also succeeded in creating corruption at the bottom. The criminal class began its war with the tyranny of that system. If financial barons could control the political process of government itself, the criminals, in precisely the same manner, corrupted the police. Police, in fact, were eager to comply. Many not only protected the gangster but often abetted his criminality. The pathetic outcome was, of course, a developing cynicism wherein Americans were no longer shocked to know that those they employed to protect their property were taking bribes from those who would steal it. It took men like Al Capone to convince America that society really wanted it this way.

Attempts at reforms were but a show of righteousness. Otherwise, the people would not tolerate such debasement as the corruption of their police, or allow the wealthy all-powerful at the top to continue to dominate the entire structure. To Capone, there was nothing but deceit and depravity in the way things worked. Had not the workingman always been beaten down? How many had been killed in the labor wars? What big businessmen had been indicted for those murders? How was Capone all that different from the merchants of death who had emerged from the war with countless millions? And what had he done but supply Americans with the beverages they chose to drink? How was his control over public officials any different from that of the Rockefellers, or the Du Ponts, or Judge Elbert Gary of U.S. Steel? Or Wayne Wheeler, for that matter? If Wheeler could get governors elected, why couldn't Al Capone elect a mayor? And if Capone was a killer, who died but a clutter of gangsters in a war of gangsters?

All the while, there were movies, the greatest invention in entertainment since the discovery of drink. Hollywood loved Prohibition, for it closed the saloons and drove millions into movie theaters. Prohibition gave the moviemaker a bootleg-gangster it could sell to Americans in place of the booze and beer now denied them. There was nothing like movies, irresistible to all classes, ages, sexes and intellects. And gangsters made ideal movie characters. They were romantic figures, no matter how evil or how brutally savage their methods; their movie lives were rich with dramatic action, beautiful sexy available women and absolutely extraordinary amounts of money that they spent in luxuries beyond all dreaming—but never without concern for dear old mothers or dying fathers, for family above all was sacred. If they died as brutally as they lived ("Crime does not pay!"), they were glorified by their creators in a way that business titans, however legitimate or philanthropic, never experienced in Hollywood. Prohibition was responsible for gangsters like Capone, and the gangsters were largely responsible for the success of movies.

Capone, as it turned out, was contemptuous of them. "You know, these gang pictures—that's terrible stuff. Why, they ought to take them all and throw them into the lake. They're doing nothing but harm to the young element. . . . These gang movies are making a lot of kids want to be tough guys and they don't serve any useful purpose."

Hollywood, it seemed, had just come up with the brilliant idea of casting Capone himself in his film biography—the first million-dollar offer in movie history. Capone, however, had more important matters to attend to, such as diversifying. The excesses of power and money demanded it. What else was his extraordinary organization designed for but to run as much of the country as possible? Booze and beer and prostitution were not enough. There was gambling, for example, almost as venerable as prostitution and even more popular. Then there was protection racketeering, one of the more sinister products of the Prohibition years. If a businessman wanted to remain in business, or even if he expected to wake up the next morning, he had to pay for the privilege. Extortion was a simple, negative tax: one paid solely for the opportunity to be able to pay again, and again. It took Capone's vast organization to lend a workable credibility to so arrogant a process.

Even more insidious was the growing gangster control over labor unions, the direct result of their decimation by the Red Scare. When A. Mitchell Palmer et al. got through with labor, Al Capone et al. moved in, taking control of union finances and working deals with employers at the sacrifice of both sides. There were "sluggers" to break up strikes and picket lines, and "counter-sluggers" to stop the scabbing. In New York, Jack "Legs" Diamond got his start by murdering union organizers for the garment manufacturers. And Arnold Rothstein multiplied his wealth and his power by paying off the police to preserve order in exchange for a piece of the subsequent profits. In Chicago, the state attorney estimated that Capone was involved in ninety-one different rackets at a cost to the citizens of the city of $136 million a year. There were so many bombs, and so much violence, and so much extortion that businessmen turned to the Capone organization for protection against the outcome of its own devices!

Herbert Hoover would call it "the great experiment," but it had been a fraud and a farce from the beginning, doomed by its own mentors, both for their excessive zealotry and the total blindness with which they failed to implement their own scenario. The

Eighteenth Amendment had hardly gone into effect when a force took shape to destroy it. In less than two years, a *Literary Digest* straw vote of a million ballots found over 60 percent in opposition, a figure that would increase dramatically in subsequent years. No matter; not one of four presidents or thousands of members of Congress had sufficient courage or leadership to denounce the damaging process so that something might be done to alleviate the disaster.

New York in the 1920s had twice as many speakeasies as it had legally licensed saloons before Prohibition.

On Fifth Avenue a saleslady stood at her counter with a brick of grape concentrate, a gallon jug and a few accessories: "Dissolve the grape brick in a gallon of water, and it is ready for consumption. However, do not store it for twenty-one days because it would turn into wine, or cork the jug with this rubber syphon hose because that will only serve to implement fermentation, and please, never never shake the jug once a day because that would stimulate the liquor." And if the customer ignored those warnings, the "Brick of Bacchus" would produce wine of 13 percent alcohol. "CAUTION: WILL TURN INTO WINE," the sign read.

Wrote Rudyard Kipling of the American: "There is a cynic devil in his blood/that bids him flout the Law he makes/that bids him make the Law he flouts."

And Walter Lippmann said, the United States had "the strongest laws and the weakest government of any highly civilized people." It also had the strongest criminal classes and the weakest public sentiment against them of any highly civilized people.

Chicago had seven thousand new "wet cabarets," and twenty-six breweries selling thousands of barrels a day at $60 a barrel. No state authority ever closed a Chicago brewery; Al Capone paid a million dollars a year in bribes.

In Detroit, where the smuggling rackets were considerably larger and not under any central control, the payoffs came to $2 million annually.

A pastor in a small parish of Sugar Notch, Pennsylvania, would testify before Congress: "Now, never in my occupation as a Catholic clergyman have I found children drinking hard liquors. . . . There were a few children last year found drunk in the schools, public schools, and had bottles of it in their pockets ... and, of course, the women are taking to it. ... I know of cases where women have run away with other men ... leaving the children behind ... and we also find that young girls, anywheres from thirteen, fourteen years old, love to go out riding, and expect the boys ... to treat them with liquor. ... Prohibition has made it very attractive to the youngsters. They hear so much about it, they read so much about it ... they think, 'We have got to try it out for ourselves.'"

In the South, the abolition of drink and the end of the liquor industry, intended to liberate the black man from its evil effects, did not alter the Southerners' desire to prevent blacks from voting. Instead of keeping blacks sober and vice free, those same Southerners put them to work as suppliers of illegal whiskey, thus training them to criminality. Nor did Prohibition deter violence: Southern states during the Prohibition years had the highest murder rates in the nation. Wrote Ellen Glasgow: "We are substituting murder for mint juleps and calling it progress."

The city of Chicago, meanwhile, had more homicides than all of England.

The ethical structure of the entire nation was caught in a fundamental contradiction. It appeared that these evils, encouraged by moral legislation, made moral legislation seem like the evil in itself. The law that was designed to secure the hegemony of the sober, reformist, law-abiding middle class had turned the country over to its opposite, the alien gangster. The eternally diligent ant became the fool, and the frivolous grasshopper became the hero. The abstemious ascetic was the new nonconformist. Like Henry Ford, for example, who in spite of his incredible successes, became vituperative about drink. Any movement for repeal of the Eighteenth Amendment (no one really believed it was possible) sent him raving to the barricades. "If booze ever comes back to the United States, I am through with manufacturing. I would not be bothered with the problem of handling over two hundred thousand men and trying to pay them wages which the saloons would take away from them. I would not be interested in putting automobiles in the hands of a generation soggy with drink."

The *New York Times* agreed—in a manner of speaking: "It would be a great pity to have Detroit's two leading industries destroyed with one blow."

It was also a wonderment why Ford sold cars to other nations that did drink, not the least of which was Canada, the biggest source of booze smuggled directly into Ford's own city. Or England, with one-eighth the number of cars as the United States, and three times the number of auto accidents. Nor was it ignored that his product was essential to the bootleggers, for it delivered the goods.

Meanwhile, Americans drank with lightheartedness, touched by a new indifference to anything that smacked of morality. The incredible scandals of the Harding administration (Teapot Dome, the Ohio Gang, the corrupt Department of Justice) rolled away like water off a duck's back. The Republican Party went unscathed, waltzing into a second term after Harding's death with the feeble candidacy of Calvin Coolidge. It didn't matter. No one cared. There was prosperity, or so it appeared, and there was jazz, baseball, movies, automobiles and lots more to go with the bootleg booze and the titillation of gangsters.

The last irony fell to the urban immigrant, presumably the principal object of the great Prohibition reform in the first place. In 1919, he found himself locked into an all but intolerable bind. Having left the old country to escape its poverty and oppressions, he came to America for its opportunity and freedom. The country was huge, richer by far than anything he could understand, full of highly acclaimed chances to make a new and better life for himself. If he had seen its restlessness and its brutality, if he had suffered its exploitations in factories and mills, if he had but barely survived in the ghetto squalor of the cities, he was nonetheless driven by hope. In Europe, there had never been hope. The poor understood a life of poverty since there had never been anything else for them. In Europe, a man knew to accept that poverty for there was no other possibility. In America, however, the first thing he learned was the potential for individual advancement. He was taught to believe he was as good as anyone else, that it was up to him to improve his life. His duty, in fact, was to stop being dirt beneath another man's feet. He would—he must—make money.

Then came the catch, the flaw in the premise: there were too many millions of immigrants vying for the thousands of so-called opportunities. The mathematics of making it set the odds over-whelmingly against any individual. Most of them, then, were ir-revocably doomed. It was all part of an impossibly stacked deck. Even the immigrant's attempt at cooperative efforts, the union movement, had been brutally destroyed. Meanwhile, in his own neighborhood, he suffered the petty corruptions of graft-ridden community action, influence peddling, deceits of officials in high places. He came to see the larger scheme of things, that the law was not an equal entity, but was designed for the prejudices of the rich. A workingman such as he could never fight the law and win.

Some immigrants learned this quicker than others. Some be-came radicals as a result of the injustices, intent on altering the inhumanities of the system so weighted against them. This, of course, became the way to get your head bashed in. It was the way of Sacco and Vanzetti, for example. To most immigrants, it seemed there had to be a better way, a more American way. If you couldn't fight the law and win, you could always go around it.

Prohibition opened the door for this underclass. It was a perfect demonstration of America's folly, an ideal creation by a hypocritical society devoted to its own righteousness. To a thug like Alphonse Capone, what could offer a better opportunity? It even served the rich, the very people who had brought on the law itself. He, for one, did not have to ponder these things. Pro-hibition was as obviously tempting as a beautiful woman hanging nude from a Christmas tree. There were fifty-five thousand peo-ple, mostly immigrants, working in the booze business in Detroit alone. There were more in Chicago and New York, Boston and Cleveland. Prohibition gave them the all-American chance they had come for.

The immigrant author Louis Adamic wrote of an Italian im-migrant who had been a radical organizer in the United States Steel strike of 1919, in Joliet, Illinois. On a picket line, he was savagely beaten by the police, the strike broken, the union de-stroyed. After years of living badly in bare subsistence, his self-respect washing away with cheap bootleg wine and self-pity, he got smart. Instead of buying rotgut wine, he took to bootlegging it. Gradually, he achieved a measure of success, gained his self-respect and the unity of his family. In time, he rose to a position of power sufficient to gain control of the Joliet Police Department. By 1927, they were working for him.

This was also the year that two other radical Italian immigrants, Sacco and Vanzetti, were executed.

In 1927, Wayne Wheeler, pundit of the Anti-Saloon League, was at his summer home in Northern Michigan, when his wife was set afire after her stove exploded. At this ghastly sight, her father fell instantly dead with a heart attack. Wheeler came rushing downstairs seconds later and he too suffered a coronary and died a few weeks later.... William Anderson, New York state superintendent of the league, was convicted of forgery and sentenced to Sing Sing Prison.... Bishop James J. Cannon, its national leader, was indicted for misappropriation of funds.... S.S. Kresge, the chain-store magnate and generous benefactor of the league, fell into disrepute in a celebrated divorce as the result of a clandestine affair with his secretary.... Al Capone, the most famous beneficiary of their accomplishments, was convicted not of murder or extortion or bootlegging, but evading income tax payments. (At his trial, it is noteworthy that his attorneys were Michael Ahearn and Thomas Nash, both of whom had served as counsel for the eight indicted baseball players known as the Black Sox.) Capone served nine years of an eleven-year sentence in federal prison in Atlanta and Alcatraz, then was released because of mental and physical incapacities, the result of a long bout with syphilis.

The Eighteenth Amendment was repealed in 1933 by the Twenty-first, the first such phenomenon in the history of the United States Constitution. During the thirteen years of Prohibition, the American people became inured to the finer points of lawlessness. It had no other lasting impact.

THE BLACK SOX SCANDAL

*As Jackson departed from the Grand Jury room, a small boy
clutched at his sleeve and tagged along after him.*
"Say it ain't so, Joe," he pleaded. "Say it ain't so."
"Yes, kid, I'm afraid it is," Jackson replied.
"Well, I never would've thought it," the boy said.

—CHICAGO HERALD AND EXAMINER

1. WHY THE 1919 WORLD SERIES WAS FIXED

I did it for the wife and kids.

—EDDIE CICOTTE before the Cook County Grand Jury

October 1, 1919, was opening day of the World Series at Redlands Field, Cincinnati. In the box behind the dugout of his team sat Charles Albert Comiskey, owner of the Chicago White Sox Baseball Club, American League pennant winner. At the age of sixty, Comiskey was the epitome of an American self-made man. No one in the history of baseball could duplicate his achievements. He had played thirteen years in the major leagues, for ten of which he was also a manager; he initiated a franchise in the newly formed American League (without a partner); built a ball-park at his own expense and in his own name; sought, purchased and developed talent to create a team that was acknowledged as the very best. No club owner had comparable knowledge or experience. (Twenty years hence he would be among the first voted into the Baseball Hall of Fame.) He was a proud, wealthy, highly respected man, especially in the city of Chicago, his birthplace and the seat of his power and prestige—so much so, in fact, that political leaders had suggested that he run for its mayoralty, to which he replied: "I would rather win a pennant than an election."

His father, known as "Honest John" Comiskey, had been an Irish immigrant; eleven years a city alderman; first president of the city council; a courtly, eloquent man with seven sons and a daughter, a believer in work and education (in that order), a man

293

who abhorred all forms of idleness and play. The story goes that seventeen-year-old Charles was driving a load of bricks (by horse-drawn wagon) to the rebuilding of the city hall (the old one had been destroyed by the Great Chicago Fire of 1871) when he passed a sandlot ballgame where a young pitcher was apparently unable to get anyone out. Young Comiskey dropped the reins, hopped down, and proceeded to reverse the slaughter in one of the more remarkable demonstrations of relief pitching in sandlot history. As for the bricks, several hours elapsed before Honest John himself discovered the source of the delay, even as his son was striking out the side.

"At the family counsel that night," wrote G. W. Axelson in his biography of "Commy," "the world lost an indifferent teamster but gained a great baseball man."

Young Commy was over six feet tall and rangy, strong and well-coordinated. His first real job as a player was in Dubuque, Iowa, where he made $50 a month on the diamond, added to the 20 percent commission he got selling magazines and candy on the Illinois Central Railroad line. Four years later, as a first baseman, he joined the St. Louis Browns in the National Association at $90 a month, managed the club to four successive pennants and two championships and eventually earned a phenomenal salary of $8,000 a season. He developed the concept of moving the first baseman deep and away from the bag, thereby covering much more territory. He trained his fielders to shift positions for different hitters, to back up throws, to prepare for making double plays, to defend against bunts. His defenses gave the game a whole new look, and because they won pennants, changed the game for all time.

They were turbulent years, for professional baseball was dominated by uncompromising businessmen who dealt with ball players the way Rockefeller dealt with immigrant copper miners. A $2,000 salary limit was imposed, plus the infamous Reserve Clause wherein a ball club owned a player's contract and held in reserve the right to renew it, year after year. At such gross exploitation, the indignation of ball players grew, leading to the formation of the National Brotherhood of Professional Baseball Players, which declared: "There was a time when the [National] League stood for integrity and fair dealing. Today it stands for dollars and cents.

Once it looked to the elevation of the game and an honest exhibition of the sport; today its eyes are on the turnstiles. Men have come into the business for no other motive than to exploit it for every dollar in sight."

In 1890, the new Players League was organized in a short-lived rebellion, and Comiskey sacrificed his managership of the St. Louis Browns to join it. "I couldn't do anything else and still play square with the boys."

Eleven years later, the American League was formed, and Comiskey returned to Chicago with a new club, the White Stockings, later changed to White Sox in deference to the needs of newspaper headline writers. He put together a makeshift team of minor leaguers, hurriedly bought land and built a makeshift ballpark, and pulled his team to the first American League pennant by his brilliance, to the accolades of what became the best baseball town in America.

Then forty-two, he moved into the front office, turning the field managing over to others. His personal style changed with new executive stature; there was a new elegance to his manner. He became known as "the Old Roman," partly with affection, partly not. His need to win was as compelling as ever. There was a story, perhaps apocryphal, that when dining at a seafood restaurant he was brought a giant lobster with only one claw. When he asked about the other, the waiter explained that lobsters frequently battled in the pond, and apparently, this one suffered the consequences. Comiskey picked up the platter and handed it back. "Bring me the winner," he said.

Although the White Sox were a second division club throughout the early years of the 1900s, Comiskey became enriched by the loyalty of his fans. As a gesture of his faith, he plowed $500,000 into the rebuilding of the ballpark, dedicated it to the people of Chicago and turned over the facilities to their activities—church festivals, community barbecues, concerts, picnics—without charge. With exceptional foresight, he built a huge, beautiful lounge for a select group of two hundred loyal supporters who called themselves the Woodland Bards, for whom he laid out festive food and drinks—and, significantly, held open house for the gentlemen of the press. As to the club offices, also in the ballpark, what George Rice, a reporter for the *Chicago Daily News*,

wrote was far more significant than anyone realized: "The furniture presented to Comiskey was so elegant that he announced
at once that he would refuse to sign any of his ball players in his
private office because it was too nice a place to do business with
the players, for they would get the idea that he should give them
a salary commensurate with his office surroundings."

But it was a winner he wanted, and having failed to build
successfully through minor league deals, he went out to buy the
best players available. From Connie Mack in Philadelphia, he got
second baseman Eddie Collins for $65,000. He sent Harry Gra-
biner, his business manager, to Cleveland with a blank check to
"bring me back this fellow [Shoeless Joe] Jackson!" who cost him
another $65,000 in cash and trades. For $15,000 he picked up
outfielder Oscar "Happy" Felsch from Milwaukee.

In 1917, the Sox literally exploded to the American League
pennant by a margin of nine games, then wiped out the New York
Giants of John McGraw, four games to two, in the World Series.

It could be said that no one in baseball had made better
investments until Yankee owner, Jacob Ruppert, the brewer,
bought George Herman Ruth from Boston for $100,000.

In 1919, Comiskey was, at long last, prepared to enjoy the
fruits of his many talents. In this, his first postwar season, his
attendance had soared to unprecedented figures. He had created
the finest team in professional baseball in the best baseball town
in America. What else was in store but a brilliant future, a dynasty
with repeating championships, a potential of unlimited fame and
fortune!

The Old Roman had become the Caesar of the baseball world.

On the mound for the White Sox in the 1919 Series opener
was Eddie Cicotte, baseball's leading pitcher with twenty-nine wins
and seven losses and a superb earned-run average of 1.82 in a
record 307 innings' work. After fourteen years in the big leagues,
he was an aging thirty-five, a "baseball player in his twilight years,"
reporters said. A native of Detroit, he was the father of two,
respected by teammates and feared by opponents, extremely lik-
able, full of pranks and jokes, though eminently serious and hardworking. Like Comiskey himself, Cicotte was pure baseball, his
entire life having been devoted to the game. He had grown up

in northern Michigan mining towns, a smallish teenager weighing no more than 135 pounds, but he would throw for nine innings, sometimes three games a week, snapping off curve balls and hard stuff, noted for bearing down on every pitch. A pitcher who wanted to move up could not acknowledge pain or throw less than his best. Cicotte developed a talent for throwing complete games, always managing to unload something extra in the final innings to hang on to a lead. He was, in fact, the kind of ball player Comiskey most admired.

After 1917, having won twenty-eight games on a meager $4,000 salary, Cicotte had asked for a raise, but the owner had snapped at him: "There's a war on! Baseball like everything else will have to pull in its belt." To prove his patriotism, Comiskey had cut all salaries and had the players marching close order drill with bats at right shoulder arms, a daily reminder of patriotic motives that justified his penuriousness. In 1919, when Cicotte again asked for more money, Comiskey referred to the pitcher's poor 1918 season and dangerously tender right arm. Cicotte would be given $5,500, but was promised $10,000 if he could win thirty games. As it turned out, that right arm proved anything but sore and Cicotte won twenty-nine. But Comiskey had him miss his last two scheduled starts, ostensibly to save him for the World Series, but everyone knew it was to save the ten-grand bonus. Nor was it inspirational to Cicotte (or anyone else on the White Sox) that the Cincinnati pitcher, Walter "Dutch" Reuther, after but two years in the majors, was making almost twice as much on a much less distinguished record.

Cicotte toed the rubber and stared at the catcher, Ray Schalk, for his sign. Schalk called for a fast ball, aware that the batter, Maury Rath, would probably take the first pitch. Cicotte nodded, then as if to let the whole world know, cut loose a fast ball that Rath could not hit on the best day he ever had. The umpire called "Strike One!"

It would be the last good pitch he would throw all day.

In New York City, the celebrated gambler Arnold Rothstein was in the Green Room of the Ansonia Hotel on Broadway and Seventy-third Street where a telegraph system had been set up to relay the World Series, play by play. The room was smoky and noisy, several hundred chairs already filled with sports fans. A large diamond-shaped chart hung on the front wall on which players would be moved from base to base as the game was wired in. Those who had seen this new procedure could testify to its excitement. It was "almost like actually being there," they said.

Rothstein declined a seat, preferring to stand in the rear, an indication as much of his uneasiness as it was of the single pitch he had come to see. This entire venture had disturbed him, right from the onset. No matter that he was a master fixer of all people and events, that he ran a variety of swindles, owned gambling dens for the rich and whorehouses for anyone, ran rackets with labor unions, was just getting started in the great new business of bootlegging; no matter that his keen supersensitive nose was forever sniffing for a chance at the big score, he was anything but enthusiastic about this venture. This was baseball. Above all, it was the World Series. He had known of the impact of gamblers in baseball for years, but he had always shied away, not only because fixing ball games seemed infinitely more complicated than fixing a boxing match or a jockey on a horse or the turn of a marked card, but because he genuinely liked baseball. He preferred not to think that a World Series could be corrupted. It was as if, for all his corruptions, he wanted to draw the line somewhere.

He was a strange and devious man. His lawyer, William J. Fallon, once said about him: "Arnold Rothstein is a man who waits in doorways . . . a mouse, waiting in the doorway for his cheese." By 1919, he had waited for enough of it to become immensely wealthy. Better than most, he comprehended the underbelly of corruption that ran the country and learned how to exploit it. This was his genius, making money through corruption.

Since his father was an eternally devout and righteous man, a psychiatrist might offer that Arnold's life was a rebellion against him. Abraham Rothstein had grown up in the ghettos of New York's Lower East Side and quit school to support his mother and siblings. In time, he prospered, but always he was admired for his integrity. In 1919, a testimonial dinner was held to honor his settlement of a garment industry labor dispute. Governor Alfred Smith was there, and Louis Brandeis, justice of the United States Supreme Court. "Abe the Just," they called him.

They called his son Arnold "The Big Bankroll."

As a young student, Arnold was poor in everything but arithmetic. He would frequently cut school for crap games. The more his pious father objected, the more he gambled. At fourteen, he was a serious and successful gambler. He understood the odds. All he ever needed was a sufficient bankroll to break any crap game. Unwittingly, his father supplied it: every Friday night Abraham Rothstein would empty his pockets of money to go to shul, whereupon Arnold would help himself to the cash, pawn the gold watch. It was his stake, as it were, for the twenty-four-hour Sabbath that ended on Saturday night.

He learned how to use money to make money. He would lend it—at 25 percent interest. If he had any trouble collecting, a moronic brute he'd found named Monk Eastman would get it back for him. He was still a kid when Big Tim Sullivan of Tammany Hall took a liking to him, affording Arnold a taste of political power he would never relinquish. He also learned how to impress important people, especially in the sporting world. John McGraw, for one. And all the while he lived frugally, saving his money, never spending anything on women. His operation escalated from a few small gambling dens on the West Side, protected by political contacts, to a big one in Saratoga, New York. Here, as with Big Jim Colosimo's café in Chicago, Arnold created a palace for the superrich who came to watch the horses run in the afternoon and the roulette wheels at night. In other seasons, he was partner in a stock fraud "bucket shop" operation wherein he swindled people looking to make easy money. In 1919, only two years older than Eddie Cicotte, he could have retired and lived like a king. He need never have placed another bet—or fixed another fight. But asking him to quit, of course, would have been like asking Woodrow Wilson to put away his Bible.

The announcer at the diamond-shaped board called out, "Strike One!" and Rothstein felt a tremor of uneasiness. He tried to put himself inside Cicotte's head, wondering at the defiance of the man. What really was going on? He could sense the possibility that this entire venture might prove to be a bad mistake. Had he not rejected the proposal when it was first offered him weeks ago? The fix had never been his idea or his doing. He saw only cheap clowns floating around the edges of surly, dumb ball players, everyone thinking they could make some easy money. Rothstein had come aboard only after he was convinced it was going to happen without him. A sure thing, then, and how could he resist that? But he was ever the fastidious man; if he hated to lose money (he had bet over $325,000 on the Cincinnati Reds already), even worse was the thought of losing because he had no sense of control. He had needed a demonstration of his mastery. A symbolic gesture of reassurance. He needed to know that the linkage through the various channels from his pocket to the pitcher's mound was a solid one. He had been advised that Cicotte was committed. Very well, let this be verified by deed. And so he had given instructions that Cicotte was to hit the first batter.

The announcer picked up the next message off the telegraph receiver and moved to the diamond-shaped board. "Roth hit by pitched ball," he said, then slid the simulated base runner down the line to first base. Curiously, Rothstein was almost surprised— but only for an instant. He left immediately for his midtown office, determined to get as much money down on the Cincinnati Reds as possible.

In baseball history, there had always been a link with betting, even as a game played in New York by gentlemen in private clubs. When baseball became highly organized, admissions charged, ball players salaried, the professional gamblers moved in. Inevitably, they devised ways to alter the odds. There were bribery schemes that proliferated with impunity until they became impossible to stop. In 1866, for example, the Louisville Club had the pennant all but cinched when they astonished everyone by falling apart in the final six-game series with Hartford, a team they had beaten all season. It was finally uncovered that four star players had been bribed, though with no more than $100 each, because their club owner had not gotten around to paying their salaries.

By 1919, baseball had become a huge entertainment business, second only to horse racing. Since Americans were always looking for something to bet on, the vastness of baseball's appeal made it all the more attractive to gamblers. There was the baseball pool, a lottery of sorts, wherein people put up a dime to a dollar on the team to score the most runs per inning, or game, or week, selling hundreds of thousands of tickets a week with agents and subagents much like the numbers racket of later years. Although community leaders tried to stop it, baseball owners did not object, knowing the paid-off political support behind it. Besides, it generated interest in the great game.

During the war, the government shut down the racetracks, but not ball games, whereupon gamblers and bookies who lived on the horses immediately came to the ballparks, applying themselves to doping the odds with the same diligence they used in handicapping horses. In the process, they intruded into the intimate circles of the baseball world, operating openly in hotel lobbies where visiting ball players hung out. They were always pleasant and friendly, ready with a warm hello and a knowledge of the local high life. In time, they got to know the ball players well, took them to dinner at the best restaurants, arranged liaisons with attractive available women. The big gamblers had long since moved in the highest social circles, many of them intimate with club owners—like the bootleggers to come.

What they sought, at first, was inside knowledge, anything to exploit the odds. Who was having trouble with his wife or the manager? Who had been drinking too much? Who had a sore arm or leg? Gamblers were masters in using such information. Then they became masters at pushing the process to the next step, the actual bribe. By 1919, they became adept at controlling games the way they had fixed horse races or boxing matches—while ball players became adept at throwing them. A shortstop would twist his body to make a simple stop seem brilliant, then make his throw a bare split-second too late to beat the runner. An outfielder might "short-leg" a long fly ball, then dive desperately for it, only to see it skid by for extra bases—and look good in the process. Such maneuvers were impossible for a fan or a sportswriter or even another ball player to detect. But even if a teammate suspected it, there was little he could do, for it was impossible to prove, and newspapers were forever stifled by libel laws.

But mostly the secrecy was maintained by the power of the owners themselves. Whatever they knew, or suspected, they concealed, terrified of losing the public faith in the game. At all costs, any suspicious incident would be buried. The probing sportswriter would be warned, or paid off, to stop his digging. Ball players who wanted to blow the whistle would be carefully thanked for their honesty, then disregarded—always in the best interests of baseball. Indeed, who would pay money to see a ball game suspected of being crooked? The official, if unspoken, policy preferred to let the rottenness grow rather than risk the dangers of exposure, for all the pious phrases about the nobility of the game and its inspirational value to youth. In fact, that too was part of the business.

The greatest illustration of this hypocrisy was the first baseman Hal Chase. He didn't even need gamblers to bribe him, but became a one-man operation, betting heavily against his ball club, then artfully throwing the game himself. Since he was a superb fielder, he would make faulty plays around the infield that made everyone else look bad but himself. Inevitably, he went too far. In 1917, while playing for Cincinnati, he approached a young pitcher, Jimmy Ring, summoned from the bullpen with the score tied, two men on. As Ring was warming up, Chase walked to the mound: "I've got some money going on this game, kid. There's something in it for you if you lose." Ring snubbed him, but ended up losing anyway. The following morning, Chase found him seated in the lobby and slipped him $50 without saying a word. When Ring reported this to manager Christy Matthewson, Matty brought the matter to John Heydler, president of the National League. At the hearing, Heydler typically found the evidence insufficient, and Chase was acquitted. But Matty knew, and hating the corruption, got rid of Chase. The great John McGraw of the New York Giants was not so squeamish, and Hal Chase came to New York in 1919 to continue his artistry.

And so it went, year after year, incident after incident. If a ball player could cheat with impunity, he would continue to cheat—especially if he made money from it.

Joseph Jefferson Jackson was anything but a cheat. At thirty-two, he was in his prime as a ball player, the greatest hitter of his time, second only to Ty Cobb in batting average but far more powerful, and an exceptional outfielder with a strong, accurate throwing arm. He had come a long way to get where he was, born on a broken-down South Carolina plantation run by an eccentric old fire-eater who drove his tenants to a fury. Joe's father eked out a mere subsistence from the barren soil in a country of corn whiskey and ignorance. If a man learned to read or write, he was looked on as a freak; young Joe was like all the others.

Then the Jacksons moved to Brandon Mill, a small cotton-mill town outside of Greenville. At the age of thirteen, Joe worked at the mill for $1.25 a day, along with his father, six brothers and two sisters. The work was unwholesome, even dangerous, but a lot better than the plantation, especially since there was baseball. Brandon Mill had a ball team, just like almost every town and factory in America. Even at thirteen, Joe was special. So too was his older brother Dave, but Dave got caught in the whirring machinery of the mill, which spun him to the roof, breaking an arm and a leg, which was never properly set. When Joe was nineteen, he was playing against a mill team in Greer, South Carolina, whose second baseman, Tom Stouch, was an old ball player who knew Connie Mack. As Stouch recalled: "This tall skinny-looking kid stepped up to the plate, he didn't appear to have much in him, but he drove the ball on a line to a spot where I was standing, like a bullet out of a gun. . . . He hit three times that game, twice for extra bases, and when he hit, he left a trail of blue flame." When Stouch became manager at Greenville, he hired Jackson at $75 a month, almost double what he was making at the mill. Toward the end of the season, Stouch called Connie Mack in Philadelphia, a scout was sent down, and Jackson was bought for $325.

Afraid of the big city, frightened by its reputation for harshness and excesses, ashamed of his rural ignorance and illiteracy, he didn't want to go. "I hardly know as how I'd like it in those big Northern cities," he told Stouch. Stouch reassured him, not believing what he'd heard. He took the trouble to escort Jackson onto the train, feed him supper and put him in his berth. But when the train arrived the next morning, Jackson was not on it. He had slipped off at Richmond and caught the first train back to Greenville. A telegram reached Philly that explained everything—and nothing. "AM UNABLE TO COME TO PHILADELPHIA AT THIS TIME. JOE JACKSON." Connie Mack sent a coach to bring him up, and this time, Jackson came all the way. He played the day he arrived, got two hits, but took an unmerciful ribbing from his teammates, exactly as he had suspected. Then it began to rain, and before it cleared two days later, Jackson had sneaked home again.

It was as if he could foretell his own doom.

A year later, Mack gave up on him and sold him to Cleveland. By this time, Jackson was happily married to a girl he'd met when the A's farmed him to Savannah. In his first full season in the majors, he had hit an astonishing .408, yet lost the American League batting title to Ty Cobb. Walter Johnson, the great pitcher for the Washington Senators, called Jackson "the greatest natural ball player I've ever seen."

Then, in 1915, Comiskey paid $65,000 to bring him to Chicago. Jackson did not want to go. He was happy in Cleveland, having learned to adjust to city life and make friends. Chicago was too big, too blustering, too much like the cities that Southerners believed were fraught with dark and evil forces. But Jackson had no say in the matter. No ball player ever did. He received not one penny of the sale price, and signed Comiskey's contract at whatever figure Comiskey deemed reasonable. That's what you had to do if you wanted to play baseball.

But Jackson remained a rube. No matter that he came to enjoy the feel of money and became a slick dresser, very conscious of good clothes. He liked the texture and style of shoes and bought far more than he needed. He was teased for this: was it in response to his famous nickname? When he returned to Greenville, he bought a house for his parents, then a pool hall and a farm (both of which were mismanaged and lost him money). In Brandon Mill, people spoke affectionately of his nature but badly of his chances. "Wait five years or so," an old mill hand commented. "Then Joe will go through all his money and he'll be back here working for a buck and quarter a day again." Another old friend from Greenville said: "Joe's record is the best example I ever saw of what a man may accomplish in this world wholly without brains." Both comments, however telling, were irrelevant. It was hardly the rube in Jackson that brought about his fall.

Like all ball players, Jackson was fully aware of his slavelike status—once bought, forever owned. The National Professional Baseball Players contract, which all ball players were forced to sign, gave them no rights whatsoever. If such an agreement violated the Sherman Anti-Trust Law as being in restraint of trade,

Congress and the courts had repeatedly declared that baseball was a sport, not a business, and thereby not subject to that law. There was even a Ten-Day Clause in the contract wherein the owner had the right to fire a ball player with ten days' notice. If a player fractured an ankle breaking up a double play, for example, since he became worthless to the team, the owner could fire him in ten days, and all payment of his year's salary would be terminated. If the player signed for two years, or three, it was the owner's option to sustain its duration. Or trade him. Or fire him. With Comiskey, the imbalanced relationships were exacerbated by his extraordinary penuriousness. As a club owner, he considered ball players to be totally beneath his concern except as investments for his expanding profits. In a classically contemptuous owner-worker scenario, Comiskey bent the fragile reed to ludicrous extremes with such irritating economies as allowing a sparce $3-a-day meal money allotment on the road when every other club gave $4, and charging players laundry fees for dirty uniforms, all the while buttering up reporters at his sumptuous groaning board, thus making his players feel like dirt. In 1919, his salary levels continued to be preposterously low, lower than those of clubs in the second division bringing in half the attendance of Comiskey Park, ostensibly because of anticipated poor postwar attendance. Early in July, it became apparent that such fears were totally unfounded. Besides, the Sox were burning up the league, making them more resentful than ever, so much so that there was an angry clubhouse meeting wherein it was agreed that action should be taken. Kid Gleason, the manager, was to take their plea for more money to the boss. Gleason could be trusted, for he too had had a salary dispute the year before, and when Comiskey refused to compromise, Gleason was forced out of baseball for his first season since he came up as a pitcher in 1888. On the following day, Gleason reported that Comiskey had refused to discuss the matter. The ball players were dressing for a game when they heard this, and were so enraged, they threatened to strike. Was this not the year of the strike everywhere else? Cicotte, in fact, was so furious, Gleason thought better of pitching him that day.

For it all, to Jackson, the idea of throwing the World Series had seemed preposterous. He first heard of it in a room at the Ansonia in New York, a week or so before the Sox clinched the pennant. In the history of American sport, it would be difficult to find another meeting that led to events so shattering. Besides Cicotte and Jackson, there were Charles Swede Risberg, shortstop; Oscar "Happy" Felsch, centerfielder; Claude "Lefty" Williams, the number two pitcher; first baseman Chick Gandil, who would turn out to be the ringleader among the players, George "Buck" Weaver, third baseman; and Fred McMullin, utility infielder, who insisted on being part of it when he overheard mention of it in the locker room. The only relevant explanation was that each would get far more money in one week than he made all season. There was none of the conspiratorial somberness that would normally attach to such a monumental occasion. There were even a few jokes concerning special bonuses to the guys who made the most errors or left the most men on base. After all, it was just an opening meeting. Nothing had been nailed down. Gandil laid out the prospects: He was to get $80,000 from a Boston gambler named Joseph "Sport" Sullivan. They would all be paid off before the opening game, or so Sullivan had promised. The details on how it would be done would be discussed later, depending on all the obvious variables, such as who was going to pitch and how the games were going.

Jackson sat there as still as a mouse, more bewildered than horrified. He would hear later that Buck Weaver, for one, wanted no part of it. That he was of two minds himself was due mostly to his friend and road roomie, Lefty Williams, who, in turn, allowed himself to get sucked in, mostly because Cicotte had agreed. Gandil, and then Risberg, kept after Jackson, calling him a fool if he stayed out, for it was going to happen for sure, and he'd only be sacrificing a bundle of money. In the end, Jackson saw the logic. He insisted on payment of $20,000. It would be Gandil's problem to obtain the money, and he assured the players that he would.

It had all been Chick Gandil's idea, cultivated in the Boston garden of Sport Sullivan, a long time associate of Chick's. Gandil loved this sort of high-handed brashness. A tough roustabout in the lawless Southwest after running away from home in St. Paul, Minnesota, he played semi-pro ball with outlaw teams in Mexico in wide-open mining towns. He was also a heavyweight boxer, taking in $150 a fight, and in the off season, a boilermaker in the copper mines. He played minor league ball until 1910, when he was picked up by the White Sox, sold to Washington, then to Cleveland, then back to Chicago in 1916. He was a reliable .280 hitter and a strong first baseman. It was as a pool player in a Boston pool hall that he attracted Sullivan's ever-roving eye. To Sullivan, Gandil became a valuable source of inside information by which he made many successful bets. Gandil enjoyed playing the role, enjoyed even more the company, which consisted of some of the most distinguished people in Boston. And then there were Sullivan's friends in New York—George M. Cohan, the great song and dance man, among them, for example.

Then, suddenly there was another offer in New York. Gandil was approached by an ex-pitcher named Sleepy Bill Burns, who had heard rumors. Gandil knew of Burns, a mediocre big-league relief pitcher known to fall asleep on the bench. Burns claimed he could get $100,000. What guarantees could Gandil offer in exchange? Burns was impressed. With his partner, an ex-pug from Philadelphia named Billy Maharg, he went to get the backing from a most likely source: Arnold Rothstein. Rothstein was known to do business at the Jamaica Race track—between races. Burns got as far as a little man in Rothstein's entourage, Abe Attell, the former featherweight champion of the world, "The Little Champ," as he was called. As a fighter, Attell had been so great that when he failed to win quickly there was reason to believe he was holding up his rival in order to do extra business. Three hundred and sixty-five professional fights, six losses, never knocked out. Only when Johnny Kilbane beat him in 1912 did he quit the ring. He was a natty dresser, a cheerful ever-smiling 116 pounds, who cultivated important friends, not the least of whom was Arnold Rothstein. Rothstein had use for him. It flattered the gambler's ego to have a champion for a lackey.

It was Attell, then, who heard Burns's proposition at the race-track restaurant. When he passed it on to Rothstein, the great gambler wanted nothing to do with it. Burns, undeterred, knew a good thing when he came across it; there had to be some way to get it financed. Like a horny john looking for a whore, he hung out in the Ansonia lobby and presto, there was Hal Chase. Chase, as it turned out, had ears as long as Burns's and had heard the fix rumors from the inception. Burns was not surprised; after all, fixing ball games was Chase's chosen avocation. Chase's advice was to pursue Rothstein. Talk to him personally. Convince him. He even knew that Rothstein would be at the Hotel Astor that very night. All he wanted was to be kept informed.

And so it was that Burns confronted Arnold Rothstein with the scheme, in person this time, but again, Rothstein politely declined. In his opinion, "whatever that was worth," Burns ought to forget it. That seemed to be the end of it. Maharg went back to Philadelphia and his job at a Ford Motor assembly plant, and Burns went about forgetting it.

Not so, Attell, however. The Little Champ had learned a few things in Rothstein's company, not the least of which was the art of deceit. Why couldn't this marvelous scheme be implemented *without* Rothstein? If it was Rothstein's backing that was so badly needed, why couldn't Attell merely pretend that he had it? Wasn't he in the perfect position to do just that? So it was that Attell contacted Burns. Once again, the Ansonia lobby was the setting for a dubious assignation as Burns picked up Attell and took him upstairs to his room. There Attell told him that A. R. had changed his mind, that he wanted to go through with it. And the money? The $100,000 cash? Attell advised Burns that it was all arranged, but that A. R. insisted that his name be kept out of it, that he didn't want to hear from Burns again, and that Attell would do all the handling for him.

With only a few days before the Series opener in Cincinnati, Burns wired Maharg in Philly to meet him in Cincinnati to get the ball rolling—unaware that it already was.

Or was it? On that very night, Rothstein received a call at his home on Riverside Drive from Sport Sullivan in Boston. Sullivan would be in New York the following day and wanted to talk with him about a matter of considerable importance. Would Mr. Rothstein consent to see him? Since A. R. had heard of him over the years, he agreed.

Again Rothstein was told of the pending fix, and this time, he came to believe in its possibility. The fact that two groups were working the same side of the street didn't bother him, and he carefully made no mention of it. He advised Sullivan that he needed to think about it. He would let him know. He discussed it with one of his partners, a man named Nat Evans. Evans objected on the grounds that with this many people involved, secrecy would be impossible. On the other hand, Rothstein reasoned, that might serve as a blessing on the theory that "If nine guys go to bed with a girl, she'll have a tough time proving the tenth is the father."

Evans, then, would go to Chicago to meet with Sullivan and the players, appraise the entire project, and call Rothstein as soon as possible. A. R. also advised him to change his name, just to muddy up the waters if there should happen to be trouble.

"My name is Brown," said Evans, and so it would be for the duration.

2. CHEATERS CHEATING CHEATERS

"I'm forever blowing ballgames
Pretty ballgames in the air.
I come from Chi
I hardly try
Just go to bat and fade and die. . . ."

—RING LARDNER,
parody of the popular song

Chicago was the ideal setting for the World Series fix. A whole city that for years had been up for grabs; a mayor, "Big Bill" Thompson, with his hand in every till; a collection of ward heelers and aldermen that could corrupt a penal colony; a racist city that just barely survived the worst race riot in America after a seventeen-year-old black boy was stoned into drowning in Lake Michigan because he had inadvertently floated across the imaginary color line; a messy city paved with brick so slippery that horses fell in the streets; a filthy congested city with insufferably heavy traffic, described in the *Atlantic Monthly* as "the ugliest in the world . . . an idiot child of cities." More than any city in America, Chicago was turning away from its moral midwestern traditions, its young people quick to find disillusionment, reaching out for the wild, jazzy sexy freedoms that would dominate the postwar years. It was a city frightened by the oncoming steel strike in its backyard, the Red Scare all around it and the jarring promise of Prohibition in a city rife with saloons and crooked leadership. At the end of September, however, Chicagoans could turn to the White Sox the way religious fanatics turn to revival meetings. Here, at least, was

310

something worthy of their enthusiasm, one last surviving boost to their dwindling pride.

The eight ball players—or seven, perhaps; no one appeared to know about Buck Weaver—were still vacillating in confusion and doubt. Was it on, or wasn't it? If so, where was the money? When Sullivan arrived with "Brown" on the twenty-ninth, the day before they would leave for Cincinnati for the opener, there was a meeting at the Warner Hotel, where several of the players lived. Brown was introduced as the man who backed them with cash. He wanted assurance that the ball players were really going to go through with this. It was an understandable precaution since a lot of money was involved. After all, what guarantee could they offer him that the series would be thrown? Gandil replied that they'd give their word. (Sullivan, of course, would vouch for it.) But Brown only smiled, somewhat dolefully. "In my book, that's not much collateral." Nonetheless, the meeting ended on an encouraging note. Brown said he was sufficiently impressed that he would recommend the support of his associates. He assured them that something would be worked out, then left with Sullivan.

The ball players, however, were less than enthusiastic, their interest dwindling with each passing day without cash. Gandil hated this kind of diddling around. He had even started to get headaches for the first time in his life.

In New York, Rothstein took the call from Evans (Brown) and decided to go through with it. He told Evans to take $40,000, turn it over to Sullivan as a commitment to the players, then secure a second payment of $40,000 in a safe at the Hotel Congress as final payment at the plan's success.

Evans then went around Chicago getting money down on the Reds at the prevailing odds of eight to five in favor of the Sox. In New York, Rothstein got on the phone and called his friend Harry F. Sinclair, multimillionaire oil baron and fellow horse enthusiast, then seduced him into a $90,000 bet on the series. Before the hour was over, he got $270,000 down on the Reds. Had he any real faith in the venture, he would have doubled the figure.

In Chicago, Sport Sullivan was washed by a fresh wave of confidence. That a smart man like Arnold Rothstein would believe in him made him feel like a king. To a gambler in such a situation, there was only one thing to do with the $40,000 Brown had given him: get it down before the odds started shifting away from the Sox. He taxied to where the big money boys hung out, Chicago's Board of Trade, arbitrarily choosing a large brokerage house where he cornered a young assistant named Harry Long. Flashing $10,000 cash, he said he wanted to bet on the underdog Reds. Long, eager for the potential commission, went to the inner offices, then returned with the news that the odds had dropped to even money. So quickly? Sullivan was angered, for it was clear that Rothstein had beaten him to the punch. Here he was, the man who had made all the contacts, and he couldn't even get in on the ground floor of his own deal. He put $29,000 on the Reds at even money.

Then, with consummate arrogance, he confronted Gandil with $10,000 as though he were doing the ball players a big favor. "You're lucky to get it!" he scowled. "Brown is plenty sore. The odds have dropped already. He said one of your players has leaked it out!" Then, drawing on another rumor: "Are you guys working with someone else?"

Gandil was stunned. He knew the cash had to go to Cicotte, leaving nothing for the others, including himself. But he pocketed the money and Sullivan knew he had won this round. "Tell 'em to keep their mouths shut," he snapped. At this, Gandil blew up, accused him of bad faith, and they stood there blasting at each other, two wary partners in the great betrayal coming near to blows. Then wisdom inspired by mutual greed got the upper hand. They made up, somewhat apologetically, Sullivan assuring him that he never went back on his word.

Gandil packed his bag for the trip to Cincinnati, the $10,000 cash staring back at him, a reminder that now he was hooked. Even if he never got another dime, there was no turning back. He had gotten that message from the man called Brown.

In G. W. Axelson's biography, *Commy*, there was a quote from Comiskey himself. "To me, baseball is as honorable as any other business. It has to be, or it would not last out a season. . . . Crookedness and baseball do not mix. . . . This year, 1919, is the greatest season of them all!" A historian could recreate the very essence of America from that statement; it was as if Kaiser Wilhelm had just been awarded the international peace prize.

Worse, in fact, for most Americans would have agreed with Comiskey. What did they know—or care—that gamblers were all over the Hotel Sinton in Cincinnati, the centerpiece of the baseball action, or that bets were flying in defiance of the odds, or even that all manner of rumors were circulating that the series was in the bag. No matter that the smart people said so. None other than the Chicago crime reporter Jake Lingle (later murdered while in Al Capone's entourage) called Gandil in his hotel room that very night to tell him that he knew it was so. Sportswriter Ring Lardner was attuned to it. So indeed was his colleague Hugh Fullerton, who would later expose it. What mattered was the people. The baseball fans. The thirty thousand who packed Redland Field that sunny October afternoon, and the millions in the rest of the country who wanted to know everything about every pitch, but were impervious to idiot rumors from sinister gamblers, who loved baseball for the joys it brought them in boyhood as players, for its purity in a world tortured by dissension and false idols and failed idealism. Baseball was America's game—born, bred and buttered between the seas. Woodrow Wilson had just destroyed himself on a tour for the League of Nations. The nation was sick of him and his pious platitudes. Millions of men were out on strike in protest to gargantuan injustices of the rigidly oppressive economic system. There were rising costs of living, and threats of Bolshevism, and the frustrations of having struggled through a war fought for nebulous purposes. Amidst all this chaos, there was baseball, and now there was the World Series, and that's what really mattered.

The series would go five games out of nine in 1919. It turned out that Cicotte would work hard to lose two, mostly on fielding errors. Lefty Williams, for the first time in his career, could not get the ball over the plate through the other three, or failed to use his best pitch, the curve ball. After the Sox lost the first two games in Cincinnati, it was clear to many that highly suspicious things were happening on the field, confirming the worst of the rumors. Catcher Ray Schalk became enraged at Williams and actually punched him out under the grandstand. Manager Kid Gleason roared at them with unprecedented fury in the locker room. Charles Comiskey saw fit to bring the matter to the attention of both John Heydler, president of the National League, and his old enemy, Bancroft Johnson, president of the American. But Johnson dismissed him: "That sounds like the whelp of a beaten cur!" Comiskey apparently did not see fit to walk into his own locker room, shut the doors to all outsiders, and take the bull by the horns. If Schalk and Gleason could rage, why not Comiskey? And if he had—? He did nothing but cover his rear. Better to yelp like a beaten cur than stir up a hornet's nest. He could always hope that the ball players would come to their senses. Then there was Ring Lardner, who staggered through the Pullman en route back to Chicago, three sheets to the wind, serenading the ball players with his pungent parody, "I'm Forever Blowing Ball Games."

Meanwhile, the gamblers of both groups failed to pay the money they promised to the players. Only Cicotte got his ten thousand, which he found under the pillow in his room at the Hotel Sinton on the night before that first game, then carefully sewed into the lining of his coat. Jackson was paid only five of the promised twenty, Felsch but five of a promised ten. Of the first six games, they won two through the pitching of the diminutive rookie Dickie Kerr, behind whom they failed to lose even though they tried. Inevitably, the tissue of the conspiracy would unravel with such blatant betrayals. Down four games to two, Cicotte reversed the fix and won the seventh game as if he had regained his old form. Jackson's hitting was unstoppable. The whole team came alive with this turnabout. No matter that the Reds needed only one more victory to clinch the series and the Sox needed two, there suddenly appeared to be little doubt but that Chicago would pull it off. The fix, in short, was over. Of the eight players, only Gandil was left to implement it, too terrified to do otherwise.

In New York, Arnold Rothstein caught the vibrations. Long realizing the slimy follies of Abe Attell and the manipulations of the Bostonian, Sport Sullivan, he sensed the oncoming fiasco precisely as he had pegged it from the beginning. He had bet over $350,000 on the Reds and had no intention of losing it. He finally reached Sullivan on the eve of the eighth game. Hat in hand, Sullivan visited A.R. and quickly received the message, polite enough, but not without menace. There was to be no ninth game, Rothstein told the Boston gambler. That would not be wise. Nor did he think it wise that the outcome of the eighth game be left in suspense, whatever the needs of a public show or the ball players' pride. He wanted to see this thing over—in the very first inning, if such a thing were possible. Did Sullivan understand?

Sullivan did, though he didn't appreciate the consequences. It was known that Lefty Williams was scheduled to pitch, and once again, therein lay the key. It was also known that Williams, like Cicotte, having lost two games, was not about to lose a third. Certainly not now, not after being cheated out of promised money. Sullivan debated the alternative: pay him off or threaten him? Unquestionably, the latter was both less expensive and more certain. He had a number in Chicago he could call, a gunsel experienced in this sort of thing. Williams, Sullivan told him, had no children but a loving wife. The gunsel replied that children were desirable in these circumstances but a wife would do. If Sullivan would wire him $500 immediately. . . .

So it was that Lefty Williams, after being slugged by Ray Schalk, was now advised that his wife would be sacrificed if he didn't sell out again. What's more, he was warned not to last through the first inning. Immediately, he understood it all. He wasn't even surprised. He was a country boy from Missouri, another rube in the big city; this was the way things worked, and there was nothing he could do about it. To go to the police was preposterous, certainly not in Chicago. To go to Kid Gleason and fake being sick was too obvious. And how could he possibly warn his wife?

As he was entering the press box, Hugh Fullerton was stopped by the sound of his name and a heavy hand on his arm. A Chicago gambler he knew. The communication, as Fullerton later reported it, said it all:

"Hello, Fullerton . . . you got your money down today?"

"I don't bet on baseball," he replied.

"Neither do I," the gambler grinned. "Except today."

Fullerton perked up. "What's that supposed to mean?"

"Cincinnati, friend. Cincinnati to win!"

3. COVER-UP, EXPOSURE AND COVER-UP

I guess the joke's on us.

—OSCAR "HAPPY" FELSCH, centerfielder

Comiskey knew. Gleason, who knew for certain, was raging in Comiskey's office in Fullerton's presence. Again, Comiskey would cover his rear with a statement regarding the rumors. But when Joe Jackson asked to see him before going home to Savannah, Comiskey kept him waiting for hours, then left by the back door. Fullerton, meanwhile, wrote what he knew but newspapers refused to publish. There was no proof, he was told. And there are libel laws. Besides, consider the resulting damage to the baseball world. Meanwhile, Comiskey hired a private investigator to check the finances of the ball players, then offered $20,000 for anyone who could bring him proof. Several volunteers for the payoff surfaced, offering inside knowledge, but no money changed hands, nor did their information get beyond Comiskey's office. Insufficient evidence, the lawyers said. Jackson had his wife write Comiskey a letter, again offering to meet with him, but Comiskey never even replied. How could he put the jigsaw puzzle together if he kept throwing away the pieces?

The cover-up was far better organized than the fix itself. The baseball establishment had years of experience to fall back on. The pot would bubble and stew for a while; a few rumors would float around from town to town; but the lid would hold fast. Who but a few hard-nosed reporters would want it otherwise? Not

Comiskey. Certainly not Comiskey. Least of all Comiskey, for those eight boys of his were worth over a million dollars. Not the ball players, who would like to forget the whole sordid mess. Not the gamblers, who shunned exposure like the plague itself.

After the series, Sullivan went with Brown to the Hotel Congress safe and removed the $40,000, which was then delivered to Gandil as promised. Gandil gave Risberg $10,000, then instead of keeping any of his promises to the others, put the remaining $30,000 in a small black bag and went home to California. Sullivan, meanwhile, had made in the neighborhood of $50,000 from bets and went to the track at Havre de Grace. It was said that he was a heavy loser. Over the long series, Abe Attell did poorly, having defeated himself by greedily betting on every game. Burns and Maharg did worse and had to borrow carfare to get out of town. So it went with cheaters cheating cheaters. Hal Chase, to be sure, did extremely well.

In New York, Arnold Rothstein won a bundle and the dubious honor of being credited as the plan's mastermind. He would vigorously deny it, of course.

The scenario played out quietly over the long winter. No new evidence was turned up. Those who knew anything were quickly disabused of talking despite hopes of receiving Comiskey's reward. The rumors died by the end of winter and the clubs went south for spring training. Of the Sox, only Gandil chose not to return. Suddenly, as it turned out, Comiskey was prepared to pay considerably higher salaries—a lesson in cynicism if there ever was one.

In 1920, the White Sox were as strong as ever—but so were the gamblers. As the pitcher Urban "Red" Faber told the author years later, "You never knew what was going to happen behind you. Especially near the end of the season, just to keep the pennant race close." Faber believed that some of the ball players were simply too frightened not to comply. And nothing was ever said. It was a lot easier to accept dirty money in silence if you were apt to get butchered for turning it down.

Then, finally, the inevitable eruption—ironically over a game between the Cubs and the Phillies. On September 21, 1920, the Cook County Grand Jury began gathering testimony about crookedness in baseball. And because American League president Ban Johnson was behind it, his old enemy, Charles Comiskey, would take the brunt of it.

Piece by piece, all the garbage that had been swept under one rug or another over the recent years began to appear. The great gamblers like Monte Tennes and George M. Cohan confessed to hearing reports, but who knew what they meant? Ban Johnson had gone all the way to New York to confer with Arnold Rothstein, after which he said: "I felt convinced he wasn't in any plot to fix the series." Rothstein had admitted he'd heard rumors, Johnson reported, but in spite of it, he had bet on the Sox. So it was that the white knight of the American League had stormed the bloody bastions only to end up in bed with the enemy.

Another cover-up. Another whitewash. Hugh Fullerton could see it happening again.

Then, on September 24, the cat finally stuck his neck out of the bag in the person of New York Giant pitcher Rube Benton, who admitted that he knew more than he had previously testified. And this time, he was unstoppable. Hal Chase, it seemed, had tipped him off that the series was in the bag, and Benton had won $3,800 as a result. Then he told of Sleepy Bill Burns's telegrams to Chase (who had won over $40,000). He described meeting a man named Hahn, a betting commissioner in Cincinnati, who had told him that the Sox had been fixed by a gambling syndicate of "professional bookmakers who advance money to major league ball players to bet on games they play in." Benton suggested that the Grand Jury summon Cicotte. Cicotte, Benton said, "knew what it was all about."

A few days later, the *Philadelphia North American* startled everyone: "THE MOST GIGANTIC SPORTING SWINDLE IN THE HISTORY OF AMERICA." It was, as it turned out, an interview with Billy Maharg, Sleepy Bill Burns's partner, in which he exposed his double-dealing with Attell. A copy of the paper was in the White Sox locker room when they came off the field, one-half game out of first place. They all read it, but no one said a word about it.

The following morning, Comiskey came early to his office, unable to sleep. Kid Gleason was there waiting for him, prepared for the funeral, as it were.

"Commy, do you want the real truth? I think I can get it for you. Today."

"How?"

"Cicotte. I know he's ready to break."

Comiskey paled. There it was, finally, there it was. The end of his pennant hopes, the end of his great ball club—or so he saw it. Or could he stall it for a few more days? Until the race ended, perhaps?

"Go get him," he mumbled.

Gleason found Cicotte in his hotel room and told him that Comiskey wanted to see him. Cicotte nodded. He didn't bother to ask what it was all about. Together they went downtown to the law offices of Alfred Austrian, attorney for the White Sox. Cicotte was asked to wait in the reception room, alone, where he sat for over twenty minutes. Then he was escorted into an inner office, and again had to wait for twenty minutes. By that time, he was shaking, sick with guilt. When he finally was led into Austrian's office, he was a beaten man. He saw Comiskey, Gleason, Austrian and cracked. "I know what you want to know ... I know," he sobbed. "Yeah, we were crooked—we were crooked."

Comiskey couldn't bear it. "Don't tell me," he snapped. "Tell it to the Grand Jury."

Then, without benefit of an attorney, Cicotte was made to sign a waiver of immunity on the promise that everything was going to be fine. He was brought into the Grand Jury room, where Judge Charles MacDonald looked him squarely in the eye. "Are you going to tell us everything, Cicotte? We want to know about the gamblers."

His testimony was a personal, anguished mea culpa. The Grand Jury sat breathlessly as he spun the painful story. "I don't know why I did it. . . . I must have been crazy." All choked up, he had trouble finishing his words. "Risberg, Gandil and McMullin were at me for a week before the series began. They wanted me to go crooked. . . . I needed the money. I had the wife and kids. The wife and kids don't know about this. I don't know what they'll think." He stopped, buried his head in his hands. For a moment it seemed as if he could not go on. When he raised his head, his eyes were wet with tears.

"Before Gandil was a ball player, he was mixed up with gamblers and low characters back in Arizona. That's where he got the hunch to fix the series. Eight of us, we got together in my room three or four days before the series started. Gandil was master of ceremonies. We talked about it, and decided we could get away with it. . . . I was thinking of the wife and kids. I'd bought a farm. There was a four-thousand-dollar mortgage on it. There isn't any mortgage on it now. I paid it off with crooked money. . . .

"The day before I went to Cincinnati, I put it up to them squarely for the last time that there would be nothing doing unless I had the money. That night the money was under my pillow. There was ten thousand dollars. I counted it. I don't know who put it there. It was my price. I had sold out, Commy. I had sold out the other boys. . . . I had been paid and I went on. I threw the game."

The Grand Jury questioned Cicotte in detail as to the manner in which he did this.

"It's easy. Just a slight hesitation on the player's part will let a man get to base or make a run. I did it by not putting a thing on the ball. You could have read the trademark on it the way I lobbed it over the plate. A baby could've hit 'em. Schalk was wise the moment I started pitching. Then, in one of the games, the first I think, there was a man on first and the Reds' batter hit a slow grounder to me. I could have made a double play out of it without any trouble at all. But I was slow—slow enough to prevent the double play. It did not necessarily look crooked on my part. It is hard to tell when a game is on the square and when it is not. A player can make a crooked error that will look on the square as easy as he can make a square one. Sometimes the square ones look crooked.

"Then in the fourth game, which I also lost, on a tap to the box I deliberately threw badly to first, allowing a man to get on. At another time, I intercepted a throw from the outfield and deliberately bobbled it, allowing a run to score. All the runs scored against me were due to my own deliberate errors. In those two games, I did not try to win. . . .

"I've lived a thousand years in the last twelve months. I would not have done that thing for a million dollars. Now I've lost everything, job, reputation, everything. My friends all bet on the Sox. I knew it, but I couldn't tell them. I had to double-cross them.

"I'm through with baseball. I'm going to lose myself if I can and start life over again."

Cicotte testified over two hours, sobbing bitterly through much of it, sometimes barely audible. Judge MacDonald, however, was not satisfied, hoping for the inclusion of big-name gamblers to expose the whole frame-up that he would be able to run through his mill. He wanted hard evidence, not mea culpa. He wanted to hear about Arnold Rothstein, not just a couple of punks like Burns and Maharg. Cicotte had failed him. "I thought you were going to tell us about the gamblers!"

But Cicotte had nothing to say about the gamblers. Whatever he knew, or might have heard, he said nothing. For his own protection and that of his wife and children, he told the judge no more.

On the following day, Jackson was totally unnerved by what Cicotte had done. He felt that Cicotte's confession of guilt needed to be countered with his own innocence. He had to tell them he was innocent. How else could he protect himself? He called the Criminal Courts Building and asked for Judge MacDonald. "This is Joe Jackson, Judge."

"What is it, Jackson? Are you ready to talk?"

"Look, Judge, you've got to control this thing...whatever they're digging up, I can tell you, I'm an honest man."

"I can tell you, Jackson, I know you are not!"

And the phone went dead.

Jackson went downstairs for coffee and ran into Risberg, who told him to keep his mouth shut. "I swear to you, I'll kill you if you squawk!"

Jackson spent the rest of the morning kicking himself around the room, partly relieved there was no game that afternoon, partly furious. He started drinking, too much too quickly. He called Judge MacDonald again. This time the judge told him to come over and talk.

Waiting for him was Alfred Austrian, Comiskey's lawyer, with a waiver of immunity. And, like Cicotte, he had no lawyer as he signed his X. In the crowded corridor outside the jury room, he was assaulted by a battery of cameras and flashlights and clawing reporters. Jackson covered his face from the flashes, then suddenly exploded, cursing them all, and charged through the crowd like a fullback, ironically seeking sanctuary in the Grand Jury room.

His testimony was not a confession but a pathetic summary of how he got shafted by Gandil and Risberg. The games would be thrown no matter what, they told him, so why be a fool? He had demanded $20,000, but they only gave him five after the fourth game. He said that he knew nothing about anyone else's involvement except Cicotte's. He knew games were being deliberately lost, but he had nothing to do with them. He didn't even know which games were thrown. He did not know of any further meetings after the early ones. He would occasionally ask Gandil or Risberg for the rest of the money they promised him. Above all, he insisted that he himself had never done anything to cause his team to lose. The record, of course, would support that, with more hits and a batting average of .375, higher than any regular on either club, and no errors or bad throws.

He came out of the room smiling after two hours on the stand. His confession to the jury had purged him. "I got a big load off my chest," he told the bailiffs who accompanied him. To newspapermen, he still felt like talking, as if he had to pour it all out to everyone who would listen—his anger, his bitterness, his fear. "They've hung it on me. But I don't care what happens now. I guess I'm through with baseball. I wasn't wise enough, like Chick, to beat them to it. But some of them will sweat before the show is over." Jackson was like a little boy flailing at the big adult world. "They," apparently, were the people who had brought him to this moment, the legal machinery, the reporters, the club magnates, all lumped into one word. The sad part was that his admiration went to Gandil, the man who had gotten away with it.

And then there was Happy Felsch, who told it all to Harry Reutlinger, a young reporter on the morning *American*. Yes, they fixed the series, but it was the pitchers, Cicotte and Williams, who pulled it off. He too believed he had been cheated, though he didn't really know who was responsible. Probably Gandil, he thought. Cicotte got his ten thousand dollars, "because he was wise enough to stand pat for it, that's all. . . . The rest of us round-heads just took their word that we were going to get an even split on the hundred thousand. . . . I got five thousand. I could have got just about that much by being on the level if the Sox had won.

And now I'm out of baseball, the only profession I knew anything about...and a lot of gamblers have gotten rich. The joke seems to be on us."

For Felsch, as with Jackson, the fix had sneaked up on him. "I didn't want to get in on the deal at first. I had always received square treatment from Commy, and it didn't look right to throw him down. But when they let me in on the idea, too many men were involved. I didn't like to be a squealer, and I knew that if I stayed out and said nothing they would go ahead without me and I'd be that much money out without accomplishing anything."

Felsch's statement was far and away the most penetrating, no doubt because it came out of an interview with a sympathetic reporter rather than the rigidity of a Grand Jury examination by a lawyer. Forty years later, this author met with Felsch in his home in Milwaukee, and the message was very much the same. The sense of guilt was still there, and the continuing bewilderment. How did it happen? Why did you do it? How could you be so stupid? He smiled and shrugged, shook his head, palms up. The answer was the same with Lefty Williams's confession, and Jackson's. As Williams had told the Grand Jury: "I was informed that whether or not I took any action, the games would be fixed.... So I told them, anything they did would be fine with me: if it was going to be done anyway, that I had no money. *I may as well get what I could.*" With Felsch too it was just another payday, no doubt sleazier than most, but there was really nothing extraordinary about it. He told me of a time when he was playing ball on a factory team in Milwaukee, where the crowd ringed the outfield, standing behind a rope. One guy called to him as he came out to start an inning, and Felsch went over to him. "He flashed a gun," Felsch said. "He said I should miss anything that came out to center field that inning. Anything!" I laughed at the incredible brashness of the scene, picturing myself chasing down a fly ball with such a threat hanging over me. "Did you?" I asked. It was his turn to laugh. "I dropped it, yeah, then I kicked it all the way to the rope." He also told me his father was a Socialist from Germany, active in the Carpenters Union. ("I had always received square treatment from Commy," Felsch had told Reutlinger. Translation: Comiskey was a club owner whose predictable function was to exploit his ball players. You couldn't blame Commy for that, could you?) "But you hated him, didn't you?" I asked. Again that big Felsch grin. "He was an owner," he explained.

What had fascinated Reutlinger was this violation of his faith that professional baseball was an honest game. From where Felsch played it, there were, in fact, two sets of rules: the written ones, rigid and properly arranged, and the real ones, open and dirty, or as Felsch made clear, whatever you could get away with. They were the same rules that applied pretty much everywhere, the rules of social Darwinism that were supposed to lend scientific justification to the exploitations of the free enterprise system. Wasn't that what made Ty Cobb so formidable, this near-psychotic contempt for all rules except what he needed to dominate? The pathetic part was the clash with America's sense of the game, the clean, sunny purity of it, then the realization that it wasn't that way at all, nor had it ever been, that professional baseball was no different than professional business. No matter how great the game and how talented its best players, in 1919, this was the stark reality. Why else would Felsch and Williams speak admirably of Gandil because, as they suspected, he had gotten away with the big money? No matter that he had suckered them all into it and then betrayed them. He was only playing by the accepted rules. As Felsch had put it, "The gold looked good to all of us." Even his defense of Comiskey emerged as an honest desire not to conceal it. How else could their failure to satisfy their greed be explained? They had moved through the contortions of the fix as though they wanted no part of it. One hand had no knowledge of what the other hand was doing. As Cicotte and Williams and Jackson had testified, they never talked about it, never had another meeting after the series began. They had simply resigned themselves to what they called a double cross, presumably by Abe Attell and Sport Sullivan, and allowed the series and the money to slip away from them. "Roundheads," as Felsch had described them, passive participants in their own destruction. They had given in to Gandil's phony promises and then let happen whatever might happen.

"Some conspiracy!" I said, an editorial comment, as it were.

He nodded, unamused this time, then came out with what were certainly the key words: "We was scared."

Of the gamblers, of course. He wasn't going to talk about it.

When I mentioned the Lefty Williams episode relating to the first inning of the last game, he waved it away. Forty years after the series, he still wanted no part of such talk.

The entire nation was shocked. Although every newspaper released the story of the confessions in banner headlines, the gravity of the betrayal was not understood. After all, this was merely a sport, a game, an entertainment. At a time of war and resolutions of war, of a climactic presidential election, of the first fitful confrontation of the farce that was Prohibition, the significance of the scandal, however depressing, was made to seem illusory. The emphasis was immediately placed on a show of compassion for the Old Roman. America had not been violated, Comiskey had. It was as if Comiskey would be the one to suffer, the grand old man who had given his life to the great game.

The depth of the problem, however, was harder to fathom. The scandal dug deeply into the American psyche, an assault on the nation's pride. Baseball was never merely a sport but a national institution, far more vital to American traditions than intellectuals had realized. In 1919, every town in the country had a ball club, every factory, every mill. There was hardly a boy who didn't play it, whatever his abilities. There were no other spectator sports (except horse-racing and an occasional prizefight) that commanded comparable attention. It was years before football, tennis, golf caught the public eye, then primarily for the greatness of a few stars. Baseball was part of the American language: "He began life with two strikes on him ... I'll take a rain check on that ... He threw him a curve ball ... That's out in left field." Baseball was as symbolically American as the presidency, the Constitution, "The Star-Spangled Banner." Our national game was revered not only by kids but by adults of all classes, rich or poor. The image was pure and patriotic. It could almost be called a religion.

Suddenly, then, that pride was shattered. The very essence of America was exposed as corrupt. The national pastime was nothing more than just another hyped-up fraud. How could that not be sickening? If baseball was corrupt, then anything might be and probably was. If you couldn't trust the integrity of the World Series, what *could* you trust?

There was no way to gauge the extent of its impact, for one

cannot add up bitterness like a batting average. But every boy's sense of security was diminished by it; a new layer of cynicism could not but settle like a giant cloud on the public mind. To grow up in the wake of the Black Sox Scandal, as it came to be called, was to accept a lie, tolerate a betrayal, believe in corruption. "Everything is fixed!" would become the conventional dictum.

With good reason, it appeared: the World Series was one fix, run by a sleazy rat pack of disorganized, mostly two-bit bunglers, primarily to their own destruction. The real fixers, the big boys whose venality and backbiting had brought on the chaos, would now go to work to fix the aftermath.

It would not be easy. In the inner offices of the millionaire club owners, there was a high quotient of panic. The fans were angry, and in their anger, they were not about to settle for pieties and public relations panaceas. They cared less about retribution for the eight men who had sold out the game than the brutalizing fact that it had happened at all. If the owners thought they could isolate the scandal by cleaning out the eight, thus purifying the game, they quickly realized this would not work. The fans were not about to see Jackson, Weaver, Cicotte, et al. as a combine of evil. The problem was obviously much bigger than that. Every day, there was new proof of it. The Associated Press reported a story from Charles "Red" Dooin, formerly playing manager of the Phillies, that gamblers had tried to bribe his team to throw the pennant race to the Giants in 1908. "Those White Sox fellas were pikers to what we passed up.... Why, the gamblers opened up a satchel must've had over one hundred fifty thousand dollars in it, told our pitchers to help themselves. At the first game at the Polo Grounds, a big man handed me eight thousand dollars, told me there was forty thousand dollars more waiting for me. I called Big 'Kitty' Bransfield who threw him down the stairs!" Another story from Horace Fogel, former Phillies president, recalled that in 1905, a group of gamblers headed by Tim Sullivan (no relation to Sport Sullivan of Boston) approached Rube Waddell, star pitcher of the A's, and offered him $17,000 merely to stay out of the World Series against the Giants; he could invent his own excuse. And Waddell, it turned out, did not play, claiming he had hurt his pitching arm "stumbling over a suitcase on a train." Then, to add sinister spice to the current world of baseball graft, Cook

County D.A. Maclay Hoyne declared in New York with categorical pomp, "I have evidence too that the coming World Series between Brooklyn and Cleveland has also been tampered with!" making it two in a row. The sporting world jumped another fifty feet in the air: "CHARGE NEW WORLD SERIES FIX!"

Meanwhile, in Chicago, there was renewed talk of what was known as the Lasker Plan, devised by Albert D. Lasker, prominent businessman and lover of baseball. It was built on the principle that the game belonged to the public and must be run by the public—a commission of leading citizens from outside of baseball headed by names that ran similar to presidential aspirants of the Republican Party: General John J. Pershing, Senator Hiram Johnson, General Leonard Wood, Judge Kenesaw Mountain Landis. Behind it were Charles Comiskey, William Veeck of the Cubs, Barney Dreyfuss of the Pirates and John J. McGraw of the Giants. The public, however, was not enchanted. For all the big names, the foxes would be guarding the chickens again. Then there was John Heydler, president of the National League, braying before the Grand Jury that the 1919 scandal was really a freak that would never have happened but for the disorganization of the National Commission. All that was needed was a strong hand at the top.

Wrote George Phair, in the *Chicago Herald and Examiner:*

> The good ship baseball lists to port,
> Its ancient hull is leaking;
> It trembles when the wild winds snort,
> Its mast and spars are creaking.
> The owners gather weak and wan
> And gaze upon the weather;
> They'll slap a coat of whitewash on
> And hope it holds together.

Meanwhile, there was the problem of what to do about the gamblers. That story began with Billy Maharg, ex-partner of Sleepy Bill Burns and an all-American loser. His telegram to Comiskey was a wondrous presumption: I ACCEPT YOUR OFFER TO TELL WHAT I KNOW OF THE CROOKED WORLD SERIES OF 1919... PROVIDED YOU HAVE A CERTIFIED CHECK FOR $10,000... TO BE TURNED OVER TO ME AFTER I TESTIFY." It was not reported whether it crossed Comiskey's mind that the reward should now properly go to Cicotte as a belated bonus. Comiskey tossed the telegram on his desk and shook his head.

In New York, Abe Attell was starting to feel the pressure. Too many mentions of his name, every day someone else was throwing it into the bubbling stew. This Maharg thing was potentially the worst. Especially now, having received a message from the Chicago D.A., who was in New York and wanted to see him. Attell hurried to Lindy's Restaurant, hoping to find his lawyer, William J. Fallon. Instead, he met a big right fist in his face from a man who'd lost $2,000 on the series. Attell never even got a chance to retaliate, for the crowd broke up the fight before it could get going—no doubt out of sympathy for Attell's assailant. Inside Lindy's, he told a reporter that the whole thing was Arnold Rothstein's doing. "I'll tell what I know of this thing," Attell said, "and it will shoot the lid sky high!"

The Great Mouthpiece, as Fallon was called, had his hands full with this affair. Attell had to be silenced, not only for his own sake, but for Rothstein's. Put a man like Attell before a Grand Jury and anything might happen. Insofar as Rothstein was concerned, Fallon realized that since baseball was a national institution (unlike Rothstein's other nefarious involvements), any mention of his name had to be muzzled—especially since the press liked to play God when it came to baseball. As he saw it, he had to start by muzzling Maharg. Who knew what a pug like Maharg would tell a Grand Jury?

In Boston, Joseph "Sport" Sullivan had also seen the papers and was astonished to read that Attell had dared to implicate Rothstein. Knowing that he too was in trouble, he caught the first train to New York, needing to be where the power was. If Attell could play this sort of game, why not Sullivan too? He checked into the Ansonia Hotel, then presented himself at Lindy's. In a few minutes, he was having a press conference. "They've indicted me and made me a goat, and I'm not going to stand for it. I know the whole history of the deal from beginning to end. I know the big man whose money it was that paid off the White Sox players— and I'm going to name him!" He had barely finished his meal when a messenger coolly requested that as soon as he was finished eating, Mr. Fallon would like to see him—at 355 West Eighty-

fourth Street. Sullivan knew the address: it was Arnold Rothstein's.

Fallon was annoyed, and so was Rothstein, first at Attell, then
at Sullivan. Too much talking. Blah, blah, blah. (Tinhorn characters always play their trump cards first.) They were all there,
the four principals. Fallon told them that they were in this together, facing a common enemy: the Chicago Grand Jury. As he
saw it, the indictments would hold up, subpoenas would be sent
out, they'd be extradicted and forced to testify—which must be
avoided at all costs. How? Simple enough: they would leave the
country. Immediately. Sullivan was to go to Mexico, Attell to Canada. Rothstein would take his wife to Europe. And just to keep it
friendly, he agreed to pick up all the tabs—a little vacation with
pay, as it were. Agreed? Rothstein was already reaching in his
pocket to withdraw that ever-ready big bankroll that gave him his
nickname.

No one recognized Sullivan in Mexico, but Attell was a cinch
to be spotted in Montreal—at a wrestling match. Wire services
relayed the message to the States. "Here I am and here I sit," he
said. "They can't touch me here." As for Rothstein, he never got
closer to Europe than Grand Central Station. The Big Bankroll
and the Great Mouthpiece went to Chicago to smother the Little
Champ.

It was Fallon's idea that A.R. would volunteer to appear before the Grand Jury, an act of defiance against the power of the
state itself. Shrewdly, he guessed what bedlam Rothstein's appearance would generate—the harassment of reporters and photographers would "violate the privacy" of his client, who would
act injured and put-upon . . . thereby turning him into a sympathetic character. Besides, Rothstein wanted to meet Comiskey's
lawyer, Alfred Austrian. For this, he and Fallon had but to show
up in Austrian's office.

Right off the bat, Rothstein told Austrian that he wished to
retain him to represent his interests in Chicago. Austrian was
miffed. Didn't Rothstein know that he was counsel for both the
Chicago baseball clubs? How could he justify such a conflict of
interests? Where was the conflict, Rothstein asked? Were they not
both facing a common enemy: exposure? The answer, Fallon em-
phasized, was mutual silence. Silence would protect Comiskey in

the future—just as it had protected him through the extremely profitable 1920 baseball season. Rothstein had come to Chicago, not to break open the World Series scandal but to assure the baseball world that such a tawdry character as himself had absolutely nothing to do with it. Any suspicion of Rothstein's involvement would be the worst possible thing that could happen to baseball. Rothstein's vindication, then, became essential to everyone—including Comiskey. Would they not agree?

As it turned out, Fallon was right about Rothstein's entrance to the Grand Jury. As Jackson had suffered through that scene, Rothstein's arrival was doubly appalling—the visiting dignitary rudely maltreated by the manhandling of the local reception committee. The better to lend sympathy to his entrance.

It was, indeed, a grand one. Chicago appreciated celebrities of both the upper- and underworlds, but preferably the latter. Never, in fact, was A.R. made to feel so distinguished. With Fallon at his side (unprecedented for a Grand Jury witness), Rothstein asked for and was granted permission to read a prepared statement.

"Abe Attell did the fixing.

"I've come here to vindicate myself. If I wasn't sure I was going to be vindicated, I would have stayed home. The whole thing started when Attell and some other cheap gamblers decided to frame the series and make a killing. The world knows I was asked in on the deal and my friends know how I turned it down flat. I don't doubt that Attell used my name to put it over. That's been done by smarter men than Abe. But I wasn't in on it, wouldn't have gone into it under any circumstances, and didn't bet a cent on the series after I found out what was under way. My idea was that whatever way things turned out, it would be a crooked series anyhow, and that only a sucker would bet on it.

"I'm not going to hold anything back from you. I'm here to clear myself and I expect to get out of here with a clean bill of health."

And so it was. Maclay Hoyne treated him like a friendly witness, presumed to be innocent, spared any show of embarrassment. In such an atmosphere, Rothstein became quite garrulous, spoke of his love for the game, of his long-term friendship and admiration for John McGraw, his warm (and highly successful) meeting with Bancroft Johnson. To a total stranger in the room, he might have been a dignified young United States senator whose motives had somehow been misunderstood.

Hoyne later declared: "I don't think Rothstein was involved in it." This was supplemented by another great Chicago legal mind, Alfred Austrian's: "Rothstein, in his testimony today, proved himself guiltless."

Picture, then, the fury of Abe Attell reading the Montreal newspapers on the following morning. Normally a fastidious man, he threw his clothes into a suitcase and caught the first train back to New York. He too would go to Chicago "to set the world straight." But he was not so stupid that, on arrival in New York, he didn't call Rothstein first, having been around long enough to know a few fundamental principles: For one, there was no action by an opponent that could not, in some way, be made to work for you. For another, to a man like Rothstein, everything was a tactic.

Rothstein, in fact, was waiting for him. And so, indeed, was Fallon. And when the Little Champ started throwing furious combinations of punches (verbal) about the prospect of being summoned, indicted, standing trial and going to jail, it was Rothstein's right hand again moving to his pocket that eventually stopped him. "Bill, I want you to take care of the Champ," said Rothstein to Fallon. "I want you to see to it that they don't extradite him. I don't want him in that Grand Jury room—and I don't want him on trial." He handed Fallon $50,000 cash. Fallon nodded, stuffed the wad of folded bills into his pocket as if it were a dirty handkerchief. Attell dropped his guard, for the bell had just rung, ending the fight. And Fallon said to him: "Your troubles are over."

During the Civil War, a Union surgeon was operating on a wounded soldier under the shadow of a Georgia hillside. A cannonball caromed off a huge rock and shattered the surgeon's leg. When Dr. Landis's son was born two years later, he named the baby Kenesaw Mountain in memory of that dramatic site. The boy grew up in Logansport, Indiana. He dropped out of school when he failed algebra, got a job as a newsboy, clerked in a general store and ran errands in a train dispatcher's office, with vague notions about becoming a brakeman in order to see something of

America. He played amateur baseball, but his greater athletic skill was as a bike rider, less for speed than for psychology: once, before a race, he bought twenty medals and pinned them ostentatiously on his uniform, which so intimidated his rivals that he beat them.

When studying law in Cincinnati, indignant at being socially ostracized for his hayseed style, he organized the nonfraternity majority and won school elections. He practiced law in Chicago, and was known as a firebrand who brought cases into court that would normally be settled outside. He was appointed federal judge by President Theodore Roosevelt in 1905 and became nationally known when he forced John D. Rockefeller to testify in a case against Standard Oil of Indiana, then slapped a fine of $29,240,000 on Rockefeller's company, which, of course, was later reversed. During the war, he sentenced Big Bill Haywood of the IWW to twenty years in prison, also reversed. During the Red Scare, he sentenced the elected congressman Victor Berger and six other Socialists for sedition. Then, curiously, in the course of postwar adjudications he discovered that lawyers who wore wrist-watches (in lieu of pocket watches) were mostly those who had avoided military service. It was an insight he took to be eminently exploitable, once ordering a clerk to "have all those wristwatch-wearing lawyers file a statement as to what branch of service they were in." One senator, Thomas of Colorado, insisted that Landis ought to be impeached for such high-handedness. (It was not known what sort of watch the senator wore.)

To the baseball magnates, however, he was the ideal man to serve as the first commissioner at this time of crisis, and they granted him absolute power for an open-ended term at the extraordinary salary of $50,000 a year.

Throughout the winter of 1920 to 1921, the district attorney's office played typical Chicago games with the Black Sox trial. The farcelike quality of the World Series fix began to repeat itself in the legal (and illegal) maneuverings. The eight ball players appeared for arraignment in February in a jammed, hero-worshipping courtroom. As Buck Weaver put it: "They oughta build bleachers in here and charge admission." To their continuing astonishment, the players were to be defended by a battery of exceedingly high-priced criminal lawyers including Thomas Nash and Michael Ahearn, and James "Ropes" O'Brien, who had suddenly and inexplicably shifted sides from the prosecution. Who, indeed, was paying them?

Then it was discovered that vital evidence had disappeared from the government files when Attorney General Maclay Hoyne left office, including the signed confessions and waivers of immunity of Cicotte and Williams and the illiterate X of Jackson— and all references to Arnold Rothstein. Even more curious was the absence of any gambler in the court: if this was to be a conspiracy trial, with whom did the ball players conspire? To resolve this unfortunate oversight, the Grand Jury reassembled in secrecy, handing down five new indictments, names hitherto unknown, all allegedly partners of Abe Attell at the Hotel Sinton—but unmentioned by the ball players. Said one, Carl Zork, a shirtwaist manufacturer from Des Moines: "I don't know what this is all about." No one as yet knew who "Brown" was, nor could he be found. Joseph "Sport" Sullivan could not be located; Hal Chase was released from extradition in San Jose, California, because of what the state called an improper warrant. Even Billy Maharg in Philadelphia released a statement indicating he had changed his mind about talking. (Fallon, it seemed had a long and effective reach.)

When it came time for Attell's extradition, Fallon showed not only reach but feints and jabs. When the Little Champ was booked in New York's West Side Police Court, the Great Mouthpiece was there: "We admit that the prisoner is Abe Attell," said Fallon. "But we will not admit that he is the Abe Attell mentioned in the Chicago indictment. The prisoner was not in Chicago at the time mentioned and knows nothing about the case. If the Chicago authorities send witnesses here who can prove that Attell is the man wanted, we will make no further objections to extradition." Legal cats can be skinned in many ways. Fallon, after all, had $50,000 to pay for the skinning. This one related to the arrival of a Chicago manufacturer-sportsman named Sammy Pass who had been suckered into a World Series bet with Attell for $3,000, Pass was sent to New York in order to properly identify the man who had done the suckering. Fallon, however, was apprised of this; he even knew what train Mr. Pass was taking; and from the "other" Abe Attell who was not even in Chicago to do the suckering, he learned exactly what Mr. Pass looked like. Fallon met the train—and Sammy Pass—at Grand Central, induced him to join him for a drink and took him to a high-class speakeasy. Fallon bought him a lot more than one. "How much," Fallon wanted to know, "did the series cost you?" A moment later, the $3,000 changed hands, and then a few pieces of free expert legal advice, and then a few thousand dollars more. On the following day, Samuel Pass testified that insofar as Abe Attell was concerned, the whole business was a mistake. He had never met this Attell. It must have been someone else who had said he was Attell. He had come to New York because "I did not want to see an innocent man go to jail." This was what constituted "insufficient evidence," and so it was that Attell, like the other gamblers, was dismissed.

The Comiskey/Austrian-Rothstein/Fallon axis seemed indomitable. The rats were escaping from the traps and fleeing gleefully into the woodwork.

There were still two rats left, however, and Ban Johnson, the bulldog American League president (who had played puppy dog to Arnold Rothstein) was more determined than ever to destroy his archenemy, Charles Comiskey, and emerge as the savior of the National Pastime. To implement the trial, he would bring in the star witness, Sleepy Bill Burns, who was allegedly hiding somewhere in the great state of Texas. How does one find a rat in the biggest state in the union? By way of Philadelphia, of course, through the aid of a rat-friend named Billy Maharg, coconspirator and a $10-a-day worker at the Ford assembly plant. Under the threat of indictment, Johnson induced him to go to Texas to find Burns, all expenses (and lost salary) paid. Maharg finally found him in a little border town doing some languid fishing in the Rio Grande. Then came Ban Johnson himself to spell out the alternatives: either Burns returned to Chicago to stand trial under indictment as a coconspirator and suffer the consequences, or he testified for the state—or he kept on running. Burns was no fool. He knew the dangers of being a stool pigeon. And since none of the other gamblers had been extradited, why would he? Johnson, however, could be very persuasive. Besides, who would he be fingering but a few minor punks who wouldn't even be there? And could he not also get even with them for crossing him up?

With a witness like Burns, Ban Johnson forced the issue. The state was finally ready to begin trial.

4. TRIAL AND ERROR

Where is Arnold Rothstein? Why was he not indicted? Why were Brown, Sullivan, Attell and Chase allowed to escape? Why were these underpaid ball players brought here to be the goats in this case?

—A. MORGAN FRUMBERG, defense attorney

July 1921. It was a trial that was not a trial. The indictments alone were artfully designed to render the prosecution helpless: a conspiracy to defraud the public, to commit a confidence game, to injure the business of Charles Comiskey, etcetera, etcetera, a deliberate legalistic obfuscation of the basis for the fix, while the celebrity status of the ball players lent a circus atmosphere to the Chicago courtroom—like putting Charlie Chaplin on trial for vagrancy in Hollywood. Judge Hugo Friend, presiding, was no older than the ball players. The opposing battery of attorneys, all of them eager to get into the act, shouted in fury at each other in suitably preposterous locutions: "You won't get to first base with those confessions!" "We'll make a home run with them!" "You may get a long hit, but you'll be thrown out at the plate!"

When Kid Gleason and a few others came in to watch on an off day, the reunion with the eight was warm and friendly. They even got to Buck Weaver, to tickle him, just as in the old days, for Buck was notoriously ticklish. Said Felsch: "I hope you win the pennant, boys!" at a time when the Sox were seventeen games out of first place. This demonstration of rapport was duly reported in the press, and severely criticized for its immoral implications. Gleason was immediately alerted to rectify the situation, whereupon he publicly denied any friendliness whatsoever. Nobody had tickled Weaver, he said. If Weaver had giggled, perhaps he'd been tickling himself. Wrote the wise old sportswriter John B. Sheriden: "I have seen prominent citizens rob a city blind and retain their positions of influence and honor. . . . It is not easy for me to feel so shocked at the fraternization of the White Sox with their former teammates." It seemed that too many Americans expected higher morals from ball players than they expected from "prominent citizens."

As for expecting higher morality from the trial, the response was a continuing farce. When Charles Comiskey took the stand as a witness for the state, the big-money defense attorneys attacked him for his defection to the Brotherhood Players League in 1890; the exploiter of the defendants was being challenged for the one significant action in his life against the plight of the exploited. The farce continued with the matter of the disappearing confessions and related evidence. Who could explain such an unprecedented happenstance? Then, finally, there on the witness stand for the prosecution was Sleepy Bill Burns. He proceeded to unravel the fix as he had experienced it. For the first time, the jury heard how it happened, the most telling moment being the testimony that it wasn't he, or even Attell, who had initiated the idea, but Gandil. The fix did not come out of a gambler's seduction, but the ball player's greed.

No one in that steaming courtroom was more astonished at this than Joe Jackson. Somehow he had always assumed it had been a gambler's deal since it was gambler's money and a gambler's betrayal. How could it be that he was on trial along with Gandil, lumped together with Gandil, innocent or guilty with Gandil? He hated himself for having confessed. He had run scared and gotten drunk, not so much because of stupidity but because of weakness. He had let himself believe a lawyer's promise that nothing would happen to him. Now he had no choice but to rely on them. That too he hated. He couldn't understand all this, and had joked with his lawyers about his own ignorance: "Hey, lawyer," he would ask his counsel. "Who's winning?" And the lawyer would shrug. At a ball game, you could always look at the scoreboard and read the numbers, but in the courtroom the answer was a shrug. The complexities of the trial seemed to him typical of what he should have expected when he first left home, all these smart city men endlessly pouring out big words he couldn't understand. He had tried hard to be what they'd all wanted him to be, the fine clothes and all those shoes, and eating in restaurants, spending money as if it were a burden to keep in his pockets. Sure, he'd had a lot of fun, especially on the diamond, but despite that, all these years were mostly seasons away from home. It was enough for him to adjust as well as he did. It had never been out of his mind that he had never wanted to come North in the first place, how he had fled that first train ride to Philly in the middle of the night. And now, a dozen years later, it seemed almost natural that he should end up this way, in a court of law, on trial for being dishonest, with a judge and a jury and hundreds of spectators with neckties on.

Eddie Cicotte too was bewildered. He was astonished at Burns, not for the content of his testimony, but the artistry of it. He had known Burns for years and he'd always been the fool, Cicotte thought, never capable of any such demonstration as this. Yet now, after making one mistake after another, he was coming up clean. And Cicotte, having slipped but once, was being turned into Burns's patsy. On the mound, Cicotte was king, where Burns had been third rate. He had grown up believing it was talent that made a man a winner. If you were good enough, and dedicated yourself, you might get to the top. But when he got there, the rewards were less than the promise. They all fed off him, the men who ran the show and pulled the strings that kept the system working. They used him and used him, and when they had used him up, they would dump him. If they had praised him and made him feel like a hero to the people of America, all the time they had paid him peanuts. The newspapermen who wrote that praise made more money than he did, and Comiskey, who broke all his promises, made a half million dollars a year in the process. Burns knew how to operate. So did Gandil. Cicotte knew he would never learn how.

Buck Weaver sat through the trial in a gathering rage. They had no right to indict him. There was no reason for him to be there. He had been neither foolish nor greedy. He had not conspired to, nor did he, defraud anyone. He had attended a meeting not knowing its purpose, then rejected its intent when he heard what it was. He had played his heart and not taken a dime. The whole thing had become a nightmare of compounding injustices.

He felt like a man being framed for a murder because he was once seen arm wrestling with the victim. Because there was not a cynical bone in Weaver's body, he could not understand how anything like this could be happening to him. He would be cleared. He would have to be cleared. To Weaver, there was no other possibility. He could be angry, but he was always optimistic. Just the other day he'd had a long talk with John McGraw, who had visited the trial ostensibly to see John Heydler. McGraw, one of the great third basemen of his time, made it clear that he wanted Weaver to play in New York. Buck knew it would happen. He wasn't kidding himself. It was his nature to believe it.

Weaver never got a chance to state any of these truths to the court since none of the ball players took the stand in their own defense. That too was part of the deal. Baseball was forever to be protected from any possible taint. The good name of Charles Comiskey was not to be threatened by the likes of these heroes. Like all trials, the truth was masked by the need to secure the system. Everything was manipulated in deference to this all-powerful overview. When big business was at stake, the courts would rally to protect it. When the public faith was being challenged, compromises would be arranged to fortify that faith. Conveniently, but only conveniently, all this would serve in the ball players' behalf. Farce, by its nature, leaves a trail of bewilderment.

The last witness for the defense was Comiskey's business manager, Harry Grabiner. It was finally put in the record that the White Sox gate receipts in 1919 had been $521,175.75. In 1920, $910,206.59. Thus it was made clear to the jury that in the year after the defendants had allegedly conspired to destroy Charles Comiskey's equity, his income had almost doubled. No one commented on how fitting this was for a denouement. One might even have suggested that if the eight ball players were to return, that figure would surely double again.

The jury was out for what seemed like an eternity. The ball players waited around with increasing anxiety, gradually losing faith in their chances with each passing hour. They joked with fans and talked baseball, especially about the amazing home runs of Babe Ruth. A fan remembered a game the year before when Ruth had hit a tremendous shot off Cicotte's fast ball, but it had blown foul. Cicotte then threw his knuckler, only to watch Ruth hit another, further than the one before, and this time fair. Cicotte remembered and grinned. Someone asked Felsch if it were really true that Jackson couldn't read or write. Happy recalled a time when a fan came up to Joe as they were going for a beer, and asked him to autograph a baseball. Joe took the ball and the kid's pen and told Hap he'd meet him inside. Felsch claimed that he had four slow brews and when he came out, Jackson was still trying to write his name.

Then, before ten o'clock, there were three loud knocks from inside the jury room indicating that a verdict had been reached. When the court was finally assembled, the judge asked: "Gentlemen of the jury, have you reached a verdict?"

"We have, Your Honor."

The court tensed as the clerk was handed a slip of paper from the foreman. He read: "We the jury find the defendant Claude Williams not guilty..."

A roar went up in the courtroom; it was as if the pitcher had just slipped a third strike past Ty Cobb with the bases loaded in the ninth inning. By the time the complete list of acquittals was read, the courtroom was in a bedlam of rousing cheers. The bailiffs kept pounding for order until they saw Judge Friend all smiles and waving at the ball players, then they too joined the jubilation. Hats were sailed into the air, papers torn up and thrown as confetti. Cicotte raced to the jury foreman to embrace him. Jackson and Williams were close behind, pounding the jurors' backs. The jurors themselves joined in the cheering, then lifted the ball players to their shoulders, parading around the room before a battery of popping flashbulbs. Weaver and Risberg grabbed each other by the arms and danced like kids at May Day. Felsch and Williams laughed until they wept. When Cicotte was asked for a statement, he laughed. "Talk? You say, talk? Not here, buddy. I talked once in this building—never again."

Never again.

There were a lot of pious phrases from everybody, but the only memorable words came from none other than Chick Gandil:

"Guess that'll learn Ban Johnson he can't frame an honest bunch of ball players."

They all went to celebrate in a nearby Italian restaurant,

where a large dinner table was set up in a private room. By some strange coincidence, or so it was reported, the twelve good men who had acquitted them were celebrating in an adjacent room in the very same restaurant. The doors between them were flung open and the party, now doubled, extended through the triumphant night.

As the party broke up, the morning newspapers were rolling off the Chicago presses, the front page noting the official end of the celebration. Judge Kenesaw Mountain Landis made his first climactic statement as commissioner of baseball:

> Regardless of the verdict of juries, no player who throws a ball game, no player that undertakes or promises to throw a ball game, no player that sits in conference with a bunch of crooked players and gamblers where the ways and means of throwing a game are discussed and does not promptly tell his club about it, will ever play professional baseball.

This, then, was the victory of organized baseball. They had rescued the eight ball players from the clutches of the law, only to make victims of them on their own terms. Baseball, as the club owners would now boast, had cleaned its own house. "Regardless of the verdicts of juries . . .," the commissioner had declared. Shoeless Joe Jackson, et al., would not go to jail, but since they had sinned, they would suffer for their sinning. Judge Landis was hailed as a hero, a savior, the man who had purged the game of its evils. The club owners need panic no longer.

But there was something about America that could not remain untouched. Baseball would remain the national pastime, and much the same as it had always been, minus the most blatant manipulation of gamblers. It was the American people who would be changed by the scandal, victimized by a savage breach of faith. As Sigmund Freud pointed out: "Mankind needs heroes, and just as the hero who is faithful to his trust raises the whole level of human life, so the hero who betrays his trust lowers the level of human life." But here, as was commonly known, the problems lay deeper than a few men in a distorted confluence of causes. Not just a few rotten apples, but the barrel itself. The need for heroes would never be dissipated, but merely the public faith in them.

No longer did they have to be pure, just larger than life, sometimes the more corrupt the better. Americans were not disenchanted with baseball but with themselves, and they found release in various new fountains of debauchery. As for honesty, they could take it or leave it. In the end, baseball would survive, and survive very handsomely, not primarily because Judge Kenesaw Mountain Landis lived up to his granitelike name and face, for all his granite-headed pronouncements, but because of a whole new phenomenon named George Herman "Babe" Ruth. And this too was fitting, for the Babe was a celebrated womanizing philanderer, a rule-breaking violator of team discipline, a gargantuan, excessive eater and drinker. To the public—and to the press that delivered the message—Babe was the perfect hero. And no matter what the Babe's transgressions, Landis was not about to bite the hand that fed his mentors.

F. Scott Fitzgerald knew Arnold Rothstein. He also knew Rothstein's partner, Edward Fuller, king of the bucket-shop men, who ended up fleecing customers with phony stock deals of over $5 million. Fuller, in fact, was arrested in Rothstein's apartment, and his attorney was William J. Fallon. Fitzgerald also knew Ring Lardner. In a highly illuminating essay, Professor Allen Boyer of New York Law School exposed the connection, the more telling because Fuller and Lardner were neighbors of Fitzgerald in the highly fashionable Long Island suburb of Great Neck. This nexus, Fuller and Rothstein with all their mysterious underworld ties, became the genesis of the great novel of the twenties, *The Great Gatsby*. Not accidentally, it was set on the North Shore of Long Island.

As a student of history, Fitzgerald knew the significance of baseball and the impact of the scandal. Baseball was a reliable key to the way Americans liked to see themselves. It reflected the pride, the honesty, the skills of American men. The national pastime transcended ethnic, class and social lines; it was a team game that perpetuated democratic values through waves of immigrants. Boyer quotes Walt Whitman in this connection:

> "Well—it's our game; that's the chief fact in our connection with it: America's game: has the snap, go, fling of the American

atmosphere—belongs as much to our institutions, fits into them as significantly, as our constitution, laws: is just as important in the sum total of our historic life."

Baseball, then, was more than a game. To suffer its corruption was more than a betrayal. That the World Series was fixed was less an aberration than a symptom of American decay. And this, of course, was the theme of Fitzgerald's great novel.

In *Gatsby,* he introduced Arnold Rothstein to the narrator through a character named Meyer Wolfsheim:

> "... he's a gambler," Gatsby hesitated, then added coolly: "He's the man who fixed the World Series back in 1919."
>
> "Fixed the World Series?" I repeated.
>
> The idea staggered me. I remembered, of course, that the World Series had been fixed in 1919, but if I had thought of it at all I would have thought of it as a thing that merely happened, the end of some inevitable chain. It never occurred to me that one man could start to play with the faith of fifty million people—with the singlemindedness of a burglar blowing a safe.
>
> "How did he happen to do that?" I asked after a minute.
>
> "He just saw the opportunity."
>
> "Why isn't he in jail?"
>
> "They can't get him, old sport. He's a smart man."

As Gatsby's (America's) tribulations unfolded through the twenties, as Prohibition disintegrated along with whatever was left of American pride, as the Teapot Dome Naval Oil Preserves were looted and President Warren Harding's cabinet members tried to steal the whole country under an administration dedicated to "normalcy," the concurrent plight of the Black Sox continued to demonstrate the hypocrisy of the system.

Take Buck Weaver, for example. With the fervor of his innocence, he finally appeared before Landis in a plea for reinstatement. He told the commissioner how he'd been approached by Gandil and offered $10,000 to get in the fix, but turned it down. Landis replied that Weaver should have done something to stop it. Weaver cringed. Talk? He couldn't have talked. He'd thought about it, but these men had been his friends. Besides, he explained, he never really knew what was happening, no one did. Nobody said anything. He hadn't known enough to talk even if he'd wanted to. Landis was sympathetic. He would review the case. He would write Weaver a letter with his decision.

But there was no letter. Just a blunt statement to the press: "Birds of a feather flock together. Men associating with gamblers and crooks [can] expect no leniency."

Weaver choked on those words, but never stopped fighting. Landis never stopped repudiating him, even to this frustrating distortion of reality: "On the trial of this case, Burns gave a detailed account of his meeting with the indicted men...Weaver was present in the Court during the testimony...and yet the case went to the jury without any denial from Weaver from the witness stand.... If the incriminating evidence was false, the public had a right to Weaver's denial under oath." How, Weaver exploded, could he have denied anything if he was denied the right to take the stand in the first place? How could he have testified if the best defense for the group was a united silence, imposed by Comiskey's chosen lawyers? Had he not repeatedly asked for a separate trial? Had he not been told by Judge Friend himself that on the basis of the evidence presented there was no chance for his conviction?

But Landis was born of Kenesaw Mountain granite.

And take Dickie Kerr, the incredible pitcher who had won two games in the 1919 series and brilliantly won nineteen games on Comiskey's losing team in 1921 but was refused a proper raise for his talent and his honesty—and so refused to sign his contract for 1922. A classic case, for if Kerr did not agree to terms, he could not play organized baseball with any club, anywhere. He ended up playing semipro, no different from the eight Black Sox, as if in some final vindication of their sellout. Enter again Commissioner Landis, who learned that Kerr had actually pitched against the outlawed ballplayers, whereupon he declared that Kerr was ineligible and therefore would not play for another year. The loyal and disloyal: Comiskey and Landis threw them all in the same pot.

Or take a man named Joseph, the new, tall, rangy center-fielder for a semipro team in Hackensack, New Jersey, in a big Sunday game against Bogota. He hit a double, then a single, then a towering home run. He stole second, threw a man out at the plate trying to score on a single to center. It wasn't until the game was over that someone told the Bogota manager that this man Joseph looked just like Shoeless Joe Jackson. Jackson had, indeed, come north in the spring on the promise of money in New York's semipro circuit. It was a feeble joke to think he could get away with it.

Meanwhile, he had heard of a Milwaukee attorney named Raymond J. Cannon who was a firebrand against the organized baseball contract system and was organizing a new ball players' union. Cannon would take Jackson's case to recoup the two years' salary, $9,000 a year, that Comiskey had owed him on his three-year contract. So Jackson filed suit for $18,000 back pay. Cannon charged that Harry Grabiner, Comiskey's business manager, had deliberately misled Jackson about the Ten-Day Clause. He put Comiskey on the stand and made him admit that the clause itself was grossly unfair. Comiskey, however, replied that this was different, for it was Jackson who had violated the contract, not Comiskey. Had he not signed a confession to selling out the World Series?

"What confession?" Cannon demanded.

Then, incredibly, there was Jackson's confession, missing since the winter of 1920, suddenly in Comiskey's lawyer's briefcase! Cannon roared: "How is it that these Grand Jury records are in *your* hands!" Comiskey paled. "I don't know."

Cannon knew. Rothstein, through Fallon, had them lifted through complicity with the district attorney for the benefit of Comiskey. "Birds of a feather flock together," Landis had said. Cannon explained to the jury how the investigation and trial had been a farce, a subterfuge to cover Comiskey's reputation. "Comiskey had actually accused Gandil of being a ringleader . . . but sent him a contract for the following year."

The jury awarded Jackson his back pay, but the judge set aside the verdict on the grounds that Jackson had perjured himself by the contradiction of his confession, while now testifying as to his innocence. In the end, he collected but a small part of what Comiskey owed him.

And none of them would ever play professional baseball again. In fact, the entire scandal faded from the news almost as if there were yet another conspiracy to cover it up. If baseball did not overly suffer its assault on the integrity of the game, it was less due to Commissioner Kenesaw Mountain Landis's iron hand than it was to the monumental appeal of Babe Ruth's magical persona. Ruth was Herculean almost beyond belief. Professional baseball needed to be saved and Ruth saved it. In the process, he became the best-known person in America—if not the world.

It seemed almost typical that, forty years after the fateful World Series, in 1959, Ford Frick, then the commissioner, managed to stop the production of a television special on the Black Sox Scandal, claiming that any such exposure would be bad for baseball and, thus, bad for America. The sponsor, Du Pont, apparantly agreed. For those who heard about it, the response was appropriately sardonic: "Say it ain't so, Ford!"

No phrase out of the sporting world would be so pervasive or have such durability.

As for the Chicago White Sox Baseball Club, Charles Comiskey never again had a winner, suffering through many subsequent second division seasons. The banned ball players played a few years of barnstorming in semipro circuits, then retired to quiet pursuits in their hometowns. They never saw or spoke to each other again. Eddie Cicotte became a game warden in Michigan. Buck Weaver, who never stopped trying for reinstatement, managed a girls' softball team around Chicago and worked at the parimutuel windows. Happy Felsch went home to Milwaukee, where he ran a tavern. Chick Gandil bought a home in the Napa Valley of California and went into the plumbing business. Joe Jackson ran a valet service in Greenville, South Carolina, and then a liquor store. Years later, Ty Cobb stopped in to buy a quart of bourbon but neither acknowledged the other until Cobb finally spoke up: "What's the matter, Joe, don't you remember me?" Jackson replied: "Sure I do, Ty, I just didn't think you wanted me to." In 1951, Jackson was invited to New York to appear on *The Ed Sullivan Show* in conjunction with a campaign to clear his name, but suffered a fatal heart attack that very week.

Meanwhile, twenty years after the scandal, professional baseball established its Hall of Fame at Cooperstown, New York, allegedly the site of the game's invention by Major Abner

Doubleday. This was, however, an unfortunate leap into mythology; not only had the major not invented it at Cooperstown, baseball was not even of American origin but, more likely, a derivative of the English game of rounders. Charles Comiskey was among the early selections to the shrine—and, largely because of him, Eddie Cicotte, Buck Weaver and Joe Jackson were declared ineligible.

Baseball, as in all sports, has had more than a few scandals since 1919 involving gamblers and athletes of infinitely less integrity than Shoeless Joe. Gangsters and gamblers had long thrived in the boxing world. (Thirty years after the Black Sox Scandal, Abe Attell, former featherweight champion of the world, and one of its leading manipulators, called me—and, no doubt, dozens of others—asking that I wire him money on the eve of what he knew was a fixed fight in Miami, thereby repeating his actions before the 1919 series exactly as he had described them to me.) Horse races are forever being tampered with. College sports are rife with payoffs and the bribing of participants to control the point spread. Professional football has covered up several highly dubious betting arrangements over the years. Parallels with the Black Sox Scandal run all the way to the current collapse of Pete Rose and his penchant for gambling, even on baseball. It is as if all of history demands its own repetition regardless of ever-changing circumstances.

There is no more telling incident in America's loss of innocence than the fixing of the 1919 World Series.

AFTERWORD

Come let us mock at the great
That had such burdens on the mind
And toiled so hard and late
To leave some monument behind,
Nor thought of the leveling wind.

—WILLIAM BUTLER YEATS
1919

It was said that the war would last a hundred years, five years of fighting and ninety-five to wind up the barbed wire.

In 1919, American began the winding and became ensnared in the barbs. How to digest such a heady year? What did it all come down to? There is no bottom line in history. In any given year, there is no beginning, no ending; there are only symbols and portents.

ITEM: Captain Joseph Medill Patterson, forty-year-old ex-socialist, scion of an American newspaper publishing family, survived the war in France with the discovery of man's unlimited capacity to absorb nonsense. He returned to New York to create his testament to the postwar world: a newspaper dedicated totally to drivel. "It can't miss," he said. "Army I.Q. tests revealed that over half the soldiers have the mentality of twelve year olds... Hollywood aimed its movies at the mentality of eleven... I am publishing a picture newspaper aimed at the ten year olds." Thus, in 1919, was born the New York *Daily News*, a tabloid so loaded with distortion that the news was relegated to what could be told in glaring headlines, the glorification of the lie with pictures. The

347

paper was an instant success, not only to the alleged child-minded masses but the sophisticated society set as well. It became the largest circulating newspaper in the world.

No one, the saying went, ever lost money underestimating the tastes of the American people.

ITEM: Americans made the following purchases in 1919:

Chewing gum	$50,000,000
Candy	1,000,000,000
Soda	350,000,000
Ice Cream	250,000,000
Cigars, cigarettes	1,000,000,000
Movie admissions	800,000,000
Sporting goods	25,000,000
Furs	300,000,000
Luxury services	3,000,000,000
Luxury foods	5,000,000,000
Automobiles	2,000,000,000

ITEM: Of the thirty million aliens in the United States, an astonishing ten million sought to leave and return to the countries of their birth—some because they had saved enough money to reestablish their families, most because of despair at what America had offered them.

ITEM: It was reported that eighteen thousand businessmen had become millionaires during the war.

ITEM: There was a conspicuous revival of anti-Semitism. In its forefront, Henry Ford found fresh vitality in the ancient Protocols of Zion alleging proof of a Jewish conspiracy to take control of the world.

ITEM: In 1919, there were more recorded lynchings of blacks than ever before.

ITEM: Also noted was the beginning of an ex-patriot colony of distinguished American writers, artists and intellectuals in Paris. Said Ernest Hemingway: "I'm patriotic and willing to die for this great and glorious nation. But I hate like the deuce to live in it."

If Europe was suffering as it crawled out from under the war, it might be said that America was dancing its way out from over. For us, the war had been much less than horrific. No nation in history ever walked away from so much devastation so enriched, so unscathed, so empowered. And no nation ever felt so worthy or believed more in its God-blessed righteousness. Did we not have all these blessings because we deserved them? Was this not spoken from the pulpits, the halls of government, the great journals of opinion? Did we not deserve our prosperity for our sacrifices?

For two decades, the Progressive movement had represented the revolt of the American conscience against the injustices and inequities of American life. In 1919, the revolt ended with a vengeance. Suddenly, the drive for reform seemed like an aberration, a period of adolescent idealism that was best forgotten. More than all others, the hopes of liberals had been crushed by the war. The subsequent Treaty of Versailles was the inevitable disaster of a disastrous war. German militarism had been mowed down but its roots were undamaged. All of Clemenceau's dogged determination to destroy Germany would not tolerate any threat to the system that nourished it lest France find herself subjected to the same revolutionary pressures. The passion of Winston Churchill to destroy the Bolshevik regime was not inspired by the violence of their revolution but by its threat to ruling classes everywhere. Better the restoration of the Romanovs, whatever their tyrannies, for Britain had always done business with the tsars. Throughout the subsequent decade, we did not grant diplomatic recognition of Russia. The history of Europe degenerated under this fear, repeating itself through the economic depression of the 1930s during which the great democracies gave way to the rise of Adolf Hitler. No matter that Hitler was an avowed enemy of all democracies, a psychopathic anti-Semite, a Führer for German world conquest, as long as he ranted against Communism he would be supported.

Twenty years after the date of our entrance into the war, George Gallup polled the American people: "Do you think it was a mistake for the United States to end the World War?" Seventy percent said yes.

How could they not? The peace treaty had become a myth. Japan was invading Manchuria. Benito Mussolini sent Italians to invade Ethiopia. Hitler was making aggressive moves as he snarled across borders. The Fascist Francisco Franco, aided by the Nazis while the democracies remained neutral, overthrew the democratic government of Spain. Meanwhile, American prosperity had collapsed like a house of cards. And the League of Nations was described as follows:

Little nation against little nation? No peace.

Little nation against big nation? No little nation.

Big nation against big nation? No league.

In 1919, someone summed up the history of America as "Columbus, Washington, Lincoln, Volstead, two flights up and ask for Gus."

Another version might go this way:

George Washington to his father re a fallen cherry tree: "I cannot tell a lie; I did it with my little hatchet."

Barbara Frietchie to Rebel soldiers: "Shoot if you must this old gray head, but spare your country's flag!"

Admiral David Glasgow Farragut to his crew: "Damn the torpedoes, full speed ahead!"

Young baseball fan to Shoeless Joe Jackson: "Say it ain't so, Joe."

BIBLIOGRAPHY

Allen, Frederick Lewis, *Only Yesterday*. Harpers, 1932.
————. *The Big Change*. Harpers, 1931.
Asbury, Herbert, *The Great Illusion*. Doubleday, 1951.
Asinof, Eliot, *Eight Men Out*. Holt, Rinehart and Winston, 1963.
Bailey, Thomas A., *Wilson and the Peacemakers*. MacMillan, 1968.
Baker, Ray Stannard, *Woodrow Wilson, Life and Letters*. Greenwood, 1968.
Beard, Charles and Mary, *The Rise of American Civilization*. MacMillan, 1937.
Birdsall, Paul, *Versailles, Twenty Years After*. Raynal and Hitchcock, 1941.
Blum, John, *Joe Tumulty and the Wilson Era*. Houghton Mifflin, 1951.
Bourne, Randolph, *War and the Intellectuals*. Harpers, 1964.
Brody, David, *Labor in Crisis, the Steel Strike*. Lippincott, 1965.
Cashman, Sean Dennis, *Prohibition, the Lie of the Land*. Free Press, 1981.
Colvin, D. Leigh, *Prohibition in the United States*. George H. Doran Co., 1926.
Cooper, John Milton, Jr., *The Warrior and the Priest*. Harvard, 1983.
————. *Causes and Consequences of World War I*. Quadrangle, 1972.
Creel, George, *The War, the World, and Wilson*. Harpers, 1920.
————. *How We Advertised America*. Arno, 1972.
Cunliffe, Marcus, *The Presidency*. Houghton Mifflin, 1968.
Dabney, Virginius, *Dry Messiah, The Life of Bishop Cannon*. Knopf, 1949.
Daniels, Josephus, *The Wilson Era*. University of North Carolina, 1946.
Dos Passos, John, *U.S.A.* Modern Library, 1930.
————, *Mr. Wilson's War*. Doubleday, 1962.
Ellis, Edward Robb, *Echoes of Distant Thunder*. Coward McCann Geoghan.
Ferber, Nat, *I Found Out*. Dial, 1939.
Ferrell, Robert, *Woodrow Wilson and World War I*. Harpers, 1985.
Filler, Lewis, *The Muckrakers*. Penn State, 1959.
Fitzgerald, F. Scott, *The Great Gatsby*. Scribners, 1925.
Fleming, D.F., *Origins and Legacies of World War I*. Doubleday, 1968.
————. *The Cold War and Its Origins*. Doubleday, 1966.
Franklin, Roger, *The Defender*. Harpers, 1986.

Freud, Sigmund (with William Bullitt), *Thomas Woodrow Wilson*. Houghton Mifflin, 1966.

Friedham, Robert, *Seattle General Strike*. University of Washington, 1964.

Furnas, J.C., *The Late Demon Rum*. Putnam, 1965.

Fussell, Paul, *The Great War and Modern Memory*. Oxford, 1975.

Ginger, Ray, *The Bending Cross*. Rutgers University Press, 1949.

Gusfield, Joseph, *Symbolic Crusade*. Greenwood Press, 1968.

Hofstadter, Richard, *The American Political Tradition*. Knopf, 1948.

———. *The Age of Reform*. Knopf, 1955.

Hoover, Herbert, *The Ordeal of Woodrow Wilson*. McGraw Hill, 1958.

Kennan, George, *The Fateful Alliance*. Pantheon, 1984.

Kennedy, David, *Over Here*. Oxford, 1980.

Kerr, K. Austin, *Organized for Prohibition*. Yale, 1985.

Keynes, John Maynard, *The Economic Consequences of the Peace*. Harcourt Brace, 1920.

Klingaman, William, *1919*. St. Martin's, 1987.

Knightly, Philip, *The First Casualty*. Harcourt Brace, 1975.

Kobler, John, *Capone*. Putnam, 1971.

———. *Ardent Spirits*. Putnam, 1973.

Kraut, Alan, *The Huddled Mass*. Harlan Davidson, 1982.

LaFollette, Robert, *LaFollette*. MacMillan, 1953.

Lansing, Robert, *The Peace Negotiations*. Houghton Mifflin, 1921.

Lasch, Christopher, *The American Liberals and the Russian Revolution*. Columbia University, 1962.

Levin, N. Gordon, Jr., *Woodrow Wilson and the Paris Peace Conference*. D.C. Heath, 1972.

Lewis, Sinclair, *Main Street*. Harcourt Brace, 1920.

Lippmann, Walter, *Men of Destiny*. MacMillan, 1927.

Link, Arthur, *Wilson the Diplomatist*. Quadrangle, 1965.

Mayer, Arno, *Politics and the Diplomacy of Peacemaking*. Vintage, 1969.

———, *Wilson vs. Lenin*. Meridian, 1963.

Mee, Charles, Jr., *The End of Order*. E.P. Dutton, 1980.

Mencken, H.L., *A Carnival of Buncombe*. Knopf, 1924.

Merz, Charles, *The Dry Decade*. University of Washington, 1930.

Morison and Commager, *The Growth of the American Republic*, V. II. Oxford, 1962.

Moch and Larson, *Words That Won the War*. Princeton, 1939.

Murray, Robert, *Red Scare*. University of Minnesota, 1955.

Nicolson, Harold, *Peacemaking 1919*. Houghton Mifflin, 1933.

Noggle, Burl, *Into the Twenties—From Armistice to Normalcy*. University of Illinois, 1974.

Pitkin and Cordasco, *The Black Hand*. Littlefield, Adams, 1977.

Ritter, Lawrence, *The Glory of Their Times*. MacMillan, 1966.

Ross, Gregory, *The Origins of American Intervention in the First World War*. Norton, 1971.

Russell, Francis, *City in Terror*. Viking, 1975.

Schuman, Frederick L. *Design for Power*. Knopf, 1942.

————, *Russia Since 1917*. Knopf, 1957.

Seldes, George, *Witness to a Century*. Ballinger, 1987.

Seymour, Charles, *The Intimate Papers of Colonel House*. Houghton Mifflin, 1926.

Sinclair, Andrew, *Prohibition, The Era of Excess*. Little Brown, 1962.

Sinclair, Upton, *The Brass Check*. Boni, 1936.

Slosson, Preston, *The Great Crusade and After*. MacMillan, 1930.

Smith, Gene, *When the Cheering Stopped*. Morrow, 1964.

Smith, Page, *America Enters the World*. McGraw Hill, 1985.

Steel, Ronald, *Walter Lippmann and the American Century*. Atlantic-Little Brown, 1980.

Steffens, Lincoln, *Autobiography*. Harcourt Brace, 1931.

Steuart, J., *Wayne Wheeler, Dry Boss*, Revell, 1928.

Sullivan, Mark, *Our Times, Over Here*, Vol. V. Scribners, 1934.

————, *Our Times, The Twenties*, Vol. VI. Scribners, 1935.

Temperly, H.V., *History of the Peace Conference of Paris*. Oxford, 1920.

Timberlake, J., Jr., *Prohibition and the Progressive Movement*. Harvard, 1957.

Tolan, John, *No Man's Land*. Random House, 1980.

Tuchman, Barbara, *The Zimmermann Telegram*. Viking, 1958.

Tumulty, Joseph, *Woodrow Wilson As I Knew Him*. Doubleday, 1921.

de Weerd, Harvey, *President Wilson Fights His War*. MacMillan, 1968.

Williams, William Appleman, *The Contours of History*. World, 1961.

————, *The Tragedy of American Diplomacy*. World, 1959.

White, William Allen, *Puritan in Babylon, The Story of Calvin Coolidge*. MacMillan, 1938.

Zilliacus, Konni, *Mirror of the Past*. Current Books, 1946.

ESSAY

Boyer, Allen, "The Great Gatsby, The Black Sox, High Finance, and American Law." New York Law School, 1988.

NEWSPAPERS AND MAGAZINES

The Chicago *Tribune*

The Daily *News*

Harpers

The Journal of American History

Literary Digest Magazine
The Nation Magazine
The New Republic
The New York *Times*
North American Review
Outlook
Review of Reviews
Survey Magazine

INDEX